C. S. LEWIS, POET

C. S. LEWIS, POET

The Legacy of His Poetic Impulse

Don W. King

The Kent State University Press

Kent, Ohio & London

© 2001 by The Kent State University Press, Kent, Ohio 44242
ALL RIGHTS RESERVED
Library of Congress Catalog Card Number 00-062025
ISBN 0-87338-681-7
Manufactured in the United States of America

Revised and expanded edition

06 05 04 03 02 01   5 4 3 2 1

The extracts from Lewis's unpublished letters and poems are reprinted by permission of © C. S. Lewis Pte. Ltd. The extracts from Warren H. Lewis are from the Lewis Family Papers and *C. S. Lewis: A Biography,* © The Marion E. Wade Center, Wheaton College, Wheaton, Illinois, 2000, and are used by permission. The Oral History Interview with Ruth Pitter, conducted by Lyle W. Dorsett for the Marion E. Wade Center, July 23, 1985, © The Marion E. Wade Center, Wheaton College, Wheaton, Illinois, 2000, is used by permission.

The Marion E. Wade Center granted permission to use material originally published in two essays for SEVEN: *An Anglo-American Literary Review:* "Making the Poor Best of Dull Things: C. S. Lewis as Poet," SEVEN: *An Anglo-American Literary Review* 12 (1995): 79–92; and "Glints of Light: The Unpublished Short Poetry of C. S. Lewis," SEVEN: *An Anglo-American Literary Review* 15 (1998): 73–96.

Appearing in this volume is adapted material originally published by the author in the following articles: "The Distant Voice in C. S. Lewis' *Poems,*" *Studies in the Literary Imagination* 22 (Fall 1989): 175–84; "A Bibliographic Review of C. S. Lewis as Poet: 1952–1995, Part One," *The Canadian C. S. Lewis Journal* No. 91 (Spring 1997): 9–23; "A Bibliographic Review of C. S. Lewis as Poet: 1952-1995, Part Two," *The Canadian C. S. Lewis Journal* No. 91 (Autumn 1997): 34–52; and "C. S. Lewis's *Spirits in Bondage:* World War I Poet as Frustrated Dualist," *The Christian Scholar's Review* 27 (Summer 1998): 454–74; "The Poetry of Prose: C. S. Lewis, Ruth Pitter, and *Perelandra.*" *Christianity and Literature* 49 (Spring 2000): 331–56; "The Religious Verse of C. S. Lewis: Part One." *The Canadian C. S. Lewis Journal* 97 (Spring 2000): 12–27.

Library of Congress Cataloging-in-Publication Data
King, Don W., 1951–
C. S. Lewis, poet : the legacy of his poetic impulse / Don W. King.
p. cm.
Includes bibliographical references and index.
ISBN 0-87338-681-7 (alk. paper) ∞
1. Lewis, C. S. (Clive Staples), 1898–1963—Poetic works.
I. Title: Clive Staples Lewis, poet.   II. Title

PR6023.E926 Z747   2001
821'.912—dc21   00-062025

British Library Cataloging-in-Publication data are available.

To Jeanine, beloved friend, wife, soulmate

Contents

Thus in their school assembled I, even I,
  Looked on the lords of loftiest song, whose style
  O'er all the rest goes soaring eagle-high.

When they had talked together a short while
  They all with signs of welcome turned my way,
  Which moved my master to a kindly smile;

And greater honour yet they did me—yea,
  Into their fellowship they deigned invite
  And make me sixth among such minds as they.
                    —Dante, *Inferno,* Canto IV, 94–102

Preface

> Poets do not merely pass on the torch in a relay race; they toss the ball to one another, to and fro, across the centuries. Dante would have been different if Virgil had never been, but if Dante had never been we should know Virgil differently; across both their heads Ezekiel calls to Blake, and Milton to Homer.
> —Dorothy Sayers, *Further Papers on Dante*

While C. S. Lewis's poetry may never be ranked with that of Homer, Ezekiel, Dante, Virgil, Milton, or Blake, it is no hyperbole to claim that from the ages of twelve to thirty, Lewis lusted to achieve acclaim as a poet. His deeply held poetic aspirations are well documented in his letters, journals, and diary entries; in addition, his first two published works, *Spirits in Bondage* (1919) and *Dymer* (1926), volumes of poetry, testify to this judgment. Scholarly interest in the poetry, while slow at first, accelerated in the 1970s and has held steady since then. Since 1952 over sixty scholarly articles and theses have been written on Lewis's poetry.

As this activity suggests, scholarly interest in Lewis as a poet has become sustained. However, scholarly investigation of Lewis's poetry has been neither thorough nor systematic. Because there is no substantial critique of his poetry, this work attempts to remedy the deficiency. My intention is to bring a new focus upon Lewis's poetry, one that embraces diverse critical readings of the poems while seeking to discover whether a unified reading is possible. Avoiding hagiography as well as the assumption that Lewis's poetry is a poor relation to his prose, this study attempts to apply thoughtful scholarship to Lewis's poetry in a comprehensive, critical manner. Furthermore, I attempt to connect Lewis's efforts at poetry to his greater success at prose. Accordingly, I survey and comment upon his significant poetry, with an eye to noting how a fuller understanding of Lewis's poetry and his desire to achieve acclaim as a poet informs a deeper understanding of his prose, both the fiction and nonfiction. In a sense I am a miner seeking to tap into the vein of Lewis's lifelong desire to achieve acclaim as a poet, in order to show the source of his golden prose.

Chapter 1 begins with a review of Lewis's early letters, diaries, and journal entries where we see his aspirations to write great poetry and achieve literary acclaim as a poet. Of special concern is Lewis's lifelong correspondence with Arthur Greeves, *They Stand Together: The Letters of C. S Lewis to Arthur Greeves (1914–1963);* Lewis's diary, *All My Road before Me: The Diary of C. S. Lewis, 1922–1927;* and "The Lewis Papers: Memoirs of the Lewis Family," Warren Lewis's eleven-volume unpublished typescript covering the history of the Lewis family from 1850–1930. As these sources confirm, Lewis initially seeks to achieve fame not as novelist but as a poet. In this regard I note that the major influences upon his maturing poetic sensibilities are Greek and Latin masters of verse, including Homer, Virgil, and Ovid; Norse literature, particularly the awe-inspiring music of Richard Wagner; and the towering English figures of Milton, Wordsworth, and Shelley. Final concerns of this chapter are with Lewis as a crafter of poetry and with his prosody.

Chapter 2 addresses Lewis's earliest poems, in which he strives with passionate energy to craft significant poems. While for the most part he models these early efforts after his favorite poets, he also fashions nonderivative pieces. This chapter also explores unpublished examples of his early narrative verse, including a lengthy poem inspired by Wagner (the complete texts of Lewis's unpublished narrative poems appear in appendix 1). Chapter 3 continues the focus upon his earliest poetry and considers Lewis's first published work, *Spirits in Bondage,* a volume unfamiliar to many and provocative in its agnostic, bitter tone. Lewis is seen in these poems as both angry adolescent and maturing young adult, troubled by his search for meaning and purpose. Indeed, this volume reveals Lewis living as a frustrated dualist. While this dualism is not particularly theological—he is not consciously advancing the notion that there are two opposing Gods in the universe, one "good" and one "bad," warring with one another—the practical result of his dualism causes him to consider this possibility in some of the poems. The real source of frustration in his dualism, however, is better expressed by his sense of being torn by two realities he cannot reconcile: Nature's beauty and mystical otherness in contradistinction to war's nightmarish horror and his perceived sense of God's delight in human misery. As a result, the poems in *Spirits in Bondage* tend to either be sanguine or morose. The source of this frustrated dualism, I argue, is Lewis's growing sense of being swept up into World War I and his eventual service at the front lines in France. *Spirits in Bondage,* while not completely devoted to WWI poetry, has at least one third of its pieces concentrating on the war or related themes. In order to establish this, I consider briefly the WWI poetry of Siegfried Sassoon and Wilfred Owen and offer their work as a lens whereby to review Lewis's own WWI poetry.

Chapter 4 reviews several poems Lewis writes after the publication of *Spirits in Bondage* through the publication of *Dymer* in 1926. Of particular note are autobiographical narrative fragments concerning his first three influential teachers and "Joy" (1924), his first literary attempt to describe the experience so central to understanding his work. However, the majority of the chapter focuses upon *Dymer;* the influence of WWI informs my reading of this difficult and complex narrative poem. While *Dymer* is not easy—in part because Lewis's artistry is deficient— I suggest that a unified reading is possible, arguing that the poem is significantly influenced by Lewis's fascination with Richard Wagner's *The Ring of the Nibelung.* Parallels between Dymer and Siegfried are explored as well as other Norse and Wagnerian elements. In the end, I argue that a central connection between Lewis's first two published volumes is his experience in WWI.

Chapter 5 considers Lewis's other published narrative poems in order to show his dedication to the grand tradition of narrative poetry. First, I show how Lewis is influenced by both Malory's *Morte D'Arthur* and Tennyson's *Idylls of the King* in his "Launcelot." Second, I consider the "The Nameless Isle" and how Lewis purposely models it after Anglo-Saxon alliterative verse. Third, I offer a careful reading of "The Queen of Drum," after *Dymer,* Lewis's most polished narrative poem.

Chapters 6 through 8 concern Lewis's topical poetry: short pieces written after *Dymer* focusing upon specific people, events, ideas, and issues important to Lewis at the time of the poem's composition. Chapter 6 considers Lewis's comical and satirical poetry that tends to be combative, public, and percussive. Chapter 7 deals with his contemplative poetry that reflects social criticism and personal rumination on the human condition. Chapter 8 centers on his profoundly powerful religious verse.

Chapter 9 concentrates upon the legacy of Lewis's poetic impulse, arguing that his prose is often poetic. Accordingly, I discuss the poetic prose of *Perelandra* and *A Grief Observed,* illustrating the presence of poetry in the midst of Lewis's most compelling prose. The chapter concludes by considering how Lewis's efforts at poetry contribute to a fuller understanding of his success as a writer per se. The book concludes with appendices concerning the location of holograph versions of the poems, the complete texts of his fragmentary unpublished narrative poems, and the texts of eleven previously unpublished lyrical poems, along with a brief commentary on each.

Acknowledgments

This book began with a presentation I made on Lewis's poetry at the invitation of Dabney Hart for the C. S. Lewis Celebration: 1898–1963–1988, Mercer University-Atlanta, October 7–9, 1988. In the years that followed I pursued an intensive review of Lewis's poetry, taught several courses at Montreat College on the legacy of Lewis's poetic impulse, published a number of essays on Lewis poetry, and made additional presentations, including one to the Oxford C. S. Lewis Society during the Fall of 1997. Much of the writing in the book was accomplished during a Fall 1997 sabbatical granted me by the College. The first "public" offering of drafts of the chapters occurred during presentations made for the 1998 annual Valyermo retreat sponsored by the Southern California C. S. Lewis Society. I am deeply grateful to Dabney Hart for sparking my interest in Lewis's poetry; to William W. Hurt, president of Montreat College, for granting my sabbatical; to my many students at the College who have shared with me their insights and enthusiasm for Lewis studies; and to the participants of the Valyermo retreat for their patient indulgence and helpful criticisms.

In addition, I am grateful to C. S. Lewis Private, Limited and the Bodleian Library for permission to quote from unpublished materials of Lewis and to the Marion E. Wade Center for permission to quote from unpublished materials of Warren Lewis.

I owe a debt of gratitude to the staff of the Marion E. Wade Center, particularly Christopher W. Mitchell and Marjorie L. Mead, who encouraged my research and provided invaluable assistance during my many visits to the Wade Center. Judith A. Priestman at the Bodleian Library offered wise counsel and generous assistance as I worked on material related to both C. S. Lewis and Ruth Pitter. I am also grateful to Mark Pitter for permission to use his aunt's poetic transcriptions of passages from *Perelandra*. Charles A. Huttar and Joe R. Christopher offered excellent critiques of early drafts; I am deeply indebted to them for their wisdom, insights, and encouragement. Walter Hooper was extremely helpful in responding to my numerous requests for assistance regarding the poems; I especially appreciate his 1997 deposit to the Bodleian Library of holograph versions of most of Lewis's poems. Finally, I have benefited from the excellent editorial advice of The Kent State University Press, particularly Julia Morton and Erin Holman.

Abbreviations

AGO   *A Grief Observed* (N. W. Clerk, pseudonym). London, Faber and Faber, 1961.

CP   *The Collected Poems of C. S. Lewis.* Memoir and ed. Warren Lewis. Revised edition, ed. Walter Hooper. 1966. Reprint, London: Fount, 1994.

DCSL   *All My Road before Me: The Diary of C. S. Lewis, 1922–1927.* Ed. Walter Hooper. New York: Harcourt Brace Jovanovich, 1991.

LB   *Loki Bound* (1914). In *The Lewis Papers,* 4:217–20. Published in appendix 2.

LKB   Letters from Lewis to Leo Kingsley Baker. Miscellaneous Letters. Marion E. Wade Center, Wheaton College, Wheaton, Ill.

LL   *Letters of C. S. Lewis.* Memoir and ed. Warren Lewis. Revised edition, ed. Walter Hooper. 1966. Reprint, London: Fount, 1988.

LP   Warren Lewis, "The Lewis Papers: Memoirs of the Lewis Family, 1850–1930." 11 volumes. Wade Center.

NP   *Narrative Poems.* Ed. Walter Hooper. New York: Harcourt Brace Jovanovich, 1969.

OB   Letters from Lewis to Owen Barfield. Wade Center.

P   *Poems.* Ed. Walter Hooper. New York: Harcourt Brace Jovanovich, 1964.

PH   *The Personal Heresy.* London: Oxford UP, 1939.

PR   *The Pilgrim's Regress.* London: Geoffrey Bles, 1933.

RP   Letters from Lewis to Ruth Pitter. Wade Center

SB   *Spirits in Bondage: A Cycle of Lyrics.* New York: Harcourt Brace Jovanovich, 1984.

SJ   *Surprised by Joy: The Shape of My Early Life.* New York: Harcourt, Brace and World, 1955.

TST   *They Stand Together: The Letters of C. S. Lewis to Arthur Greeves (1914–1963).* Ed. by Walter Hooper. New York: Macmillan, 1979.

WLB   "C. S. Lewis: A Biography." Unpublished manuscript. Wade Center.

CHAPTER ONE

C. S. Lewis, Poet

Although C. S. Lewis is best known as a prose writer for his clear, lucid literary criticism, Christian apologetics, and imaginative Ransom and Narnia stories, he actually began his publishing career as a poet. His first two published works, *Spirits in Bondage* (1919) and *Dymer* (1926), were volumes of poetry published under the pseudonym of Clive Hamilton. In addition, he wrote many other poems that were later collected by Walter Hooper and published as *Poems* (1964). Hooper also published *Narrative Poems* (1969), a volume that reprints *Dymer* as well as three other narrative poems. Most recently Hooper has published *The Collected Poems of C. S. Lewis* (1994), a work that reprints *Spirits in Bondage* and *Poems*, but includes for the first time "A Miscellany of Additional Poems," a supplement of seventeen other short poems (eleven previously unpublished). With one exception, the previously unpublished poems date from the time Lewis was seventeen to nineteen years old. In addition, a recent essay, "Glints of Light: The Unpublished Short Poetry of C. S. Lewis," has published another ten poems and fragments.[1]

Despite this body of work, Lewis has not achieved acclaim as a poet. While Thomas Howard calls *Poems* "the best—the glorious best—of Lewis,"[2] other critics view his poetry less favorably. Chad Walsh refers to Lewis as "the almost poet,"[3] and Dabney Hart believes that Lewis "will never have a major place in the canon of . . . poets."[4] Charles Huttar says that, given current critical taste, Lewis as a poet is viewed as a "minor figure" and, "barring a revolution in taste, he will never be accorded a higher position."[5] On the other hand, George Sayer's brilliant study of *Dymer* argues "the time may come when it will be ranked higher than much of Lewis's prose work."[6] W. W. Robson, a Lewis colleague and friend, has published an article, "The Poetry of C. S. Lewis," in which he reevaluates his own earlier negative view of Lewis's poetry, arguing that in some of Lewis's poems he "touches greatness."[7] Luci Shaw has celebrated Lewis's poetic "ability to see and probe reality and express it in vivid and illuminating metaphors."[8]

Aspirations and Influences

While critics debate the quality of Lewis's poetry, anyone interested in Lewis as a writer should become aware of the important role poetry had in shaping his literary life, particularly his aspirations to achieve acclaim as a poet, and the literary influences that shaped him. Owen Barfield remembered Lewis when he first met him as one "whose ruling ambition was to become a great poet. At that time if you thought of Lewis you automatically thought of poetry."[9] Tracing these aspirations and influences as he moved from boyhood to mature adult is fascinating and sheds significant light upon the prose for which he later became best known. His autobiography, *Surprised by Joy*, letters (particularly to Arthur Greeves), diaries, and journal entries provide ample chronological evidence of his early enthusiasm for poetry, the writers most influencing him, and his sustained desire to achieve acclaim as a poet. Furthermore, throughout we see his attempt to establish his own theory of poetry, something he pursued throughout his life via a number of different forums culminating in his published debate with E. M. W. Tillyard, *The Personal Heresy*. What all these sources make clear is how integral poetry was to Lewis's life. He did not sip or taste poetry in a casual, off-handed manner; rather, poetry was a stream intricately threaded through his life that fed a literary well— a nourishing reservoir almost without bottom—one from which he drank deeply and passionately.

In *Surprised by Joy* he recalled how his imagination developed from the ages of six to eight, in part through his writing about Animal-Land. At first there was an absence of poetry: "I was training myself to be a novelist. Note well, a novelist; not a poet. My invented world was full (for me) of interest, bustle, humor, and character; but there was no poetry, even no romance, in it. It was almost astonishingly prosaic" (15). Yet during this same period he says his "third glimpse [of joy] came through poetry," specifically the lines "I heard a voice that cried, / Balder the beautiful / Is dead, is dead," from a translation of Tegner's *Drapa*. The impact of these lines was electrifying: "I knew nothing about Balder; but instantly I was uplifted into huge regions of northern sky, I desired with almost sickening intensity something never to be described" (17). While it may be argued that this example is less about poetry's role in his early life and more about his awakening to the pangs of joy around which much of Lewis's life came to revolve, poetry was in fact the primary vehicle by which this intense longing was felt.

Still, prose, not poetry, demanded Lewis's attention in these early years. Whatever interest in poetry the reading of Balder may have prompted remained dormant through Lewis's early education. The critical years 1908–10, which he spent under the tutelage of Robert Capron at Wynyard School—"Oldie" and "Belsen"[10] in *Surprised by Joy*—effectively squelched almost all his literary interests. Lewis says that while at Wynyard, "the only stimulating element in the teaching consisted of a few well-used canes which hung on the green iron chimney piece of the single schoolroom."[11] Lewis speaks volumes in this regard by naming the chapter covering these years in *Surprised by Joy* "Concentration Camp." In a diary he kept while at Wynyard, Lewis provides additional insight into his life there:

> It was on a bleak November morning in the year of grace 1909 that I pulled myself from my bed in an uncomfortable corner of the dormitory at the abominably early hour of 7:30 a.m. Mindful however that a half-penny fine awaited me if I was late, I began to wash in icy water with all reasonable despatch [*sic*]. . . . I had a shop egg for breakfast, today being Sunday; for breakfast most weekdays we have bad ham. We . . . marked to Church in a dismal column. We are obliged to go to St. Cuthbert's, a church which wanted to be Roman Catholic but was afraid to say so. A kind of church abhorred by all respectful Irish Protestants. . . . In this abominable place of Romish hypocrites and English liars, the people cross themselves, bow to the Lord's Table (which they have the vanity to call an altar) and pray to the Virgin . . . . [For dinner the next evening] we had enormous helpings of boiled beef with thick, sickening yellow fat, and little grey puddings known as slime balls, not to mention an adjoining complement of black, adamantine parsnips.[12]

While some of this may be dismissed as adolescent sarcasm, clearly such living conditions did little to nurture literary, much less poetic, sensibilities. Still the diary entry itself is remarkably mature, an early indication of his writing potential.

Mercifully, Lewis's father sent him to Campbell College, Belfast, in September 1910, and while there only through December, for the first time he experienced poetry in a profoundly significant way through reading Matthew Arnold's *Sohrab and Rustum*: "I loved the poem at first sight and have loved it ever since. As the wet fog, in the first line, rose out of the Oxus stream, so out of the whole poem there rose and wrapped me round an exquisite, silvery coolness, a delightful quality of distance and calm, a grave melancholy. . . . Arnold gave me at once (and the best of Arnold gives me still) a sense, not indeed of passionless vision, but of a passionate, silent gazing at things a long way off" (*SJ*, 53). He goes on to use this occasion to describe "how literature actually works." To those who argued that only classicists could enjoy a poem such as *Sohrab and Rustum* for its Homeric echoes, he counters: "[I] knew nothing of Homer. For me the relation between Arnold and Homer worked the other way; when I came, years later, to read the *Iliad* I liked it partly because it was for me reminiscent of *Sohrab*. Plainly, it does not matter at what point you first break into the system of European poetry. Only keep your ears open and your mouth shut and everything will lead you to everything else in the end" (53). This commendation, that readers practice an unfiltered, objective reading of great literature, especially poetry, was one Lewis held throughout this life. Moreover, it is important to note he did not say we should read poetry uncritically, but instead that we should use great poetry to find great poetry. It is not literary criticism that should capture our attention; instead, we should give our full attention to great literature itself.

Beginning in January 1911, now enrolled at Cherbourg House, Malvern, Lewis had an even more important encounter with poetry, perhaps the defining moment in his literary life.[13] While idling in the school library, his "eye fell upon a headline and a picture, carelessly, expecting nothing. A moment later, as the poet says, 'The sky had turned round'" (*SJ*, 72). In the passage that follows, Lewis connects his reading of the words *Siegfried and the Twilight of the Gods* and Arthur Rackham's illustrations for that volume with birthing in him a zeal for Norse literature: "Pure 'Northernness' engulfed me: a vision of huge, clear spaces hanging above the Atlantic in the endless twilight of Northern summer, remoteness, severity . . . and almost at the same moment I knew that I had met this before, long, long ago (it hardly seems longer now) in Tegner's *Drapa*, that Siegfried (whatever it might be) belonged to the same world as Balder" (73).[14] What has not been sufficiently noted before is how profoundly Lewis was drawn to Wagner's music through this event. He relates how fortuitously his father's purchase of a gramophone gave him ample opportunity to indulge his new passion. Indeed, he connects for the first time his love of poetry with his growing interest in music: "Gramophone catalogues were already one of my favorite forms of reading; but I had never remotely dreamed that the records from Grand Opera with their queer German or Italian name could have anything to do with me" (73–74). Only several weeks later he says he is "assailed from a new quarter" when he begins reading a magazine that contains synopses of Wagner's *The Ring of the Nibelung*.[15] Lewis was completely overwhelmed: "I read in rapture and discovered who Siegfried was and what was the 'twilight' of the gods. I could contain myself no longer—I began a poem, a heroic poem on the Wagnerian version of the Niblung [*sic*] story. . . . I was so ignorant that I made Alberich rhyme with *ditch* and Mime with *time*" (*SJ*, 74).[16] Although he never completed the poem, Lewis comments on the powerful effects it had on him as a writer:

> Since the fourth book [of his poem] had carried me only as far as the last scene of *The Rhinegold*, the reader will not be surprised to hear that the poem was

never finished. But it was not a waste of time, and I can still see just what it did for me and where it began to do it. The first three books (I may, perhaps, at this distance of time, say it without vanity) are really not at all bad for a boy. At the beginning of the unfinished fourth it goes all to pieces; and that is exactly the point at which I really began to try to make poetry. Up to then, if my lines rhymed and scanned and got on with the story I asked no more. Now, at the beginning of the fourth, I began to try to convey some of the intense excitement I was feeling, to look for expressions which would not merely state but suggest. Of course I failed, lost my prosaic clarity, spluttered, gasped, and presently fell silent; but I had learned what writing means. (74)[17]

That Lewis engaged in such an effort at age thirteen clearly reveals how deeply poetry gripped him. What makes this more surprising is he that tells us he still had never heard a note of Wagner's music, though the composer's name became to him "a magical symbol." Upon first hearing a recording of the *Ride of the Valkyries*, he remembers it came "like a thunderbolt," and all his pocket money went toward purchasing Wagnerian records: "'Music' was one thing, 'Wagnerian music' quite another, and there was no common measure between them; it was not a new pleasure but a new kind of pleasure, if indeed 'pleasure' is the right word, rather than trouble, ecstasy, astonishment, 'a conflict of sensations without name'" (75). In addition, he says that, at this time, "Asgard and the Valkyries seemed to me incomparably more important than anything else in my experience," so "I passed on from Wagner to everything else I could get hold of about Norse mythology" (76, 78).

In September 1913 Lewis moved to Malvern College, still nurturing his discovery of Wagner and Norse poetry. Here he encountered the first of his two greatest teachers, Henry Wakelyn Smith (Smewgy in *Surprised by Joy*) who is discussed in more detail later.[18] Of note is Lewis's gratitude to Smith for teaching him Latin and Greek poetry, especially Horace's *Odes*, Virgil's *Aeneid*, and Euripides' *Bacchae*: "I had always in one sense 'liked' my classical work, but hitherto this had only been the pleasure that everyone feels in mastering a craft. Now I tasted the classics as poetry. . . . Here was something very different from the Northernness. Pan and Dionysus lacked the cold, piercing appeal of Odin and Frey. A new quality entered my imagination: something Mediterranean and volcanic, the orgiastic drum beat" (113). The other great contribution to his developing poetic sensibility was the school library where he discovered "Milton, and Yeats, and a book on Celtic mythology, which soon became, if not a rival, yet a humble companion, to Norse." Together these influences led him to begin "an epic on Cuchulain and another on Finn, in English hexameters and in fourteeners respectively. Luckily they were abandoned before these easy and vulgar meters had time to spoil my ear" (114).

A year later, in September 1914, Lewis went to live with his greatest teacher, W. T. Kirkpatrick.[19] Kirkpatrick's influence on Lewis's intellectual development is everywhere present and need not be recounted here; however, noteworthy is what Lewis said about Kirkpatrick's teaching: "Homer came first. Day after day and month after month we drove gloriously onward, tearing the whole *Achilleid* out of the *Iliad* and tossing the rest to one side, and then reading the *Odyssey* entire, till the music of the thing and the clear, bitter brightness that lives in almost every formula had become a part of me" (145). However, by far the most important poetry at this time is Lewis's *Loki Bound*.[20] Because his primary literary interest centered upon Northernness, he modeled *Loki Bound* after an ancient literary form: "Norse in subject and Greek in form . . . as classical as any Humanist could have desired, with Prologues, Parodos, Epeisodia, Stasima, Exodus, Stichomythia, and (of course) one passage in trochaic *septenarii*—with rhyme. I never enjoyed anything more" (114–15).[21]

Concurrent with Kirkpatrick's influence, Lewis began a lifelong correspondence with Arthur Greeves, an amazing record of his developmental years with particularly rich material about Lewis's consuming love of poetry. In his letters to Greeves (*They Stand Together,* hereafter *TST*), we find him freely sharing his latest poetic discoveries. For instance, in a letter dated June 1914, he writes: "I have here discovered an author exactly after my own heart, whom I am sure you would delight in, W. B. Yeats. He writes plays and poems of rare spirit and beauty about our old Irish mythology. . . . His works have all got that strange, eerie feeling about them, of which we are both professed admirers" (*TST,* 47–48). Many letters further reveal the important literary influences shaping his poetic sensibilities. For instance, we find he enjoyed reading Homer's *Iliad*, Malory's *Morte D'Arthur*, Spenser's *The Faerie Queen*, the Pearl Poet's *Sir Gawain and the Green Knight*, Milton's "Comus" and *Paradise Lost*, Shelley's "Prometheus Unbound," Wordsworth's "The Prelude," and the poetry of Tennyson, Morris, Arnold, Swinburne, and Yeats. About reading aloud in Greek the *Iliad*, Lewis writes to Greeves on September 26, 1914: "Those fine, simple, euphonious lines, as they roll on with a roar like that of the ocean, strike a chord in one's mind that no modern literature approaches" (50).[22] Of the *Morte D'Arthur,* he notes on January 26, 1915, "It has opened up a new world to me" (*LL,* 63). A month later he says, "It is really the greatest thing I've ever read" (Feb. 2, 1915, 64).

However, the most profound early influence was Milton.[23] Lewis tells Greeves that "Comus" is "an absolute dream of delight" (Sept. 27, 1916, *TST,* 130) and that "it is agreed to be one of the most perfect things in English poetry" (Aug. 4, 1917, 198). His praise of *Paradise Lost* was more frequent and sustained. For example, he writes Greeves after reading the first two books of *Paradise Lost* that "[I] really love Milton better every time I come back to him" (Feb. 7, 1917, 165). A month later he adds: "I have finished 'Paradise Lost' again, enjoying it even more than before. . . . In Milton is everything you get everywhere else, only better. He is as voluptuous as Keats, as romantic as Morris, as grand as Wagner, as weird as Poe, and a better lover of nature than even the Brontes" (Mar. 6, 1917, 176). In reading of Lewis's early delight in poetry, we are struck by the depth of his enthusiasm; his passion for poetry was visceral, and it fed and nourished his aesthetic taste. Letter after letter communicated his love of literature, music, and art, but especially poetry. He consumed it greedily, and his appetite was perhaps never sated.[24]

Lewis's deep affection for the poetry he read stimulated his own aspirations as a poet. Once again, his letters and diary entries are filled with these longings. He frequently writes Greeves about the poems he is writing. Concerning *Loki Bound,* he wrote seven letters between June 1914 and November 1916. In one, he writes: "I was very glad to hear your favourable criticism of 'Loki.' . . . Your idea of introducing a dance after the exit of Odin etc, is a very good one, altho' it will occasion some trifling alterations in the text" (Oct. 14, 1914, 54). Twelve letters were written about his efforts to write "The Quest of Bleheris."[25] Apparently Lewis struggled throughout as he composed this prose romance: "I think Bleheris has killed my muse—always a sickly child. At any rate my verse, both in quality and quantity for the last three weeks is deplorable" (June 6, 1916, 107). He adds later that he regrets he "began Bleheris in the old style [as opposed to a modern style]: I see now that though it is harder to work some effects in modern English, yet on the whole my way of writing is a sort of jargon" (July 4, 1916, 118). Eventually he records the death of Bleheris: "As to Bleheris, he is dead and I shan't trouble his grave" (Oct. 12, 1916, 136). In addition, several letters concern his effort to write "Medea": "The subject [of the poem] is 'The childhood of Medea,' & it will leave off where the most poems about her begin—shortly after her meeting with Jason. It will describe her lonely, frightened childhood away in a castle with the terrible old king her father & how she is gradually made to learn magic against her will" (Feb. 15, 1917, 167). In a later letter he records the fate of this poem: "'Medea's Childhood' after struggling on for 300 turgid lines has been quietly made into spills for my 'tobacco pipe'—all those fine landscapes and vigorous speeches, devoted to real use at last!" (Feb. 28, 1917, 173).

Other early letters to Greeves revealed Lewis devoted himself to writing lyrics, many later published in *Spirits in Bondage.* Consciously turning away from writing narrative poetry, he confesses to Greeves: "I begin to see that short, slight stories & poems are all I am fit for at present & that it would be better to write & finish one of such than to begin & leave twenty ambitious epic-poems or romances" (Oct. 4, 1916, 133). However, he did not abandon narrative poetry; instead he began work on a prose version of *Dymer* late in 1916 or early in 1917, after matriculating at University College, Oxford. Yet in April 1917, while involved in officer training, he found it easier to focus upon short lyrics rather than narrative poetry. He tells Greeves: "I am in a strangely productive mood at present and spend my few moments of spare time in scribbling verse. When my 4 months course in the cadet battalion is at an end . . . I propose to get together all the stuff I have perpetrated and see if any kind publisher would like to take it" (June 10, 1917, 192). In addition, he continued his interest in Wagner, writing Greeves about a performance he saw: "Now will I make you envious. On Friday night I went to Drury Lane to hear 'The Valkyries.' The dream of years has been realized, and without disillusionment: I have had thrills and delights of the real old sort, I have felt as I felt five years ago" (June 17, 1918, 221). Despite Macmillan's rejection of this collection, Lewis was not dejected, writing to Greeves: "I am determined not to lose heart until I have tried all the houses I can hear of. I am sending it off to Heinneman [sic] next" (Aug. 7, 1918, 227).

Happily, William Heinemann accepted this work less than a month later, and Lewis's letters show his increasing ambition to achieve acclaim as a poet. For example, he writes his father: "This little success gives me a pleasure which is perhaps childish, and yet akin to greater things" (Sept. 9, 1918, LL, 88). To Greeves he says: "You can imagine how pleased I am, and how eagerly I now look at all Heinneman's [sic] books and wonder what mine will be like" (Sept. 12, 1918, TST, 230). Several weeks later he gives his father a qualified evaluation of the poems: "I am not claiming that they are good poems—you know the schoolboys' definition— 'prose is when the lines go on to the end of the page; poetry is when they don't'" (Oct. 3, 1918, Warren Lewis, unpublished "C. S. Lewis: A Biography," hereafter WLB, 73). When asked by John Galsworthy for permission to publish one of the poems from Spirits in Bondage, "Death in Battle," in a war poetry anthology, Lewis writes his father that "I naturally consented because it is pleasant laudari laudato viro" (Oct. 27, 1918, LL, 94).[26] He tells Greeves later when recalling his first meeting with the publisher: "You will understand well how pleasant it was to walk in under a doorway . . . feeling I had some right to be there" (Nov. 2, 1918, TST, 237).

Spirits in Bondage was eventually published in March 1919. Once a published poet and enjoying the first taste of fame, however modest, Lewis continued his poetic maturation. In a series of letters to Leo Baker, Lewis reflected upon the classical poets he so admired and the role and function of poetry. In April 1920 he confides to Baker: "All poetry is one, and I love to see the great notes repeated. Homer and Virgil wrote lines not for their own works alone but for the use of all their followers. A plague on these moderns scrambling for what they call originality—like men trying to lift themselves off the earth by pulling at their own braces: as if by shutting their eyes to the work of the masters they were likely to create new things themselves."[27] In September 1920 he writes Baker and thanks him for his theory of poetry: "The most valuable part of it, and the part which shd. be insisted on is that 'a poet who is only a poet is not the greatest poet': the assumption that a great poem must have nothing in it but poetry has 'worked like madness in the brain' of too many of us" (*LKB*, 0092). A poet, Lewis suggested, cannot afford to be a poet only; he must be involved in the lives of men and women. In addition, Lewis intimated how longing to achieve acclaim as a poet can interfere with writing poetry. That is, as he worked to write great poetry, the focus had been too much upon *him* and too little upon poetry.[28]

Later in the same letter Lewis attempts to describe the peculiar function of poetry as compared to other arts: "What we want to find is—that which is proper to poetry alone: what is the method by which poetry *and no other art* [Lewis's emphasis] performs the duties shared with all art? Doubtless you would answer that in the same way as I wd. & come to a definition something like this: 'Poetry is the art of utilizing the informal or irrational values of words to express that which can only be symbolized by their formal or conventional meanings.' These values include chiefly sound & association: also of course their—'group'—sounds or rhythms which are above and beyond their individual sounds: here is the meaning & justification of metre. Hence the value of the test 'could this be said as well in prose?': if the answer is in the affirmative the poem is condemned" (*LKB*, 0093). Here Lewis reflects a workman's view of how poetry happens. That is, he implies that the poet uses language in a particularly structured and precise way to produce a desired emotional effect. Form, therefore, becomes a central interest for Lewis.[29] His interest in form may explain why Lewis eventually turned his attention back to narrative poetry. Having finished a prose version of *Dymer* in 1917, Lewis finished a verse version in December 1918.[30] However, still not content, from 1920 to 1926 Lewis pursued a final poetic version with intensity and deliberate single-mindedness. His diary, *All My Road before Me: The Diary of C. S. Lewis 1922–1927*, contains over seventy-five direct references to this effort. In these entries he recounts an almost daily obsession with both his progress on the poem and his ambition to achieve fame as a poet. A study of the diary shows that he completed initial drafts of the first two cantos by the end of June 1922; Canto III by the end of July 1922; Canto IV by the end of August 1922; Cantos V and VI by the end of June 1923; and Cantos VII, VIII, and IX by mid-April 1924.[31] Of course during this process he went back and forth between one canto and another, revising here and there as he saw the need. Often he was assisted in this process by the sympathetic but frank criticism of colleagues, including Leo Baker, Owen Barfield, Alfred Hamilton-Jenkin, Cecil Harwood, Rodney Pasley, and Arthur Greeves. He completed a final version in the summer of 1925.

At times he wrote about his struggles. For instance, early on he notes that "I am very dispirited about my work at present. . . . I have leaned much too much on the idea of being able to write poetry and if this is a frost I shall be rather stranded"

(*DCSL*, Apr. 15, 1922).[32] Three months later he is rewriting Canto IV, "with which I am finding great difficulties" (July 30, 1922, 77). Eighteen months later he is at his most dissatisfied: "[I am] discontent with the whole plan of 'Dymer': it seems 'full of sound and fury, signifying nothing'" (Jan. 6, 1924, 281). When revising the proofs just prior to publication, Lewis shares a feeling many writers have as they look over their labors: "I never liked it less. I felt no mortal could get any notion of what the devil it was all about. I am afraid this sort of stuff is very much hit or miss, yet I think it is my only line" (July 6, 1926, 422). Yet, more often than not, he is at least upbeat if not jubilant about his progress. Many entries include comments such as "made some progress," "pleased myself fairly well," "felt fairly satisfied," "pleased myself with it," and "with considerable satisfaction." After several months of work, he writes: "After supper I worked on 'Dymer,' bringing it to the end of the storm. I was so transported with what I considered my success that I became insolent and said to myself that it was the voice of a god" (Sept. 30, 1922, 111). A week later he adds, "I read the whole thing through and felt fairly satisfied with the general movement of the story" (Oct. 9, 1922, 115). The following summer Lewis says that Harwood "covered me with enough praise to satisfy the vainest of men" (July 8, 1923, 255).

It is a mistake, however, to think that Lewis's only poetic preoccupation during this time was *Dymer*. While it is true he published no poetry between *Spirits in Bondage* in 1919 and "Joy" in 1924, *All My Road Before Me* contains over fifty references showing him at work on several other poems. For instance, apparently he spent a good deal of time working on two poems that have not survived, "Misfire" and "Offa," submitting them for publication to the *London Mercury* (Apr. 4, 1922, 16). While he waited to hear their fate, he asked his friend William Stead how he managed to get his poems published by the *London Mercury*. Lewis wrote in his diary that Stead called on the editor, John Squire, and said: "'Look here Mr. Squire, you haven't taken these poems of mine and I want to know what's wrong with them!!' If the story ended there, it would be merely a side light on Stead, but the joke is that Squire said, 'I'm glad you've come to talk it over: that's just what I want people to do' and actually accepted what he'd formerly refused. Truly the ways of editors are past finding out!" (Apr. 5, 1922, 17). After this, several entries chronicle his work on "Joy."[33] "Nimue," first mentioned in a letter to Greeves of June 2, 1919, was the subject of eight entries (*TST*, 254).[34] When it was eventually rejected by the *London Mercury*, Lewis despairs: "I was thinking seriously of how I could face the prospect of having to give up poetry, if it came to that" (May 10, 1922, *DCSL*, 32). Six months later Lewis refers to "a new poem on my old theme of 'Alone in the House.' I soon found that I was creating rather too well in myself the creepy atmosphere wh. I was trying to create in the poem, and gave it up" (Jan. 3, 1923, 169).[35] Lewis also recalls Owen Barfield's comments after reading several poems sent him for review: "He said it always surprised him that my things were as good as they were, for I seemed to work simply on inspiration and did no chipping. I thus wrote plenty of good poetry but never one perfect poem. He said the 'inspired' percentage was increasing all the time and that might save me in the end" (Jan. 26, 1923, 186).

Lewis took such criticism to heart as he revised one poem: "Worked as hard as I have ever done on a poem, trying to resist all my clichés, shortcuts and other original sins" (Feb. 11, 1923, 195). Still, self-doubt plagued his efforts at poetry: "I am haunted by fears for the future . . . and whether I shall ever be able to write good poetry" (Feb. 15, 1923, 200). Yet, a year later when "Foster," a poem he spent considerable effort writing, was rejected by the *London Mercury*, he was not crestfallen, seeing in the rejection a silver lining because "an unknown publisher called Stockwell wrote saying that 'a mutual friend' had told him I would soon have enough poems for a book and telling me he would be pleased to see them" (Jan. 28, 1924, 286).[36] One particularly ambitious project was a sequence of sonnets "which was to be put in the mouth of a man who is gradually falling in love with a bitch, tho' quite conscious of what she is. I don't care for sonnet sequences and it is not the sort of thing I ever imagined myself writing: but it would be jolly if it shd. come off" (May 29, 1926, 403).[37] However, and unexplainably, after several weeks, he abandoned the sequence. Other poems he worked on during this period were "Wild Hunt," "The King of Drum," "Sigrid," and variations on the myth of Cupid and Psyche.[38]

However, the most penetrating insights into Lewis's poetic aspirations are found in his diary entry of March 6, 1926. Here Lewis is brutally honest in analyzing his feelings when *Dymer* was rejected by Heinemann (it was later published by Dent in 1926). As he analyzed his reactions to the rejection, he posited five reasons for why he was so disturbed.[39] In a process reminiscent of his logical parry-and-thrust apologetic dialectic, he at first discounted each motive. But as he probed deeper, he finally admitted that he did desire fame as a poet: "I desire that my value as a poet should be acknowledged by others" (*TST,* 383). What follows is one of Lewis's longest passages of self-analysis:

As far as I can see both these are manifestations of the single desire for what may be called mental or spiritual rank. I have flattered myself with the idea of being among my own people when I was reading the poets and it is unpleasing to have to stand down and take my place in the crowd. . . . The completion of the poem, Coghill's praise of it, and the sending off to a publishers [*sic*] (after so many years) threw me back into a tumult of self-love that I thought I had escaped. . . . Worst of all I have used the belief in such secret pre-eminence as a compensation for things that wearied or humiliated me in real life. . . . The cure of this disease is not easy to find. . . . I was free from it at times when writing Dymer. Then I was interested in the object, not in my own privileged position as seer of the object. But whenever I stopped writing or thought of publication or showed the MS. to friends I contemplated not that of which I had been writing, but my writing about it: I passed from looking at the macrocosm to looking at a little historical event inside the "Me." The only healthy or happy or eternal life is to look so steadily on the World that the representation "Me" fades away. Its appearance at all in the field of consciousness is a mark of inferiority in the state where it appears. Its claiming a central position is disease. (383–84)

Lewis went on to say the only way to cure this disease was to look away from self to the greater world so that thoughts of self would fade. What is so striking here is his brutal self-assessment. He confessed that his desire for fame as a poet was nothing less than spiritual pride, a key theme he explored later in prose fiction and apologetics. Equally, he noted that poetry per se, even his poetry, had not been nearly as interesting to him in this process as *he* had been. Additionally, we see that his hopes for literary fame had been a kind of sop for other disappointments. Indeed, he was clearly embarrassed by the recognition that his desire to be a poet veiled an intense self-absorption. Although this realization was certainly a watershed in the life of Lewis the poet, it did not mark the end of his desire for fame as a poet. Instead, it provided Lewis with a point in time for occasions later in life when his thirst for fame as a poet or more broadly as a writer was tempered by the realization that such a desire was an unhealthy exaltation of self.

After 1926, references to his efforts at writing poetry drop off substantially in his letters and diary entries as a direct result of his being elected a fellow of Magdalen College. Lewis had feared his time for poetry would be limited by this election, as a diary entry from February 29, 1924 reveals: "I saw that it [a Trinity College fellowship] would mean pretty full work and that I might become submerged and poetry crushed out" (*DCSL,* 293). Still he did not abandon writing poetry. In a letter on August 18, 1930, Lewis attempted to encourage Greeves, who had just experienced rejection of a writing project.[40] Lewis, who by this time was nearing conversion to Christ, openly admitted his belief that because achieving success as a poet had become for him an idol, God had to kill it: "From the age of sixteen onwards I had one single ambition, from which I never wavered, in the prosecution of which I spent every ounce I could, on wh[ich] I really deliberately staked my whole contentment. . . . Suffering of the sort that you are now feeling is my special subject, my profession, my long suit, the thing I claim to be an expert in" (*TST,* 378–79). Foreshadowing his later phrase a "severe mercy," Lewis counseled Greeves that perhaps God was dealing kindly with them by denying their desires for literary fame. Such a denial saved them from the disappointment and despair attendant upon those who briefly flame up with literary fame, only to flicker quickly before fading into oblivion.

We know, of course, that he continued to write poetry, as his pieces appeared regularly in newspapers, literary magazines, and scholarly journals.[41] In letters to other friends, he recorded this continuing impulse to write poetry. At times he was very confident of his ability as a poet. Tongue in cheek, he writes to Owen Barfield: "I have written about 100 lines of a long poem in my type of Alexandrine. It is going to make the Prelude [by Wordsworth] (let alone the *Tower* [by Barfield]) look silly" (Mar. 16, 1932).[42] Yet his discouragement about poetry in general was pronounced when he wrote Barfield seven years later: "I am more and more convinced that there is no future for poetry" (Feb. 8, 1939, *OB,* 0088). Lewis's debate with E. M. W. Tillyard published in 1939 as *The Personal Heresy* (hereafter *PH*) offers additional evidence of the primacy of poetry in Lewis's life.[43] Although this debate did not explicitly reveal Lewis's passion to be known as a poet, it clearly demonstrated how seriously he considered the necessity for right thinking about the nature of poetry and the role of the poet. Lewis rejected modern poetry's emphasis on the poet's personality or character; he came to call this emphasis the "personal heresy." Instead, he argues "that when we read poetry as poetry should be read, we have before us no representation which claims to be the poet, and frequently no representation of a *man*, a *character*, or a *personality* at all" (Lewis's emphasis).[44] Citing his as an "objective or impersonal theory of poetry," he admits that this notion "finds its easiest application in the drama and epic" (*PH*, 8). Given Lewis's consistent early efforts at narrative poetry, his point of view is not surprising. Furthermore, it is not difficult to posit that Lewis's personal heresy argument germinated in part from the diary entry of March 6, 1926, quoted above; Lewis's self-indictment provided the basis for his critical distaste for poetry focusing upon the author's personality.

Yet he did not totally dismiss the significance of the poet's personality. Instead, he articulated effectively how a poet's personality may affect the reading of a poem: "[However, when reading a poem], let it be granted that I do approach the poet; at least I do it by sharing his consciousness, not by studying it. I look with his eyes, not at *him*. . . . The poet is not a man who asks me to look at him; he is a man who says 'look at that' and points; the more I follow the pointing of his finger the less I can possibly see of *him*" (11, Lewis's emphasis). Later, he adds that while looking to where the poet points, "I must make of him not a spectacle but a pair of spectacles. . . . I must *enjoy* him and not *contemplate* him" (12, Lewis's emphasis).[45] Throughout, Lewis argued that poetry was not a private matter, but instead a public one: "[In a poem] it is absolutely essential that each word should suggest not what is private and personal to the poet but what is public, common, impersonal, objective" (19).[46]

Lewis's view of the role of the poet has been under attack since the great Romantic poets; Wordsworth claimed that poets wrote about "both what they half create, / And what they perceive." Lewis believed the elevation of the poet's personality led to "Poetolatry" and "the cult of poetry" displaying "religious characteristics" (65). When Lewis turns to a theory of poetry in *The Personal Heresy*, he sounds very much like he did in his early letters: "[Poetry is] a skill or trained habit of using all the extra-logical elements of language—rhythm, vowel-music, onomatopoeia, associations, and what not—to convey the concrete reality of experiences. . . . [A poem is] a composition which communicates more of the concrete and qualitative than our usual utterances do. A poet is a man who produces such compositions more often and more successfully than the rest of us" (108–9). Lewis's view suggests that a poet is primarily a workman using the tools of language to reflect on the universal concerns of all men and women. Because the poet is more gifted in the use of language, he can speak poignantly to universal human concerns. However, the poet as a person is no more worthy of our interest than a plumber; the poet simply articulates more effectively the same basic concerns he shares with the plumber. Near the end of *The Personal Heresy*, Lewis says there are only two questions to ask about a poem: "Firstly, whether it is interesting, enjoyable, attractive, and secondly, whether this enjoyment wears well and helps or hinders you towards all the other things you would like to enjoy, or do, or be" (119–20). It was this pragmatic view of poetry that Lewis consistently supported, and, at the same time, this view may have kept him from achieving acclaim as a poet. That is, it may be that Lewis's workmanlike efforts to write poetry, to make himself into a poet, inevitably thwarted his poetic sensibilities.

Even so, Lewis's public discussion with Tillyard complemented his continued private correspondence. For instance, he carried on a lengthy correspondence with Ruth Pitter, an accomplished poet. In response to her critiques of several of his poems, he writes: "In most of these poems [that he has sent her] I am enamoured of metrical subtleties—not as a game: the truth is I often lust after a metre as a man might lust after a woman" (*RP*, Aug. 10, 1946).[47] He writes to Rhona Bodle commenting on the way poetry makes language concrete: "Indeed, in a sense, one can hardly put anything into words: only the simplest colours have names, and hardly any of the smells. The simple physical pains and (still more) the pleasures can't be expressed in language. I labour the point lest the devil shd. hereafter try to make you believe that what was wordless was therefore vague and nebulous. But in reality it is just the clearest, the most concrete, and most indubitable realities which escape language: not because *they* [Lewis's emphasis] are vague but because language is. . . . Poetry I take to be the continual effort to bring language back to the actual" (June 24, 1949).[48] In writing to Martyn Skinner about his *Two Colloquies*, Lewis says, "I didn't want to write until I had given them a sympathetic reading and somehow I never was in quite the mood for them till tonight. (Reading collection papers, like marking School Cert., I have always found a great whetter of appetite for poetry. Fact! I don't know why). The right mood for a new poem doesn't come so often now as it used to. There is so little leisure, and when one comes to that leisure untired—well, you know *Ink* is a deadly drug. One wants to write. I cannot shake off the addiction" (Oct. 11, 1950).[49] In a letter to Dom Bede Griffiths, Lewis expresses his well-known distaste for modern British poetry and a surprisingly positive evaluation of some modern American poetry: "I feel as you do about modern English poetry. American is better. [Robert] Frost and Robinson Jeffers all really have something to *say* and some real art" (Apr. 22, 1954, Lewis's emphasis).[50] During a dry period, he writes Pitter: "It is a long time since I turned a verse. One aches a little, doesn't one? I should like to be 'with poem' again" (Mar. 19, 1955, *RP*, 0073).

Lewis the Craftsman

Lewis's penchant to be "enamoured of metrical subtleties," his lusting "after a metre as a man might lust after a woman," his ache to turn a verse and "be 'with poem' again," was lifelong, so before we consider the content of his poetry, it is appropriate we consider his focus upon crafting his poetry, including both his tendency to revise his poems and his fascination with prosody. While he certainly dashed off quick initial drafts of poems, he labored to make the final draft as polished as possible. Hooper has noted that while Lewis the prose writer worked quickly and wrote few drafts, Lewis the poet was painstaking, often writing several versions of the same poem: "Most of Lewis's prose came from his head almost exactly as it appears on the printed page, with only an occasional word being changed. It was not like this with his poetry. They went through endless revisions."[51] We know, for example, that Lewis sent friends drafts of poems and asked for criticism. In the mid-twenties, he writes Leo Baker: "I am sending you the revised version of the Wild Hunt and await your criticism. . . . I have not time today to discuss your theory of poetry; we seem to be agreed on fundamentals, tho' there are still points of difference—real ones, not 'misunderstanding'" (*LKB*, 090). About an autobiographical poem concerning, in part, his spiritual pilgrimage, Lewis writes Barfield: "It really takes a load off my mind to hear that you like the poem ["I Will Write Down"]. Couplets, however dangerous, are needed if one is to try to give to the subjective poem some of the swing and narrative

zest of the old epic. . . . I send . . . the opening of the poem. . . . I am not satisfied with any part I have yet written and the design is ludicrously ambitious.
But I feel it will be several years anyway before I give up" (May 6, 1932, *OB*, 0063,
0064).[52]

Lewis's extensive correspondence with Ruth Pitter also shows him seeking
criticism about drafts of poems. Given Lewis's deep affection for Pitter's poetry, it
is not surprising that he seeks her advice about his own poetry.[53] In her he found
one who shared similar poetic sensibilities, so he felt comfortable asking her to
critique his verse. In fact, he asked her to be straightforward in her criticisms:
"Now remember . . . you won't wound a sick man by unfavourable comment. . . .
I know (or think) that some of these contain important thoughts and v. great
metrical ingenuity. That isn't what I'm worrying about. But are they real poems
or do the content and the form remain separable—fitted together only by force?"
(July 24, 1946, *RP*, 005). At one point he asks her to judge between two versions of
his poem "Two Kinds of Memory": "I want some advice. I have written two different versions of a poem and all my friends disagree, some violently championing
A and some B, and some neither. Will you give a vote? Firstly, is either any good?
Secondly, if so, which is the good one? Don't be in the least afraid of answering
NO to the first question: kindness wd. only be an encouragement to waste more
time. . . . I could almost make myself hope for your sake—and lest you spend more
time and attention on them than is reasonable for me to exact—that both are
bad!" (Feb. 2, 1947, 017, 019). In her recollection of this letter, Pitter writes, "Both
versions are very fine, of course: the skill in form alone is enough to drive a small
poet to despair: and then the melody, so strong and so unforced, and the solemn
images and the contrasting moods. Strange how memory is here *polarised,* as
though he could not have encompassed the paradisal without retaining a hellish
pain in recollection, an ever-fresh wound. (NB. These poems should be read aloud,
but only by a strong male voice.) And see how he deprecates giving trouble, when
one was of course only too eager: I have sometimes thought he would devise little
jobs because he knew very well what pleasure it would give."[54] In another instance,
she recalls being flattered that Lewis would think her view on his poems important: "'Donkey's Delight,' 'Young King Cole,' 'Vitraea Circe,' [are] magnificent
poems to my mind, the technique staggering, vocabulary so wide, learned, &
choice, discrimination (moral or spiritual) so lofty. As well might a lion request a
mouse to criticise his roaring: and yet I can imagine a lion doing so."[55]

On the basis of such criticisms as well as his own desire to write the best poetry
possible, Lewis frequently reworked poems.[56] While any number of poems could
be cited to show Lewis working as a craftsman, we will consider one here as representative. In *Poems,* Hooper published the poignant sonnet "As the Ruin Falls,"
an agonizing recollection about a beloved one's suffering.[57] Three holograph ver-

sions of the poem survive, but all are undated.[58] However, based on the internal evidence of the three versions, I surmise the following order of the drafts:

Draft A (written on very thin typing paper)
This is all flashy rhetoric about loving you;
I never had a selfless thought since I was born.
I am mercenary and self-seeking through and through,
I want God, Man, and you, only to serve my turn.

Pleasure, ease, reassurance are the goals I seek,
I cannot crawl one inch outside my proper skin.
I talk of "love" (a scholar's parrot might talk Greek)
But, self-imprisoned, end always where I begin.

But this at least: you have shown me, dearest, what I lack,
Revealed the gulf, and me on the wrong side of it,
Shown me the impossibility of turning back,
And pointed me the one way from[?] the noisome pit.

For this I bless you for my broken heart. The pains
You cause me are more precious than all other gains.

Draft B (written on a scrap of paper)
All this is flashy rhetoric, about loving you.
I never had a selfless thought since I was born.
I am mercenary and self-seeking through and through:
I want friends, you, and God only to serve my turn.

Pleasure, peace, re-assurance are the goals I seek;
I cannot crawl one inch outside my proper skin.
I talk of love—a scholar's parrot may talk Greek—
But, self-imprisoned, always end where I begin.

Only that now you have shown me (oh how late) my lack:
I see the chasm; and everything you are was making
Each moment a long bridge by which I might get back
From exile and grow man. And now the bridge is breaking.

Yet so, I bless you for my hammered heart: the pains
You give me are more precious than all other gains.

Draft C (written on lined, greenish paper)
All this is flashy rhetoric about loving you.
I never had a selfless thought since I was born.
I am mercenary and self-seeking through and through:
I want God, you, all friends, merely to serve my turn.

Peace, re-assurance, pleasure, are the goals I seek,
I cannot crawl one inch outside my proper skin:
I talk of love—a scholar's parrot may talk Greek—
But, self-imprisoned, always end where I begin.

Only that now you have taught me (but how late) my lack.
I see the chasm. And everything you are was making
My heart into a bridge by which I might get back
From exile, and grow man. And now the bridge is breaking.

For this I bless you as the ruin falls. The pains
You give me are more precious than all other gains.[59]

Each draft is written in alexandrines and uses the rhyme scheme of an English sonnet. In the first quatrain, there are few differences between the drafts. "B" and "C" change the opening from "This is all flashy rhetoric" to "All this is flashy rhetoric," and in line four "only" becomes "merely" in "C." In the second quatrain, the "ease" of line five becomes "peace" in "B" and "C"; the alliteration of "pleasure, peace, reassurance" in "B" is weakened in "peace, re-assurance, pleasure" in "C." The only other significant difference is that "(a scholar's parrot might talk Greek)" becomes "—a scholar's parrot may talk Greek—" in "B" and "C."

However, the minor tweaking Lewis did in the drafts of the first two quatrains contrasts to major changes in the third quatrain and final couplet. In the initial draft, the third quatrain is weak. In line nine "but this at least" is jarring, and "dearest" edges the poem to the brink of sentimentality. "Revealed the gulf" in line ten could work, but "me on the wrong side of it" is forced. Line eleven suggests the beloved has shown the speaker "the impossibility of turning back" from his love for her, and this works well with the sentiment expressed in line twelve: that their relationship has saved him from hell on earth ("pointed me the one way from[?] the noisome pit"). Also, the *it:pit* rhyme is odd. The third quatrains of "B" and "C" are considerable improvements. Both drafts remake lines nine and ten-A into the more poetically powerful "Only that now you have taught me (but how late) my lack. / I see the chasm." The next clear sign the poem evolves from weak to stronger occurs when lines ten-B and eleven of "B," "and everything you are was making / Each moment a long bridge by which I might get back" becomes "and everything you are was making / My heart into a bridge by which I might get back" of "C." The shift from the impersonal "each moment a long bridge" to "my heart into a bridge" suddenly transforms the poem from an objective, clinical analysis to a subjective, personal confession. The power of both "B" and "C" is highlighted by the shared conclusion: "And now the bridge is breaking." Lewis deftly describes the pain of heartbreak yet avoids being maudlin.

The final couplet in the three drafts undergoes the most change, particularly line thirteen. In "A," Lewis again verges on the sentimental when he writes, "For this I bless you for my broken heart." "B" is a qualitative improvement as we read, "Yet so, I bless you for my hammered heart." Indeed, the notion his heart has been hammered by a smith shaping molten iron ameliorates the hackneyed use of "bless." However, Lewis nears perfection in "C" when the line evolves to its most powerful expression: "For this I bless you as the ruin falls." Now it all comes out: As he watches her suffering—her physical ruin—he faces squarely his own ruin: his broken life as he anticipates losing her. Yet in the midst of this knowledge, the poem's final line shares the secret of one of life's greatest ironies—the pain of losing one's beloved reinforces the inestimable worth of human love: "The pains / You give me are more precious than all other gains." In reviewing the three drafts of this poem, it is clear a craftsman was at work—shaping, honing, and molding words into the best combination of sounds and meanings he could. This same dedication to making the best poetry he could informed all of Lewis's serious efforts at verse.

LEWIS'S PROSODY

As a crafter of verse, Lewis was extremely conscious of prosody, especially meter, rhyme (exact and slant as well internal and final), and stanza form.[60] As early as March 7, 1916, he writes Greeves and critiques the prosody of several of George MacDonald's poems appearing in *Phantastes*: "There are . . . poems in the tale . . . which with one or two exceptions are shockingly bad, so don't TRY [Lewis's emphasis] to appreciate them: it is just a sign, isn't it, of how some geniuses can't work in metrical forms" (*TST*, 93). Three months later he tells Greeves, "My verse, both in quality and quantity for the last three weeks is deplorable!" (June 6, 1916, 107). On October 12, 1916, Lewis's praise to Greeves of Shelley's *Prometheus Unbound* is tempered by his criticism of the prosody: "Shelley had a great genius, but his carelessness about rhymes, metre, choice of words etc., just prevents him being as good as he might be. To me, when you're in the middle of a fine passage and come to a 'cockney' rhyme like 'ru*in*' & pursu*ing* [Lewis's emphasis], it spoils the whole thing" (136).

While Lewis's youthful criticism of Shelley may be querulous, it nonetheless demonstrates how important prosody was to him. Lewis's interest in the making of verse, especially prosody, was lifelong and is reflected in many of his scholarly writings. In "The Alliterative Metre," Lewis took it upon himself to expound "the principles of this metre to a larger public than those Anglo-Saxon and Old Norse specialists who know it already."[61] Throughout this essay he tries to make the technical aspects of alliterative meter understandable, and he gives a detailed explanation of how the half-line meter works. In addition, he explains lifts and dips, providing multiple examples (A–E plus variations of each) of how lifts and dips may be arranged in the half-line. In something of a tour de force, he ends the essays with his own model alliterative poem, "The Planets." Throughout this essay we follow the serious passion of a poet intent upon demonstrating how important a knowledge of prosody is for those who want to understand alliterative verse. In "The Fifteenth-Century Heroic Line," he offers another thoughtful discussion of prosody: "I shall give the arbitrary name 'Fifteenth-Century Heroic' to the line we find in *The Temple of Glas*, *The Pastime of Pleasure*, Barclay's *Ecologues*, Wyatt's *Complaint upon Love to Reason*, and, in general, all those poems which appear at first sight to attempt the decasyllabic line without success. The question I propose is whether the Fifteenth-Century Heroic is, in fact, an attempt at our decasyllabic; and, if it is not, what else it may be."[62] Lewis offers at one point in the essay to demonstrate what he means by an "experiment" in which he offers two contrasting four-line stanzas; while the content of each is roughly the same, the differing meters of each illustrate the point he wishes to make.

In his massive *English Literature in the Sixteenth Century* (1944), Lewis moves easily between literary history, evaluation of various poets (he dismisses some rather abruptly), and commentary on prosody. For example, about the poulter's measure (alternating lines of hexameter and heptameter), he writes, "The vices of that metre are two. The medial break in the alexandrine, though it may do well enough in French, quickly becomes intolerable in a language with such a tyrannous stress-accent as ours: the line struts. The fourteener has a much pleasanter movement, but a totally different one; the line dances a jig. Hence in a couplet made of two such yoke-fellows we seem to be labouring up a steep hill in bottom gear for the first line, and then running down the other side of the hill, out of control, for the second" (232–33). In "Metre," published near the end of his life, Lewis is still focusing upon prosody.[63] The essay attempts to consider the somewhat thorny question of how to scan lines of poetry. After admitting that scansion depends upon phonetic facts and individual differences of pronunciation, he posits, "I am going to suggest that metrical questions are profitable only if we regard them, not as questions about fact, but as purely practical. That is, when we ask 'What is the metre of this poem?,' we are not, or should not be, asking which analysis of the paradigm is 'true' but which is most useful" (281).

Lewis's earliest poems illustrate this lifelong fascination with prosody. For example, he enjoyed experimenting with meter from the heroic couplets of "Descend to Earth, Descend, Celestial Nine" to the eight-stressed catalectic trochees of "'Carpe Diem' after Horace" to the rhyme royal of "In Winter When the Frosty Nights Are Long" to the blank verse of *Loki Bound*.[64] Other examples of Lewis's earliest verse, the ten poems that survive from "Metrical Meditations of a Cod"[65] and the lyrics of *Spirits in Bondage*, offer additional insights into Lewis's youthful concerns with prosody. Of these fifty-one poems, thirty-five are tetrameter or pentameter, most often iambs, with trochees less frequent. The other sixteen poems include trimeter, hexameter, heptameter, and several cases where the meter is mixed.

Tetrameter and Pentameter Poems

Several of Lewis's iambic tetrameter and pentameter poems employ rhyming couplets. For instance, the tetrameter couplets of "Satan Speaks" (I) and the heroic couplets of "Satan Speaks" (XIII) indicate that the two poems share more than a common title (*SB*, 3, 22). Both open similarly, including the use of a medial caesura. The "I am Nature, the Mighty Mother / I am the law: ye have none other" of the former sets the stage for "I am the Lord your God: even he that made / Material things, and all these signs arrayed" of the latter. In "The Hills of Down," Lewis disguises his heroic couplets by printing the poem as though lines of iambic dimeter alternate with iambic trimeter:

> I will abide
>> And make my dwelling here
> Whatso betide,
>> Since there is more to fear
> Out yonder. Though
>> This world is drear and wan,
> I dare not go
>> To dreaming Avalon. (*CP*, 229)

What we actually have are heroic couplets with internal rhyme. Lewis weaves the fabric of this poem even tighter when we note the assonance of *abide, my,* and *betide* in the first three lines as well as the final *-er* sound of *here, there, fear, yonder,* and *drear* in lines two through six. This assonance and sound repetition occurs throughout the other sections of the poem.

Lewis used tercets less often but to powerful effect, as in "Spooks": "Last night I dreamed that I was come again / Unto the house where my beloved dwells / After years of wandering and pain" (*SB,* 11). While the rhyme scheme here is *aba* and not the typical *aaa* of the true tercet, Lewis may have been experimenting with a kind of terza rima, since the rest of the poem rhymes *acc, dde, ffe, acca.* However, "De Profundis" utilizes the true tercet rhyme, with several sounds repeated in the twelve stanzas: *abcdefgdhige.* In addition, one stanza uses the unusual perfect rhyme: "Yet I will not bow down to thee nor love thee, / For looking in my own heart I can prove thee, / And know this frail, bruised being is above thee" (20). Another example of the true tercet is found in "Hymn (for Boys' Voices)" where Lewis uses trochaic catalectic tetrameter: "Every man a God would be / Laughing through eternity / If as God's his eye could see" (58). We also see tercets in the longest poem of *Spirits in Bondage,* "Song of the Pilgrims."

Oddly, although Lewis admired Tennyson's poetry, in these early poems we never see him attempt the *In Memoriam* stanza: iambic tetrameter with the *abba* rhyme scheme. At the same time, most of Lewis's pentameter poems, such as "Of Ships," "French Nocturne," "Victory," "Apology," and "Milton Read Again," use the *abba* rhyme. Also, among his early poems Lewis wrote two Italian sonnets, "Sonnet—To Philip Sydney" and "Sonnet" ("The stars come out; the fragrant shadows fall"), both employing the *abbaabba cdcdee* rhyme (*CP,* 237; *SB,* 33). In the sonnet to Sydney, Lewis appears to be working strictly to form, so much so that the poem is only two sentences: The octave is the first sentence and the sestet is the second. In the sonnet "The stars come out," he more freely uses the caesura, producing a poem with five sentences and medial caesuras in lines one, eight, and eleven. A final connection between the two sonnets is his use of the feminine rhyme *hour:bower* in both. While Lewis wrote other sonnets later, it was not a form he particularly favored, so these two early specimens suggest poetic "finger exercise" where he imitated and experimented with the form.

We also see Lewis experimenting with a medieval poetic form—the ballade— in his "Ballade of a Winter's Morning" and "Ballade Mystique" (*CP,* 234–35; *SB,* 53–54). The ballade, which Lewis may have encountered in imperfect form in Chaucer and almost certainly knew from Swinburne's "Ballad of Dreamland," Henley's "Ballade of Dead Actors," and Lang's "Ballades of Blue China," is highly structured. Most commonly, the ballade consists of three stanzas and a final envoy. Each stanza is eight to ten lines, and the envoy contains half as many lines as the stanzas. The rhyme in all the stanzas must be identical in the corresponding lines, although the rhyming words may vary from stanza to stanza; the most common rhyme scheme for the stanza is *ababbcbc* and for the envoy *bcbc.* However, the one element that marks the ballade is the refrain, which forms the last line of each stanza and the envoy. The envoy "is not only a dedication, but should be the peroration of the subject, and richer in its wording and more stately in its imagery than the preceding verses, to convey the climax of the whole matter, and avoid the suspicion that it is a mere postscript."[66]

Both "Ballade of a Winter's Morning" and "Ballade Mystique" are iambic tetrameter stanzas of eight lines with the *ababbcbc* rhyme scheme, and both four-line envoys use the *bcbc* rhyme scheme. The refrain in "Ballade of a Winter's Morning" undergoes progressive mutations from "A merry morning we shall spend" to "And make us merry friend by friend" to "To make us merry friend by friend" to "Of him who sang Patroklos' friend" to "Than thine or mine, oh friend, my friend" to the final line of the envoy, "We'll tread them bravely, friend by friend." In a poem almost certainly celebrating Lewis's friendship with Greeves, the refrain is most appropriate. In "Ballade Mystique," Lewis experiments with the refrain as it moves from a question to a declarative to a final combined declarative and question: "What do they know? What do they know?" (repeated in the second stanza) to "They do not know, they do not know" to the envoy's "They do not know: how should they know?" This poem, ostensibly also about friendship, uses the refrain to contrast the distance between the speaker and his friends.

Similarly, the envoy of the former is upbeat ("So while the wind-foot seasons wear / Be glad, and when towards the end / Adown the dusky ways we fare, / We'll tread them bravely, friend by friend!"), while that of the latter is dark ("The friends I have without a peer / Beyond the western ocean's glow, / Whither the faerie galleys steer, / They do not know: how should they know?"). Yet both poems link friendship with love for literature. "Ballade of a Winter's Morning," obviously set in winter when all is cold and dead outside, fairly exalts in the anticipation of rich sessions inside where the friends will "take fit books" and "old tomes full oft re-read with care," those perhaps of Spenser, Horace, Malory, and Virgil, as a remedy for the outer cold. Ironically, however, in "Ballade Mystique," the speaker, whose friends think he needs to leave his house in order to enjoy Spring and "the wakening of the year," does not feel the need for their fellowship. He is not, as they believe, "piteously alone / Without the speech of comrades dear." Instead, literature is his comfort:

> That I have seen the Dagda's throne
> In sunny lands without a tear
> And found a forest all my own
> To ward with magic shield and spear,
> Where, through the stately towers I rear
> For my desire, around me go
> Immortal shapes of beauty clear.

As a result, both ballades, highly structured literary forms, center upon the value of literature. While "Ballade Mystique" underscores the speaker's isolation and alienation from his friends, "Ballade of a Winter's Morning" highlights the fellowship and camaraderie the speaker enjoys with one friend.

Poems with Other Meters

Although Lewis favored iambic tetrameter and pentameter, he enjoyed writing poems in other meters. "Exercise," for example, utilizes iambic trimeter: "Where are the magic swords / That elves of long ago / Smithied beneath the snow / For heroes' rich rewards?" (*CP*, 242). The trimeter six-line stanzas of "Hesperus" employ a unique *ababcb* rhyme scheme (*SB*, 65–66). Three poems, "To Sleep," "Our Daily Bread," and "How He Saw Angus the God" (18, 60–62), use a kind of English form of the Sapphic stanza with rhyme: four-line stanzas of alternate rhyme, with the first three lines in pentameter and the fourth line a trimeter. Lewis plays with an even shorter form in the couplet lines of "The Autumn Morning," where we find quatrains with the first three lines in trimeter and the fourth line in dimeter: "See! The pale autumn dawn / Is faint, upon the lawn / That lies in powdered white / Of hoar-frost dight" (34–35).

Lewis's only example of hexameter in these early poems is the appropriately entitled "Alexandrines" (41). In addition to experimenting with iambic hexameter in this poem, Lewis also plays with the sonnet form by modifying both the rhyme scheme and the length of the poem. His *ababbccddeeff* is a loose adaptation of the typical English sonnet rhyme scheme, and his thirteen-line format is one short of the sonnet. The alexandrine is typically characterized by a regular and strongly marked medial caesura, and Lewis's poem includes medial caesuras in lines three, seven, nine, ten, eleven, and twelve. The effectiveness of the medial caesura is best seen in the last four lines: "For in that house I know a little, silent room / Where Someone's always waiting, waiting in the gloom / To draw me with an evil eye, and hold me fast— / Yet thither doom will drive me and He will win at last."

More frequent in these early poems is Lewis's exploration of the heptameter (or septenary). Like the hexameter, the heptameter is marked by a regular and strong medial caesura evident in "Ode for New Year's Day":

Woe unto you, ye sons of pain that are this day in earth,
Now cry for all your torment: now curse your hour of birth
And the fathers who begat you to a portion nothing worth.
And Thou, my own beloved, for as brave as ere thou art,
Bow down thine head, Despoina, clasp thy pale arms over it. (13)

"World's Desire" is written primarily in septenarian couplets, with occasional octameters as well: "And the cold ravine / Echoes to the crushing roar and thunder of a mighty river / Raging down a cataract. Very tower and forest quiver / And the grey wolves are afraid and the call of birds is drowned, / And the thought and speech of man in the boiling water's sound" (72). Lewis uses heptameter tercets throughout "The Roads": "I stand on the windy uplands among the hills of Down / With all the world spread out beneath, meadow and sea and town, / And ploughlands on the far-off hills that glow with friendly brown" (63). In "Prologue" he employs an irregular heptameter:

As of old Phoenician men, to the Tin Isles sailing
Straight against the sunset and the edges of the earth,
Chaunted loud above the storm and the strange sea's wailing,
Legends of their people and the land that gave them birth—
Sang aloud to Baal-Peor, sang unto the horned maiden,
Sang how they should come again with the Brethon treasure laden. (xli)

To this oddity Lewis adds lines of octameter as in "Toiling at the stroke and feather through the wet and weary weather."

One of the most interesting heptameter specimens is "The Satyr," where Lewis, as he does with the heroic couplets in "The Hills of Down," disguises the meter by printing the poem so it appears we are reading tetrameter quatrains rhyming *aaba:* "When the flowery hands of spring / Forth their woodland riches fling, / Through the meadows, through the valleys / Goes the satyr carolling" (5). In fact, the meter is heptameter couplets with internal rhyme occurring in the first line of each couplet as in *spring:fling.* Furthermore, Lewis emphasizes particular sounds in each couplet as in *fl*owery, *f*orth, *fl*ing, and va*ll*eys and caro*ll*ing. He extends the connection of sounds by creating internal rhyme between pairs of couplets. For instance, the couplet following the one cited above is: "From the mountain and the moor, / Forest green and ocean shore / All the faerie kin he rallies / Making music evermore." In addition to the internal rhyme of *moor: shore*, the alliteration of *m*ountain, *m*oor, *m*aking, and *m*usic, and the emphasis on the sound—*or* as in m*oor*, f*or*est, sh*or*e, and everm*or*e, Lewis links the couplets by rhyming *valleys* in the second line of the first heptameter couplet with *rallies* in the second line of the second heptameter couplet. This use of internal rhyme to connect the septenarian couplets continues in the rest of the poem as in *cloven:woven* in lines six and eight and *asunder:wonder* in lines ten and twelve. As this review of Lewis's earliest poetry illustrates, he enjoyed experimenting with meter, rhyme, and lyric forms, and this interest extended throughout his poetic career.

Nevill Coghill in "The Approach to English" commented upon Lewis's poetry, recalling as young men in the 1920s that both he and Lewis "hoped to be poets. . . . It was not until six or seven years later that Lewis said sadly to me 'When I at last realized that I was not, after all, going to be a great man. . . .' I think he meant 'a great poet.'"[67] He also recalled Lewis's "'gusto' for poetry" (62). Coghill's comments are a helpful gloss to Lewis's poetic aspirations, influences, craftsmanship, and prosody. In combination they illustrate the degree to which writing poetry and being a poet were fundamental to the way Lewis saw himself. While the tepid critical reception of *Dymer* in 1926 forced him to suppress his desire to be known as a poet publicly, privately he longed to be a good one as his sustained efforts at verse demonstrate. He wanted to be a great poet in the tradition of the ancients he so admired. Consequently, he drew from the cistern of poetic impulse by frequently reading Virgil, Dante, Milton, Wordsworth, Yeats, and others. At the same time, he worked consciously as a crafter of verse, especially at prosody, in order to shape poems worthy of the same well.[68] It is now time to turn to his initial efforts in verse, poetry written and in some cases published before *Spirits in Bondage*, in order to see the earliest outpourings of his poetic impulse.

CHAPTER TWO

Early Poems, 1908–1919

In *Collected Poems,* Walter Hooper begins by noting that "this volume brings together for the first time all C. S. Lewis's short poems into a single volume." In addition to *Poems* and *Spirits in Bondage,* he includes "a 'Miscellany' of seventeen short poems previously either unpublished or uncollected. The poems cover the whole of Lewis's life, from those he wrote as a young man of sixteen to those written within a few weeks of his death" (ix).[1] Hooper's choice for the title of *Collected Poems* is judicious, since it is the "collected" rather than the "complete" poems of Lewis.[2] As was noted in the last chapter, a number of short poems and fragments as well as four narrative poem fragments have also survived.[3] From these several sources we can explore Lewis's earliest efforts at verse. In particular, eighteen early poems, written between 1908 and 1919, offer readers fascinating insights into Lewis's poetic development.[4] While some of the poems are not Lewis at his best, in part because they are school exercises imitating classical models,[5] they illustrate the importance of Lewis's poetic aspirations.

"The Old Grey Mare" (1908?)[6] is his earliest surviving poem. Warren Lewis says this "poem I judge from internal evidence to be the earliest of Clive's attempts in verse which survives. It is certainly not later than 1909, and a careful comparison . . . suggests that it may be as early as 1907. In any case it was written at Little Lea, and not at Wynyard, for the paper is of a pattern which was never used at the school" (*LP,* 3:166–67). As a poem, "The Old Grey Mare" is a pedestrian celebration of the valor of a knight's battlefield charger: "Rushing in some dreadful fray, / She's a living shield I say, / Rushing o'er the bloody field, / She will face the foeman's shield." Though simple, it reflects a lively imagination and has obvious affinities with Lewis and his brother's fascination with Animal-Land and Boxen dating from the same time. This poem is about what we might expect of a boy between eight and eleven.

In contrast, his "Descend to Earth, Descend, Celestial Nine," is the heroic narrative poem inspired by Wagner that Lewis refers to in *Surprised by Joy*. Its seven hundred ninety-four lines of heroic couplets date to 1912–13 and show unusual maturity.[7] As has been mentioned, we know from *Surprised by Joy* that some time early in 1911 after his move to Cherbourg House, Malvern, Lewis, one day musing in the library, came across the title of a new book listed in a literary periodical, *Siegfried and the Twilight of the Gods*.[8] When he read the title he was suddenly transported into realms of pure "northernness" (72–73), and he attempted his version of *The Rhinegold* (the "prelude" of the *The Ring of the Nibelung*) without having read a line-by-line translation or heard a score.[9] Furthermore, Warren Lewis reproduced a lengthy essay on Richard Wagner that his brother wrote while at Cherbourg House (*LP*, 3:233–35). As a piece of writing for someone this young, the essay is remarkable, although it adds little to our critical understanding of Wagner. In the essay Lewis surveyed Wagner's important work, made general comments upon opera, and finished by priggishly dismissing those incapable of appreciating opera. About the *Ring* he says: "His next, and perhaps his greatest work, was his immortal 'Nibelung Ring,' a trilogy whose three parts, the 'Walkyrie,' 'Siegfried,' and the 'Twilight of the Gods' are preceded by a prelude, 'The Rhinegold.' It is based on the great Scandinavian epic, the Nibelungen Lied or Lot, and is a beautiful piece of work" (233–34). Lewis was so enthralled by *The Ring of the Nibelung* through reading synopses of it in *The Soundbox* that he immediately began work on "Descend to Earth, Descend, Celestial Nine" (*SJ*, 74–75). Considering all this, "Descend to Earth" is an impressive accomplishment. Warren Lewis thought so, noting it was written "between the summers of 1912 and of 1913. Its absolute merit and its astonishing maturity make it . . . a remarkable production for a boy of between 14 and 15" (*LP*, 3:321).

Unlike Wagner's opera, Lewis's "Descend" is narrative rather than dramatic.[10] Three complete books survive as well as a fragmentary fourth, suggesting that Lewis was structuring a work of twelve books imitating the Greek and Latin epics he so admired. Accordingly, we are not surprised when he begins with a six-line invocation to the Muses:

> Descend to earth, descend, celestial Nine
> And sing the ancient legend of the Rhine:
> What races first upon the world did dwell
> In earliest days, descend Oh Muse and tell.
> Who did the mighty hills inhabit, who
> The earth's deep clefts: narrate the story true.

Recalling Milton's "Sing, Heavenly Muse" opening to Book 1 of *Paradise Lost*, Lewis follows by merging his love of classical narrative poetry in the next six lines with his new passion for Norse literature:

> Upon the mountain tops in happy light
> Abode the gods with majesty and might,
> Whom Wotan ruled as chief. The sluggish Rhine
> Rhine maidens sheltered, nymphs of form divine,
> Who for their sire a noted treasure held,
> The Rhinegold, and in watch of this they dwelled.[11]

As he wrote this, it is not hard to imagine Lewis seeing himself in the tradition of great epic poets. Homer had his Odysseus, Virgil his Aeneas, Milton his Adam, Tennyson his Arthur, and Lewis his Wotan.

Book 1 introduces Alberich, the misshapen king of the Nibelung: "A stunted race who never see the light / Of hideous visage and puny height: / Abide they thus in corners dark and deep, / . . . cunning they, and full of vicious greed." One day Alberich, rising from the river's depth, sees the beautiful Rhine maidens swimming, and he is inflamed with lust. Once aware of him, the maidens mock and tease him: "'Does Alberich indulge in dreams of love / And steer his mind through thoughts of his state above?' / . . . They tantalize with dance the tiny king, / The waters wide with wanton laughter ring." Alliteration, particularly effective here, is notable throughout the poem. While Wagner's opera then has the maidens one by one cruelly feign love for Alberich, effectively lacerating his emotions and humiliating him, in Lewis's version they collectively taunt him, all the while inflaming his lust. Tiring of the Nibelung king's pursuits, Lewis's maidens decide to give him a vision of the Rhinegold, hoping this will deflect interest away from them. This fatal error is compounded when they foolishly reveal the awful power of the gold:

> Knows he not the key
> By which alone the hoard his own may be?
> Knows he not as he tries to grasp in vain
> The treasure, that who would the Rhinegold gain
> Must first curse love before his hands may hold
> The glistening and so much desired gold.
> And he, should he but gain the pile he wants
> (If there be truth in legendary vaunts)
> If to a RING he forge it by the art
> Of goldsmith, then to rule shall be his part;
> Whoe'er the treasure keeps and wears the RING
> Shall rule the world, an everlasting king.

Having seen Alberich's lust, the maidens are confident he can never renounce love. However, the book ends with him seizing the gold, the maidens fleeing in disarray, and Alberich returning to the underworld in proud arrogance, this latter detail Lewis's addition.[12]

In Book 2, as the scene shifts to Asgard, Lewis summarizes Wotan's agreement with the giants, Fasolt and Fafnir: If they build him a castle, he will give them his sister-in-law, the goddess Freia. The action begins with Lewis's description of the sleeping Wotan:

> Thus, as the dawn was breaking, lay the god
> Before the castle on the verdant sod;
> The light caressed with gentle touch his form,
> His noble visage, free from passion's storm,
> His golden beard, and arms and limbs divine.
> As on the herbage lay the god supine
> Closed were his eyes, and sweet, refreshing sleep
> The mighty king in soft embrace did keep.

Nearby, Frika, his "everlasting spouse," is also sleeping. She awakens to Wotan's exclamation upon first seeing his newly created castle:

> Fit shelter for the lord and king of all!
> Valhall! My home! Oh be thou strong and blessed,
> Standing so firmly by the light caressed
> See! How vermilion grows each stony point.
> How flames like fire each wooden beam and joint.

Both, however, soon are uneasy about the agreement Wotan has made with the giants and blame Logie, god of fire and Wotan's favorite counselor, for advising him to accept the giants' conditions.[13]

Freia then enters hysterical and shrill, indignant over Wotan's bargain. Before Wotan can respond, Fasolt and Fafnir appear. While the former is a somewhat kindly figure, seeking Friea motivated by love, Fafnir reveals a darker motive for his interest:

> Tis Freia who the golden apples tends,
> Of which the gods immortal eat and live.
> Were she not there the duteous care to give,
> The gods must some day pass in death away,
> I, with Fasolt, will hold unbounded sway
> O'er all the world.

Together, they demand payment: "Oh mighty lord of Valhall blessed. / We come the bargained price you owe to claim, / Fulfill your vows or yield t'eternal shame." Wotan withdraws to retrieve Freia, in the meantime sending out Freia's brothers, Froh, god of joy, and Donner, god of thunder, advising them to buy time while Wotan waits for Logie to appear. Using "oily words and counsels fair," Freia's brothers for a time have limited success, but Fasolt's desire (his "blue eyes the fire flames fiercer still") will not be thwarted.

As the four of them prepare to fight, Wotan returns with Logie:

> For by the hand he led a slender god,
> In burning robe, in burning sandals shod:
> His frame was thin, nor was his stature great,
> His raven eyes with varied thoughts dilate.
> He counts and counts again his every wile,
> And whispers in his master's ear the while.

Wotan demands that Logie tell if he has discovered any way to void the agreement with the giants. Although he has scoured the earth, Logie has not been successful. However, in his journeys he has learned of the story of the Rhine maidens and Alberich, even having pledged on Wotan's behalf to help the maidens. Fafnir, fascinated by Logie's story of the powerful gold, offers Wotan an unexpected deal:

> I had fondly hoped
> Freia to gain: But since you do not choose
> To give her up, I will not therefore lose
> My whole reward. Freia to thee I'll give,
> (So may she always in Valhalla live).
> Give me that treasure which the god of fire
> Hath told us of: for that I most desire.

Wotan points out that the treasure is not his to give; in addition, he appears weak: "The cunning gnomes may snare / Our person by their wiles, did we but dare / Their noisome caverns where in gloom they dwell; / I fear their hidden, untried depths of hell." After the giants lead Freia away, Logie urges Wotan to reconsider, reminding him that without Freia's harvest of golden apples, the gods of Valhalla will grow weak and lose power. The book ends with Wotan reluctantly agreeing to take on the quest and to descend to the Nibelheim.

Book 3, as in *Paradise Lost*, begins with an invocation, but while the latter is a request for the Heavenly Muse to enlighten Milton's view of Heaven, Lewis's request takes him in the opposite direction:

Guide me, my muse, down yonder sloping way,
Far lead me from the happy light of day.
Let us descend by clefts, where fathoms deep
The Nibelungs their hollow city keep.
Here, in the regions of eternal night,
By pumice rocks enclosed: where never light
With shining radiance spreads its warming ray,
Nor morning dawns, nor differs night from day.

Once there, we find Alberich lording his new power over his goldsmith Mime, who he has commissioned to forge a magic helmet. Mime, while cognizant that the gold has power, does not know what the power is, so he is physically abused by Alberich for not having the helmet ready when he demands it. The helmet's power is substantial: "For the Tarnhelm—so the cap was named / This virtue for the golden helmet claim; / Whoe'er the headgear wore, at any time / What form he wished could take." When Alberich puts it on for the first time, he becomes invisible and rewards Mime for his hard work by beating him senseless.

Into this dark, noxious atmosphere, Wotan and Logie suddenly appear: "What light, what radiancy divine, / Fails to recite this earthly pen of mine, / Which that dark cavern flooded as the forms / Of two fair gods appeared." The Nibelung, upon seeing such glory, like "rats with evil patterings haste away, / Recoiling from the glare in wild dismay."[14] Pretending to care about Mime's mistreatment by Alberich, Logie offers to conspire with Mime against his cruel king. Before they can come to an agreement, Alberich reenters, pitilessly driving a crew of Niblungs before him with a whip and holding a ring of gold above his head. Logie tries to flatter Alberich: "Hail, mighty king. We know your stirling worth, / Nor, being wise, despise your dwarfish birth. / We come our due respect as brother kings / To pay. Valhalla worthy homage brings." However, Alberich rejects false homage and bitterly scorns Asgard:

> Do gods
> Descend the dark and unfrequented roads
> That lead to my dark realm, respects to pay
> To Alberich? Or leave the glowing day
> To seek the caverns of a king they hate?
> Or doth the eagle with the beetle mate?
> Am I a child that I should thus believe
> Ye come love-laden spirits to relieve
> With kindly words? Nay: never was there yet
> A god but did all misery beget

With lofty schemes. The price of Asgard's good
Is running rivulets of human blood.

These lines, perhaps the best in the poem, reveal Lewis writing almost effortlessly, using effective imagery, unforced rhymes, and pointed rhetoric. Furthermore, Alberich's bitter criticism of Asgard and its gods, who "all misery beget with lofty schemes" at the price of "running rivulets of human blood," ties the poem to *Spirits in Bondage* where, as we shall see, the only slightly older Lewis rails against a God he hates. There, as here, God is for God, Asgard for Asgard.

Though Alberich scorns Wotan and Logie, he cannot resist demonstrating his newly acquired power, so he threatens to use his ring and helmet against them. Fate, he says, has permitted Asgard to rule until the present, but now "Fate hath prepared its downfall and its shame: / The ring hath made me monarch of ye all." Wotan, his pride offended, is enraged at this threat; to illustrate this, Lewis employs an epic simile worthy of the *Aeneid* or *Paradise Lost*:

> And at this jeer
> The rage swelled up in Wotan's godly heart;
> Forgets the god to play his subtler part,
> And, like as when the hounds with barking stand
> About the antlered deer, on either hand,
> And vex the mighty monarch of the glades
> Who, for a time, resists their paltry raids
> With only lazy strength. Then rears his head
> Above the throng, the meadows swims with red
> And curdling gore as charges he the throng,
> Invades their ribs with cruel horns and strong.

Before Wotan can strike, however, Logie intervenes and cleverly demands that Alberich give a demonstration of his power; unless they see him change shape, they will not believe his words. Initially, Alberich rejects this demand, wisely seeing through Logie's scheme: "And think ye, friends, / I do not know your avaricious ends: / Shall I a small and feeble beast become, / That you may bear the treasure from my home?" Logie, undeterred, presses Alberich, shaming his pride so that he forgets his own warning. In a scene reminiscent of Canto XXV of the *Inferno* where thieves are transfigured into loathsome giant serpents, or Book 10 of *Paradise Lost* where Satan and the fallen angels unwillingly become huge snakes driven to consume ash and cider as a part of God's judgment upon them for having perverted Adam and Eve, Alberich willfully transforms himself into a vicious fox.[15] Wotan is horrified when he witnesses this, but Logie seizes the chance to appeal to Alberich's vanity. Feigning awe, Logie flatters Alberich and asks for another demonstration. Alberich, his reason blind to the danger, foolishly does exactly what he said he would not: "And where the dwarf in form of fox had been / There writhed a slimy toad upon the floor."[16] At this Wotan rushes forward, pinning Alberich to the floor, and Logie seizes the helmet. The book concludes as the gods embrace, grab the toad, ascend from Nibelheim, and rejoice "once more to breathe the upper air."

Book 4 is a fragment of forty-three lines and departs radically from Wagner. It begins with Wotan and Logie bringing the toad to Valhalla while Valkyries, Brunhilda in particular, are seen riding in the distance. As Wotan is about to speak to Frika, the manuscript breaks off. That Lewis never returned to the poem, although he does deal with related characters and issues in *Loki Bound* several years later, is our loss, for he achieves much, especially in the three complete books. For example, we see him handling rather effectively the demands of narrative poetry, combining an effective meter and rhyme with a compelling story. Furthermore, his characterization suggests insights into human nature we might not expect from one so young and that far exceed Wagner's flat, melodramatic characters. While Lewis can be criticized for lacking his own creative impulse and thus writing a derivative narrative, within the limits of the genre and his age, "Descend to Earth" is unusually powerful. Practice with a narrative this long was fertile ground for a novelist in training.

The next poem, "*Quam Bene Saturno*," is Lewis's first published poem; it appeared toward the end of his time at Cherbourg House, Malvern, where he was a student between January 1911 and July 1913.[17] The title comes from Tibullus 1.3.35 and means "How well they lived when Saturn (was king)." It celebrates the benevolent rule of Saturn in the days of the Titans before the successful rebellion of Jove: "Alas, what happy days were those / When Saturn ruled a peaceful race, / Or yet the foolish mortals chose / With roads to track the world's broad face." Since that time peace has been replaced with strife and contention: "But now . . . With Jove our haughty lord / No peace we know by many a wound: / And famine, slaughter, fire and sword / With grim array our path surround." Characteristic of several of Lewis's earliest poems, this poem is probably a response to a school exercise written in iambic tetrameter, employing a simple rhyme scheme.

"'Carpe Diem' after Horace" is included in a letter postmarked October 19, 1913 that the young Lewis sent his father, and it may be a piece encouraged by the disciplined instruction of Henry Wakelyn Smith.[18] In the letter he is clearly pleased with himself since the poem had achieved distinction as a school exercise at Malvern College: "The poem after Horace was, I am glad to tell you, somewhat in the nature of a success. It was top of the form and was sent up to the James. 'Being sent up for good' is a priveledge [*sic*] . . . and is rather a ceremony"

(*LP,* 4:87). The poem, modeled after Tennyson's "Locksley Hall" (twelve lines of eight-stressed catalectic trochaic meter) is an example of the kind of school writing exercise (a set piece) Lewis was doing at this time:

> When, in haughty exultation, thou durst laugh in
>   Fortune's face,
> Or when thou hast sunk down weary, trampled in
>   The ceaseless race,
> Dellius, think on this I pray thee—but the
>   Twinkling of an eye,
> May endure thy pain or pleasure; for thou knowest
>   Thou shalt die
> Whether on some breeze-kissed upland, with a
>   Flask of mellow wine,
> Thou hast all the world forgotten, stretched be-
>   Neath the friendly pine,
> Or, in foolish toil consuming all the springtime
>   Of thy life,
> Thou hast worked for useless silver and endured
>   The bitter strife
> Still unchanged thy doom remaineth. Thou art
>   Set towards thy goal,
> Out into the empty breezes soon shall flicker
>   Forth thy soul,
> Here then by the plashing streamlet fill the
>   Tinkling glass I pray
> Bring the short lived rosy garlands, and be
>   Happy—FOR TODAY.[19]

Lewis used Horace's "Aequam Memento Rebus" (Book 2, Ode 3) as his model, though he slightly shifted the sober, at times depressing, Horatian tone to an upbeat, seize-the-day affirmation. This is most apparent in a comparison of the final stanzas. Horace says: "Omnes eodem cogimur, omnium / Versatur urna serius ocius / Sors exitura et nos in aeternum / Exsilium impositura cumbae."[20] We notice, however, that while Lewis maintains the notion that Dellius is surely heading for death ("still unchanged thy doom remaineth"), he includes an imperative that tries to thwart the inevitable, if only for a moment: "Here then by the plashing streamlet fill the / Tinkling glass I pray / Bring the short lived rosy garlands, and be / Happy—FOR TODAY." This final shout urges Dellius to take advantage of the day and to find happiness, though fleeting and transient. Lewis's "'Carpe

Diem' after Horace" reflects youthful exuberance and earnest effort. While a poetic derivative, it is a fine poetic finger exercise preparing the way for Lewis's later mature poetic efforts.

Another poem Smith may have encouraged Lewis to write is "In Winter When the Frosty Nights Are Long," a thirty-line fragment of rhyme royal (appropriately complementing the poem's cadence and diction) written about the same time as "'Carpe Diem' after Horace." Warren Lewis says it is a poem "written on the type of paper in use for exercises in the Upper Fifth at Malvern," and he dates it "tentatively in the winter of this year [1913] or in the spring of 1914" (*LP*, 4:121). The poem is a dream vision revealing Lewis's deep love for the beauty of Nature:

> In winter when the frosty nights are long
> And sedge is stiff about the frozen meres,
> One night above a volume of old song
> Of legendary loves and magic fears
> Sweetened by long elapse of slumbering years,
> I nodded in the frosty firelight beam
> And fell on sleep and straightway dreamed a dream.
>
> I thought it was a luminous summer night,
> And in the star-flecked welkin overhead
> A fading sickle of soft golden light
> Its wonder over all the landscape spread,
> While fleecy clouds athwart its paleness sped:
> Ten thousand thousand points of light did peep
> Out of the boundless heaven's velvet deep.
>
> Meseemed I stood upon a goodly plain
> Full of soft streams and meadows deep in corn,
> While the far thunder of a foaming main
> Across the calm, delicious air was born.
> Beyond the plain, a mountain waste forlorn
> Clear seen beneath the trembling silver light,
> Rose, and yet rose with height still piled on height.
>
> Higher than mountains seemed, than Alpine peaks
> Or fabled mountains spied from the moon,
> And tortured into grim fantastic freaks
> Of rock: oerhanging cliffs that seemed to swoon
> Towards me, ready with vast ruin soon
> To fall and whelm the plain, and vallies steep
> Engulphed with icy torrents swift and deep.

> The eye could hardly reach, and senses failed
> In gazing on those unimagined. . . .[21]

The first stanza suggests the powerful influence of literature upon the dreamer ("a volume of old song / Of legendary loves and magic fear"), while the second takes him from a wintry present to an enchanted summer evening, the sky filled with "ten thousand thousand points of light." In the third and fourth stanzas, Nature, while beautiful, suddenly appears terrifying and contrasts with the serenity portrayed in the first two. The dreamer feels the mountains are about to overwhelm him ("tortured into grim fantastic freaks / Of rock"), and the stone and earth are on the verge of burying him. The paradox of nature's beauty and awful power connects this fragment to Wordsworth's *The Prelude*:

> One summer evening (led by her [Nature]) I found
> A little boat tied to a willow tree
>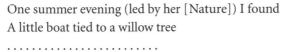
>   I fixed my view
> Upon the summit of a craggy ridge
> . . . .
> She was an elfin pinnace; lustily
> I dipped my oars into the silent lake
> . . . .
> When, from behind that craggy steep till then
> The horizon's bound, a huge peak, black and huge,
> As if with voluntary power instinct
> Upreared its head. I struck and struck again,
> And growing still in stature the grim shape
> Towered up between me and the stars, and still,
> For so it seemed, with purpose of its own
> And measured motion like a living thing,
> Strode after me. (I, 357–58; 359–60; 373–74; 377–85)

We know from letters, journals, and diaries that Lewis admired Wordsworth's poetry, especially *The Prelude*. Moreover, as we saw in the first chapter, Lewis desired early in life to write an important narrative poem, so it is not surprising to detect the influence of this poem on the young Lewis.[22] Yet, while Wordsworth completed his terrifying vision of Nature's hidden power in the remainder of *The Prelude*, Lewis did not.

As a poem, "In Winter When the Frosty Nights Are Long" is unsatisfying. While the young Lewis managed to create an appropriately enchanted mood for the poem, it is too derivative, imitative, and unconvincing.[23] At the same time, it

does anticipate themes Lewis deals with later in *Spirits in Bondage,* where a third
of the poems reflect an angry adolescent, shaking his fist at a God he denies, rejects, hates, and fears; the other two thirds suggest that Nature is beautiful and
benevolent, in the lyrical and Romantic tradition of Wordsworth, Shelley, Keats,
and Yeats. For example, in "Noon" this love of Nature's beauty and lyricism are
combined:

> And the honey-bee
> Hums his drowsy melody
> And wanders in his course a-straying
> Through the sweet and tangled glade
> With his golden mead oe'r laden,
> Where beneath the pleasant shade
> Of the darkling boughs a maiden
> —Milky limbs and fiery tress,
> All at sweetest random laid—
> Slumbers, drunken with the excess
> Of the noontide's loveliness. (*SB,* 31)

The lyricism of "In Winter When the Frosty Nights Are Long" is admittedly forced
and uneven, but its focus upon the beauty of Nature links it with Lewis's similar
poems in *Spirits in Bondage.*[24] This poem reveals the soul of an earnest if imperfect poet.

Also during this time period and under Smith's influence is "Ovid's '*Pars Estis
Pauci.*'"[25] In the tradition of the earlier Horatian poem, this twenty-line poem uses
Ovid's poetry as the model. In a letter to his father postmarked June 22, 1914, Lewis
writes: "I enclose a few verses in imitation of Ovid, which were top of the form
last week. . . . Do you care for that metre? There are a great many rhymes in it,
which makes it difficult; but the thing I want to learn is 'to move easily in shack-
les'[26] (I wonder who said that? Do you know?)" (*LP,* 4:191). This time, rather than
a Tennysonian meter, Lewis uses one patterned after the seventh chorus of Swinburne's "Atalanta in Calydon":

> Of the host whom I NAMED
>   As friends, ye alone
> Dear few!, were ashamed
>   In troubles unknown
> To leave me deserted; but boldly ye cherished my cause as your own.
>
> My thanks shall endure
>   —The poor tribute I paid

To a faith that was pure—
            Till my ashes be laid
In the urn; and the Stygian boatman I seek, an impalpable shade.

But nay! For the days
            Of a mortal are few;
Shall they limit your praise
            Nay rather to you
Each new generation shall offer—if aught be remembered—your due.

For the lofty frame
            That my VERSES ENFOLD,
Men still shall acclaim
            Thro' ages untold:
And still shall they speak of your virtue; your honour they still shall uphold.[27]

The first stanza, reflecting a warrior's *comitatus*, praises the devotion of real friends when trouble comes. The second pledges lifelong thanks to these loyal friends until his body, following the Roman tradition, is burned, and his spirit, "an impalpable shade," is ferried by Charon, the classical boatman of hell, to the shore where "hope never comes." The third and fourth stanzas employ a literary dissembling used by Horace, Spenser, Shakespeare, and other poets; that is, Lewis says lines of poetry themselves immortalize the persons written about, since every time future generations of readers enjoy the poem the persons come "alive" again. So it is he writes "that my VERSES ENFOLD," forever immortalizing the virtue of his friends' loyalty and their "honour they still shall uphold." As with "'Carpe Diem' after Horace," this poem illustrates Lewis's early pattern of writing set pieces.

Along with "*Quam Bene Saturno*," both "'Carpe Diem' after Horace" and "Ovid's '*Pars Estis Pauci*'" prefigure his penchant throughout his life to write poems imitating or inspired by the writers he admired. For instance, later he turned his hand to translation in "From the Latin of Milton's *De Idea Platonica Quemadmodum Aristoteles Intellexit*" (1945),[28] his translation of Milton's "On the Platonic Idea as Understood by Aristotle" (probably a school exercise by Milton dated between 1628–30). In still another instance, we see him writing an "Arrangement of Pindar" (1949).[29] Accordingly, these early efforts imitating Horace and Ovid, while perhaps not great poetry, reveal Lewis's lasting affection for classical poetry.[30] Moreover, these poems introduce his use of literary allusion, a characteristic that often aids in the success of his poems.

Loki Bound (1914) was written around the time Lewis began studying under his second and greatest teacher, W. T. Kirkpatrick, and its skepticism reflected in part his tutor's.[31] As mentioned above, Lewis proposed that he and Greeves collaborate on this poem with an eye toward making it an opera, Wagner's influence and his experience writing "Descend to Earth" obviously operating upon his imagination. Warren Lewis, in commenting upon the letter to Greeves (Oct. 6, 1914) where his brother makes this proposal,[32] writes:

> Whether Arthur Greeves ever attempted any part of his share in this music drama is not known; Clive completed his part, which we have before us. It occupies thirty-two pages of a folio note book, and is elaborately written, in black ink, with the characters names, episode headings etc. in red.[33] The volume bears for title, "LOKI BOUND and other poems" by C. S. Lewis. The stage directions for this tragedy read as follows:—
>
>> The scene of this tragedy is laid in a wild, volcanic valley, surrounded by mountains of the most precipitous description. In the background is a vast mountain on the top of which stands a very beautiful and mysterious city, from whose gate a bridge in the form of a rainbow leads down to the neighbouring hills. The left of the stage is supposed to lead off to this bridge. Therefore the gods and the chorus make their entrance through it. The right, whence Fasholt enters, leads to Jottumheim. The scene is the same throughout, and action begins in the evening. In the foreground must stand an altar, a lake, or some such mark, to serve as a centre for the grouping of the chorus. (*LP*, 4:217)

Still referring to the stage directions, Warren Lewis then gives "Loki's opening speech, for which 'sombre and eerie' music is required [Lewis is anticipating, perhaps, the operatic version with Greeves]." Unfortunately, Warren Lewis did not preserve the entire work, reproducing only an eighty-three-line fragment, followed by a second eight-line fragment, a third sixteen-line fragment, and finally a twelve-line fragment (*LP*, 4:217–20).

One of the first things we notice about what survives of *Loki Bound* is that Lewis abandoned the heroic couplets of "Descend to Earth" in favor of blank verse, indicating a maturing of his style. Furthermore, Logie in "Descend to Earth" becomes Loki in this poem.[34] Working almost like a dramatic monologue, the poem's opening lines grab our attention and set the stage for Loki's defiance:

> This is the awful city of the gods,
> Founded on high to overlook the world;
> And yonder gabled hall, whose golden roof
> Returns the sinking sun's red glare again
> With twofold force, is Valhall. Yonder throne

That crowns th'eternal city's highest peak
Is Odin's throne, whence once the impious Frey
With ill-starred passion eyed the demon maid.[35]

Loki continues, noting how impregnable and mighty Valhalla appears, "perched high above all fiends and monsters dire / Out of their reach," but moving on to predict "not long shall she be fair, not long have peace." He sees the storm clouds of war approaching from "the fierce brood from Surtur," yet he plans not to join in Asgard's defense. Instead,

I shall shed no tear at Asgard's fall:
Nay rather will I join the demon band,
And with my monster children at my back
Defy my erstwhile masters. For know this,
All mortals, that tho' I enjoy the name,
The glory, and the hollow, hollow pomp,
The worship and the common reverence paid
To gods, yet I have never been of them.

Loki goes on to explain that though he was made "ere time began" as Odin's brother (Wotan of "Descend") and initially enjoyed friendship with him, conflict occurred when Odin decided to mold the chaos. His decisions to "build a world a home for man," to "create the gods / Companions to himself," and to establish sanctuaries for giants, dwarfs, and beasts led Loki to oppose Odin. The fire-god said he saw in such a plan "awful error and injustice dread":

Then, knowing what I knew, addressed the god.
"Odin! And who art thou to make a soul
And force it into being? Who art thou
To bring forth men to suffer in the world
Without their own desire? Remember this,
In all the universe the harshest law,
No soul must ever die: it can but change
Its form and thro' the myriad years
Must still drag on for aye its weary course,
Enduring dreadful things for thy caprice."[36]

Lewis's later comments on the poem are instructive: "My Loki was not merely malicious. He was against Odin because Odin had created a world though Loki had clearly warned him that this was a wanton cruelty. Why should creatures have the burden of existence forced on them without their consent?" (*SJ*, 115).[37] Furthermore, Loki's attitude toward Odin is an instance of how Lewis's early poetry anticipated a central theme of *Spirits in Bondage:* God does not exist but how dare He create a world. Lewis says, "I was at this time living, like so many Atheists or Antitheists, in a whirl of contradictions. I maintained that God did not exist. I was also very angry with God for not existing. I was equally angry with Him for creating a world" (115).

The conflict between the two gods escalates when Loki attempts to void Odin's universe; for his pains, Loki is subdued by Odin and

> Bound as his slave, bound me to work for him.
> Thus, therefore have I lived thro' all these years,
> Forced to obey the mighty criminal,
> The father of injustice, he who makes
> Sorrow and pain on earth, in heaven strife.

Loki believes Odin does not know of Loki's plan to lead a rebellion against Valhalla: "In Asgard, stone on stone shall not be left / And all the gods shall perish— haste that day. / Let all of them such pains as they have caused / Soon taste in full and learn what sorrow is!" However, this fragment ends with an ominous image that promises ill for Loki:

> Curse them, the light-souled gods! Yea, curses on them!!
> What form is this that glistens up aloft,
> Athwart the gathering darkness? What that cry
> Echoing wild across the riven clouds?
> Lo! The bald ravens flutter down to earth:
> 'Tis Odin that I see. The cloud grey steed
> Flies through the storm clouds, and upon his back
> The grim creator of the world is borne.

The loss of the rest of this section of *Loki Bound* and indeed of most of the remainder of the poem is regrettable, for it would be fascinating to read how Lewis handles the story and the poetry from this point forth.

Fortunately, the three remaining fragments throw partial light on these issues. For instance, the second and third fragments focus upon Fasholt [Fasolt from "Descend"] who, almost having built a wall around Valhalla in one year for the gods upon the advice of Loki with Freya [Freia] for payment as his concubine, says in the second fragment: "It shall be done, / For I am bent on gaining that dear prize, / To cheer my lonely home in Jottumheim."[38] About the third fragment, Warren

Lewis says : "Then follows the episode of the maddened horse and Fasholt's exit, after which succeeds the following song for the chorus" (*LP*, 4:219).[39] The song is notable since we see Lewis experimenting with dactylic hexameter:

> Lo! He is coming at last, the sun, and wherever he touches
> Mountain or wall with his rays, with his life giving breath he ignites it.
> Now from the vale and the hill, from the throat of many a songster
> Poureth the song of the dawn, the song that is old as the mountain.
>
> Gone is the night of our fear: let us greet the day with rejoicing.
> Praising, each from her heart, the Norns[40] that have pitied our sorrow.
> Who cometh hither in haste, so wild and so eager for tidings?
> Surely over the brow of the mountain Loki appeareth.

The fourth fragment contains the last lines of the poem spoken by Odin, after Loki, bound Promethean-like to a rock for his deceptions, rejects the opportunity for pardon and renewed friendship:

> So be it then. The day
> Of doom at last has fallen. Wo is me,
> Never again as in the days of yore,
> To clasp thy hands in friendship, or to walk
> Together through the chaos, as of old
> Ere yet the worlds were builded! Thou alone
> Couldest be my friend, or understand. For these—
> Gods, men, or beasts, what are they but my self,
> Mirrored again in myriad forms? Alas,
> How weary is my soul . . . .
>   But let us come,
> Oh, maidens, and repair to heaven's halls.

Loki Bound continued Lewis's obvious fascination with Norse mythology and is a sequel to "Descend to Earth," revealing Lewis's further maturation as an aspiring narrative and dramatic poet. Employing literary allusion of a different sort from his earlier narrative poems, *Loki Bound* shares with "Descend" easy rhythm, a strong story line, and depth of characterization, again remarkable for a sixteen year old. While other boys at school gave themselves over to sports, "bloodery," or other interests, these two poems show the "bookish" Lewis investing himself deeply in imaginative and creative narrative poetry. These poems give credence to his claim in *Surprised by Joy* that he overcame his inherited manual clumsiness by making narrative and dramatic stories instead: "You can do more with a castle in a story than with the best cardboard castle" (*SJ*, 12). In addition to Wagner's influence and *Siegfried and the Twilight of the Gods*, books such as H. M. A. Guerber's *Myths of the Norsemen from the Eddas and Sagas* supplied Lewis with rich literary and mythic sources. While Lewis turned to writing versions of *Dymer*, he did not abandon Norse mythology. Indeed, with the efforts of "Descend" and *Loki Bound* behind him, he continued to explore Norse mythology. He writes Greeves on July 8, 1917: "All morning I have been reading the German text of 'Siegfried.' The splendid first Act has quite stured [*sic*] up my old Wagnerian enthusiasms . . . it is lovely wild poetry &, like everything else, much better in its own language" (*TST*, 193–94). Moreover, his dedication to Norse mythology resurfaced in the final published version of *Dymer*.

We now turn to the ten early poems recently published in the "Miscellany" from *Collected Poems*.[41] Warren Lewis dates the writing of "Hills of Down" as Easter 1915 during one of his brother's school holidays at Little Lea (*LP*, 4:306–7). In the poem Lewis again anticipated *Spirits in Bondage*, since it indicates both a longing for the "faery town" and a love for the immediate beauty of Nature.[42] While the former frightens him ("I dare not go / To dreaming Avalon"), the latter grips him:

> Not I alone,
>   If I were gone, must weep;
> Themselves would moan
>   From glen to topmost steep.
> Cold, snow pure wells
>   Sweet with the spring tide's scent,
> Forsaken fells
>   That only I frequent—
> And uplands bare
>   Would call for me above,
> Were I not there
>   To roam the hills I love.
> For I alone
>   Have loved their loneliness;
> None else hath known
>   Nor seen the goodliness
> Of the green hills of Down.
> The soft low hills of Down. (*CP*, 229–30)

In a similar vein, the persona in "Death in Battle" from *Spirits in Bondage* notes his own heightened, when solitary, love of Nature: "Ah, to be ever alone, / In flowery valleys among the mountains and silent wastes untrod, / In the dewy upland places, in the garden of God, / This would atone!" (74). Lewis's youthful lyrical poetry often reveals the tension between the physical and/or mental ugliness of his present reality and the beauty and wonder of Nature and/or the faery world. As we will see in chapter 3, given the fact that much of his early lyrical poetry was written under the shadow of World War I, either in his anticipation of serving or during his time at the front, this tension is not surprising. His search for joy was often realized through the beauty he found in Nature or the faery world.

"Against Potpourri," which Warren Lewis dates as having been written at Little Lea in August 1915 (*LP*, 5:14), begins by describing someone's gathering summer flowers for a potpourri. Employing a familiar literary allusion, Lewis writes: "These were no worser weeds than those they say / Sad Proserpine was culling on that day / When, plucking such to deck her maiden bower, / Herself by swarthy Dis was born away" (*CP*, 231–32). A mild invective against those who believe they capture the essence of flower's summer beauty through a potpourri follows: "Folly! Though they shed / Some fragrance yet, there is no man shall find / Delight and beauty here among the dead." In fact, Lewis says faded petals can never hope to conjure back the past season. The futility of such effort is underscored in the poem's dark conclusion:

Why do ye garner then the leaves that fall?
They should be left to weave the dead year's pall
And dance upon the Autumn's frosty breath.
For but one flower shall outlive them all—
The eternal poppy, deathless weed of death.

Again, with Warren Lewis at this time serving in France in World War I with Fourth Company Seventh Division Train, British Expeditionary Force, and with the shadow looming of being inevitably drawn into active service himself, it is not surprising Lewis wrote such a poem.

"A Prelude," according to Warren Lewis written in 1915 at the same time as "Against Potpourri" (*LP*, 5:14), chronicles how thoughts before bed can charm away the winter's chill and night's phantoms, and how they can lead to writing poetry. With its eerie beginning ("When casements creak and night winds shriek"), the poem focuses upon how "forgotten lore," "ancient stories," and "kings of eld, dance through my brain." In his dreamy thoughts he sees "sorcerer, and lady white / And churl or clown of low degree" as well as "dusky gallies . . . [sailing] / Full freighted on a faery main." All could be well if he could be content with these dreamy thoughts, but "I must moil and labour long / With tongue untought [*sic*] and careful pain / To beat my fancies into song." So it is as the icy wind rattles his window, "upon my bed I wrought these rhymes— / Ill-done mayhap, and held too dear: / But foolish dreams will not be still" (*CP*, 233–34). This urge to write poetry is neatly expressed elsewhere in a letter to Greeves dated October 12, 1915: "I write up my diary for the day, and then turning to the other end of the book devote myself to poetry, either new stuff or polishing the old" (*TST*, 85). As both "A Prelude" and the letter to Greeves indicate, Lewis was driven to express his poetic muse, perhaps even falling asleep with thoughts of writing.

"Ballade of a Winter's Morning" (*LP*, 5:46–47) celebrates friendship, almost certainly with Arthur Greeves in mind, the essential link being love of books. Warren Lewis thinks as much when he writes that the poem occurs along with seven others in his brother's "'meditations' under the general date 'Christmas 1915'. . . . This which follows ["Ballade of a Winter's Morning"] is doubtless reminiscent of mornings spent with Arthur Greeves either at Little Lea or Bernagh" [Greeves's home] (*LP*, 5:46). The poem starts with reference to how wet and bare it is outside and how this allows two friends to draw up chairs side by side to spend "a merry morning together." The rain beats against the windows:

> We this crackling blaze will share
> And take fit books for drowsy heads
> To bend above an easy chair—
> Old tomes full oft re-read with care,
> Where hoary rhymes and legends blend
> With noble pictures rich and rare
> To make us merry friend by friend. (*CP*, 234–35)

These lines recall Lewis's description of his first meeting with Greeves when they discovered a mutual affinity for Northernness through a copy of *Myths of the Norsemen* Lewis noticed lying on a table next to Arthur's bed: "'Do *you* like that?' said I. 'Do *you* like that?' said he. Next moment the book was in our hands, our heads were bent close together, we were pointing, quoting, talking—soon almost shouting—discovering in a torrent of questions that we liked not only the same thing, but the same parts of it and in the same way. . . . Many thousands of people have had the experience of finding the first friend, and it is none the less a wonder. . . . Nothing, I suspect, is more astonishing in any man's life than the discovery that there do exist people very, very like himself" (*SJ*, 130–31). The poem continues with the two friends unhurriedly considering their reading options: "What songcraft sweet shall be our fare?" They consider Spenser, Horace, Malory, and Homer, and while we never know which writer they chose, we would not be surprised if they tasted a bit of each.[43] The ballade concludes with an envoy suggesting that as they approach the end of life they will face it bravely, bolstered by the memory of their friendship and the literature they have shared.

Warren Lewis says *"Laus Mortis"* ("In praise of death") dates from Easter 1916 (*LP*, 5:73–74). It is an almost clinical description of "the wone of old horse-mastering Hades," inspired no doubt by Lewis's readings of Dante's *The Divine Comedy* and Virgil's *Aeneid*. The atmosphere in the poem is peacefully calm "where the soft, wan wraiths to Lethe river / Throng to quench their sorrows and desires" (*CP*, 236–37). Unlike the frenzied pace of the life above, the life of living flesh, "time this people knoweth not, nor treason / Of his guile that steals swift joys away, / Nor this garish pomp of changing season / And the interflow of night and day." Like the figures on Keats's urn, those who inhabit these shadowy lands are rocked neither by joy nor sorrow, love nor hate, laughter nor tears, bliss nor pain. In contrast to human existence where these realities are in tension, the realm of Hades is dark, quiet, and inviting: "Cut thy shallop from the shores asunder / Child of man, and drift towards the West / Where the pale lights gleam, and drifting wonder / Why so long thou tarriedst from thy rest." Here Lewis's allusions are effective, and his Hades is ever in the background, a benevolent if fatal friend. While it goes too far to link this poem to a death wish, *"Laus Mortis"* may be another poem at least partially inspired by the shadow of World War I.[44]

Another poem indicating Lewis's love of literature, particularly for Sydney's *Arcadia* (1590), is his "Sonnet—To Sir Philip Sydney," which dates from Autumn 1916 (*LP*, 5:123).[45] Lewis honors Sydney because he "did not dream in any rose-sweet bower / Sequestered, all thy days, but even as we / Did battle in the self same troublous sea / And loved the terrible voices of its power" (*CP*, 237). Indeed, in his revised *Arcadia,* Sydney shared some of his seasoned thoughts on statecraft, all the while pretending his work was intended for light reading. However, Lewis praises the poet, "stainless knight of God," more for his military exploits than his political ones. Sydney's "silver chimes of old romance" do not mitigate that "the singer's arm was strong / To break in real lists no fabled lance." For "treading a nobler path than Milton trod, / To justify the ways of man to God," Lewis praises Sydney. Given Lewis's deep appreciation for Milton, this is high praise indeed.

In "Of Ships," written Christmas 1916 upon his return to Little Lea from his studies with Kirkpatrick in Bookham, Lewis mused on the nobility of ships (*LP*, 5:170–71). It is not hard to imagine Lewis, who had sailed over the Irish Sea several times by this time, writing this poem in honor of heroic ships and sailors of the past. In particular he thinks of Odysseus:

A thousand hammers ringing all for joy
Because the soul of a ship is still the same
As when among his father's shiprights came,
To watch the work, Odysseus, then a boy.

He loved to see the master galley grow
And felt perhaps, in dreams, the spicy breeze
Of lotus-isles, and thought on endless seas
And nearest down to the ocean river flow. (*CP*, 238–39)

He claims that regardless of the type of ship, "the man of honest heart shall love them all. / 'Argo' or 'Golden Hind' or 'Mary Lee', / From every country where man's foot has trod, / Sure they're all ships to brave the winds of God / And have their business in his glorious sea." The soul of a ship, its potential for exotic travel, fascinated the young Lewis and reinforced his longing for both heroic adventure and joy.

A second Christmas poem from 1916, "Couplets," celebrates spring, friendship, and faery (*LP*, 5:171–72); in addition, in it Lewis appears to hold the notion that life continues after death. In many ways this is a poem that could have appeared in *Spirits in Bondage* because it shares so many characteristics with poems in that volume. The first thirteen lines focus upon the speaker's call to his friend to consider the vitality of early spring: "Oh friend, the spring is mad today; the trees / Like wintry waves are tossing in the breeze / With rushing music round us and above" (*CP*, 240).[46] He then invites his friend to look upon the distant hills as they rise above the dirty air of the city "and all the turmoil of the enthralled folk / Who labour." In the next sixteen lines, he imagines the two of them up on the hills enjoying "the little copses newly dressed / In baby-green," places visited nightly by "fairy men" and "earthy gods" who "leave their cloven print in the dewy sods." If the folk of the city are "enthralled" by their labor, he and his friend by contrast will be enthralled by the lovely hillside, a spot frequented by Pan. Once there, the two of them will while away the time in lazy reverie:

To gaze our full upon the windy sky
Far, far away, and kindly, friend with friend
To talk the old, old talk that has no end,
Roaming without an aim, without a chart
The unknown garden of another's heart.

The last twelve lines of the poem shift to the speaker's musings on what will happen after they die. If "it be truth, as some have taught / That these frail seeds of being are not caught / And blown upon the cosmic winds in vain," then he says be sure "we should return again whence we were flown / Leaving the bauble of a sainted crown / To walk and talk upon the hills of Down."[47]

"Couplets" is one of the best early poems. Its lyricism is rich and easy, capturing beautifully the sentiments explored. Highlighted by phrases such as "trees like wintry waves are tossing," the earth "newly cloven, rich and kind and brown," "little copses newly dressed in baby-green," "the unknown garden of another's heart," and "the bauble of a sainted crown," the poem is a lovely lyric. Thematically it anticipates poems such as "The Satyr," "Dungeon Grates," "Noon," "The Autumn Morning," "Song," and "World's Desire" from *Spirits in Bondage*. Furthermore, Lewis's focus on friendship (the "couple" the poem written in "couplets" celebrates), again probably with Arthur Greeves or Warren Lewis in mind, prefigured ideas in *The Four Loves*. There he says friendship is when two persons with common interests "discover one another, when, whether with immense difficulties and semi-articulate fumblings or with what would seem to us amazing and elliptical speed, they share their vision—it is then that Friendship is born. And instantly they stand together in an immense solitude" (97). Finally, because of its setting, it links to "The Hills of Down" discussed above, both poems underscoring Lewis's affection for these hills northeast of Belfast.

"Circe—A Fragment," which Warren Lewis dates April 1917, is primarily a descriptive two-stanza piece, inspired no doubt by Lewis's reading of the *Odyssey*, where the witch, Circe, enchanted men, turning them into swine (*CP*, 241). Since the poem is a fragment, it lacks a thematic focus; instead it uses rich imagery to describe Circe's castle:

> Her couch was of the mighty sea beast's tusk
> With gold and Tyrian scarlet overlaid
> Set in a chamber where the wafted musk
> With scent of pines a wanton medley made
> [Born on the breeze of every breath that played]
> Through the wide pillared arches of her hall. (*CP*, 241)[48]

This heavy, sleepy atmosphere continues outside her castle: "Without, the unbeclouded afternoon / Of an eternal summer drenched with light / Her drifting island, ready half to swoon / Beneath such heavy burden of delight."[49] Even "drunken bees forgot their toilsome flight / To slumber in the countless, drooping flowers." Lewis returned to Circe thirty year later in "*Vitrea Circe*."[50]

"Exercise," also from April 1917, approaches a medieval *ubi sunt* (where have they gone?) with Lewis asking a series of rhetorical questions about where the glory and romance of faery have gone (*LP*, 5:197–98). Perhaps Lewis had in mind his own service in World War I, as this is about the time he matriculated at University College, Oxford, and began officer's training. He may have wondered if what awaited him in France had any connection with those issues he so longed to know more deeply: "Where are the magic swords / That elves of long ago / Smithied beneath the snow / For heroes' rich rewards?" (*CP*, 242). Though many of the brutal realities of the front lines and much of the horrific loss of life in the trenches were shielded from the British public, enough truth came through so that Lewis's answers link his poem to the tradition of the Anglo-Saxon lament, *The Wanderer;* his rhetorical questions have a melancholy reply akin to that older work: "The loves, the wisdoms high / The sorrows, where are they? / They are nothing at all today, / They are less than you and I." This poem is an "exercise" in form, practicing the style of rhetorical question and answer, and it is an "exercise" in substance, pondering the dark uncertainty he faced, wondering where he might go as the trenches loom on the horizon.

As noted earlier, Lewis expended much energy working on a poem about Nimue. In a letter to Greeves of September 18, 1919, Lewis writes he is turning "Nimue" from a monologue into a narrative: "It appears in 'stanzas' of my own invention and is rather indebted to 'St. Agnes Eve' with touches of Christabel and some references to contemporary politics—by way of showing how much better I could manage the country if they made me Prime Minister. Sounds promising, DON'T it? It relates the events of a single evening—Merlin coming back & catching Nimue at last. This is the first stanza, do you think it any good?" (*TST*, 261).[51]

> There was none stirring in the hall that night,
> The dogs slept in the ashes, and the guard
> Drowsily nodded in the warm fire-light,
> Lulled by the rain and wearied of his ward,
> Till, hearing one that knocked without full hard,
> Half-dazed he started up in aged fear
> And rubbed his eyes and took his tarnished spear
> And hobbled to the doorway and unbarred. (261)

Although Lewis says the stanza is of his own invention, the *ababbccb* rhyme scheme in the sole stanza that survives is a variation of "The Monk's Tale" stanza (*ababbcbc*). In a later letter Lewis confesses he struggled with the poem: "I am still working at my poem on Merlin and Nimue. It has been in succession— rhymed monologue—rhymed dialogue—blank verse dialogue—long narrative in stanzas—short narrative in couplets—and I am at present at work on a blank verse narrative version. I hope I am not wasting my time: but there must be some good in a subject which drags me back to itself so often" (Apr. 11, 1920, 273). Entries in his diary, *All My Road before Me,* show he completed a version, probably in blank verse, and submitted it to the *London Mercury* on May 3, 1922 (29).[52] It was rejected, and we can only regret the poem has not survived, for it surely would have contributed substantially to our understanding of Lewis's poetic development.

These eighteen early poems advance our understanding of Lewis's maturation as a poet. While many are flawed, they indicate the devotion Lewis had to poetry, and the halting, faltering nature of them as poems is useful in measuring his growth as a poet. For instance, Lewis's reliance on literary allusion, his experiments in meter, and his practice with rhyme illustrate a poet in training. In a sense these early poems are an aesthetic drill field for the practice of poetry. Moreover, though some are unfinished fragments, they tend to focus upon themes Lewis dealt with later in finished poems. Throughout, we see his characteristic love of language and classical literature marking him as an apprentice poet who becomes a prose master. What these eighteen poems, as well as the lost poems, "Foster," the blank verse version of "Nimue," "Medea" (one version running seven hundred lines), "Sigrid," "The Wild Hunt," and numerous short poems, reveal is a young mind investing itself deeply into poetry. That this poetry was close to Lewis's heart is further clarified when we consider Lewis's repeated reference to some of these poems in *Surprised by Joy;* interestingly, there he emphasizes how important "Descend to Earth" and *Loki Bound* were to his developmental years, never referring to any of his later published works, poetry or prose. While these poems falter at various points, they glisten, if not with gold, then as glints of light, illuminating his later poetry.[53] It is to these later poems we now turn.

CHAPTER THREE

Spirits in Bondage:
Frustrated Dualist at War

Surprisingly, in the eighty years since these poems were published, only thirteen critical essays or book chapters on *Spirits in Bondage* have appeared.[1] The paucity of critical commentary on these poems may be in part due to the relative obscurity of the volume until it was reprinted in 1984; however, even since then scholars have been reticent about discussing them.[2] Yet this neglect is shortsighted since *Spirits in Bondage,* the culmination of Lewis's earliest efforts at verse, is a watershed in his literary life. While limited in its scope and technique, *Spirits in Bondage* reveals much about Lewis the young poet and prepares the way for *Dymer* seven years later. Above all else, it shows Lewis living as a frustrated dualist. On the one hand, many *sanguine* poems in this collection show his delight in Nature's beauty and mystery; still others expose his longing to know more intimately a reality that transcends the merely physical, often characterized by the world of faery. On the other hand, in a number of *morose* poems he rails against man's inhumanity to man and against a God he denies yet blames for man's painful condition.[3] Central to this frustrated dualism and before now not thoroughly explored is how Lewis's experiences on the front line in France during World War I impact the poems.[4] In addition, the war poetry of Lewis's contemporaries, Siegfried Sassoon and Wilfred Owen, further informs our understanding of Lewis's frustrated dualism. Accordingly, after tracing Lewis's growing sense of being drawn into the war, we will explore the poetry of *Spirits in Bondage* from the perspective of his own war experiences and the insights afforded by Sassoon and Owen.

Lewis's Experiences in WWI

The failure to see a connection between Lewis's wartime experience and *Spirits in Bondage* has occurred, in part, because we have accepted too quickly Lewis's statements in *Surprised by Joy* where he masks the horrors of the battlefield.[5] The fact that Lewis does not write about WWI until well over halfway through *Surprised by Joy* is a red flag suggesting that masking is occurring.[6] Furthermore, Lewis never adequately explains why he decided to enlist, since as a native Irishman he was not obliged to do so, nor did conscription appear to be a certainty in the early days of the war. When he adds, "I did feel that the decision absolved me from taking any further notice of the war . . . [and] accordingly I put the war on one side to a degree which some people will think shameful and some incredible," we are left unsatisfied. Equally unsatisfying is his comment: "I said to my country, in effect, 'You shall have me on a certain date, not before. I will die in your wars if need be, but till then I shall live my own life. You may have my body, but not my mind. I will take part in battles but not read about them'" (*SJ*, 158).

In addition, if we accept what Lewis says in "Guns and Good Company," the chapter in *Surprised by Joy* where he deals most openly with his wartime experiences, we come away with the sense that WWI for him was a rustic camping adventure punctuated by pneumonia, camaraderie, and the occasional falling bomb. For example, he summarizes his entire service in two sentences (187–88). Then, while admitting he did meet some unpleasant people in the army, he asserts, "Every few days one seemed to meet a scholar, an original, a poet, a cheery buffoon, a raconteur, or at the least a man of good will" (189). He catalogs the books he reads, friends he makes, and comforts he manages with an easy breeziness. Nowhere, for instance, does he write of the great loss of his friend Paddy Moore, his worries about his brother, or his father's pathological obsession with his welfare. Lewis mollifies this to a degree near the end of the chapter when he says, "I must not paint the wartime army all gold" (194). He recalls how cold, fatigue, and rain were the "chief enemies." In addition, he speaks frankly about the dead: "Familiarity both with the very old and the very recent dead confirmed that view of corpses which had been formed the moment I saw my dead mother" (195–96).

But he leaves describing the realities of the battlefield to "those who saw more of it than I" (195). Only in the last paragraph of "Guns and Good Company" does he mention the brutal nature of his experience, and even here he ameliorates it: "For the rest, the war—the frights, the cold, the smell of H [igh] E [xplosives], the horribly smashed men still moving like half-crushed beetles, the sitting or standing corpses, the landscape of sheer earth without a blade of grass, the boots worn day and night till they seemed to grow to your feet—all this shows rarely and faintly on the memory" (196). Though this catalogue of details is intended to be a stripped account, it actually reveals how much the war remained with him regardless of his attempts to block out or mask such memories. He ends the chapter by admitting that his memories of the war show "rarely and faintly," noting that "one imaginative moment seems now to matter more than the realities that followed. It was the first bullet I heard—so far from me that it 'whined' like a journalist's or a peacetime poet's bullet. At that moment there was something not exactly like fear, much less like indifference: a little quavering signal that said, 'This is War. This is what Homer wrote about'" (196). This bookish, "literary response" to war illustrates how Lewis, typical of many who experienced WWI battlefield brutalities, tried to suppress the unpleasant memories.[7]

Notwithstanding these assertions by the older Lewis, the real impact of the ravages of war went much deeper, and the many letters he wrote at the time give this evidence. A review of his letters to Greeves and Albert Lewis shows them peppered with concerns about the war. Concurrent with these letters and references to war, Lewis began working in earnest on a number of poems that later appeared in *Spirits in Bondage*. The *Lewis Papers* affirm that from Easter 1915 until Lewis matriculated at University College, Oxford, in 1917, he spent his holidays at Little Lea writing verse, culminating in his putting fifty-two of the poems into a notebook entitled "The Metrical Meditations of a Cod."[8] While the notebook containing the "Meditations" has not survived, it contained early versions of some poems later appearing in *Spirits in Bondage*. Accordingly, as Lewis admitted to the presence of the war in his letters, we can be certain he considered the war in the poetry he was writing. For example, one of his earliest references to the war appears in correspondence to his father and shows Lewis swept up in anti-German propaganda. He writes on October 18, 1914 (he is now studying with Kirkpatrick): "Young Kirk [Kirkpatrick's son] was employed at his camp the other day in unloading a train of seriously wounded soldiers from the front: from whom he learned that the newspaper stories of German atrocities (mutilation of nurses, killing wounded etc.) were not in the least exaggerated." In the same letter he encourages his father to maintain the proverbial British "stiff upper lip": "I hardly think that the siege of Bookham will begin before Xmas, so that I need not come home just yet. And seriously, why not study the lilies of the field? All your worry and anxiety will not help the war at all; and the truest service that we who are not fighting, can do is to conduct our lives in an ordinary way and not yield to panic" (*LP*, 4:232). Later that month he chides his father for worrying over rumors of an invasion: "The one thing that Britain can depend upon is her fleet: and in any case Germany has her hands full enough. You will perhaps say that I am living in a fool's paradise. 'Maybe thon [*sic*].' But, providing it only be a paradise is that not preferable to a wise and calculating inferno? Let us have wisdom by all means, so long as it makes us happy: but as soon as it runs against our peace of mind, let us throw it away and 'carpe diem'" (234).

In over two dozen references in his correspondence with Greeves between February 5, 1915 and December 2, 1918, Lewis tried to maintain the literary focus of the letters, although he gradually acknowledged the war. For instance, his first reference to the war was rather glib. In connection with his father's worries about the German submarines firing on Irish ships, he writes "that, though I do not usually take much interest in the war, yet it would be unpleasantly brought home to me if I had to spend my holydays [*sic*] in England" (*TST,* 65). Several months later he tells Greeves to give his regards to friends enlisting in the ambulance corps, hoping they "get on famously and come back with Victoria crosses and eye-glasses, which seem to be the two goals of military ambition" (May 25, 1915, 73). On June 9(?), 1915, he writes his father, wishfully noting, "I think we may reasonably hope that the war will be over before it begins to concern me personally. . . . There is the possibility that Europe will be at peace before I am eighteen" (*LP,* 4:319–20). A few days later he adds to his father, "A propos of conscription, I sincerely hope that one of two things may happen. Either that the war may be over before I am eighteen, or that conscription may not come into force before I have volunteered. I shouldn't fancy going out to meet the others—as a conscript" (June 17[?], 1915, 322–23).

All these fears began to wear on Lewis. For instance, in a diary entry of July 19, 1915, he writes, "Had ghastly dreams about the front and getting wounded last night" (cited in *SB,* xxi). Moreover, he confesses that his dreams are beginning to include fears of Germans: "[In my recent dream] everyone had escaped and we were hurrying along in terror through the deserted streets with the German soldiers always just round the corner, going to catch us up and do something terrible" (Oct. 12, 1915, *TST,* 85). This ominous admission was followed in late winter of the next year when Lewis, in the full throes of his blissful time with Kirkpatrick in Bookham, wonders to his father, "This business about matriculation and enlisting is 'very tiresome.' . . . Are you (sure?) that it applies to those who are under age, and who are also Irish? If so, as you say, we must think it over together. Of course in dealing with such a point we must always remember that a period of something more than a year elapses between the time of joining up and one's getting any where near the front" (Feb. [?], 1916, *LP,* 5:52). Weeks later he recognized the specter he feared, writing Greeves, "In November comes my 18th birthday, military age, and the 'vasty fields of France, which I have no ambition to face" (Mar. 7, 1916, *TST,* 94). Apparently Lewis and his father considered various strategies whereby he could continue to study for the Oxford scholarship for which Kirkpatrick was preparing him, without the war intruding. On May (?), 1916, he writes his father, "It is a great relief to hear your news about the exact terms of the Military Service

Act [of May 24, 1916], as in this case I ought to be able to get a commission of some sort at home, or even a nomination from Oxford" (*LP,* 5:86).

Albert Lewis, however, was so concerned about his son's future that he seriously proposed his going to the war college at Sandhurst (where Warren Lewis attended) if the Oxford scholarship was not successful. In response Lewis replies, suggesting they "pull whatever strings" available to them:

> All things considered I think we should look on the Sandhurst scheme as a "pis aller" if it be found impossible to get a commission by influence or any other way. You see the difficulties of entrance, though not insurmountable, are still serious, and it is well to remember that . . . if I get a permanent commission, it may not be easy to leave the army immediately after the war. Do you think we could manage to work the business through our political friends? Kirk assures me that even now this is not difficult, and if it could be done, it would certainly be far the best plan. Failing this, I should suggest some volunteer institution from Ulster if any of these are still in existence. . . . [Being wounded] is by far the best thing that can happen to a man in the trenches, and the really unlucky ones are those who "bear the labour and heat of the day" unhurt for over a year—always it would seem in the long run to be killed after returning from a leave. (June ? 1916, *LP,* 5:92)

A letter to Greeves on November 8, 1916, referred to the certainty of conscription coming to Ireland. Such war preparations and concerns culminated in his letter of June 10, 1917, written after Lewis had joined a cadet battalion in Keble College. Here he made a direct link between the poetry he was writing and the war: "I propose to get together all the stuff I have perpetrated and see if any kind publisher would like to take it. After that, if the fates decide to kill me at the front, I shall enjoy a 9 days immortality while friends who know nothing about poetry imagine that I must have been a genius" (*TST,* 192). Apparently Lewis sent his "Meditations" (undoubtedly containing some of the "stuff" he wanted to publish) to Greeves for safekeeping, so once actually on the battlefield he advised Greeves "better not send the MS. book till we're sure where I'll be" (Oct. 28[?], 1917, 201).

After matriculation Lewis wrote regularly to his father; the subject of these letters moved progressively from the mundane daily details of his move from being a student at University College to his officer's training at Keble to his accounts of shipping out to battlefield. His accounts of his activities in Oxford were light-hearted and punctuated with humor, but Albert Lewis failed to understand the urgency of a telegram his son sent him on November 16, 1917, informing him of an unexpected change in orders. As a result, they did not see each other before Lewis was shipped across the channel. Once in France he writes his father: "This is really a very sudden and unpleasant surprise. . . . I suppose we have no reason to grumble: this was bound to come sooner or later. There is no need to worry for a good time yet, and I'll try and let you hear every day when there is" (Nov. 21, 1917, *LL*, 69). Albert Lewis's propensity to worry, one which Lewis said in *Surprised by Joy* was characteristic of his family, led him to try to arrange for his son's move to an artillery battalion. When Lewis learned of this, he wrote his father explaining why he preferred not to try for such a move: "I should be sorry to cut so poor a figure in [the C.O.'s] eyes as I must do in trying to back out as I get nearer to the real part of my job" (Dec. 13, 1917, 70). Subsequent letters reaffirmed his decision to remain in the infantry, detailed life in the trenches, and informed his father of his eventual admission to a hospital for "trench fever."[9]

Many of the letters from this period are chatty, but the tone began to change just before the offensive occurred in which Lewis was wounded. In a letter Albert Lewis received before his son was "cured" of trench fever, Lewis writes, "I have discovered that optimism about the war increases in an inverse ratio to the optimist's proximity to the line . . . [and] I can't see any bright prospects at present" (Feb. 22, 1918, *LL*, 76). Back at the front and during a battle near Arras in northern France, Lewis writes his father, "I have been living at such a rush since I left the hospital that it needed this battle and your probable anxiety to make me write. I am out of the fighting area, but of course we are not enjoying the old peaceful trench warfare I knew before Le Treport [the hospital]. We have just come back from a four days' tour in the front line during which I had about as many hours' sleep: then when we got back to this *soi-disant* rest, we spent the whole night digging. Under these conditions I know you will excuse me from much letter writing: but I will try and let you know that I am safe from time to time" (Mar. 25, 1918, 77). The realistic details of a letter like this are further evidence that Lewis's recollections of his wartime experiences noted in *Surprised by Joy* were heavily filtered.

The foresight regarding Greeves keeping "Meditations" was realized when Lewis was wounded during the Battle of Hazebrouck on April 15, 1918.[10] His first letter to Greeves after this, one Walter Hooper calls "one of the most bookish and unlikely letters to be written by a soldier,"[11] contained several remarks about his battlefield experiences as well as the thematic kernal of *Spirits in Bondage*. First, in response to an apparent request by Greeves, Lewis agreed to tell him face to face about "war impressions," though he maintained his own disinterest in the subject. Second, and more significantly, he shared a genuine insight into how his thinking about moral conduct was being impacted by his experience on the front lines: "You will be surprised and I expect, not a little amused to hear that my views at present are getting almost monastic about all the lusts of the flesh. They seem to me to extend the dominion of matter over us: and, out here, where I see spirit continually dodging matter (shells, animal fears, animal pains) I have formulated my equation Matter = Nature = Satan. And on the other side Beauty, the only spiritual & not-natural thing that I have yet found" (*TST*, 214). This bifurcation between matter and beauty is the essential dualism of *Spirits in Bondage*; frustrated by this tension, Lewis's poems vacillate between polar opposites. Third, the letter ends with a poem he had just penned, an early version of "Song" (later appearing in *Spirits in Bondage*) illustrating how the horrible reality of the battlefield drove Lewis to beauty:

> Atoms dead could never thus
> Wake the human heart of us
> Unless the beauty that we see
> Part of endless beauty be,
> Thronged with spirits that have trod
> Where the bright foot-prints of God
> Lie fresh upon the heavenly sod. (216)

When he first informed his father about the nature of his wounds, he was not as prosaic, either intentionally or carelessly misinforming his father about the nature of his injuries. Later he writes to clarify his condition: "In one respect I was wrong in my last account of my wounds: the one under my arm is worse than a flesh wound, as the bit of metal which went in there is now in my chest. . . . This is nothing to worry about as it is doing no harm. They will leave it there and I am told I can carry it about for the rest of my life without any evil results" (May 14, 1918, *LL,* 79). His spirit may have dodged matter for a time, but his body did not; this battlefield experience was not easily dismissed and influenced the poetry he wrote.

Lewis's next letter to Greeves clarifies a bit further his thinking about beauty and shows him admitting to the possibility of transcendent reality: "You see the conviction is gaining ground on me that after all Spirit does exist. . . . I fancy that there is Something right outside time & place, which did not create matter, as the Christians say, but is matter's great enemy: and that Beauty is the call of the spirit in the something to the spirit in us" (May 29, 1918, *TST,* 217). The gritty reality of battle had obviously awakened in Lewis the sense there was more to human existence than no-man's-land.[12] The tension between beauty and matter as the poetic focus of *Spirits in Bondage* had its genesis at this time.

After his return to England to recover from his wounds, his letters to Greeves continued to reflect how his poetry was influenced by the war. On June 3, 1918, he asks Greeves again about the notebook containing his "Meditations": "By the way, haven't you got a reddy-brown MS. book of mine containing 'Lullaby' [a version later appears in *Spirits in Bondage*] and several other of my later poems? I wish you would send it here, as I have decided to copy out all my work of which I approve and get it typed as a step toward possible publishing" (*TST,* 220). Whatever revisions occurred to the poems in "Meditations" that survive in *Spirits in Bondage,* we may be sure they were shaped by Lewis's battlefield experiences. For instance, later in this letter he returned to the tension between beauty and matter, this time linking explicitly the former with God, in spite of protests to the contrary: "I believe in no God, least of all in one that would punish me for the 'lusts of the flesh': but I do believe that I have in me a spirit, a chip, shall we say, of universal spirit; and that, since all good & joyful things are spiritual & non-material, I must be careful not to let matter (= Nature = Satan, remember) get too great a hold on me, & dull the one spark I have" (221). Moreover, he tells his father, "If I had not been wounded when I was, I should have gone through a terrible time. Nearly all my friends in the Battalion are gone" (June 29, 1918, *LL,* 85). He laments one in particular, Laurence Bertrand Johnson: "I can hardly believe he is dead. Don't you find it particularly hard to realize the death of people whose strong personality makes them particularly alive: with the ordinary sons of Belial who eat and drink and are merry, it is not so hard" (85–86).

Several weeks later he wrote to Greeves and apologized for his recent silence, but excused himself on the grounds that "'my hand aches and my eyes grow weary' with writing for I am at present busily engaged in copying out the final version of my poems [*SB*]: in a few days the new MS. will be ready for the typist and when it returns thence it will begin the round of the publishers. I shall start with the famous houses and go on until I have exhausted all that I can hear of" (July 17?, 1918, *TST,* 225). The exact nature of Lewis's revision process for *Spirits in Bondage* remains unknown since the notebooks have not survived, but in this letter he does indicate the amount of time and energy he spends working on the volume: "Of course the book is now very different from the one you have, by the insertion of several new pieces and alteration or omission of some of the old. The arrangement I find particularly difficult and besides I am beginning to grow nervy and distrust my own judgment. It is hard to know whether you are improving or spoiling a thing" (225–26).[13] After Macmillan rejected his poems, he sent them to Heinemann, who accepted them. He wrote his father with this good news and briefly summarized how he had worked on the poems on and off the battlefield: "I don't know when I may hope actually to see the book, but of course I will send you a copy at once. It is called *Spirits in Prison: a cycle of lyrical poems by Clive Staples. . . .* This little success gives me a pleasure which is perhaps childish and yet akin to greater things" (Sept. 9, 1918, *LL,* 88).

He writes Greeves similarly with the news, adding Heinemann's proviso that he reconsider "some of the pieces 'which are not perhaps on a level with my best work'" (Sept. 12, 1918, *TST,* 230).[14] In the same letter he offered more about the nature of the volume, details he could not share with his father: "[My book] is going to be called 'Spirits in Prison' by Clive Staples & is mainly strung round the idea that I mentioned to you before—that nature is wholly diabolical & malevolent and that God, if he exists, is outside of and in opposition to the cosmic arrangements. I am afraid you will find a good many of your favourite ones left out: I thought very carefully over them but I think we all have to follow our own judgement in the end" (230). Worthy of note here are several things. We see, for example, the subtle change Lewis permitted in his thinking about God; that is, whereas in earlier letters he denied God, now he condescended to allow for a God as long as he did not interfere with the universe. This condition implicitly linked such a God with his previous notions of beauty. Furthermore, the contents of *Spirits in Bondage* altered considerably from the "Meditations" Greeves had in his keeping, clearly suggesting he included more poems influenced by his wartime experiences and omitted some written before he went to the trenches.

As the volume slowly dragged toward publication, Albert Lewis, wishing to be helpful, suggested the title be reconsidered, since a novel by Robert Hichens, *A Spirit in Prison*, had been published in 1908. To this his son quickly agreed. He also comments on the subtitle:

> The sub-title "A cycle of lyrical poems" was not given without a reason: the reason is that the book is not a collection of really independent pieces, but the working out, loosely of course and with digressions, of a general idea. If you can imagine *In Memoriam* with its various parts in different metres it will give you some idea of the form I have tried to adopt. Such merit as it has depends less on the individual than on the combined effect of the pieces. To call it a cycle is to prepare the reader for this plan and to induce him to follow the order of the poems as I have put them. Probably he will not, but we must do our best. . . . Of course one could dispense with a sub-title altogether, but I rather approve of the old practice by which a book gives some account of itself—as *Paradise Lost—a heroic poem in twelve books—The Pilgrim's Progress—being an account of his journey from this world to the next*. (Lewis's emphasis; Sept. 18, 1918, *LL*, 90)

We will return later to Lewis's explanation of the subtitle, but it is worth noting here he connected his use of a subtitle with older works of literature he admired, especially Milton's. This letter demonstrates his deliberate work on the final published version of the poems. Also, a letter several weeks later reveals a melancholic Lewis relating to his father the death of "Somerville, whom I have mentioned to you. . . . With him the old set [friends in his battalion] completely vanishes" (Oct. 3, 1918, 91–92). The shadow of war even off the battlefield was never far from Lewis at this time.

Demonstrating the anxiety of a soon-to-be-published writer, Lewis shared his fears that Heinemann might reverse the decision to publish his poetry when he wrote Greeves ten days later, adding a cryptic comment: "*Of course* there is none of the fighting element in my book, but I suppose it has some indirect bearing on the war" (Lewis's emphasis; Oct. 13, 1918, *TST*, 234). Did Lewis mean his poems intentionally neglected battlefield details (in contrast to those of Siegfried Sassoon), or was he being glib and saying fighting elements in his poems must have *some, even if insignificant,* connection with the war? The most likely explanation is that he meant his poems were influenced by the war because many were written while on the battlefield. Regardless, he soon met Heinemann and discussed all the publication details, including financial ones; writing to his father about this, Lewis reveals that others saw war's influence in *Spirits in Bondage*: "[Heinemann] told me that John Galsworthy (who publishes with them) had seen my MS and wanted to publish a certain poem ["Death in Battle"] in a new monthly called *Reveille* which he is bringing out in aid of disabled soldiers and sailors" (Oct. 27, 1918, *LL*, 94).

After the Armistice agreement was signed on November 11, 1918, Lewis wrote Albert Lewis several letters before he was discharged. In a letter of November 17?, 1918, Lewis soberly reflects: "I remember five of us at Keble, and I am the only survivor: I think of Mr. Sutton, a widower with five sons, all of whom are gone. One cannot help wondering why. Let us be silent and thankful." The same letter ends with him recounting his own personal injuries and introducing a new concern: "On the nerves there are two effects which will probably go with quiet and rest. . . . The other is nightmares—or rather the same nightmare over and over again. Nearly everyone has it, and though very unpleasant, it is passing and will do no harm" (96–97). The last time he mentioned the war to Greeves was in a letter he wrote shortly after this: "It is almost incredible that the war is over, isn't it—not to have that 'going-back' hanging over my head all the time. This time last year I was in the trenches, & now—but, come!, the tendency to moralize is getting the best of me" (Dec. 2, 1918, *TST*, 239). Having the sword of Damocles withdrawn was liberating to Lewis, although we should not think the impact of the war was over. Lewis, like many soldiers of his generation, carried with him the lingering legacy of the Great War for the rest of his life, an idea to which we will return when we explore *Dymer.*

THE WORLD WAR I POETRY OF SIEGFRIED SASSOON AND WILFRED OWEN

As we consider the impact of Lewis's front-line experiences upon *Spirits in Bondage,* it is proper to note how similar experiences affected other soldier poets. The sheer butchery of World War I is almost without equal, so grotesque it borders on being an outrage to the imagination; estimates place the number killed on the battlefield at 8.75 million (including 750 thousand British) with another 21 million wounded. Even those brought up on World War II and the Vietnam war, wars with their own particular nightmares of death, recoil at this incredible loss of life and the seemingly absurd battlefield tactics. Literary responses to this debacle were not, of course, confined to poetry. Countless letters, diaries, and journals survive, and later memoirs and fictional accounts provide a rich cache of material detailing battlefield experiences. However, the poetry of World War I offers the most personal and poignant interpretation of those suffering its grip. If "every war is ironic because every war is worse than expected,"[15] then World War I poetry suggests this as one of history's greatest irony. The poetry of Sassoon and, to a lesser extent, Wilfred Owen, reflects this ironic shift. The former becomes "the most articulate spokesman for the mood of protest and rejection that animates the later poetry of the war," while the latter moves beyond Sassoon's anger and accusation to throw "all of his resources into the struggle to express the deeper significance of the war."[16] Taken together, their poems offer a useful context wherein to examine both Lewis as a war poet as well as the frustrated dualism of *Spirits in Bondage*.

The literature of England for the first fifteen years of the twentieth century has come almost by default to be known as Georgian, so named after George V who ascended the throne in 1910. Georgian poetry—beautiful, dreamy, and abstract but also insipid, fatuous, and ornamental—initially embraced the war, highlighting a romanticized view of war better suited to medieval conflicts where courage, valor, and honor ruled the battlefield. Rupert Brooke's five sonnet sequence "1914" best demonstrates this, culminating in the most famous poem of the war, "The Soldier":

> If I should die, think only this of me:
>   That there's some corner of a foreign field
> That is for ever England. There shall be
>   In that rich earth a richer dust concealed;
> A dust whom England bore, shaped, made aware,
>   Gave, once, her flowers to love, her ways to roam,
> A body of England's, breathing English air,
>   Washed by the rivers, blest by suns of home.[17]

Though Brooke had seen limited action when he wrote this poem, its context was well before the war settled down into the trenches with death, damp, and stench filling the "corner of a foreign field" where most British soldiers lived. However, according to a contemporary account, Brooke captured the essence of how many felt: "I wish to assure you with all the sincerity I can command that [April 1914] seems to me now, as then, a just, dazzling and perfect expression of what we then felt."[18] However, another soldier poet, Charles Sorley, found little to praise in Brooke's sentiments: "[Brooke] is far too obsessed with his own sacrifice, regarding the going to war of himself (and others) as a highly intense, remarkable and sacrificial exploit, whereas it is merely the conduct demanded of him (and others) by the turn of circumstances, where non-compliance with this demand would have made life intolerable. . . He has clothed his attitude in fine words: but he has taken the sentimental attitude."[19] Nonetheless, after Brooke's death in the Dardanelles in April 1915, the poem became a rallying cry for enthusiastic supporters of the war, inducing many to enlist in what they believed was a noble, honorable conflict.

Events of the war, though, soon soured such idealism. As one disaster followed another on the battlefield and the number of killed and wounded mounted—for example, at the battle of the Somme on July 1, 1916, the British casualties included sixty thousand men killed or wounded, a battlefield catastrophe unique even in this war of battlefield catastrophes—other poets were compelled to write poems reflecting the reality of war, especially since back home the press was heavily censored. For example, the official communiqué issued on the evening of July 1, 1916, said little and approached a lie: "Attack launched north of River Somme this morning at 7:30 A.M., in conjunction with French. British troops have broken into German forward system of defenses on front of 16 miles. Fight is continuing. French attack on our immediate right proceeds equally satisfactorily."[20] A soldier poet like Sassoon, witnessing the sickening horrors on the battlefield and functioning as an "independent contemplator," wrote poems giving a realistic, virtually photographic picture.[21] Sassoon's poems have a biting, harsh edge, with the intent of telling the truth, at least as seen by men on the field.

For example, in "Editorial Impressions," his irony is turned on those reporters who tell those back home "'all was going well'" during "the glorious time he'd [the reporter] had / While visiting the trenches." One such reporter is working on a book called *Europe on the Rack*, and he intends to communicate "the feeling of the [Front] Line, / And the amazing spirit of the troops." Moreover, his prose will highlight "those flying chaps of ours" and their daring dogfights, all the time feeling "that splendour shine / Which makes us win." Sassoon's ironic understatement about such hype is given by a soldier who has listened to the reporter's plans: "Ah, yes, but it's the Press that leads the way!"[22] John Johnston in *English Poetry of the First World War* effectively summarizes the kind of war poetry Sassoon and others like him wrote:

During the second winter of the war, when the true nature of the struggle was becoming apparent, poets began to react to the horrors around them with a directness almost unprecedented in verse. This literature of angry protest employed the weapons of satire, irony, and a savage realism. . . . Most frequent of all, and most significantly from a literary point of view, we have accounts of the experiences of the common soldier amidst a new kind of warfare—a warfare that utilized to the maximum every species of concentrated scientific violence. As a partial and natural consequence, we have a tentative, episodic, disconnected, emotional kind of writing, a desperate insistence on the shocking facts of life and death, a compulsive focus on the obscene details of crude animal needs and reactions, on wounds, death, and decomposition. Never before in literature had war been described with this painful compression of action and incident, with this narrowing of focus, this fragmentation of reality, this obsessive emphasis on isolated and irrelevant sensory details. (13)

Indicative of such realism is "Attack," in which Sassoon used only thirteen lines to create a startling visual picture of a crowd of men swelling to confront the enemy. From the beginning we sense an ominous undercurrent: "At dawn the ridge emerges massed and dun / In wild purple of the glow'ring sun, / Smouldering through spouts of drifting smoke that shroud / The menacing scarred slope" (*War Poems*, 95; written at Craiglockhart, 1917). Then, almost in slow motion, he reports the movement of creeping tanks, the deafening artillery barrage, and the awful human predicament: "Then, clumsily bowed / With bombs and guns and shovels and battle gear, / Men jostle and climb to meet the bristling fire." Moving out, "they leave their trenches, going over the top, / While time ticks blank and busy on their wrists, / And hope, with furtive eyes and grappling fists, / Flounders in mud. O Jesus, make it stop!" Perhaps nowhere else in the poetry of World War I can we see so finely condensed and visually imagined the brutal experience of soldiers leaving their trenches for an almost certain death.

Sassoon, however, saved his bitterest irony for those he counted most responsible for the war. In "Base Details" he mocks those old men at home who "speed glum heroes up the line to death"; yet "when the war is done and youth stone dead, / [They] toddle safely home and die—in bed," the poem's ironic title coming sharply into focus with this ending (71; written Mar. 4, 1917). More pointedly, he attacks military intelligence in "The General":

"Good-morning, good-morning!" the General said
When we met him last week on our way to the line.
Now the soldiers he smiled at are most of 'em dead,
And we're cursing his staff for incompetent swine.
"He's a cheery old card," grunted Harry to Jack
As they slogged up to Arras with rifle and pack.
But he did for them both by his plan of attack. (*War Poems*, 78)

Sassoon's sympathy for common foot soldiers appears often, while he reserves bitter scorn for those away from the front, from incompetent commanders on the staff to idealistic women at home. Of the latter he writes in "Supreme Sacrifice," when a young woman, after being told a battalion has been decimated, is only momentarily shocked: "Her tired eyes half-confessed she'd felt the shock / Of ugly war brought home. And then a slow / Spiritual brightness stole across her face. . . . / 'But they are safe and happy now,' she said" (81).[23] Indeed, denial or the inability of those back in England to perceive the truly horrible nature of the war stimulated Sassoon to write acerbic, bitter poems, whether he was describing how the lie must be given to those back home as "In the Pink," the excruciating pain of an injured soldier in "Died of Wounds," the false story told the mother whose son was actually a coward in "The Hero," or the self-serving ire of "The Tombstone-Maker" back in England, angry he is missing out on so much business away from the front.

Of particular note is Sassoon's consideration of religion. In one of his most famous poems, "They," he begins by having a bishop pontificate on the justness of the war since it opposes the "anti-Christ," and he continues by preaching how the boys will return from the conflict changed, the implication being they will be ennobled for having "challenged Death and dared him face to face." Again, Sassoon's irony bristles:

> "We're none of us the same!" the boys reply.
> "For George lost both his legs; and Bill's stone blind;
> Poor Jim's shot through the lungs and like to die;
> And Bert's gone syphilitic: you'll not find
> A chap who's served that hasn't found *some* change."
> And the Bishop said: "The ways of God are strange!" (57, written Oct. 31, 1916)

Yet, at times Sassoon found God in the midst of the trenches. "The Redeemer" chronicles an experience in which the poem's persona, struggling under fire one black night during a rainstorm to move down a trench, turns and catches a silhouette of a figure as a flare explodes overhead: "[It] lit the face of what had been a form / Floundering in mirk. He stood before me there; / I say that He was Christ." Sassoon's Christ, however, wears "no thorny crown, only a woolen cap," for he is an English soldier willing to die to defend England, this particular night bearing as his cross a heavy load of planks to place in the trenches to keep them all from sinking in the mud. In the sacrifice of such a soldier, Sassoon sees Christlikeness: "I say that He was Christ, who wrought to bless / All groping things with freedom bright as air, / And with His mercy washed and made them fair" (16–17, written Nov. 1915–Mar. 1916). In many other poems Sassoon considered the role of religion and the presence or absence of God on the battlefield.[24] When we examine Lewis's war poems, we will see that he also addressed the subject of God and war, and while his skepticism was as strong as Sassoon's, his approach to the relationship between God and war was different from Sassoon's.

If poems by Brooke romanticize the war and those by Sassoon give it a dark, bitter edge, those by Wilfred Owen, perhaps the best poet of World War I, present an integrated vision of the conflict. Though only four of his poems were published during his short lifetime (he was killed in action a week before the Armistice in November 1918), his complete war poems are marked by "the originality and force of their language, the passionate nature of the indignation and pity they express, [and] their blending of harsh realism with a sensuousness unatrophied by the horrors from which they flowered."[25] Eschewing for the most part Sassoon's irony, Owen instead targeted the human condition; he sought to understand the impact of the war on soldiers and noncombatants alike, often capturing poignant and startling revelations. For instance, in "Strange Meeting," he pictured a soldier who stumbled into a deep tunnel where he found a number of groaning sleepers (*Collected Poems*, 35–36). Discerning that he was in Hell, the soldier tried to comfort one of the sleepers who awakened, telling him there is now "no cause to mourn" since the battlefield terrors cannot touch them in this place. In reply, the sleeper says "None . . . save the undone years, / The hopelessness. Whatever hope is yours, / Was my life also; I went hunting wild, / After the wildest beauty in the world." He goes on to list all he will miss of the world above and leads to the poem's dramatic end: "I am the enemy you killed, my friend. / I knew you in this dark: for so you frowned / Yesterday through me as you jabbed and killed." Yet the poem is not bitterly ironic, since both the soldier and sleeper are presented sympathetically. It is Owen's fine sense of delineating such incongruities and ambiguities that give his war poetry such power.

This is not to say he never took the bitter way. Indeed, after Owen met Sassoon in spring 1917 at Craiglockhart in Edinburgh, where both were recovering from "neurasthenia," several poems have a sharper edge. The best of these and perhaps his most famous poem, "Dulce Et Decorum Est," begins as a powerful description of the awful conditions of a battle:

> Bent double, like old beggars under sacks,
> Knock-kneed, coughing like hags, we cursed through sludge,
> Till on the haunting flares we turned our backs
> And towards our distant rest began to trudge.
> Men marched asleep. Many had lost their boots
> But limped on, blood-shod. All went lame; all blind;
> Drunk with fatigue; deaf even to the hoots
> Of tired, outstripped Five-Nines that dropped behind. (*Collected Poems*, 55)

As the poem continues, the men are suddenly gassed and fumble to get their masks on in time; one man does not. In describing the death of this soldier, Owen strikes deeply at the senselessness and brutality of war:

> If in some smothering dreams you too could pace
> Behind the wagon that we flung him in,
> And watch the white eyes writhing in his face,
> His hanging face, like a devil's sick of sin;
> If you could hear, at every jolt, the blood
> Come gargling from the froth-corrupted lungs,
> Obscene as cancer, bitter as the cud
> Of vile, incurable sores on innocent tongues,—
> My friend, you would not tell with such high zest
> To children ardent for some desperate glory,
> The old Lie: Dulce et decorum est
> Pro patria mori.

From Horace's *Odes*, 3.2.13, the Latin phrase "It is sweet and meet to die for one's country" is shown to be a damnable lie. Owen, like Sassoon, penetrated the veneer of war's respectability and showed its horrific side for all to see.[26]

Owen also considered religion and God, and like Sassoon, he discovered God in the image of his fellow sufferers. "Apologia Pro Poemate Meo" is his rejoinder to Sassoon's "The Redeemer": "I, too, saw God through mud,— / The mud that cracked on cheeks when wretches smiled" (39). "Greater Love" laments the battlefield as a place "where God seems not to care" (41). Unlike Sassoon, however, Owen used direct biblical stories as in "The Parable of the Old Man and the Young." In this poem he retells the story of Abram (European powers) and Isaac (its young soldiers), with the sardonic ending that when the angel calls out for the "Ram of Pride" to be sacrificed, "the old man would not so, but slew his son, / And half the seed of Europe, one by one" (*Collected Poems*, 42). "At a Calvary Near the Ancre" portrays a crucifix near a crossroads, a common sight during the war, where the persona mocks the church and its disciples who have left Christ on the battlefield. Jesus' new disciples are "the Soldiers [who] bear with Him." Nearby the priests evidence pride and are finally condemned: "The scribes on all the people shove / And brawl allegiance to the state, / But they who love the greater love / Lay down their life; they do not hate" (82). "Soldier's Dream" turns out to be a bad one:

> I dreamed kind Jesus fouled the big-gun gears;
> And caused a permanent stoppage in all bolts;
> And buckled with a smile Mausers and Colts;
> And rusted every bayonet with His tears.

And there were no more bombs, of our or theirs,
Not even an old flint-lock, nor even a pikel.
But God was vexed, and gave all power to Michael;
And when I woke he'd seen to our repairs. (84)

"Kind" Jesus is overruled here by a vexed God who inexplicably directs Michael to insure the fighting goes on. Noticeably absent in this trinity is the Holy Spirit, his place taken by the warrior angel.

Unique to Owen, however, was his ability to see deeply into the many dimensions of the battlefield, even to find beauty there. Indeed, his discovery of beauty on the battlefield sets him apart from Sassoon, the latter's distress so great he frequently cannot see beyond bitter outrage. For instance, "Apologia Pro Poemate Meo" finds beauty in the clash of mud, bullets, and flesh. The poem notes that men involved in such a hell have their own beauty: "I have perceived much beauty / In the hoarse oaths that kept our courage straight; / Heard music in the silentness of duty; / Found peace where shell-storms spouted reddest spate" (39). Furthermore, Owen's language communicates a beauty not typically seen in Sassoon. For instance, lines like "Red lips are not so red / As the stained stones kissed by the English dead," "For his teeth seem for laughing round an apple. / There lurk no claws behind his fingers supple," and "The pallor of girls' brows shall be their pall. . . . And each slow dusk a drawing-down of blinds" are beyond Sassoon. Nor does Sassoon ever approach the poignant ending of "Futility":

Think how it [the sun] wakes the seeds,—
Woke, once, the clays of a cold star.
Are limbs, so dear-achieved, are sides,
Full-nerved—still warm—too hard to stir?
Was it for this the clay grew tall?
—O what made fatuous sunbeams toil
To break earth's sleep at all? (58)

The range of Owen's poetic achievements in his war poetry surpassed Sassoon's, though both gave powerful indictments of the carnage they witnessed.

SPIRITS IN BONDAGE

It is too much to say that *Spirits in Bondage* was solely driven by Lewis's own battlefield experiences, since we know more than half the poems were written before Lewis went to France. Nor do we know how much war poetry Lewis read, though in a letter to Greeves he writes, "I saw a book of poems 'Counter-Attack' by Siegfried Sassoon (a horrid man) published by [Heinemann] in a red cover and horrid type" (Oct. 6?, 1918, *TST*, 232).[27] However, because fourteen poems in *Spirits in Bondage* deal directly with war, it would be an egregious oversight not to see a clear connection between Lewis's battlefield experiences and these poems. Moreover, though Lewis avoided direct descriptions of battlefields scenes like those portrayed by Sassoon and Owen, there is a real sense in which our understanding of their war poetry informs our reading of *Spirits in Bondage*. That is, these poems reveal Lewis as a frustrated dualist. On the one hand, like Sassoon, he uses bitter irony to declaim against a God he denies yet blames for the war, while on the other hand, like Owen, he can see beauty, and this capacity enables him to make repeated imaginative leaps over the dirt, grit, and angst of the battlefield.

In discussing *Spirits in Bondage*, the most logical approach might appear to consider the poems in light of the subtitle, a cycle of lyrics. In perhaps the most ambitious essay on these poems thus far, Stephen Thorson attempts to follow the thematic pattern of *Spirits in Bondage* as a cycle of lyrics.[28] Thorson attempts to give a reading of the volume as a whole by tracing the poems, one by one, in light of the tripartite thematic structure provided by Lewis. In this regard he takes us through the poems in each section (Part 1: The Prison House; Part 2: Hesitation; Part 3: The Escape), makes most often a very brief comment on each (in some instances only a phrase), and tries to show their interconnectedness; in this latter effort he fails, probably more because the poems are only loosely connected than because Thorson's attempt is flawed. In the letter to Greeves cited earlier, Lewis says, "The sub-title 'A cycle of lyrical poems' was not given without a reason: the reason is that the book is not a collection of really independent pieces, but the working out, loosely of course and with digressions, of a general idea" (Sept. 18, 1918, *LL*, 90). While Lewis intended these poems to function "loosely" as a cycle, a close reading suggests that *Spirits in Bondage* is not cyclical in the sense of his comparison to *In Memoriam*. There Tennyson consciously takes us through his grieving for Arthur Hallam, using among other markers the three Christmas poems progressively indicating Tennyson's eventual coming to terms with Hallam's death. Readers who think of a thematic cycle as a movement through identifiable stages where they consider multifaceted aspects of the theme, struggle with inherent contradictions and ambiguities, and then return to the beginning enlightened or renewed will be disappointed with *Spirits in Bondage*. It is not such a cycle; indeed, some poems placed in one section could as easily be placed in another.[29] Yet these poems are "not a collection of really independent pieces" since most of the lyrics loosely touch upon Lewis's frustrated dualism, the three-part structure suggesting the connections.

However, rather than offering an analysis of *Spirits in Bondage* within the context of the three-part structure, it seems that the poems can best be considered in terms of the thematic bifurcation Lewis created. That is, regardless of where Lewis placed them in his cycle, the poems fall into either one of two categories:

those that are *morose*, dealing often with his battlefield experiences and his athe-ism; and those that are *sanguine*, dealing often with his affection for Nature and redemptive beauty. Poems in the former group see life as demeaning, futile, and empty, primarily as a result of wartime brutalities. Other morose poems comment upon a God who is hateful, cruel, and red; He "kills us for His sport." In the latter group, some sanguine poems see Nature as kindly and benevolent in the lyrical and Romantic tradition of Wordsworth, Shelley, Keats, and Yeats. Other sanguine poems intimate that beauty is the evidence there is "something" beyond the mate-rial world, often connected to faery, and experiencing such beauty is the only way to transcend life's bleak reality. A small handful of poems bridge both themes and merit special consideration.[30]

The prologue conveniently establishes the thematic bifurcation of *Spirits in Bondage.* Lewis identifies himself with ancient Phoenician sailors, who, after set-ting out for England to recover "Brethon treasure" (tin), sing of their homeland and gods as well as their looked-for adventures and eventual success. They sing "above the storm and the strange sea's wailing" in order to forget "their burden" and the hardship of a long sea journey. Like them, Lewis will use the poems of *Spirits in Bondage,* his "coracle of verses," to sail "in mighty deeps alone on the chainless breezes" where he "will sing of lands unknown." He lessens his task by referring to a coracle, a diminutive watercraft for one that barely displaces enough water to keep from sinking, but his is a worthy effort since he strives to flee "from the scarlet city where a Lord that knows no pity / Mocks the broken people praying round his iron throne, / [and to]—Sing about the Hidden Country fresh and full of quiet green. / Sailing over seas uncharted to a port that none has seen" (*SB*, xli). These lines clearly illustrate Lewis's intention to use the poetry of this collection in order to transcend an ugly reality characterized by a cruel god and impover-ished people. In seeking the hidden country, he alludes to the world of faery where he can experience a redemptive beauty far from the flux and flow of a mean, di-minished present. Though "Prologue" lacks the grandeur of the opening lines of *Paradise Lost* (and Lewis is not so vain as to consider himself Milton's equal), his desire to "sing of lands unknown" and to sail "over seas uncharted to a port that none has seen" are transparent echoes from the prologue of *Paradise Lost.* In effect, Lewis pays homage to Milton and his invocation to the "Heavenly Muse" [the Holy Spirit], where he similarly requests assistance in his "adventurous song" to "pursue things unattempted yet in prose or rhyme."[31]

MOROSE POEMS

"French Nocturne (Monchy-Le-Preux)" may be the first poem Lewis wrote di-rectly focusing upon his trench experiences, and, thus it becomes the natural place to begin considering Lewis's morose poems focusing upon war.[32] It opens with a Sassoon-like portrayal of what an "independent contemplator" sees: trenches stretch out in either direction in an apparently endless fashion. Nearby "the jaws of a sacked village, stark and grim, / Out on the ridge have swallowed up the sun, / And in one angry streak his blood has run / To left and right along the horizon dim" (*SB*, 4). Lewis's image of the sunset is characteristic of World War I poetry, according to Paul Fussell: "When a participant in the war wants an ironic effect, a conventional way to achieve one is simply to juxtapose a sunrise or sunset with the unlovely physical details of the war. . . . These sunrises and sunsets . . . move to the very center of English poetry of the Great War" (55).[33]

Sassoon's poem "Break of Day" is the best example of this, as a soldier who is waiting for the beginning of an attack notices how peaceful the countryside before him appears: "Now a red, sleepy sun above the rim / Of twilight stares along the quiet weald, / And the kind, simple country shines revealed / In solitudes of peace, no longer dim" (*War Poems*, 95). An ominous sunrise occurs in his "Attack": "At dawn the ridge emerges massed and dun / In wild purple of the glow'ring sun" (95). Owen's sunset in the last line of "Anthem for Doomed Youth" is equally disturbing: "And each slow dusk [is] a drawing-down of blinds" (*Collected Poems*, 44). Indeed, the poems of both Sassoon and Owen are full of sunrises and sunsets, in part because "stand-to," the practice of looking twice a day toward enemy lines to discern any movement, normally occurred at dawn and dusk. Accordingly, Lewis's sunset with its angry streak of blood marks this as a war poem in the tradition of both Sassoon and Owen.

"French Nocturne" continues with the persona following a plane that appears to fly straight into the moon; this leads him to associate the plane's upward movement with the world of dreams he once held dear. However, it is only a brief reprieve, since the reality of the battlefield quickly recalls itself:

> False, mocking fancy! Once I too could dream,
> Who now can only see with vulgar eye
> That he's no nearer to the moon than I
> And she's a stone that catches the sun's beam.
>
> What call have I to dream of anything?
> I am a wolf. Back to the world again,
> And speech of fellow-brutes that once were men
> Our throats can bark for slaughter: cannot sing. (*SB*, 4)

War reduces everything to the merely physical. For instance, there is nothing enchanting about the moon; it is simply a cold, reflective rock. Furthermore, soldiers cannot dream, a distinguishing human quality, since now they are vicious animals, brute predators intent on blood and destruction. Even their capacity to sing, to make harmonious music, has been reduced to the rasping, grating snapping of wolves.

"Victory" continues this theme by noting how war has stripped life of its magic, mystery, and wonder. Lewis illustrates this loss of the numinous by noting the death of two mythic warrior heroes: Roland, hero of Charlemagne's army and *The Song of Roland*, and Cuchulain, ancient Irish hero noted in *The Cattle Raid of Cooley* for single-handedly defending Ulster from the forces of Medb, queen of Connaught. In addition, he laments the passing of the mythic beauty of Helen of Troy and Iseult, and the absence of faery-inhabited woodlands, dryads, Triton, and King Arthur. All the poetry written to celebrate these figures has been useless; even Shakespeare is deprecated: "All poets have been fools who thought to mould / A monument more durable than brass."[34] While decay marks such human efforts, what does endure is the "yearning, high, rebellious spirit of man." Lewis is recalling his own Loki from *Loki Bound* and Prometheus from Shelley's *Prometheus Unbound*, figures representing the indomitable, unbroken will of man. It is this spirit that strives mightily in the midst of war with "red Nature and her ways," a phrase intentionally echoing Tennyson's "Lyric 56" from *In Memoriam*. "Victory" is Lewis's answer to this lyric. Tennyson suggests the human spirit will not endure against "Nature, red in tooth and claw." Lewis, while admitting "in the filth of war, the baresark shout / Of battle, [the spirit of man] is vexed" (*SB*, 7),[35] affirms that the human spirit will not be crushed, a theme he returns later in "De Profundis." In fact, the poem ends with an affirmation negating much of the poem's earlier morose tone: "Though often bruised, oft broken by the rod, / Yet, like the phoenix, from each fiery bed / Higher the stricken spirit lifts its head / And higher—till the beast become a god" (8). This sentiment is notably different from any expressed by either Sassoon or Owen, perhaps reflecting Lewis's still somewhat adolescent attitude on matters of universal significance.

Another morose war poem that can be glossed to *In Memoriam* is "Spooks." Tennyson's "Lyric 7" imagines him standing at the door to Hallam's home looking to grasp "a hand that can be clasped no more." Similarly, Lewis's poem is set outside the home of a beloved: "Last night I dreamed that I was come again / Unto the house where my beloved dwells / After long years of wandering and pain" (*SB*, 11).[36] However, the lover cannot enter the "warmth and light" of his true love's house, at first believing some "secret sin" or "old, unhappy anger" keeps him outside. However, his alienation is explained when it "suddenly came into my head / That I was killed long since and lying dead." No doubt influenced by the many corpses Lewis saw in the trenches and on the battlefield, "Spooks" ends with the dead lover still standing outside his beloved's home "unseen amid the winter night / And the lamp burned within, a rosy light, / And the wet street was shining in the rain." Though moving, Lewis's poem lacks the poignant power of Tennyson's ending: "He is not here; but far away / The noise of life begins again, / And ghastly through the drizzling rain / On the bald street breaks the blank day." Sassoon also addresses the issue of the death of a friend in "The Last Meeting." Like Lewis, he imagined himself journeying back to his friend's home, "a ghostly hulk," and even entering its empty rooms and speaking his name: "I called him, once; then listened: nothing moved: / Only my thumping heart beat out the time. / Whispering his name, I groped from room to room" (*War Poems*, 31). The loss of a loved one, painful regardless of the context, is heightened during war, since battlefields are places where death is manufactured, leading to alienation, estrangement, and isolation. Consequently, this poem demonstrates that the longing to see loved ones causes some to seek them in places once shared; in effect, both the dead and the living become spooks.

"Apology" is Lewis's most Sassoon-like war poem. Its tone is bitter and ironic, giving an explanation for why he will not write verse celebrating the glory of war. He begins by addressing Despoina, another name for Persephone, Queen of Hades,[37] telling her he has a reason for speaking "of nothing glad nor noble in my verse / To lighten hearts beneath this present curse / And build a heaven of dreams in real hell" (*SB*, 12).[38] The poem may work on two levels. On the one hand, he directs Despoina to tell the dead why his verse is morose and cannot bring them comfort, while on the other hand, he, in the role of Despoina, explains why he will not give the lie about the glory of war to soldiers in nightmarish battlefield conditions (their "real hell"). Just as it is a cruelty to remind the dead "down in the rotting grave where the lithe worms crawl, / [Of] green fields above that smiled so sweet," so it is to remind soldiers, living in vile trenches where rats gorge on human flesh, of green fields back home.[39] Neither the dead nor soldiers want to be told how wonderful and vital life is for those not experiencing their hell. To emphasize this, Lewis asks what good is it "to tell old tales of Troynovant / Or praises of dead heroes, tried and sage," a slight variation on the same point he makes in "Victory." The old stories of war's valor, heroism, and honor ring hollow: "Can it be good / To think of glory now, when all is done, / And all our labour underneath the sun / Has brought us this—and not the thing we would." "This" is their "present curse": for the dead, hell, and for the soldier, the trenches. It is as futile for them to build a case for the glory of their deeds as it was for Mammon in book 3 of *Paradise Lost* to argue the fallen angels can build a literal Heaven in Hell: "As he [God] our darkness, cannot we his light / Imitate when we please? . . . / What can Heaven show more?"[40] Though Lewis's final comments are not as sarcastic as Beelzebub's who mocks Mammon for "hatching vain empires," he does reject the idea of using the old myths of glory: "All these were rosy visions of the night, / That loveliness and wisdom feigned of old. / But now we wake. The East is pale and cold, / No hope is in the dawn, and no delight." His use of "feigned" links the poem to Owen's declamation against the "old Lie: Dulce et decorum est / Pro patria mori," and the final idea of waking at dawn to no hope shows Lewis again using sunrise in the ironic manner of other World War I poets. Because of its nihilistic ending, this is Lewis's most morose battlefield poem.

Other morose poems illustrate Lewis's attempt to come to grips with a God he does not want to exist, yet blames for human misery. Unlike Sassoon and Owen who contrasted the compassionate Christ they saw in battered soldiers with the stern, unfeeling God they identified with organized religion, Lewis saw only a cruel, malicious, and inexorable God. Nowhere did he consider Christ, underscoring his efforts at this time to live consistently as an atheist. That is, while he was willing to accuse and defame an evil God, he rejected the idea of a personal, intimate Christ. Two poems with the same title offer us the chance to see how Lewis's thoughts about his malicious God developed. "Satan Speaks" (I) begins by recalling Lewis's comments to Greeves when he writes "I have formulated my equation Matter = Nature = Satan" (*TST*, 214), and his later *Spirits in Bondage* "is mainly strung round the idea that I mentioned to you before—that nature is wholly diabolical & malevolent and that God, if he exists, is outside of and in opposition to the cosmic arrangements" (230). The poem opens with Lewis emphasizing a God of rules, laws, and universal force: "I am Nature, the Mighty Mother, / I am the law: ye have no other" (*SB*, 3). After clearly establishing there is no grace, no charity, no empathy in this Darwinian God of Nature, he follows with couplet stanzas underscoring this God's mechanistic nature, making frequent use of war imagery: "I am the battle's filth and strain, / I am the widow's empty pain. / I am the sea to smother your breath, / I am the bomb, the falling death." This God is brutish, oppressive, insatiable, unapproachable, and destructive.

However, the later "Satan Speaks" (XIII) presents a slightly different God, revealing Lewis's evolving thoughts about his "diabolical & malevolent" deity. The God here is also connected to Nature—"I am the Lord your God: even he that made / Material things"—but Lewis's blasphemous parody goes on to demonstrate that this God is more "personal," being malicious, proud, and condescending (*SB*, 22). He harangues his creatures, reminding them he uses pain and suffering to remind them that he, and only he, is God: There is no softer, gentler deity as they would like to believe. He mocks their "dreams of some other gods" by giving them a miserable existence, calls them vermin, and then appears surprised "they hate my world!" As if to prove his ultimate authority, he sardonically challenges "that other God" to come from his realm of glory to "steal forth my own thought's children into light." Then he claims that the softer, gentler God (if He exists) is detached, unconcerned for man as "he walks the airy fields of endless day." The poem ends with the malicious God reasserting his supremacy: "My order still is strong / And like to me nor second none I know. / Whither the mammoth went this creature too shall go." Whether "this creature" refers to man or the softer, gentler God, the malicious God countenances no competitors.[41] He prophesies man or the other God will follow the mammoth into extinction.[42]

The God of both "Satan Speaks" poems is further developed in two other morose poems in *Spirits in Bondage*. "Ode for New Year's Day" returns to Despoina and advises her and all "ye sons of pain" to curse the hour of their birth as well as the parents who brought them into existence, because "God's hate" is now descending:

> Body and soul shall suffer beyond all word or thought,
> Till pain and noisy terror that these first years have wrought
> Seem but the soft arising and prelude of the storm
> That fiercer still and heavier with sharper lightnings fraught
> Shall pour red wrath upon us over a world deform. (*SB*, 13–15)[43]

He then contrasts the present horrors with past myths, an idea linking the poem to "Apology"; in the "golden age . . . both maid and man / And beast and tree and spirit in the green earth could thrive." But this is no more, for "now one age is ending" and the malicious God has loosed his ire so that

> madness is come over us and great and little wars.
> He has not left one valley, one isle of fresh and green
> Where old friends could forgather amid the howling wreck.
> It's vainly we are praying. We cannot, cannot check
> The Power who slays and puts aside the beauty that has been.
> It's truth they tell, Despoina, none hears the heart's complaining
> For Nature will not pity, nor the red God lend an ear. (12)

With perhaps the scarred image of a no-man's-land battlefield before him, Lewis pictured here a scene stripped, denuded, sterile; to intercede in prayer with the malicious God is futile, since He is the author of all suffering and pain.[44]

The tone of the poem now changes; the speaker, who until this time has advised Despoina to be passive, interjects his own story, noting "I too have been mad in the hour of bitter paining / And lifted up my voice to God, thinking that he could hear / The curse wherewith I cursed Him because the Good was dead." What he has come to realize, however, is that such intercession is based on fantasy: "I am grown wiser, knowing that our own hearts / Have made a phantom called the Good." In fact, the malicious God, intent on ruling his universe, is not even consciously aware of his suffering creatures: "And what should the great Lord know of it / Who tosses the dust of chaos and gives the suns their parts? . . . Here he builds a nebula, and there he slays a sun / And works his own fierce pleasure." He is utterly above and beyond human pain: "And O, my poor Despoina, do you think he ever hears / The wail of hearts he has broken, the sound of human ill? / He cares not for our virtues, our little hopes and fears, / And how could it all go on, love, if he knew of laughter and tears?" The poem ends with the speaker longing to cheat this malicious God by fleeing into "some other country beyond the rosy West" away from the "rankling hate of God." This ending anticipates later poems where beauty becomes the means whereby man transcends an ugly, God-stricken world.

While the speaker in "Ode to New Year's Day" considers breaking from his passive endurance of the whims of the malicious God, the speaker in "De Profundis" frankly challenges the authority of such a deity, reflecting Lewis's reading of Shelley's *Prometheus Unbound*.[45] In effect, he damns the malicious God: "Come let us curse our Master ere we die, / For all our hopes in endless ruin lie. / The good is dead. Let us curse God most High" (*SB*, 20–21). The shocking tone of this opening explains Warren Lewis's reaction to his first reading of *Spirits in Bondage* when he writes his father: "While I am in complete agreement with you as to the excellence of part of IT's book, I am of the opinion it would have been better if it had never been published. Even at 23 [Warren's age when writing this letter] one realizes that the opinions of 20 are transient things. Jack's Atheism is I am sure purely academic, but, even so, no useful purpose is served by endeavouring to advertise oneself as an Atheist. Setting aside the higher problems involved, it is obvious that a profession of a Christian belief is as necessary a part of a man's mental make-up as a belief in the King, the Regular Army, and the Public Schools" (Jan. 28, 1919, cited in *SB*, xxxvii–xxxviii, and from *LP*, 6:84). When Lewis learned of Warren's "misreading," he attempted to mollify his father: "You know who the God I blaspheme is and that it is not the God that you or I worship, or any other Christian" (Mar. 5, 1919, 96). This is, of course, only a partial truth, since Lewis was not worshipping the "Christian" God at this time.

Lewis's reassurances aside, the tone of "De Profundis" reflects an angry adolescent, shaking his fist at a malicious God he denies, rejects, hates, yet fears. In a patent slap at meliorism, the popular prewar notion that the world was gradually getting better and could be improved further by human effort, Lewis says, "Four thousand years of toil and hope and thought / Wherein men laboured upward and still wrought / New worlds and better, Thou hast made as naught." All human effort to build beautiful cities and to acquire knowledge and wisdom are nothing but offal to the malicious God, for "the earth grew black with wrong, / Our hope was crushed and silenced was our song." The speaker momentarily entertains the thought that perhaps somewhere there is "a just God that cares for earthly pain," but this, too, is rejected, since, even if true, "yet far away beyond our labouring night, / He wanders in the depths of endless light, / Singing alone his musics of delight." What is left man against this malicious God, this "universal strength"? Though admitting "it is but froth of folly to rebel," this is precisely what he advocates. The indomitable spirit of man will resist forever the interfering, capricious hand of a cruel, malicious God:

> Yet I will not bow down to thee nor love thee,
> For looking in my own heart I can prove thee,
> And know this frail, bruised being is above thee.
>
> Our love, our hope, our thirsting for the right,
> Our mercy and long seeking of the light,
> Shall we change these for thy relentless might?
>
> Laugh then and slay. Shatter all things of worth,
> Heap torment still on torment for thy mirth—
> Thou art not Lord while there are Men on earth. (*SB*, 21)

Though foolhardy, man's best shall not be traded for the malicious God's might. He may kill man, even delighting in the carnage, but he will not conquer man's will. Indeed, although it is false bravado, the speaker claims the malicious God will never truly be Lord as long as men live. The malicious deity of *Spirits in Bondage* is like Moloch of Milton's *Paradise Lost*—angry, bloodthirsty, vindictive.[46]

The last two morose poems are short meditations on the futility of life and the fear of death. "In Prison" concerns one who cries out "for the pain of man" that leads "from death to death." One evening he imagines he transcends the earth and views in "endless depths of nothing" the earth falling as "a lonely pin-prick spark of light" through the "wide, enfolding night." Although light is associated with it, the earth's isolation and insignificance among the stars is emphasized:

> And if some tears be shed,
> Some evil God have power,
> Some crown of sorrows sit
> Upon a little world for a little hour—
> Who shall remember? Who shall care for it? (*SB*, 19)

With the angry passion of the speaker from "De Profundis" spent, all that remains "In Prison" is ennui. Instead of Christ, the world is crowned with thorns the malicious God intends for it, and what remains is for man to accept this judgment. "Alexandrines" relates the fears of the speaker about "a house that most of all on earth I hate" (41).[47] Though he has known pain and anguish "in bloody fields, sad seas, and countries desolate," clear allusions to wartime experiences, "Yet most I fear that empty house where the grasses green / Grow in the silent court the gaping flags between, / And down the moss-grown paths and terrace no man treads / Where the old, old weeds rise deep on the waste garden beds." This description takes us to a cemetery, and we realize the house he fears is his own grave. However, his is not fear of annihilation. Instead, it is the inevitable confrontation with the malicious God: "For in that house I know a little, silent room / Where Someone's always waiting, waiting in the gloom / To draw me with an evil eye, and hold me fast— / Yet thither doom will drive me and He will win at last."[48] The broken, almost docile tone of the speaker here is a far cry from the defiant one of "De Profundis." Taken together, however, they reveal the range of Lewis's attitude toward the malicious God he confronted in his morose poems.

Lewis's war poems and those dealing with a malicious God reveal the extent to which he was living as a frustrated dualist. Without question, Lewis's atheism was profoundly influenced by Kirkpatrick's as well as the philosophical ideas he encountered elsewhere. Yet the battlefield horrors he witnessed inform these poems even more deeply, exposing a young man grappling to understand his place in a world that appeared to be teetering on the brink of collapse. Although his angry, defiant responses in some of the poems are immature and adolescent, they are a measure of the passion with which he imbued his poetry. It was poetry, not prose, he used to work through the crises he was experiencing, giving outward expression to deeply internalized feelings. What saves *Spirits in Bondage* from turning merely into teenage angst, however, is the sanguine poetry representing the other dimension of Lewis's dualism. Here, too, we find immaturity, but even greater maturity as Lewis focused upon his love of Nature and beauty. Indeed, Lewis's sanguine poems are among his first poetic attempts to put in writing his longing for joy he later recounted in *Surprised by Joy*; as such, these poems reveal his yearning to experience transcendent truth. In these poems, therefore, we see the genesis of Lewis the theist.

Sanguine Poems

The first group of sanguine poems is primarily lyrical and celebrates landscapes, rest, literature, music, Nature (Wordsworthian instead of Darwinian), stars, and human love. For instance, "Irish Nocturne" celebrates Lewis's homeland. It begins with a description of an eerie landscape with mist filling a valley, like "evil drink in a wizard's hand," and then alludes to ghosts, demons, Grendel (the *Beowulf* monster), and other ominous supernatural creatures. Lewis then uses the mist as metaphor to indicate Ireland's obscured understanding of itself:

> Bitter and bitter it is for thee, O my heart,
> Looking upon this land, where poets sang,
> Thus with the dreary shroud
> Unwholesome, over it spread,
> And knowing the fog and the cloud
> In her people's heart and head
> Even as it lies for ever upon her coasts
> Making them dim and dreamy lest her sons should ever arise
> And remember all their boasts. (*SB,* 9–10)

The poem ends with Lewis lamenting this mist, since it breeds "lonely desire and many words and brooding and never a deed." Lewis's complaint against his countrymen for being dreamers and talkers rather than doers is stereotypical; however, because Lewis does not connect this poem to a specific incident, it is difficult to know how seriously we should take his lament. Another landscape poem, "The Roads," returns us to Lewis's favorite spot near Belfast: "I stand on the windy uplands among the hills of Down / With all the world spread out beneath, meadow and sea and town, / And ploughlands on the far-off hills that glow with friendly brown" (63–64). From this vantage point, Lewis looks out upon roads extending to the horizon in several directions. As his eye follows them, he feels a strong pull: "And the call of the roads is upon me, a desire in my spirit has grown / To wander forth in the highways, 'twixt earth and sky alone, / And seek for the lands no foot has trod and the seas no sail has known." The urge to explore, to find adventure, to discover, suggests that this is an early poem, perhaps written in 1915, and marks it, as well, as one where Lewis articulated early his yearning to find deep satisfaction in unknown external experiences.[49] If related to "Irish Nocturne," it also intimates that travel down these roads can be the escape from the homeland he loves yet laments.

Moving from an affection for the landscape, Lewis's "Night" (IX) and "To Sleep," a pair he intends to be read together, are sanguine pieces on rest. In "Night" (IX) he pictures night as a necessary comforter: "After the fret and failure of this day, / And weariness of thought, O Mother Night, / Come with soft kiss to soothe our care away / And all our little tumults set to right" (*SB,* 16). Like Shakespeare and Keats before him, Lewis finds sleep a metaphor for death when he calls sleep "most pitiful of all death's kindred fair." Imitating Keats's lyricism in particular, Lewis envisions Night as a goddess who drives a pair of magic steeds:

> Thou from the fronting rim
> Bending to urge them, whilst thy sea-dark hair
> Fall in ambrosial ripples o'er each limb,
> With beautiful pale arms, untrammeled, bare
> For horsemanship, to those twin chargers fleet
> Dost give full rein across the fires that glow
> In the wide floor of heaven, from off their feet
> Scattering the powdery star-dust as they go.

The poem ends as it begins, as Lewis underlines night as a solace to man's weary life: "Thou still art used to bind / With tenderest love of careful leeches' art / The bruised and weary heart / In slumber blind." Though a derivative, this poem gives evidence both of Lewis's working hard at the craft of poetry as well as its own dualism: The peace of night contrasts with the busyness of day. "To Sleep" continues this focus upon rest and is influenced by Keats's "Sonnet to Sleep" and "Ode to Psyche." Here Lewis seeks to retreat to "a hidden wood among the hill-tops green, / Full of soft streams and little winds that creep / The murmuring boughs between" where "in the fragrant twilight I will raise / A secret altar of the rich sea sod, / Whereat to offer sacrifice and praise / Unto my lonely god" (*SB*, 18). His earnest devotion to build such an altar, covering it with poppies,[50] is not altruistic, for he hopes such worship will be rewarded by "dreams of dear delight / And draughts of cool oblivion, quenching pain, / And sweet, half-wakeful moments in the night / To hear the falling rain." Although not directly a war poem, Lewis's desire for "draughts of cool oblivion, quenching pain" could mark this as more than a poem about his wanting sleep to refresh him from a particularly stressful day of academic study. The poem's concluding lines are a request that sleep silence the day's pain, extending perhaps to a similar desire at his death: "And when he meets me at the dusk of day / To call me home for ever, this I ask— / That he may lead me friendly on that way / And wear no frightful mask." "Sonnet" is still another Keatsian poem about sleep, and while sanguine, its tone is darker and may contain a veiled death wish. In the poem, set in a "dreaming garden still and sweet," the speaker longs "for a chamber dim, a pillow meet / For slumbers deep as death, a faultless sheet, / Cool, white and smooth" (33). This time the poppies of sleep are like a "magic sponge" and can wipe away the hours or even the years: "Why not a year, / Why could a man not loiter in that bower / Until a thousand painless cycles wore, / And then—what if it held him evermore?" While "Night" (IX) and "To Sleep" portray rest as a necessary antidote to life's tumult, "Sonnet" suggests there is a more permanent way to achieve rest, one that is lasting.

Another poem urging retreat, though not through sleep, is "The Ocean Strand," in which Lewis calls us to "leave the labouring roadways of the town, / The shifting faces and the changeful hue / Of markets, and broad echoing streets that drown / The heart's own silent music" (*SB*, 29). Echoing ideas from "Couplets" and "The Roads," Lewis says it is time to withdraw:

> Far, far away among the valleys green
> Let us go forth and wander hand in hand
> Beyond those solemn hills that we have seen
> So often welcome home the falling sun
> Into their cloudy peaks when day was done—
> Beyond them till we find the ocean strand
> And hear the great waves run,
> With the waste song whose melodies I'd follow
> And weary not for many a summer day,
> Born of the vaulted breakers arching hollow
> Before they flash and scatter into spray. (29)

Set in summer, the languid tone of the poem deepens with its last image of discovering on the remote beach "a lonely nereid drowsing half a-swoon / Buried beneath her dark and dripping locks."[51] Similarly, another poem that celebrates not so much the action of retreating as the place of retreat is "Noon." In addition, its languid lyrical tone is even more pronounced than "The Ocean Strand." Lewis sets it in a garden bower, using ornamental description to paint a picture of a silent, static, sultry, and heavily aromatic Eden-like oasis. Heat is especially utilized to create the sense this is a place where all activities gradually cease:

> Noon! and in the garden bower
> The hot air quivers o'er the grass,
> The little lake is smooth as glass
> And still so heavily the hour
> Drags, that scarce the proudest flower
> Pressed upon its burning bed
> Has strength to lift a languid head. (31)[52]

Indeed, roses and violets faint, swoon, and sink in such heat. Even the bees, so necessary to pollinating the flowers, are affected; these are not "busy bees" since their buzz is a "drowsy melody" as they stagger drunkenly with "golden mead o'er-laden." The poem, like "The Ocean Strand," ends by picturing a drowsing female figure. Lewis's gifts as a poet are demonstrated here, as the elaborate figurative language and rhyming iambic tetrameter reflect the poem's winding down to a halt: "A maiden / — Milky limb and fiery tress, / All at sweetest random laid— /

Slumbers, drunken with the excess / Of the noontide's loveliness." This garden of retreat experienced at noon in the full heat of summer's sun is a bower of nature's excess, an apt spot for delightful retirement.

This sequence of sanguine poems urging rest and retreat leads to two lyrics whose themes are withdrawal. "Milton Read Again (in Surrey)" is in the tradition of Keats's "On First Looking into Chapman's Homer" or Wordsworth's "London, 1802" (another panegyric to Milton); that is, it is a poem praising an author who influenced the writer.[53] Lewis's delight at being sent to study with Kirkpatrick, and his withdrawal from Malvern and all he detested there, created the context for this poem. Since we have already seen how highly Lewis regarded Milton, the poem is no surprise. In particular, Lewis appears to be celebrating his recent rereading of *Paradise Lost*: "Three golden months while summer on us stole / I have read your joyful tale another time, / Breathing more freely in that larger clime / And learning wiselier to deserve the whole" (*SB*, 32). Of course here Lewis's debt to Milton is primarily poetic, not theological, though given Lewis's eventual turn to faith in Christ and his later *A Preface to Paradise Lost*, we may see in "Milton Read Again" the dormant seeds of his conversion. Regardless, Lewis credits Milton with guiding him to the treasures of poetry, opening his eyes to a rich imagination where, before, his has been barren. He compares his reading of Milton to one who returns to walk a familiar wood, suddenly overcome with "the weird spirit of unexplained delight, / New mystery in every shady place, / In every whispering tree a nameless grace, / New rapture on the windy seaward height." "Lullaby," another poem of withdrawal, focuses not upon literature, but instead upon the power of music.[54] Recalling Tennyson's "The Lady of Shalott," the poem describes three maidens who inhabit the upper chamber of a tower, who "spin both night and day," though in the evening they are transformed into swans.[55] They fly to the woods nearby, "singing in swans' voices high / A lonely, lovely lullaby" (71). More lyrical than "Milton Read Again," "Lullaby" has affinities with "The Ocean Strand" and "Noon" for both its language and its use of female figures.

Moving from sanguine poems emphasizing rest or retreat, we see in "Hymn (For Boys' Voices)" a poem in which Lewis says the wonders of Nature's beauty are ever before us and accessible to us, if only we will open our eyes and see. The things magicians do, the games faeries play, Nature's power, immortality, even God's perspective—all these and more—can be ours: "If we could but understand! / We could revel day and night / In all power and all delight / If we learned to think aright" (59). Affirming this, however, does not make it happen, and the poem gives us no way to do what he recommends other than the poem's circular argument. Directly related to "Hymn" and following it in *Spirits in Bondage* is "Our Daily Bread," beginning, "We need no barbarous words nor solemn spell / To raise the unknown. It lies before our feet" (60).[56] This poem also does not give us a coherent means to see what Lewis does. However, it surpasses "Hymn" in its personal view, as Lewis explains that his visits to favorite spots in nature create the context where "the Living voices call" him, and he catches "a sight of lands beyond the wall, / I see a strange god's face." Furthermore, he intimates that the allure of such visions will one day pull him out of the workaday world:

> And some day this will work upon me so
> I shall arise and leave both friends and home
> And over many lands a pilgrim go
>   Through alien woods and foam,
>
> Seeking the last steep edges of the earth
> Whence I may leap into that gulf of light
> Wherein, before my narrowing Self had birth,
>   Part of me lived aright. (60)

Lewis returns to the idea of being a pilgrim looking for beauty below in "Song of the Pilgrims." Also of note is Lewis's clear debt to Wordsworth's "Ode: Intimations of Immortality":

>   Though inland far we be,
> Our Souls have sight of that immortal sea
>   Which brought us hither,
> Can in a moment travel thither,
> And see the Children sport upon the shore,
> And hear the mighty water rolling evermore. (162–67)

Lewis's longing to become a part of the mysterious beauty of Nature he saw is given expression more effectively in later poems, where he directly connected Nature to faery.

"The Ass" and "How He Saw Angus the God" are sanguine poems where fellowship with two creatures of the field brings Lewis contentment. In "The Ass" the speaker slips away early in the morning to heathery hills where he encounters a gentle ass. While stroking its nose and scratching its ears, the speaker wonders aloud what it is like to be an ass. He asks if it is true "as the wise men tell, / That you are a mask of God as well, / And, as in us, so in you no less / Speaks the eternal Loveliness" (SB, 51). Though he realizes this is not Baalam's ass, he wishes it peace and protection "from violent men / Who'd put you back in the shafts again." The poem ends with the ass, giving no sign he understands, turning blithely back to its thistles and grass. "How He Saw Angus the God" concerns not an ass but a bull.[57]

As in "The Ass," a speaker arises early in the morning and steals away, enjoying the dew-laden trees and lengthening shadows "at that pure hour when yet no sound of man, / Stirs in the whiteness of the wakening earth" (61). Delighting in his morning on the mountain heath and in the little wood nearby, he unexpectedly has a vision of what he believes is a god:

> Suddenly, from out the shining air
> A god came flashing by.
>
> Swift, naked, eager, pitilessly fair,
> With a live crown of birds about his head,
> Singing and fluttering, and his fiery hair,
> Far out behind him spread,
>
> Streamed like a rippling torch upon the breeze
> Of his own glorious swiftness: in the grass
> He bruised no feathery stalk, and through the trees
> I saw his whiteness pass.

Yet when the speaker follows the god into the wood, he finds instead "he was changed into a solemn bull / That there upon the open pasture stood / And browsed his lazy full." In both poems, Lewis suggests his experiences with "brother" ass and the bull are positive, fruitful natural times of fellowship, implicit contrasts to human relationships.

Stars are the topic of two sanguine poems. "Hesperus" is a meditation on "Hesperus the bright," here identified as the evening star, and his "garden of delight." Lewis enjoys Hesperus, since he often sees it:

> Hesperus the fairest
> Of all gods that are,
> Peace and dreams thou bearest
> In thy shadowy car,
> And often in my evening walks
> I've blessed thee from afar. (65)[58]

In his musings on Hesperus, he imagines the Garden of Hesperides, in mythology a garden containing a tree producing golden apples that is guarded by Hesperus's three daughters and a dragon.[59] He ends by longing to transcend the earth and follow Hesperus "through the starry hollow / Of the summer night, / Sloping down the western ways / To find my heart's delight!" However, "The Star Bath" takes an entirely different approach. Lewis remembers a desolate place among ancient mountains where a frigid, dark pool is visited at fixed times by all the stars of the universe so they can "wash in that cold wave their brightness clean" (67).[60] A simile describes what he sees:

> Even as a flock
> Of falling birds, down to the pool they came.
> I saw them and I heard the icy shock
> Of stars engulfed with hissing of faint flame
> —Ages ago before the birth of men
> Or earliest beast.

This lyric ends inconclusively, but both poems illustrate Lewis's affection for Nature.

A sanguine poem of a different sort follows in "*Tu Ne Quaesieris.*" The title, based on the opening lines of Horace's Eleventh Ode, means "ask not," and the poem in effect is a rejection of the psychical research put forth by Joseph Lodge and Frederick Myers, at different times president of the Society for Psychical Research.[61] Lewis says that psychical phenomenon and the promise he will prosper "in fields beneath a different sun / By shores where other oceans run" after he dies cannot "heal his torn desires" (68). Moreover, he asks, what is the use of endless lives if all his urgings and desires in this world are never realized? Thus, he rejects such thinking. Instead, he opts for a Wordsworthian solution:

> But when this searching thought of mine
> Is mingled in the large Divine,
> And laughter that was in my mouth
> Runs through the breezes of the South,
> When glory I have built in dreams
> Along some fiery gleams,
> And my dead sin and foolishness
> Grow one with Nature's whole distress,
> To perfect being I shall win,
> And where I end will Life begin. (68–69)

If he can commune directly with Nature, he can achieve a unified vision of his life and experience renewal.

Sanguine poems unified by a focus upon faery, including specific faery creatures, general observations about faery, and the longing for faery have a central place in *Spirits in Bondage*. Lewis's affection for faery culminates in a series of poems illustrating his idea that the faery world proves transcendent beauty exists.[62] "The Satyr" describes the mythological creature normally thought of as a personification of Nature, appearing in literature under various names, Pan chief among them.[63] In the poem a satyr is pictured as heralding the arrival of spring by dancing through forest, meadow, and valley "carolling" and "making music evermore" as a means of rallying his "faerie kin." Lewis's physical description of the satyr is traditional—half man/half goat—combining both native beauty with the darker suggestion ("his dreadful feet are cloven") of veiled power and mystery:

> Though his brow be clear and white
> And beneath it fancies bright,
>   Wisdom and high thoughts are woven
> And the musics of delight,
>
> Though his temples too be fair
> Yet two horns are growing there
>   Bursting forth to part asunder
> All the riches of his hair. (5)

The cloven feet and horns interrupt the reverie, not necessarily suggesting the demonic but hinting at danger. This is heightened when the poem concludes by emphasizing another traditional attribute of the satyr, sexual licentiousness: "Faerie maidens he may meet / Fly the horns and cloven feet, / But, his sad brown eyes with wonder / Seeing—stay from their retreat." The power of the satyr to lure maidens with "his sad brown eyes" is the first instance in *Spirits in Bondage* ("The Satyr" is the third poem in the volume) of a concept Lewis repeatedly underscores: the power of faery to draw us out of this world and into one of beauty, mystery, and danger.

"The Witch" alludes to Medea, the subject of a much longer poem that has not survived, and complements "The Satyr."[64] Here "a deadlier sorceress" than Medea has finally been captured by townspeople. Although she eluded them for seven months, only occasionally glimpsed "crouched in godless prayer alone / At eve before a Druid stone," now they have her at the stake:

> The quarry's caught, her magic's done,
> The bishop's brought her strongest spell
> To naught with candle, book, and bell;
> With holy water splashed upon her,
> She goes to burning and dishonour
> Too deeply damned to feel her shame. (23)

The conquest of faery by orthodoxy is highlighted here and reminiscent of what happens in Matthew Arnold's "The Forsaken Merman." While not an idea Lewis returns to often, given his own theological questioning and interest in the occult at this early point in his life, this interest is not surprising. However, the poem is not about the witch meekly submitting; rather, even as she burns, she is "proud [and] impenitent." Actually, the poem shifts from her to the reaction of the townspeople as they observe her burn. As they reflect upon her indomitable spirit and her journeys into mysteries they will never know, a note of envy surfaces: "'Alas!' the full-fed burghers cry, / 'That evil loveliness must die!'" In her death the townspeople question whether or not something so beautiful can harbor evil, an idea Lewis returns to in later poems. The witch, with her unbroken will, serves as well to suggest a type for the unconquerable spirit of man, another instance of the influence of *Loki Bound*, Shelley's *Prometheus Unbound*, or Henley's "Invictus."

"The Autumn Morning" has similarities to "The Hills of Down"; both poems picture a solitary walker in nature who senses faery all around him yet is unafraid. Set in late autumn with its "lawn / That lies in powdered white / Of hoar-frost dight," the poem shows the speaker moving through an early morning of "ghostly mist" that might cause discomfort and terror to others (*SB*, 34).[65] In this heavy mist of "wizard things" and "magic dances," eerie, unnatural aspects of nature are comforting and familiar:

> Yet these should know me too
> Lover and bondsman true,
>   One that has honoured well
>   The mystic spell
>
> Of earth's most solemn hours
> Wherein the ancient powers
>   Of dryad, elf, or faun
>   Or leprechaun
>
> Oft have their faces shown
> To me that walked alone
>   Seashore or haunted fen
>   Or mountain glen. (35)

These are friendly environs, so he reaches for them: "Wherefore I will not fear / To walk the woodlands sere / Into this autumn day / Far, far away." This is like the end of "The Hills of Down" where the walker affirms "for I alone / Have loved their loneliness; / None else hath known / Nor seen the goodliness / Of the green hills of Down." As in "The Witch," "The Autumn Morning" contains the notion that faery, while appearing mysterious and evil, is actually something to embrace and enjoy, for it contains a beauty unknown in this world.

"The Philosopher" is ironically titled, since this sanguine poem asks a series of questions concerning who is going to be the next "great man," perhaps in the tradition of a Thomas Arnold, to train people to reason properly:

> Who shall be our prophet then,
> Chosen from all the sons of men
> To lead his fellows on the way
> Of hidden knowledge, delving deep
> To nameless mysteries that keep
> Their secret from the solar day! (27)

Who, the poem asks, will help us make sense of a meaningless, painful existence? Who will clarify the issue of what happens after we die? At this point the poem wonders if this philosopher will be "an elder, bent and hoar" schooled on old books and traditional ideas, thus incapable of understanding nature and faery:

> For he rejoiceth not in the ocean's might,
> Neither the sun giveth delight,
> Nor the moon by night
> Shall call his feet to wander in the haunted forest lawn.
> He shall no more rise suddenly in the dawn
> When mists are white and the dew lies pearly
> Cold and cold on every meadow,
> To take his joy of the season early,
> The opening flower and the westward shadow,
> And scarcely can he dream of laughter and love,
> They lie so many leaden years behind. (28)

As these lines suggest, what is really needed is a "philosopher" who communes with Nature intimately; such a person will be able to comprehend a hidden deeper truth than the elder one whose "monstrous books can never know / The secret we would find." Accordingly, the poem's resolution is to "let our seer be young and kind," virile, alert—untainted by "the gnawing, peasant reason" and not by training set against the imagination. This person "may live a perfect whole, / A mask of the eternal soul, / And cross at last the shadowy bar / To where the everliving are." Lewis's preference for relying on faery or the imagination is clearly unlike where his studies under Kirkpatrick took him, suggesting a lifelong bifurcation between reason and imagination.[66]

In one of the few sanguine poems in *Spirits in Bondage* linked to dreams, "L'Apprenti Sorcier" concerns the power of faery to tempt the dreamer from bitter, dark dreams to ones suggesting harmony. A dreamer hears the sound of mighty ocean breakers crashing on the distant shore of a realm inhabited by "frightful seraphim" and a fierce, cold God whose eyes promise "hate and misery / And wars and famines yet to be." As he stands before the deafening breakers, he catches a vision of faery: "Out of the toiling sea arose / Many a face and form of those / Thin, elemental people dear / Who live beyond our heavy sphere" (39). They speak, inviting him to join them:

> Leap in! Leap in, and take thy fill
> Of all the cosmic good and ill,
> Be as the Living ones that know
> Enormous joy, enormous woe,
> Pain beyond thought and fiery bliss:
> For all thy study hunted this,
> On wings of magic to arise,
> And wash from off thy filmed eyes
> The clouds of cold mortality. (40)

Their invitation to submerge with them—to learn of good and evil, to know ultimate happiness and sorrow, to experience ecstatic sensory realities—is extremely attractive, for the dreamer has been searching for this all his life. Their call, therefore, to discover with them "real life," and their scorn if he slinks "again / Back to the narrow ways of men," pull strongly at him. With them he can enter faery and realize the opportunity to experience final truth. However, the poem ends much as dreams do: "So all these mocked me as I stood / Striving to wake because I feared the flood." His desire to awaken before he had to make a choice leaves the ending inconclusive; nonetheless, we see the pull Lewis's fascination with faery had on him.[67]

"Song of the Pilgrims" continues this longing for faery; indeed, it is Lewis's fullest expression of this yearning. The poem portrays a group of pilgrims who have been journeying endlessly trying to discover faery peoples and their land, here personified as "dwellers at the back of the North Wind" (47).[68] The pilgrims have been told by some that there is no realm of faery, "but, ah God! we know / That somewhere, somewhere past the Northern snow / Waiting for us the red-rose gardens blow." Because of this conviction, the pilgrims

Have forsaken all things sweet and fair,
We have found nothing worth a moment's care
Because the real flowers are blowing there.

Land of the Lotus fallen from the sun,
Land of the Lake from whence all rivers run,
Land where the hope of all our dreams is won! (47–48)

The promise of real life, the fulfillment of all desires, and the living out of dreams are more than enough to stimulate the pilgrims in their quest. Like Odysseus's sailors enchanted by the island of the Lotus eaters, so these pilgrims do not want to be deflected in their search for faery. While they go on to admit that day-to-day life deadens them to perceiving faery and that even as they approach faery it causes them to tremble, they long to "wake again in gardens bright / Of green and gold for infinite delight, / Sleeping beneath the solemn mountains white." In faery they imagine a realm untouched by time where songbirds never cease singing, where queens rule without break, and where poets write forever and "whisper a wild, sweet song" revealing the deepest truths of the universe. It is their longing to merge with the eternal that drives the pilgrims.

In their review of why they keep missing faery, they note having journeyed near places associated in the past with faery, wondering if they miss it because they have sinned. Or, they consider, "Is it all a folly of the wise, / Bidding us walk these ways with blinded eyes / While all around us real flowers arise?" Perhaps *this* world is where they find "real flowers." Such self-doubt is only momentary, and the poem ends with their powerful affirmation: "But, by the very God, we know, we know / That somewhere still, beyond the Northern snow / Waiting for us the red-rose gardens blow." The pilgrims' search for a real, eternal, nonchanging world indicates Lewis's own deeply felt Platonism, but their desire is not for a Platonic realm of forms; instead, they seek the richly imagined world of faery, one in a sense beyond both the earthly and Platonic. Though the pilgrims never answer the question of whether or not it is their sin that keeps them from entering faery, we should remember that pilgrims traditionally move from a state of sin to one of grace *through* the act of pilgrimage itself. It could be that these pilgrims are nearer to faery than they know.

The next sanguine poem, "In Praise of Solid People," returns to the idea that faery is frightening, but gives it a homely twist. At one level the poem can be read as Lewis playfully mocking those who live comfortably in this world: "Thank God that there are solid folk / Who water flowers and roll the lawn, / And sit and sew and talk and smoke, / And snore all through the summer dawn" (42). This could be a pejorative assessment of such people "who pass untroubled nights and days," eating well, happy with each other, and living respectable, innocent lives. These are people who live on "stock responses" and who "think in well-worn grooves of thought," naïve but also undisturbed by life's mysteries. However, the speaker admits there had been a time he scorned such lives, but now his own "weariness and strife" has caused him to "learn your worthiness indeed, / The world is better for such life / As stout, suburban people lead." In fact, he confesses it is his own unrealized longings to enter the faery world that so frustrate him:

Too often have I sat alone
When the wet night falls heavily,
And fretting winds around me moan,
And homeless longing vexes me

For lore that I shall never know,
And visions none can hope to see,
Till brooding works upon me so
A childish fear steals over me. (43)

That is, as he sits in his room longing for faery, he wonders if he manufactures visions and fantasies, one leading to yet another, and all unfulfilled. In the end, he feels such fantasies cannot satisfy his longings for faery, for they take him "still no nearer to the Light, / And still no further from myself, / Alone and lost in clinging night." Because his fantasies bring no truth, no deeper self-knowledge, and no sense of belonging, he envies "solid folk," who, although they live compromised lives, are superior to him for they "are not fretted by desire." Lewis in "In Praise of Solid People" is one who longs for faery and its accompanying raptures but who realizes in his disappointment the practical necessity of normal, solid, even staid living.[69]

In the only poem of *Spirits in Bondage* dealing with romantic love, Lewis imagines in "World's Desire" a kind of Valhalla of love; that is, the poem concerns a castle "built" in a desolate country, the whole scene strongly reminiscent of Wagner's influence upon Lewis:

Where the trees are grim and great,
Blasted with the lightning sharp—giant boulders strewn between,
And the mountains rise above, and the cold ravine
Echoes to the crushing roar and thunder of a mighty river
Raging down a cataract. (72)

In the midst of this rugged, wild land, a castle rises, its towers strong, its gates "made of ivory, the roofs of copper red." Guarded by warders and "wakeful dragons," nothing can assail it, for it is "a resting-place, dear heart, for you and me." Faery touches the poem when a wild faery maiden who, homeless and torn by the forests, wanders beneath the castle: "Often to the castle gate up she looks with vain endeavour, / For her soulless loveliness to the castle winneth never." The castle is an escape, a retreat for the speaker and his beloved: "Within the sacred court, hidden high upon the mountain, / Wandering in the castle gardens lovely folk enough there be, / Breathing in another air, drinking of a purer fountain / And among that folk, beloved, there's a place for you and me." In this pinnacle of love, this fortress of passion, the speaker and his beloved will find the best place to dwell. Human love signals beauty, Lewis suggests, and in the midst of daily routine, love is its own castle of desire. If this is a battlefield poem, Lewis's longing to escape his terrible present for a palace of love is surely understandable.

As we draw to the close of this discussion of Lewis's sanguine poems, we find three that are his best expression of faery's capacity to enhance human life, and each is a progessively stronger argument for faery being the proof of transcendent beauty. "Song," one of the few sanguine poems we can document as having been written while Lewis was serving in France,[70] begins by affirming "Faeries must be in the woods. . . . / Else how could the dead things be / Half so lovely as they are?" (*SB*, 50). In like manner he questions how it is that stars fill us with delight and cause us "dreams divine" unless each of them is a "happy isle" where "the Other People go / On the bright sward to and fro?" The notion that earthly beauty is a reflection of faery, as if the latter infuses the former, has Platonic connotations, but Lewis is not concerned here with Platonism. Instead, he is saying earthly beauty as expressed in our apprehension of faery proves the reality of transcendent beauty:

> Atoms dead could never thus
> Stir the human heart of us
> Unless the beauty that we see
> The veil of endless beauty be,
> Filled full of spirits that have trod
> Far hence along the heavenly sod
> And seen the bright footprints of God. (50)

In the midst of war, Lewis reaches for beauty as that which brings sense to a senseless situation. His yearning for beauty mitigates the horror he sees regularly on the battlefield. Closely related is "Ballade Mystique," and its setting is perhaps Little Lea.[71] The poem presents a speaker living in a big, red house with a wasted garden and a desolate look. He says his friends are concerned for him living in such a spot, as they believe such isolation is unhealthy: "It grieves them thinking of me so / While all their happy life is near" (53). Ironically, however, the speaker's refrain

"What do they know? What do they know?" indicates that his friends have it all wrong. What they do not realize is that such isolation gives him ample opportunity to pursue faery through literature, more than compensating for his lonely life:

> That I have seen the Dagda's throne
> In sunny lands without a tear
> And found a forest all my own
> To ward with magic shield and spear,
> Where, through the stately towers I rear
> For my desire, around me go
> Immortal shapes of beauty clear:
> They do not know, they do not know. (53)

His friends cannot know that through faery he travels to the realm of Dagda (one of the chief Irish gods) where in his imagination ("the stately towers I rear / For my desire") he experiences unspeakable beauty. Even more, his friends can never know of "the friends I have without a peer / Beyond the western ocean's glow, / Whither the faerie galleys steer." His friends from faery are more real to him than his earthly friends.

The dangers of all this, of course, are losing one's self in wish fulfillment and the inevitable frustration associated with trying to live constantly in the faery world, the central idea of "In Praise of Solid People" and, as we will see later, an important concept in *Dymer*. Nevertheless, "Night" (XXIX) reinforces such wish fulfillment and is another strong expression of how faery is the evidence of transcendent beauty. With an opening that recalls the beginning of Yeats's "Lake Isle of Innisfree," Lewis employs elaborate lyricism to set the context for the faery world:

> I know a little Druid wood
> Where I would slumber if I could
> And have the murmuring of the stream
> To mingle with a midnight dream,
> And have the holy hazel trees
> To play above me in the breeze,
> And smell the thorny eglantine. (*SB*, 55)[72]

In this wood he hears "the wild, strange, tuneless song / Of faerie voices" that call him to "leave the world and come away!" Stories of those who leave the world of men for faery he knows, and the poems ends with an obvious allusion to Keats's "La Belle Dame Sans Merci":

Kings of old, I've heard them say,
Here have found them faerie lovers
That charmed them out of life and kissed
Their lips with cold lips unafraid,
And such a spell around them made
That they have passed beyond the mist
And found the Country-under-wave . . . ,

Kings of old, whom none could save! (*SB*, 55–56)

The ending clearly intimates that the longing for faery can be so powerful it draws some to escape the common world of man for transcendent beauty.

Three poems include details about both war and beauty; as a result, they may be efforts by Lewis to bridge the bifurcation of *Spirits in Bondage*. "Oxford" shows bifurcation in that its first, fourth, and fifth stanzas concern how an enclave like Oxford serves as a citadel for beauty, while the second and third stanzas present war as a threat to such beauty. Lewis begins by saying it is good there are "palaces of peace / And discipline and dreaming and desire, / Lest we forget our heritage and cease / The Spirit's work—to hunger and aspire" (57). His use of "Spirit" is that of the "something" we have seen previously, and it links his aspirations not with Christian faith but instead with transcendent beauty. In the second stanza he notes that places like Oxford remind us beauty lives on, in spite of the fact we now are "tangled in red battle's animal net, / Murder the work and lust the anodyne." The third stanza continues this thought, noting that unlike the battlefield where men are reduced to surviving on animal instincts, Oxford "has nothing of the beast, / That was not built for gross, material gains, / Sharp, wolfish power or empire's glutted feast." The final two stanzas leave the battlefield entirely ("we are not wholly brute"), focusing rather upon Oxford's function as a lighthouse of dreams, visions, aspirations, and beauty; if it is a kind of fortress in the midst of war, it is "a refuge of the elect." Oxford becomes an emblem of beauty's survival regardless of the swirl of war: "She was not builded out of common stone / But out of all men's yearning and all prayer / That she might live, eternally our own, / The Spirit's stronghold—barred against despair." This is not Lewis's attempt "to build a heaven out of hell" so much as it is his effort to remind himself and others that wartime brutality is not the only reality. It may be the most immediate one for soldiers, even one not easily put aside, but in "Oxford" he recalls that there is another reality, a place where men aspire for beauty rather than gunshot, and one that gives motivation to him to live beyond the brute.

"Dungeon Grates" is Lewis's most comprehensive attempt to illustrate how faery is the evidence of transcendent beauty and how such beauty contradicts the

sense produced by war that human existence is meaningless. Man's essential condition, heightened by war, the opening lines suggest, is one of loneliness, grief,
burden, and pain; these beat him down toward death except for those moments
when he captures "a sudden glimpse of spirit faces" (*SB*, 25). That is, though
his life may appear to be lived in a cell behind dungeon bars, the apprehension
of beauty, "the fragrant breath" of "flowery places," the longing "for which the
hearts of men are always sore," reminds man of another reality beyond time. Anticipating what he comes to hammer home consistently in *Surprised by Joy*, however, Lewis says this reality is not one to seek actively:

> It lies beyond endeavour; neither prayer
> Nor fasting, nor much wisdom winneth there,
> Seeing how many prophets and wise men
> Have sought for it and still returned again
> With hope undone. (25)

In fact, beauty comes unlooked for, serendipitously: "But only the strange power /
Of unsought Beauty in some casual hour / Can build a bridge of light or sound or
form / To lead you out of all this strife and storm." For the first time he attempts
to explain how beauty leads us, claiming that when we mesh with beauty, when
"we are grown a part" of it until "from its very glory's midmost heart / Out leaps
a sudden beam of larger light / Into our souls," then we will see all things as they
really are, "seven times more true than what for truth we hold / In vulgar hours."
This Wordsworthian ethos culminates in lines reminiscent of "Tintern Abbey":

> The miracle is done
> And for one little moment we are one
> With the eternal stream of loveliness
> That flows so calm, aloof from all distress
> Yet leaps and lives around us as a fire
> Making us faint with overstrong desire
> To sport and swim for ever in its deep. (26)

Although such epiphanies are momentary and rare, we feed off them for a long
time, sustained by them because through them "we know we are not made of
mortal stuff." Indeed, such momentary visitations of beauty help us survive our
otherwise burdensome human condition: "And we can bear all trials that come
after, / The hate of men and the fool's loud bestial laughter / And Nature's rule
and cruelties unclean, / For we have seen the Glory—we have seen." As we shall
see later, Lewis's poem "Joy" (1924) reexamines this same notion with a rather

different and unexpected resolution. Here, however, Lewis honors the visitations of beauty as harbingers whereby man can endure an otherwise dark, meaningless world.

"Death in Battle" we know is a war poem, because it was for that very reason first published by John Galsworthy in *Reveille*.[73] From the beginning the poem is escapist, with a particular longing to transcend the battlefield for "the peaceful castle, rosy in the West, / In the sweet dim Isle of Apples over the wide sea's breast" (*SB*, 74). This desire is a direct result of battlefield experiences that have pressed "and driven and hurt" him almost beyond bearing; he has been blindly fighting "among men cursing in fight and toiling." As a consequence, he longs to escape, to be alone, "to be ever alone," above and beyond the turmoil of the fray, "in flowery valleys among the mountains and silent wastes untrod, / In the dewy upland places, in the garden of God." In such a retreat he no longer will have to see "the brutal, crowded faces around me, that in their toil have grown / Into the faces of devils—yea, even as my own." This realm of transcendent peace blots out war's tumult: "O Country of Dreams! / Beyond the tide of the ocean, hidden and sunk away, / Out of the sound of battles, near to the end of day, / Full of dim woods and streams." As he does in "Oxford" and "Dungeon Grates," Lewis resolves his frustrated dualism in "Death in Battle" via beauty. Only beauty can atone for war's hell.

An overall evaluation of *Spirits in Bondage* suggests several things. First, the title underscores the bifurcation discussed above; that is, the book is about how the spirit of man—variously portrayed in the poems as either proud and indomitable or longing for beauty—is shackled by an earthly existence marked by suffering and theological uncertainty. *Spirits in Bondage* shows Lewis disturbed by his sense that human life was directed by a malicious God, yet the many poems focusing upon faery show his belief in a mitigating, transcendental beauty. Second, his use of the lyric leads to many poems in which we glimpse his deeply felt emotional life, but it also limits his range of poetic sensibilities. For instance, though he grappled with theological and aesthetic conundrums, the short nature of the lyric prevented him from anywhere working out a resolution to the tensions he was experiencing. Third, *Spirits in Bondage* gives Lewis hope he might some day achieve acclaim as a poet. The rigor of academic study at Oxford after the war, while not a death knell to his muse, certainly muted his poetic efforts; quite properly he invested most of his time into high-level achievement as an undergraduate. Still, we know he continued to write poetry, as his letters and diaries indicate, and he actively sought to see his poetry published. Fourth, while Lewis clearly does not rank as a World War I poet on the level of Sassoon or Owen, the fourteen poems in *Spirits in Bondage* influenced by his wartime experiences are deeply felt and communicate more immediately the reality of his experiences in

France than his memories of the war later recorded in *Surprised by Joy*. Finally, his experience in writing *Spirits in Bondage*, particularly the war poems, served him well, though he largely abandoned lyric poetry between 1922 and 1926 to devote himself to a long narrative poem, *Dymer*, where he attempted to consider again the tensions he first explored in *Spirits in Bondage*. It is to the poems of his student days at Oxford and to *Dymer*, Lewis's most sustained effort in verse, that we now turn our attention.

CHAPTER FOUR

Early Oxford Poems and Dymer, 1920–1926: Siegfried Unbound

Before we focus on *Dymer,* a poem ten years in the making, we turn to others Lewis worked on after *Spirits in Bondage* and his return to Oxford. "On Robert Capron," "On Henry Wakelyn Smith," and "On W. T. Kirkpatrick" all date between 1920 and 1923. Warren Lewis says his brother began work on "an autobiographical poem . . . in the 'twenties and then abandoned [it]" (*WLB,* 12).[1] These three autobiographical fragments appear to be parts of this larger autobiographical poem.[2] Because they focus upon the three pivotal teachers in Lewis's early life, they are important, since they illustrate Lewis's desire to use poetry to explain the story of his life.

Robert Capron was headmaster of Wynyard School, Watford, Hertfordshire, where Lewis was a pupil from 1908 to 1910; in *Surprised by Joy* Capron becomes the tyrannical Oldie of Belsen. The end of Warren Lewis's lengthy recollection of Capron's brutality provides an apt preface to his brother's poem: "I have failed . . . if I have not shown you a powerful, violent, brutal man, without intellectual tastes or attainments, regarding his school as at once a mere livelihood, and a safety valve for his ill temper, who by secluding himself from all who were not under his domination, had reached such a degree of tyranny that the kindest verdict I can pass on him, is to agree with my friend Balfour that he was not quite sane" (*LP,* 3:41). Warren Lewis then writes: "Capron is dismissed more briefly, but perhaps more contemptuously, by Clive Lewis in a fragmentary autobiographical poem":

> Heart-breaking school
> Received me , where an ogre hearted man held rule,
> Secret and irresponsible, out of the call

Of men's reproach, like Cyclops in his savage hall:
For at his gate no neighbour went in, nor his own
Three fading daughters easily won out alone,
Nor if they did, dared wag their tongues, but, in a trice
Their errand done, whisked home again, three pattering mice,
Pale, busy meek: more pitiable far than we
From whom he ground the bread of his adversity,
Himself a theme for pity: for within him boiled
The spirit of Genghis Khan or Timur, ever foiled
And forced back to the dogs-eared Virgil and the desk
To earn his food: ridiculous, old, poor, grotesque,
A man to be forgiven. Here let him pass, by me
Forgiven: and let the memory pass. Let me not see
Under the curled moustaches on the likerous, red,
Moist lips, the flat Assyrian smile we used to dread
When in the death-still room the weeping of one boy
Gave the starved dragon inklings of ancestral joy,
Antediluvian taste of blood.[3]

There are several fascinating implications to consider in this twenty-one-line alexandrine fragment. First, these lines are greatly expanded upon in the chapter "Concentration Camp" of *Surprised by Joy*. Given the bitterness of the memory of Capron, it is not surprising that this is the longest chapter in Lewis's autobiography (*SJ*, 22–41).[4] Second, we see Lewis using numerous literary and historical allusions, including comparing Capron to Cyclops, the historical marauders Genghis Khan and Timor, and the biblical Assyrian conqueror Sennacherib,[5] all reflecting the growing depth of his learning and tendency toward literary and historical allusion. Third, and perhaps because this piece was written when Lewis was older, there is a surprising objectivity. He appears to feel compassion for Capron's pitiful daughters who had to endure his cruelty constantly, and, what is more, he appears to forgive Capron: "ridiculous, old, poor, grotesque, / A man to be forgiven." Yet while some filtering may have occurred in Lewis's mind, the trauma of Capron's educational methods lived long in Lewis's memory, as his reincarnation as Oldie in *Surprised by Joy* indicates.

"On Henry Wakelyn Smith" is a forty-two-line alexandrine panegyric honoring Lewis's favorite teacher at Malvern College, where he enrolled in September 1913. In *Surprised by Joy*, Smith became Smewgy and Malvern became Wyvern. Warren Lewis notes "the memory of [Smewgy] was to be the only pleasant one which Clive . . . brought away with him after his short stay at Malvern, and the [excerpt from the] unfinished autobiographical poem . . . shows vividly the impression which Mr. Smith was capable of making on a clever and sensitive boy" (*LP,* 3:262). In the first twenty-six lines, Lewis pays homage to how Smith exposed him to classical poetry and its "mediterranean metres" as well as to "cold Platonic forms" and the wonder of Virgil's poetry. Lewis's debt to Smith is expressed in the opening lines: "And after this they sent me to another place, / New miseries, another school. But I retrace / Only the good which there I found; one master dear, / At thought of whom the bird of memory sings."[6] The rest of the poem credits Smith, "an old man with a honey-sweet and singing voice," with infusing into Lewis "beauty and melodious thought," as he recalls the way Smith urged the young boys to pursue poetry earnestly and not to rest "save where the springs of beauty flow." Lewis remembers Smith's favorite phrase, "Never let us live with *amousia,*"[7] and ends by asking a blessing upon his spirit:

> Therefore the ancient beauty brought him clear delight
> Each day, and all day long, and in the wakeful night
> Forgetfulness of the unhappy thousand things
> Age thinks of, making equal to the wealth of Kings
> His poverty. Oh Master, may the earth be green
> Above thy grave! Far hidden in the lands unseen,
> Far off now, and mature among the ghosts, yet fare
> Well and thrice well forevermore and everywhere.[8]

To find a teacher like Smith was an unexpected blessing after Capron. In *Surprised by Joy* Lewis supplements these recollections of Smith's influence:

> Except at Oldie's I had been fortunate in my teachers ever since I was born; but Smewgy was "beyond expectation, beyond hope." He was a gray-head with large spectacles and a wide mouth which combined to give him a froglike expression, but nothing could be less froglike than his voice. He was honey-tongued. Every verse he read turned into music on his lips: something midway between speech and song. It is not the only good way of reading verse, but it is the way to enchant boys. . . . He first taught me the right sensuality of poetry, how it should be savoured and mouthed in solitude. Of Milton's "Thrones, Dominations, Princedoms, Virtues, Powers" [*Paradise Lost,* 10:460] he said, "That line made me happy for a week." It was not the sort of thing I had heard anyone say before. (*SJ,* 110–11)

Lewis also recalls that Smith "could also analyze. An idiom or a textual crux, once expounded upon by Smewgy, became as clear as day" (112). As we saw with the fragment on Capron, Lewis used poetry to recall early memories, this time the pleasant ones concerning Smith.[9]

Except for Smith, Lewis had little good to say about his year at Malvern College (see *SJ*, 83–117). Therefore, after repeated requests from his son, Albert Lewis decided to remove him from Malvern College, sending him instead to study under his and Warren Lewis's former tutor. So it was that Lewis went to study under Kirkpatrick, his greatest teacher, in September 1914. "On W. T. Kirkpatrick," the last autobiographical poetic fragment, is the longest and the best. In fifty-four alexandrines Lewis presents a vivid picture of Kirkpatrick, immortalized as "The Great Knock" in *Surprised by Joy,* describing him with both wit and respect. For example, on the one hand, he says Kirkpatrick was like "father Time himself" trailing "clouds of cheap tobacco smoke" and planting a garden "with green utilitarian kale." On the other hand, he notes the old man was a Charon-like figure, and he follows this with a wonderfully evocative metaphor, perhaps the best in the whole poem: "[He was] a leathery, lean / Northeaster of a man." The fragment also augments our picture of Kirkpatrick's spiritual experience since his heritage was that of "the brave, bitter Presbyterian race who stood / for Calvin to the gallow's foot"; this heritage notwithstanding, Lewis notes "Kirk allowed / No God in the world, nor spirit in man." Furthermore, Lewis's respect for Kirkpatrick's honest disbelief is clear: "He did not shroud / That unbelief in pious frauds, as teachers love. / He thought the reverence owed to boys was Truth."[10] Yet, in the telling conclusion to the first half of the fragment, Lewis notes that even Kirkpatrick tipped his hat to the Almighty he rejected, since "each seventh day / A Presbyterian shift of suits from rusty grey / To rusty black [occurred]. He gardened differently clad / On Sundays."[11]

In the second half of the fragment, Lewis emphasizes how Kirkpatrick went about training his "uncorrected mind" to think logically:

> On the iron coast
> Of such a man, with noise of yeasty waves, the young
> Spring-swellings of my uncorrected mind were flung
> So often that even now I see him as he spoke
> Fling up his arm, and hear him from the cloud of smoke
> Break in. "I hear you well enough. Stop there! I hear!
> Have you read this—and that—and the other?—Hah! I fear
> You've got no facts. Give me the FACTS!" Repeated shame
> Silenced my babbling: months wore on, and I became
> Aware how the discourse of men (what none before
> Of all my teachers showed me), asks for something more
> Than lungs and lips. Across my landscape, like the dawn,
> Some image of the sovranty of truth was drawn,
> And how to have believed an unproved thing by will

> Pollutes the mind's virginity; how reasons kill
> Beloved supposals: day makes tawdry lesser lights,
> And mountain air is med'cinal.[12]

Time after time, session after session, class after class, Kirkpatrick would drum into his pupil his own methodical logic. Such demanding treatment to a lesser mind might have been stunting but, oddly, Lewis admired the way Kirkpatrick demonstrated the supremacy of debate in discovering truth: "I had my spurs / Of intellectual knighthood in that bannered field / From Kirk's strong hand." Lewis confesses an eternal indebtedness to his old teacher and offers his highest praise as the fragment ends: "Blameless champion of a pitiful cause."[13]

In *Surprised by Joy* Lewis expanded on these lines to give a lengthy portrait of Kirkpatrick. For instance, about Kirkpatrick's philosophy he writes, "If ever a man came near to being a purely logical entity, that man was Kirk. Born a little later, he would have been a Logical Positivist. The idea that human beings should exercise their vocal organs for any purpose except that of communicating or discovering truth was to him preposterous" (*SJ*, 135–36). However, Lewis did see in Kirkpatrick a curious contradiction: "I have said that he was almost wholly logical; but not quite. He had been a Presbyterian and was now an Atheist. He spent Sunday, as he spent most of his time on weekdays, working in his garden. But one curious trait from his Presbyterian youth survived. He always, on Sundays, gardened in a different, and slightly more respectable, suit. An Ulster Scot may come to disbelieve in God, but not to wear his weekday clothes on the Sabbath" (139). One striking thing about the Kirkpatrick fragment is its concrete imagery: "Clouds of cheap tobacco," "claps of laughter," "the iron coast of such a man," and "maiden shield [of intellectual knighthood]" are richly evocative; one wishes Lewis had included them in *Surprised by Joy*, as it is poorer for their absence.

The value of these fragments referring to Lewis's teachers is fourfold. First, they underscore the primary role poetry played in Lewis's developing literary life. As the three fragments make obvious, when as a young man he contemplated telling his life's story, Lewis turned to poetry as his natural medium. Second, they illustrate how significant these three teachers were in shaping Lewis's intellectual life: From his reaction against Capron he learned how literature could help him survive a brutal reality; from Smith he learned how poetry could open to him the experience of beauty; and from Kirkpatrick he learned how learning could help him engage in intellectual discourse and discovery. Third, they supplement the extended prose versions of the same persons in *Surprised by Joy*. Fourth, these three fragments offer telling biographical insight into Lewis's development as a writer. As poetry, however, they are uneven. On the one hand, Shaw notes the "vivid imagery" of lines such as "where the hammered hills / Grow hot like metal, and metallic sunshine fills / The basin of the burning sky till the blue is dark" and "may the earth be green / Above thy grave" from the poem on Wakelyn.[14] On the other hand, the alexandrines become tired, and Lewis's literary allusions are sometimes forced.

"The Carpet Rises in the Draught," probably dates from 1922–23.[15] Warren Lewis connects this fragment with "the aloof and solitary nature of Clive's life during his adolescence . . . [as it describes] the emptiness and silence of Little Lea as it was after [our mother's] death in 1908" (*LP*, 11:251). The thirteen-line heptameter fragment echoes passages from *Spirits in Bondage,* especially the morose poems questioning the meaning of life:

> The carpet rises in the draught. The little scarlet leaf,
> That's blown in from the window sill, is wicked past belief:
> That old face in the picture there is bad as bad can be,
> And thro' its chromolithic eyes it says strange things to me.
> Beyond this room, if I went out, there's thirty feet or more
> Of passage thro' the empty house and many an open door
> And many an empty room that's full of breeze and sunless light
> With empty beds for visitors all neat and cold and white.
> And sometimes now a door will bang and then at other whiles
> A little bit of wind gets lost—strays in beneath the tiles
> And among beams and water pipes it makes a fretting sound
> Behind the walls, between the laths it wheezes round around,
> There's so much room about a house.[16]

The fragment reinforces what Lewis writes in *Surprised by Joy* about how Little Lea, for all its other benefits to him and Warren, was bereft of beauty: "This absence of beauty, now that I come to think of it, is characteristic of our childhood. No picture on the walls of my father's house ever attracted—and indeed none deserved—our attention. We never saw a beautiful building nor imagined that a building could be beautiful" (*SJ*, 6). In particular, the image of the draught cutting through the house is chilling.[17] However, as a poem, "The Carpet Rises in the Draught" is flawed. While Shaw says, "I rather like this," perhaps because of the eerie, forsaken mood it creates, lines such as "the little scarlet leaf . . . is wicked beyond belief," "as bad as bad can be," and "among beams and water pipes" are unsatisfying.[18] In addition, the heptameter suggests that Lewis was floundering with the lengthy meter. Nonetheless, the poem is valuable for the additional light it sheds on Lewis's sense of home, his nostalgia for the past, and his impulse to record these in poetry.

Lewis's interest in writing a poem on Psyche dates at least to May 6, 1922, when he writes in his diary, "Tried to work on 'Psyche' . . . with no success" (*DCSL*, 30). Six months later he toys with another idea: "After lunch I went out for a walk . . .

thinking how to make a masque or play of Psyche and Caspian" (Nov. 23, 1922, 142). Ten months later he still is looking for the right formula for the poem: "My head was very full of my old idea of a poem on my own version of the Cupid and Psyche story in which Psyche's sister would not be jealous, but unable to see anything but moors when Psyche showed her the Palace. I have tried it twice before, once in couplets and once in ballad form" (Sept. 9, 1923, 266). Warren Lewis adds that, in 1923, his brother was "very full of the idea of re-writing the story of Cupid and Psyche. To what state of completion the scheme was brought is not known, but I have found the following draft in one of his note books" (*LP*, 8:163). What follows, "On Cupid and Psyche," is seventy-six lines of heroic couplets.[19]

Lewis begins by taking issue with Lucius Apuleius Platonicus's version as found in *Metamorphoses* or *The Golden Ass:* "The tale of Psyche is unjustly told /And half the truth concealed by all who hold / With Apuleius." Poets following Apuleius have perpetrated false versions of the story, claiming Venus, jealous of Psyche's beauty, caused her to be sacrificed to a serpent to appease the goddess's wrath. Actually, says Lewis, it was not the goddess's envy but man's desperation that caused Psyche's problems: "It was no fabled Venus' spite / That drove them to this thing; but summer rains / Withheld and harvest withering on the plains. / The streams were low." There were rumors among the people of an old custom requiring human sacrifice to insure that the land's fertility surface; the priests first tried using prisoners and slaves as sacrifices, but they were unworthy:

> But this was vain
> They must give more, give all, to get the rain,
> Give the land's best and first—give anything—
> Even to the royal blood. Now let the king
> Deny them, and within the hour he's dead.
> "What. Shall the king be spared? Our sons have bled
> To build his throne. His turn has come today.
> Children are dying. Lead the girl away." (*LP*, 8:163)

So it is that Psyche is led in chains near the serpent's den to await her fate.

Happily, however, no serpent but a god, "some strange helper came and took her part," his face never seen, hidden by clouds. After he freed her, he wooed her as his lover. Here, Lewis says, the story has gotten even more distorted, blurred by slanderers who say Psyche's two ugly sisters force her to look upon the forbidden face of her god husband, thus causing a breach between them. Such poetry is

> Like the work of some poetic youth,
> Angry, and far too certain of the truth,

Mad from the gleams of vision that claim to find
Bye ways to something missed by all mankind.
He thinks that only envy or dull eyes
Keep all men from believing in the prize
He holds in secret. In revenge he drew
—For portrait of us all—the sisters two,
Misunderstanding them: and poets since
Have followed. (164)

Ironically, we can read in these lines Lewis himself as an angry, poetic youth determined to "set right" the injustices he claims have been done to Psyche's story.
Accordingly, when he turns to tell the "truth" of Psyche's story, he introduces completely new elements:

Now I say there was a prince
Twin brother to this Psyche, fair as she,
And prettier than a boy would choose to be,
His name was Jardis. Older far than these
Was Caspian who had rocked them on her knees,
The child of the first marriage of the king. (164)[20]

Lewis's new elements are fascinating. What might have occurred to her brother,
Jardis, "prettier than a boy would choose to be"? And what of this Caspian? Was
she the prototype for Orual in *Till We Have Faces?* Though these questions remain
unanswered, since Lewis never completed this poem, "On Cupid and Psyche"
gives evidence of another halting attempt by Lewis to write narrative verse; unfortunately, like his earlier efforts, this one was stillborn. As a poem it is noteworthy
in its easy rhyme and quick pace, though it is clearly the work of an apprentice.
  "The Silence of the Night," which also uses heroic couplets and dates from the
same time as "On Cupid and Psyche," is a ninety-five-line fragment concerning
Hippolytus, probably the source poem for Lewis's later "The Queen of Drum."[21]
As poetry, "The Silence of the Night" is not very good. It describes the nightmarish
wakening of Hippolytus to a cacophony of harsh noises, and then his naked dash,
accompanied by his snarling dogs, out of the city and up a great hill. Then, with no
explanation, we read:

Running beside the prince there seemed to be
Innumerable hordes of beast and man.
Under his feet the little foxes ran:
Wings smote upon his temples. Often he felt

The hoarse breathed mountain bear with shaggy pelt
Brushing his thighs. Women with skirts caught up
And revellers fresh crowned from the full cup
And maudlin pipe, ancients with silver head,
Young children, priests, merchants, and maids unwed
Ran there with labouring breath, wide gaping mouth,
Some naked, wounded some, all parched with drouth
In the burning throat. (166–67)[22]

The fragment ends incoherently: "Brother, I have grown hound. I smell the track /
I am all nose—Look. Look; with flanks of snow / See where the quarry flies—it is
a doe— / It is a lion—it's a man." The frenzied pace and theme of the poem suggest
connections to the "Wild Hunt" poem that has not survived, and the race up the
hill may prefigure both the Queen of Drum's escape in "Canto V" and the Great
Dance motif Lewis used in the *Chronicles of Narnia* and *Perelandra*. Interestingly,
however, the wild hunt aspects of the poem link it to Lewis's Norse interest, since
one of the myths associated with Odin is actually called the Wild Hunt, and details
related to it parallel Lewis's fragment. For instance, Odin, in the character of the
Wild Huntsman, gathers all disembodied spirits and sweeps through the landscape
so "when people heard the rush and roar of the wind they cried aloud in super-
stitious fear, fancying they heard and saw him ride past with his train, all mounted
on snorting steeds, and accompanied by baying hounds."[23] Lewis has a passage
very similar to this:

        Then more and more
    Came other noises through the wuthering wind,
    Cat calls that raised the hair and drums that dinned,
    Struck cymbals, screaming voices and the sounds
    Of divine beasts at mort and gaining hounds
    Baying their thirst, that nearer, nearer rang
    Now in the street, now at the door. (164)

"The Silence of the Night," while weak, does offer us the opportunity to see Lewis
take an early idea, work it, struggle with it, let it sit, and later turn it into a successful narrative poem, "The Queen of Drum." It is a work in progress. Furthermore,
its possible origin as an Odinic myth undergirds the pervasive impact Norse literature had upon his poetic sensibilities.

    "Joy," published in 1924, is a watershed poem, because in it we see Lewis rename
the longing for transcendent beauty he wrote about so passionately in the sanguine
poems of *Spirits in Bondage;* indeed, this poem was Lewis's earliest published
attempt to describe the essence of joy.[24] While the later *Surprised by Joy* is an al-

most exhaustive attempt by Lewis to chronicle his determined pursuit for joy, here he sketches a sleeper's awakening to unexpected joy and beauty.[25] Alluding to the myth of Leda and the swan, where Zeus in the form of a gigantic bird ravishes a beautiful girl, Lewis compares the sleeper's wakening to this event: "As I woke, / Like a huge bird, Joy with the feathery stroke / Of strange wings brushed me over."[26] As Leda is overcome by the swan, so the sleeper is by Joy, which then touches "the lair / Of each wild thing and woke the wet flowers everywhere." Drunk with such joy, the speaker believes he will have this vital sense of joy so constantly "that this mood could never die." Indeed, at least briefly, he glories in believing joy makes him master of all, liberating him to see clearly: "Like Christian when his burden dropt behind, / I was set free. Pure colour purified my mind." Yet he pauses quickly and realizes:

> We do not know the language Beauty speaks,
> She has no answer to our questioning,
> And ease to pain and truth to one who seeks
> I know she never brought and cannot bring.
> But, if she wakes a moment, we must fling
> Doubt at her feet, not answered, yet allayed.
> She beats down wisdom suddenly. We cling
> Fast to her flying skirts and she will fade
> Even at the kiss of welcome, into deepest shade. (ll. 28–36)

This passage recalls Shelley's "Hymn to Intellectual Beauty" in several ways. On the one hand, Lewis takes issue with Shelley's claim that only Beauty can give "grace and truth to life's unquiet dream," since for him beauty "has no answer to our questioning." On the other hand, he supports Shelley's vow to "dedicate my powers / To thee and thine" so that when Beauty comes, one can find in her an "awful LOVELINESS, / [That] wouldst give whate'er these words cannot express" (ll.71–72). For Lewis, Beauty is the swan beating wisdom down on the passive receiver; for Shelley, Beauty is "the awful shadow of some unseen Power . . . Which like the truth / Of nature on my passive youth / Descended, to my onward life supply / Its calm" (ll.1–2, 78–79).

As Lewis's poem continues, the speaker's sober realization that Beauty "will not stay" echoes Shelley's lament: "Spirit of BEAUTY, that dost consecrate / With thine own hues all thou dost shine upon / Of human thought or form,—where art thou gone?" (ll.13–15). However, at this point the two poems diverge radically. Shelley, while admitting Beauty is imperceptible, inconstant, and shadowy, still affirms it is ever present, although we may not realize this since it "floats . . . unseen amongst us." Lewis's speaker disagrees:

> And then I knew that this was all gone over.
> I shall not live like this another day.
> To-morrow I'll go wandering, a poor lover
> Of earth, rejected, outcast every way,
> And see not, hear not. Rapture will not stay
> Longer than this, lest mortals grow divine
> And old laws change too much. The sensitive ray
> Of Beauty, her creative vision fine,
> Pass. I am hers, but she will not again be mine. (ll.46–54)

For Lewis, the breath of joy Beauty brings carries with it the melancholic realization it cannot last. Joy, full of aching beauty, is fleeting. The sense that the speaker will never again experience Beauty contrasts sharply with Lewis's views in *Surprised by Joy* and elsewhere. This is not surprising when we recall that this poem is written before Lewis connects his lifelong pursuit of joy with realizing in Christ the joy he desires: "But what, in conclusion, of Joy? for that after all, is what the story has mainly been about. To tell you truth, the subject has lost nearly all interest for me since I became a Christian. . . . It was valuable only as a pointer to something other and outer" (*SJ*, 238). As a young man in his twenties, still struggling to achieve both academic success and literary acclaim and laboring under a genetic and philosophic moroseness exacerbated by the recent horrors of World War I, Lewis's misgivings about joy's capacity to offer him solace are to be expected.

These early Oxford poems, with the exception of "Joy" and "The Carpet Rises in the Draught," illustrate Lewis's continued fascination with and commitment to narrative verse. The alexandrines of the three autobiographical poems dealing with Capron, Smith, and Kirkpatrick are handled competently; Lewis favored hexameters at this time and enjoyed practicing the meter. In addition, his verse reflections on these teachers indicate the primacy of poetry in his early literary life. "On Cupid and Psyche" and "The Silence of the Night" lack an autobiographical signature, and Lewis's return to heroic couplets is a deficiency rather than an advance. That neither was ever finished indicates Lewis's own misgivings about them. "The Carpet Rises in the Draught" never becomes a compelling lyric because it is hobbled by its fourteeners; Lewis largely abandons heptameter after this poem. "Joy," notwithstanding Shelley's influence, is delightful and a fitting poetic exploration of the theme that so defined Lewis's experience.

DYMER

Lewis's primary verse preoccupation from 1920 to 1926 was *Dymer*. Yet scholars have given *Dymer* even less critical scrutiny than *Spirits in Bondage,* no doubt because the poem is both lengthy and obscure.[27] However, those who have studied the poem closely find much to admire. The earliest essay on *Dymer* was Marjorie Milne's laudatory personal reaction to how powerfully the poem affected her as myth. She quoted Lewis's own distinction between myth and poetry, noting in particular his claim that "in a myth the pattern of events is all that matters. . . . Any means which succeeds in lodging these events in our imagination has, as we say, done the trick" (Milne, 170).[28] Nevill Coghill said "[*Dymer*] is a good story well told, and supported by the sense of there being a powerful mind behind it, flashing out occasionally with an original expression . . . or in a well-sustained passage of natural description, in a vein that harks back to the countryside tradition of poetry and to the sentiment of nature" ("The Approach to English," 59). Similarly, Owen Barfield said *Dymer* was "an extremely good, though not quite a great, poem. There is not a single flat line in it" (*Owen Barfield on C. S. Lewis*, 6). Furthermore, he argued elsewhere that *Dymer* is worth reading because "it is practically the only place where the voice of the earlier Lewis [preconversion to Christ] . . . is heard speaking not through the memory of the later Lewis but one could say in his own person."[29] Accordingly, in *Dymer* we hear a voice stripped of religious dogma, utterly unbound by conventional, orthodox Christianity.

However, George Sayer's essay is without question the best piece of criticism yet published on *Dymer*. He begins with helpful references to how the poem was initially reviewed, including citations, and then he briefly traces in Lewis's letters and diaries the origin of the ideas behind the poem.[30] Also, Sayer mentions the important philosophical influences upon Lewis at the time of the poem's composition (in addition to Kirkpatrick's atheism, he lists Hegel, F. H. Bradley, and J. Cook Wilson) as well as the fact that Lewis was "in full flight from his romantic sensibility."[31] With this extremely effective introduction behind him, Sayer succinctly states what he believes to be the main subject of the poem, "which is without doubt the temptation of fantasies—fantasies of love, lust, and power." Specifically, Sayer argues that *Dymer* is centrally concerned with the "Christina Dream, the fantasy of sexual love" (97).[32] Using this as his critical perspective, Sayer then offers an intelligent though not entirely systematic analysis of the poem. He freely uses the verse to support his critical insights, frequently making perceptive comments. For example, about the mysterious bride Dymer enjoys sexually and who later is transformed into a hideous old hag, Sayer says: "Whom does she represent? Not, I am sure, Lewis's friend, Mrs. Moore, as has sometimes been suggested. The poem is not written at this crude biographical level. She represents the strong sense of guilt he experiences after having broken the conventional social and moral laws, and still more the guilt that is often felt by those who indulge in sexual fantasies. He feels guilty because of the inadequacy of his relationship with the mysterious bride" (104).[33] Indeed, much of Sayer's analysis focuses upon how guilt drives Dymer into often reckless and purposeless action. He ends by calling on readers to read *Dymer* aloud: "Experienced in this way (of course you have to find a reader who knows how to read rhyme royal, nowadays no easy thing) it will still make a great impression on the sensitive listener, even though he may not dance with delight, as Owen Barfield is reported to have done when he first heard parts of it read to him" (114).

While Sayer's essay is thorough and comprehensive, it is primarily informed by Lewis's introduction to the 1950 edition where Lewis himself glossed *Dymer* to the idea of the Christina Dream and summarized what the poem meant to him.[34] However, an author's reading of his own poem is always suspect, since rarely can he know all that goes into it; even less under his control is all that comes out of the poem as the text is engaged by various readers. The intentional fallacy reminds us to accept an author's evaluation of his own work cautiously. Accordingly, it seems that a better approach to *Dymer* is one informed by viewing Dymer as a haughty adolescent intent on living an autonomous life. As he faces the consequences of his selfish, cruel actions, however, he achieves humility and wisdom, albeit at high personal cost. In addition, the impact of Lewis's World War I experiences and the influences of Norse mythology and literature are intrinsic to a full understanding of the poem. Indeed, *Dymer* is profoundly influenced by the poetry of *Spirits in Bondage;* this is clearly evident in the emotional undulations of Dymer himself, reflected by his alternating sanguine highs and morose lows. Furthermore, there are battlefield descriptions surpassing those Lewis includes in *Spirits in Bondage* and rivaling those written by other WWI poets. The first hint that Lewis's love of Norse literature is at work in *Dymer* is found opposite the title page in the first edition published by Dent in 1926. There we find this epigram from *Havamal,* Odin's High Song from *Edda,* essentially a code of laws and ethics his people are to use to govern their conduct: "Nine nights I hung upon the Tree, wounded with the spear as an offering to Odin, myself sacrificed to myself."[35] This epigram offers a key to understanding *Dymer*'s cryptic conclusion. In the canto by canto discussion of *Dymer* that follows, these influences are considered at length.

CANTO I

Canto I begins by echoing several qualities of Byron's *Don Juan.*[36] First, the narrator, whose appearance gradually fades into the background, attempts to create a friendly, conspiratorial relationship between himself and his readers: "This moment, if you join me, we begin / A partnership where both must toil to hold / The clue that I caught first. We lose or win / Together; if you read, you are enrolled" (2, 1–4).[37] Given the struggles many have understanding the poem, "toil" is not hyperbole. Furthermore, readers unaccustomed to reading narrative poetry welcome the narrator's promise of assistance. Unfortunately, however, unlike the intrusive narrator of *Don Juan,* the narrator of *Dymer* rarely intrudes after this introduction; even when he breaks into the narrative to offer commentary, our understanding of the poem is not appreciably enhanced. Second, the rhyme schemes of the two poems, while not identical, are similar; both the rhyme royal of *Dymer* (*ababbcc*) and the ottava rima of *Don Juan* (*abababcc*) rely primarily on end rhyme and effectively portray the alternating morose and sanguine moods. In effect, both poems contain passages fluctuating between violent agitation and sublime longing. Finally, both poems employ satire, though that of *Don Juan* is fuller and more consistent than that in *Dymer*, where it is limited primarily to the first few cantos.

In brief, Canto I introduces us to Dymer, a nineteen-year-old student (only a little older than Don Juan) living in a repressed, constrained, totalitarian state. Stimulated by Nature's fecundity, he rebels against his situation, murders his teacher in class, and escapes to Nature. There, he strips off his clothes and wanders about in a mad desire for desire. In a forest clearing he discovers and enters a castle. Dymer's emotional upheaval in this stanza is stimulated, no doubt in part, because he has been repressed for nineteen years, but also it is awakened by the longing for beauty that nature inspires in him. For instance, the narrator appears to excuse Dymer's inattention in a rigid classroom one April morning, since "who ever learned to censor the spring day?" (7, 7). Challenged by his teacher, Dymer murders him, echoing the actions of Siegfried against his teacher and foster parent, Mime, from Wagner's *Siegfried*.[38] Furthermore, both Dymer and Siegfried experience an inarticulate longing to be fulfilled, although they do not know how to slake their desires.

Both turn to Nature as a first resort. Dymer, seeking to divorce himself from his previous life, strips naked and wanders about a forest, crushing "wet, cool flowers against his face: / And once he cried aloud, 'O world, O day, / Let, let me,'—and then found no prayer to say" (17, 5–7). Similarly, Siegfried notices a bird and asks:

Bird sweet and friendly,
I ask thee a boon:
Wilt thou find for me
A comrade true?—
Wilt thou choose for me the right one?
So oft I have called,
And yet no one has come![39]

While Siegfried follows the music of the bird and is told his love will be realized when he wins Brunnhilde for his bride, Dymer, still hoping "some answer yet would come to his desire" (20, 4), is overcome, like Shakespeare's Caliban, by powerfully evocative music coming from an unidentified source:

The curtained air
Sighed into sound above his head, as though
Stringed instruments and horns were riding there.

It passed and at its passing stirred his hair.
He stood intent to hear. He heard again
And checked his breath half-drawn, as if with pain.

That music could have crumbled proud belief
With doubt, or in the bosom of the sage
Madden the heart that had outmastered grief,
And flood with tears the eyes of frozen age
And turn the young man's feet to pilgrimage—
So sharp it was, so sure a path it found,
Soulward with stabbing wounds of bitter sound.

It died out on the middle of a note,
As though it failed at the urge of its own meaning.
It left him with life quivering at the throat,
Limbs shaken and wet cheeks and body leaning
With strain towards the sound and senses gleaning
The last, least, ebbing ripple of the air,
Searching the emptied darkness, muttering "Where?" (23–25)

Lewis almost certainly has in mind passages from Wagner's *Ring;* specifically, he is alluding to the Ride of the Valkyries. As we saw earlier, Lewis wrote Greeves about the joy he had upon first hearing a live performance of the *Valkyries,* and Dymer is similarly stabbed by the music he hears, so that he is left with a mounting urge to understand and fulfill his longing. Additionally, for the remainder of Canto I he follows "the music, unendurable / In stealing sweetness wind from tree to tree" (27, 3–4) until it leads him to a light coming through an arch in a forest glen. The connection between Dymer and Siegfried established in Canto I should not be overemphasized; at the same time it should not be ignored, particularly since both characters eventually come to associate fulfilling their inarticulate longings with romantic love. Siegfried, who follows Mime into the forest to learn fear for the first time, transfers this to the newly awakened feelings the bird's song produces: "With longing I burn / Now from Brunnhild' to learn it" (Wagner, 231). Dymer, as we shall see, transfers his unnamed desire into an unbridled, yet hopelessly sentimentalized, sexual union.

CANTO II

In Canto II, Dymer boldly moves through the arch; inside he finds great beauty enclosed by a high dome, further exciting his desire. After admiring his naked reflection in a huge mirror, he dresses himself in rich clothing he finds nearby.

Haughty yet guilty, he eats and drinks at a rich banquet table, exciting a heightened stimulation to consummate his still unnamed desire. Passing through a low curtain, he enters a dark room where an unidentified girl slips into his arms; there, he is "surprised by lust" and quickly experiences sexual gratification with this imagined beauty, imagined because he never sees her face. The canto, therefore, begins with Dymer initially attracted by idealized beauty and moves him to the end where he experiences the intensity of raw sexual passion. Lewis employs lines worthy of sanguine poems in *Spirits in Bondage,* even echoing the end of "Dungeon Grates" and its devotees of beauty: They "have seen the Glory." Dymer, admiring the beauty of the dome within the arch, "wondering round around he turned: / Still on each side the level glory burned" (1, 7). In fact, the beauty of the dome momentarily makes Dymer stupidly good: "The shouting mood had withered from his heart" and the Wagnerian music continues its power over him: "The sound / Of music, never ceasing, took the role / Of silence and like silence numbed his soul" (4, 1, 5–7).

However, the power of ideal beauty is broken when he catches a glimpse of himself in the mirror, since, Narcissus-like, he becomes fascinated with his own physical beauty. Finding lavish clothing hanging near the mirror, he vainly dresses himself and "wondered that he had not known before / How fair a man he was" (9, 4–5). Moreover, this self-love expresses itself by glorifying in lawlessness: "'Here is no law, nor eye to see, / Nor leave of entry given. Why should there be?'" (7, 6–7). Dymer, in full flight from the totalitarian state that bred him, instead embraces total self-indulgence, even planning to return to the city as a self-proclaimed hero to "drive them all to freedom on this track" (9, 7). Believing himself an autonomous man, Dymer thinks he can be the savior of the ignorant, deluded beings he left in the city. In one of his rare intrusions, however, the narrator prepares us for Dymer's eventual fall and disillusionment by pointing out his adolescent posturing:

> Thus feeding on vain fancy, covering round
> His hunger, his great loneliness arraying
> In facile dreams until the qualm was drowned,
> The boy went on. Through endless arches straying
> With casual tread he sauntered, manly playing
> At manhood. (12, 1–6)

This cocky manchild soon comes upon a rich banquet that attracts his palate: "When Dymer saw this sight, he leaped for mirth, / He clapped his hands, his eye lit like a lover's. / He had a hunger in him that was worth / Ten cities" (13, 1–4). The language of this passage is revealing. While on the one hand it literally refers to

Dymer's physical hunger, so long unsated in the forest, on the other hand, it figuratively refers to his unrealized sexual desires. Accordingly, his binge at the table foreshadows his sexual encounter at the end of the canto, and the guilt he feels at the former—"There in the lonely splendour Dymer ate, / As thieves eat, ever watching, half in fear" (16, 1–2)—is dead during the latter.

In addition to his overeating, he liberally consumes strong drink as well. Contrasted with the Spartan "rations" and "scientific food, / At common boards, with water in his cup, / One mess alike for every day and mood" (17, 2–4) he had in the past, he eagerly tosses back flagon after flagon of "some liquor that foamed blue" (18, 2). The culmination of all his indulgence, ever stimulated by the ubiquitous Wagnerian music, overwhelms Dymer: "There was a riot in his heart that brought / The loud blood to his temples" (19, 5–6). He realizes for the moment that all his thoughts of going back to "free" those still living under totalitarian rule is a fool's errand. Instead, though he has been warned in the past about living to realize unfulfilled desire, all the stimulation to his senses has further heightened his desire for desire: "A thousand times they have warned me of men's greed / For joy, for the good that all desire, but never / Till now I knew the wild heat of the endeavor" (20, 5–7). Rejecting his past, he intends instead to push forward to unrestrained desire:

> I was a dull, cowed thing from the beginning.
> Dymer the drudge, the blackleg who obeyed.
> Desire shall teach me now. If this be sinning,
> Good luck to it! O splendour long delayed,
> Beautiful world of mine, O world arrayed
> For bridal, flower and forest, wave and field,
> I come to be your lover. Loveliest, yield! (22)

Drunkenly, he thinks to find in nature the fulfillment of his desires, even personifying nature as his beloved,[40] and using bizarre sexual images to describe what he seeks: "Somewhere, before the world's end, I shall fill / My spirit at earth's pap" (25, 5–6).

Such language prepares us for the dramatic conclusion of the canto. Dymer sees a low door hidden by "dark curtains, sweepy fold, night-purple pall" (27, 3) and is mysteriously attracted to it: "Sudden desire for darkness overbore / His will, and drew him towards it. All was blind / Within. He passed. The curtains closed behind" (27, 5–7). This passage will be variously interpreted, and no doubt those informed by Freud have much grist for the mill here. At the least, this can be seen as Dymer's descent into Hell, albeit it is one he fails to recognize, for the realm he enters is a void:

> Darker than the night
> That is most black with beating thunder-showers,
> —A disembodied world where depth and height
> And distance were unmade. No seam of light
> Showed through. It was a world not made for seeing
> One pure, one undivided sense of being. (28, 2–7)

This is a delicious Hell, richly evocative with a cool smell "that was holy and unholy," and a soft thicket of "broad leaves and wiry stems" (29, 3, 6). Sensuous and sensual, this lush, dark place causes Dymer's body to thirst for sensual fulfillment: "With body intent he felt the foliage quiver / On breast and thighs. With groping arms he made / Wide passes in the air." In addition, as he senses consummation coming to his long burning desire, "a sacred shiver / Of joy from the heart's centre oddly strayed / To every nerve" (30, 1–3 and 3–5). Groping forward with excitement and fear, he finds "a knee-depth of warm pillows on the ground" (30, 7). He sinks down into the luxurious bedding, feeling it a "sweet rapture to lie" there. Then, unexpectedly, out of the silent darkness "as if by stealth" a hand touches his, and he hears "a low grave laugh and rounded like a pearl / Mysterious, filled with home" (32, 1–2). Dymer, now in a fever pitch of longing, does not wait to respond:

> He opened wide
> His arms. The breathing body of a girl
> Slid into them. From the world's end, with the stride
> Of seven-leagued boots came passion to his side.
> Then, meeting mouths, soft-falling hair, a cry,
> Heart-shaken flank, sudden cool-folded thigh. (32, 2–7)

The canto ends with one of the best passages of poetry in the entire poem:

> The same night swelled the mushroom in earth's lap
> And silvered the wet fields: it drew the bud
> From hiding and led on the rhythmic sap
> And sent the young wolves thirsting after blood,
> And, wheeling the big seas, made ebb and flood
> Along the shores of earth: and held these two
> In dead sleep till the time of morning dew. (33)

Dymer's descent into Hell is masked to him, since he is consumed by passion. However, details like the impenetrable darkness and the "grave" laugh clearly connect this experience to a more sinister end. In addition, the passage can easily be seen as autoerotic since initially the hand that touches him as well as the source of the laugh is not identified; even after the girl is introduced, we do not know if she is the source of the initial touch and laugh. Regardless, in this creature Dymer realizes his inarticulate longing for desire as sexual passion, unimpeded and all consuming. His heretofore unfocused longing finds outlet in this mysterious girl.

By contrast, Siegfried, once shown the fiery circle surrounding the sleeping and enchanted Brunnhilde, acts heroically, disregards the fire, and plunges through to awaken her. However, even though he is as passionate as Dymer, his is a purer, less selfish love. While initially he longs to overpower her, he waits until she is ready to receive him willingly. He learns the fear he has long heard about yet never known: Love might be unrequited. *Siegfried* ends with his affirmation of love:

> Hail, O world
> Where Brunnhilde dwells! . . .
> She is for ever
> And for aye
> My wealth, my world,
> My all in all,
> Love ever radiant,
> Laughing death! (Wagner, 258–59)

Dymer is an adolescent seeking self-fulfillment; Siegfried is a man seeking redemptive love. Both are instructive cases of the power of romantic love.

CANTO III

Canto III marks the peak of Dymer's emotional high in the poem, but it also begins his descent into despair; indeed, the wild swings of mood characteristic of *Dymer* are best seen in this canto. Curious by its absence is the music that had once charmed Dymer. The action begins the morning after his spent passion with the unidentified girl. Dymer awakens to a sanguine morning of still, lovely beauty, conscious of a warm, breathing body next to him. Oddly, however, he never looks at the girl; instead he arises to go out and to enjoy the forest beauty alone, "Just for one glance" (2, 7). Again, Lewis's lyrical description of nature is effective: "Out into the crisp grey air and drenching grass. / The whitened cobweb sparkling in its place / Clung to his feet. He saw the wagtail pass / Beside him and the thrush" (3, 1–4). He lingers here leisurely stretching, yawning, sighing, laughing softly to himself, apparently completely satisfied:

> The wood with its cold flowers had nothing there
> More beautiful than he, new waked from sleep,
> New born from joy. His soul lay very bare

That moment to life's touch, and pondering deep
Now first he knew that no desire could keep
These hours for always, and that men do die
—But oh, the present glory of lungs and eye! (5)

Dymer little knows how prophetic these thoughts are. As an adolescent, he does not understand that the joy he revels in is cheaply purchased, unable to sustain him. This knowledge, however, is not long in coming, for as he suddenly remembers the girl, he longs to return to her. He sentimentalizes his affection for her when he reflects the forest would be a frightful place, "but now I have met my friend / Who loves me, [and] we can talk to the road's end" (6, 6–7).

Thus, "quickening with the sweetness of the tale / Of his new love" (7, 1–2), he returns to a low door, but is unsure whether it is the same one he entered the night before. At the same moment, he realizes he does not even know the girl's name, so he hastens to find her. The path to his bower of bliss is blocked, however: "Across the quiet threshold something lay, / A bundle, a dark mass that barred the way. / He looked again, and lo, the formless pile / Under his eyes was moving all the while" (11, 4–7). Lewis goes on to describe a creature the opposite of what Dymer imagines he enjoyed the previous evening:

And it had hands, pale hands of wrinkled flesh,
Puckered and gnarled with vast antiquity,
That moved. He eyed the sprawling thing afresh,
And bit by bit (so faces come to be
In the red coal) yet surely, he could see
That the swathed hugeness was uncleanly human,
A living thing, the likeness of a woman. (12)

In addition, she is mantled in thick cloth that draped to the ground, giving the impression she is rooted to the earth. Ominously, her face is not visible. Dymer shrinks from her, turns, and runs to another entrance, "a hungry lover, / And not yet taught to endure, not blunted yet, / But weary of long waiting to discover / That loved one's face" (16, 1–4). To his horror, he finds the same enigmatic creature blocking his path; when he goes to other doors, she is always waiting: "The thing sat there / In every door, still watching, everywhere, / Behind, ahead, all round" (18, 4–6).

Oddly, he recalls he has dreamed of such a place, even knowing how it will all end. Even so, "all the more / He raged with passionate will that overbore / that knowledge" (19, 4–6). Sick with despair and anticipation, he calls to his unidentified lover, again sentimentalizing their relationship: "Where? Where? Dear, look once out. Give but one sign. / It's I, I, Dymer. Are you chained and hidden? / What have they done to her? Loose her! She is mine" (20, 1–3). He also boldly claims he will come to her, even if means going past the old, grotesque creature. Dymer at this point really has no concern for his unidentified lover; he only wants her so he can be satisfied again, not to save her from danger. He tries another door, but the hag is there as well. He strives to convince himself there is nothing to fear since she is "only an old woman," but her size, "the old, old matriarchal dreadfulness, / Immovable, intolerable . . . the eyes / Hidden, the hidden head, the winding dress, / Corpselike" daunted him (23, 2–5). Putting aside his belligerence, he tries to talk his way past her, recounting his meeting of the unknown girl and justifying their illicit union:

> The woman answered nothing: but he saw
> The hands, like crabs, still wandering on her knee.
> "Mother, if I have broken any law,
> I'll ask a pardon once; then let it be,
> —Once is enough—and leave the passage free.
> I am in haste. And though it were a sin
> By all the laws you have, I must go in." (25)

Dymer's false humility does not mask his lack of repentance; he is trying to live as an autonomous man, unbound by the laws of man, intent upon realizing again and again his newly discovered passion. He is in haste because he can barely control his desire for consummation.

As a result, he returns to swagger and bravado: "Out of my path, old woman. For this cause / I am new born, new freed, and here new wed, / That I might be the breaker of bad laws" (26, 2–4). He claims she will "not wrest / My love from me. I journey on a quest / You cannot understand, whose strength shall bear me / Through fire and earth. A bogy will not scare me" (27, 4–7). Nevertheless, the assertion that his lawlessness is stronger than old rules as well as his pompous, vain claims of autonomy are ineffectual. While he may think he is "the sword of spring," his posturing "I am the truth" (28, 1) is both blasphemous and comic. Seeing the hag intractable, he falters "like a man / Unnerved, in bayonet-fighting," and he is left "drained of hope" (29, 1–2 and 7). His last desperate plea is for pity and shows him willing to "recant—confess his sin," if only she will let him pass. Still she remains silent. Driven wild by desire, Dymer attempts to force his way by the old hag:

> Then when he heard no answer, mad with fear
> And with desire, too strained with both to know
> What he desired or feared, yet staggering near,

He forced himself towards her and bent low
For grappling. Then came darkness. Then a blow
Fell on his heart, he thought. There came a blank
Of all things. As the dead sink, down he sank. (32)

The canto ends with an image recalling the eviction of Adam and Eve from the garden of Eden; Dymer is pictured going away from the entrance "slowly, drunkenly reeling, / Blind, beaten, broken, past desire of healing, / Past knowledge of his misery, he goes on / Under the first dark trees and now is gone" (33, 4–7).

Who is this old woman? In addition to Sayer's view given above, I offer the following. Her physical description clearly has affinities to Sin in book 2 of *Paradise Lost,* though Lewis's hag lacks the serpentine qualities of Milton's portress to Hell.[41] Actually, the old hag has strong connections to Erda of Wagner's *Siegfried* and the Norns of Norse literature. Erda, ancient prophetess of the underworld, is sought out by Wotan in the third act of the play when he comes and asks her how he can conquer his fear of the future, particularly his knowledge that the twilight of the gods is certain. While Erda does speak to him, unlike the old hag who remains silent, her words are evasive and without comfort. Interestingly, however, she defends Brunnhilde from Wotan's anger and attempts to reconcile him to her. The Norns, the three Northern goddesses of fate, are not subject to the other gods, and their main tasks are "to warn the gods of future evil, to bid them make good use of the present, and to teach them wholesome lessons from the past" (Guerber, *Myths of the Norsemen,* 166). Daily they weave the web of fate, albeit it blindly and not according to their own wishes; instead they are subject to Orlog, the eternal law of the universe. Urd (wurd or weird), later portrayed by Wagner as Erda, is the Norn with the most affinities to Lewis's old hag. As a personification of time, she appears "very old and decrepit, continually looking backward, as if absorbed in contemplating past events and people" (167). If Lewis based his old hag upon Urd, her silence indicates Dymer's spent passion is just that: spent, finished, over, with no hope of repeating itself in spite of his eagerness to consummate it again. He can no longer hope to return to the past, either to his unidentified lover or to the totalitarian state; he is alone, without comfort, finally realizing in full the awful loneliness of attempting to live as an autonomous man. The old hag, therefore, is the first concrete evidence in his experience giving the lie to Dymer's quest for autonomy.

CANTO IV

Cantos IV and V function together, first portraying Dymer's descent into morose emotional despair; and then, after he realizes his nadir, his mood lightens as Canto V ends. In addition, Lewis draws upon his WWI battlefield experiences for

much of the imagery, metaphor, and story line in these stanzas. Canto IV begins
with Dymer, who is now devastated and wandering about the forest, suffering the
deluge of a fierce rainstorm, symbolic of the terrible tempest in his mind.[42] Nature, his friend in early portions of the poem, appears intent on persecuting him:

> Aha! . . . Earth hates a miserable man:
> Against him even the clouds and winds conspire.
> Heaven's voice smote Dymer's ear-drum as he ran,
> Its red throat plagued the dark with corded fire
> —Barbed flame, coiled flame that ran like living wire
> Charged with disastrous current, left and right
> About his path, hell-blue or staring white. (4)

Like King Lear on the heath, Dymer longs for the storm to punish him for his folly;
indeed, for the first time in the poem we see him engage in honest self-criticism:
"All lost: and driven away: even her name / Unknown. O fool, to have wasted for
a kiss / Time when they could have talked!" (6, 1–3). The description that follows
reflects the awful experiences of soldiers in the trenches during World War I who
had to endure extended time up front under constant bombardment. This is evident as the storm drives him through the forest:

> The storm lay on the forest a great time
> —Wheeled in its thundery circuit, turned, returned.
> Still through the dead-leaved darkness, through the slime
> Of standing pools and slots of clay storm-churned
> Went Dymer. Still the knotty lightning burned
> Along black air. He heard the unbroken sound
> Of water rising in the hollower ground. (7)

Note the echoes to Owen's "The Sentry":

> We'd found an old Boche dug-out, and he knew,
> And gave us hell, for shell on frantic shell
> Hammered on top, but never quite burst through.
> Rain, guttering down in waterfalls of slime,
> Kept slush waist-high and rising hour by hour,
> And choked the steps too thick with clay to climb. (Owen, 61)

Eventually the storm lessens but not Dymer's morose despair; in fact, "then came
the worst hour for flesh and blood" (9, 7). Dymer is in his worst hour because he

now knows he is totally alone, and his dream of autonomy carries the bitter price of isolation, estrangement, alienation. He no longer hopes to find the fulfillment of his dreams in an inarticulate longing, since the everyday, humdrum world is all about him.

Yet he has not experienced the worst, for at the moment he thinks he is most alone in his misery, "weary to death," he hears someone nearby breathe out in pain and whiffs "the raw smell of blood" (11, 1 and 4). He soon discovers a horribly wounded soldier. When Dymer beckons him to reach out his hands for help, the soldier curses him and says: "They've done for me. / I've no hands. Don't come near me. No, but stay, / Don't leave me. . . . O my God! Is it near day?" (12, 5–7) Lewis's own wartime experiences certainly inform this passage and illustrate that, while *Spirits in Bondage* avoids explicit battlefield scenes, in *Dymer* Lewis draws upon his vivid memories of the trenches to create this compelling episode. Dymer, stunned by this man's mutilations, has yet not reached the depth of his own despair, for as the wounded soldier tells his story, Dymer learns the ironic truth: He is responsible not only for this man's injuries but for the slaughter of many. The wounded soldier recounts how the story of Dymer's rebellion and longing for personal fulfillment had infected many, spreading like disease through the society:

> Then . . . I was lying awake in bed,
> Shot through with tremulous thought, lame hopes, and sweet
> Desire of reckless days—with burning head.
> And then there came a clamour from the street,
> Came nearer, nearer, nearer—stamping feet
> And screaming song and curses and a shout
> Of "Who's for Dymer, Dymer?—Up and out!" (20)

As many of the young in the society joined the rebellion, exulting in their own newly discovered autonomy, the leaders of the totalitarian state cracked down; the young learned "the old world could not die / And . . . we were no gods" (22, 4–5). Still, led on by a charismatic leader, Bran, the rebellion proceeded, ostensibly inspired by Dymer:

> As Dymer broke, we'll break the chain.
> The world is free. They taught you to be chaste
> And labour and bear orders and refrain.
> Refrain? From what? All's good enough. We'll taste
> Whatever is. Life murmurs from the waste
> Beneath the mind . . . who made the reasoning part
> The jailer of the wild gods in the heart? (24)

This rejection of reason in favor of feeling, says the wounded soldier, was enough to spur on many against the keepers of the totalitarian state.

Once the actual fighting occurs, Lewis again draws upon battlefield memories. The soldier's description of the fierce fighting recalls vivid passages from Sassoon and Owen. As the rebels press forward amid "charge and cheer and bubbling sobs of death, / We hovered on their front. Like swarming bees / Their spraying bullets came—no time for breath" (27, 1–3). Instead of men, they become brutes: "I saw men's stomachs fall out on their knees; / And shouting faces, while they shouted, freeze / Into black, bony masks. Before we knew / We're into them. . . . "Swine!"—"Die, then!"—"That's for you!" (27, 4–7). The wounded soldier recalls seeing "an old . . . man / Lying before my feet with shattered skull" while Bran moves to commit atrocities against prisoners; he wants "to burn them, wedge their nails up, crucify them" (28, 2–3 and 7).[43] When this unbridled revenge occurs, the "noble rebellion" becomes simply a blood bath. As the rebels win victory after victory, they torch the city and become ever more bloodthirsty: "We had them in our power! / Then was the time to mock them and to strike, / To flay men and spit women on the pike, / Bidding them dance" (30, 3–6). To Dymer's horror, he hears the wounded soldier say, "wherever the most shame / Was done the doer called on Dymer's name" (30, 6–7). After the rebels claim bloody victory, however, Bran's paranoia causes him to solidify his power by making an example of a few in order to intimidate all the rest. So it is, says the soldier, he had been randomly selected and "they cut away my two hands and my feet / And laughed and left me for the birds to eat" (33, 6–7). He dies cursing Dymer, who "sat like one that neither hears nor sees. / And the cold East whitened beyond the trees" (35, 6–7).

The powerful battlefield passages of this canto recall *Spirits in Bondage*. For instance, "French Nocturne" ends "I am wolf. Back to the world again, / And speech of fellow-brutes that once were men / Our throats can bark for slaughter: cannot sing," and "Oxford" refers to soldiers "now tangled in red battle's animal net, / Murder the work and lust the anodyne, / Pains of the beast 'gainst bestial solace set." The war imagery of Canto IV may be Lewis's less filtered recollections than ones he draws upon for *Spirits in Bondage* and contradicts to some degree his claims in *Surprised by Joy* about the impact of the war upon him.

CANTO V

Canto V offers additional insight into war's impact on Lewis. The canto begins with Dymer having wandered aimlessly away from the corpse until he comes to a deep valley; he is driven by "wonder and keen shame," while "little thoughts like bees / Followed and pricked him on and left no ease" (2, 5–7). When he gazes down into the valley, he experiences a "deep world-despair" that leaves him with "no hope, no change, and no regret" (3, 4 and 7). Like Manfred from Byron's play, Dymer looks upon Nature and is ready to die. However, before he can indulge this death wish, he falls asleep. But this is no peaceful sleep; rather, he has a nightmare filled with battlefield horror:

> For he had dreamt of being in the arms
> Of his beloved and in quiet places;
> But all at once it filled with night alarms
> And rapping guns: and men with splintered faces,
> —No eyes, no nose, all red—were running races
> With worms along the floor. (6, 1–6)

Such dreams, it is not hard to imagine, have their basis less in Dymer's experience with the dying soldier than in Lewis's own battlefield memories.

When Dymer awakens, "wailing like a child . . . heart-sick with desolation" (7, 4–5), he indulges in self-pity, regretting his loss of fulfilled longing with the unknown girl and his actions that have caused the slaughter of so many. Tormented by the thought of the latter, he tries to comfort himself with sentimental thoughts of his beloved. Unfortunately, he has no solid memory of her to comfort him: "He ran / For refuge to the thought of her; whence came / Utter and endless loss—no, not a name, / Not a word, nothing left." He is left pathetically alone "crying amid that valley of cold stone" (8, 3–6 and 7). Still, Dymer has much to learn, for instead of admitting his own responsibility in both disasters, he blames a cruel, malicious God. "Ode for New Year's Day" from *Spirits in Bondage* says that such a God does not listen to human suffering: "Do you think he ever hears / The wail of hearts he has broken, the sound of human ill? / He cares not for our virtues, our little hopes and fears" (15). Here Dymer has a similar thought: "They, they up there, the old contriving powers, / They knew it all the time—for someone knows / And waits and watches till we pluck the flowers, / Then leaps" (9, 2–5). He blames this "someone" for his joy denied and attempts to move back into his position as an autonomous man. He rejects the dead soldier's implication that he is responsible for the rebellion, claiming he acted only for himself: "What's Bran to me? I had my deed to do / And ran out by myself, alone and free" (11, 5–6). He defends his actions, claiming innocence:

> What have I done? No living thing I made
> Nor wished to suffer harm. I sought my good
> Because the spring was gloriously arrayed
> And the blue eyebright misted all the wood.
> Yet to obey that springtime and my blood,

This was to be unarmed and off my guard
And gave God time to hit once and hit hard. (13)

Indulging in further blame shifting, he says "a man must crouch to face / Infinite malice" (14, 2–3), and, again Manfred-like, he prepares himself for death, since nothing left on earth can satisfy his longings: "Great God, take back your world. I will have none / Of all your glittering gauds but death alone" (15, 6–7). The narrator, who has been long in the background, suddenly comes forth and gently mocks Dymer's self-pity, noting how the world is beautiful and will continue on regardless of Dymer's rejection. Furthermore, we see the sham of his death wish, since he does nothing active to seek it; rather, he reverts to the fetal position as "he crouched and clasped his hands about his knees / And hugged his own limbs for the pitiful sense / Of homeliness they had" (19, 1–3). Except for the impulsive murder of his teacher and his almost accidental liaison with the unknown girl, Dymer is no man of action.

Moreover, once his desire is spent, he wanders purposelessly. The remainder of the canto describes his descent into the deep valley, gradual at first, but then, when he slips on a steep slope, we find his death wish is empty. As he clutches desperately to the hillside, "his idle feet / Dangled and found no hold. The moor lay wet / Against him and he sweated with the heat / Of terror, all alive." In this moment of crisis, he finds impetus to go on: "By God, I will not die" (24, 1–4 and 5). He hugs the earth to him, feeling "it was the big, round world beneath his breast, / The mother planet" who saved him at the moment of his greatest need. Humility finally follows: "The shame of glad surrender stood confessed, / He cared not for his boasts. This, this was best, / This giving up of all. He need not strive; / He panted, he lay still, he was alive" (25, 1–2 and 4–7). After this and for the first time since he murdered his teacher, Dymer sleeps a deep, restful slumber, marked only by a comforting dream where he hears a lark sing the promise of the world never ending. In this song Dymer captures a vision of longing that is peaceful and pacifying instead of fierce and raging:

It seemed to be the low voice of the world
Brooding alone beneath the strength of things,
Murmuring of days and nights and years unfurled
Forever, and the unwearied joy that brings
Out of old fields the flowers of unborn springs,
Out of old wars and cities burned with wrong,
A splendour in the dark, a tale, a song. (29)

After this dream, Dymer awakens cleansed, reconciled with himself, and prepared to face the consequences of his previous actions. Moreover, he no longer seeks to live autonomously. Cantos I–V take Dymer through emotional extremes, beginning with haughty spiritual and personal pride, moving through profound depression and despair, then finishing with calm acceptance. Reminiscent of the emotional roller coaster that Coleridge's Ancient Mariner endured, Dymer's story might best be finished at the conclusion of Canto V. However, Dymer has more to learn about himself and the consequence of his rebellious, self-willed actions earlier in the poem.

CANTO VI

Cantos VI and VII must be considered together since they illustrate to Dymer through the appearance of a great magician that he is not yet free from destructive dreams. Indeed, in this magician, Dymer sees the frightening image of what he will become if he continues such dreams. In brief, Canto VI finds Dymer following the song of the lark in a search for food. In a house he meets a magician, and, while they eat, Dymer tells his story. The magician offers to help Dymer control his dreams; though Dymer refuses, the magician tells him the only way to rediscover his beloved is through dreams. On the other hand, Dymer believes his only hope of seeing her is through repentance. The magician belittles him for such morality and, as the canto ends, convinces Dymer to drink from his cup of dreams. In Canto VII the magician joins Dymer in drinking. While Dymer's dreams are somewhat unsettling, the magician's dreams are fantastic, and he teeters on the edge of madness. Dymer awakens and relates his dream of meeting his beloved. Although he was initially enchanted by her in his dream, he came to see that the beloved of his dream was actually himself.[44] He was in love with his own lust. The magician, descending into total madness, pulls out a gun and fires upon Dymer, badly wounding him as he flees the house.

   A closer look at Canto VI shows him believing he is now healed of his earlier dreams:

> He was whole.
> No veils should hide the truth, no truth should cow
> The dear self-pitying heart. "I'll babble now
> No longer," Dymer said. "I'm broken in.
> Pack up the dreams and let the life begin." (2, 3–7)

His first decision after this is to seek food; unlike the fabulous feast of Canto II, however, this time Dymer desires not self-indulgence but rather sustenance. Still following the lark (perhaps symbolic of the new life he seeks) he heard at the conclusion of Canto V, Dymer moves forward with "hope at heart" (4, 3). His peaceful search has a shadow fall across it when he hears in the distance a gun fired, and a short time later he comes to the house of a magician. This magician "was a mighty man whose beardless face / Beneath grey hair shone out so large and mild / It made a sort of moonlight in the place. / A dreamy desperation, wistful-wild, / Showed in his glance and gait" (7, 1–5).[45] Furthermore, "over him there hung the witching air" (8, 1). In this magician, Dymer encounters the image of what he might become: an autonomous man completely divorced from the concerns of the world and other human beings, selfishly indulging his egoistic appetites. The magician lives only for himself and the constant pursuit of realizing in full the dreams he seeks.

In his first words, the magician reveals the extent of his self-focus. He asks how Dymer discovered him, wondering if he heard the gunshot. Dymer is horrified when the magician casually explains, "It was but now I killed the lark" (10, 2). Again reminiscent of the Ancient Mariner and his murder of the albatross, the magician's action is capricious and selfish; he excuses the shooting by saying "they sing from dawn to dark, / And interrupt my dreams too long" (10, 4–5). His egoism is further exposed when he takes Dymer to his garden and explains his plantings are intended to enclose the house from the outside world "because this too makes war upon / The art of dream" (12, 2–3). Interestingly, he confesses that nothing he plants in the garden grows; this detail suggests that his attempt to live an autonomous life is sterile. One who lives only for himself and his dreams in the end atrophies and withers. Dymer, however, even though offended by the execution of the lark, never passes moral judgment upon the magician. He accepts the invitation to eat supper there and soon finds himself affected by the food he eats: "He ate and never knew / What meats they were. At every bite he grew / More drowsy and let slide his crumbling will" (14, 4–6). He listens to the magician's "tales of magic words" until he "had stolen quite away / Dymer's dull wits and softly drawn apart / The ivory gates of hope that change the heart" (16, 5–7).

So powerful are the magician's words that Dymer forgets his earlier resolution to forswear his dreams, quickly telling the magician about the girl he loved but never saw. As he listens, the magician, perhaps to lure Dymer ever deeper into his dreams, claims the girl of his dreams is not imaginary but heavenly: "Why this must be / Aethereal, not aerial!" (17, 5–6). He also recognizes the old hag, noting "always the same . . . that frightful woman shape / Besets the dream-way and the soul's escape" (18, 6–7). However, when Dymer tries to discuss Bran and the rebellion, the magician loses interest. Why? Because Bran and the rebellion have to do with the real world, not the realm of dreams. For the magician, the real world has little interest. Unlike Prospero from *The Tempest*, a powerful enchanter who does not succumb to the temptation to use his power selfishly, Lewis's magician falls prey to his own art and rejects human fellowship. Isolation is the substance of his enclosed, restricted life. Consequently, he offers to assist Dymer to find "that heavenly ghost / Who loves you" (19, 5–6). Through the magician's art, Dymer can learn the technique of living constantly in dreams:

Listen! For I can launch you on the stream
Will roll you to the shores of her own land. . . .
I could be sworn you never learned to dream,
But every night you take with careless hand
What chance may bring? I'll teach you to command
The comings and the goings of your spirit
Through all that borderland which dreams inherit. (20)

Based on his most recent experiences, however, Dymer initially resists the magician's suggestion. Dymer wants to live in the world with other human beings, not autonomously in a world of dreams: "Dreams? I have had my dream too long. I thought / The sun rose for my sake. . . . But that's behind. / I'm waking now. They broke me. All ends thus / Always—and we're for them, not they for us" (23, 1–2 and 5–7).

Consequently, Dymer exposes a flaw in the magician's thinking, because he claims his beloved "was no dream. It would be waste / To seek her there, the living in that den of lies" (24, 1–3). Still, the magician presses his point and makes powerful arguments: "In dreams the thrice-proved coward can feel brave. / In dreams the fool is free from scorning voices. / Grey-headed whores are virgins there again" (25, 7; 26, 1–2). He even ascribes to dreams biblical merit: "There the stain / Of oldest sins—how do the good words go?— / Though they were scarlet, shall be white as snow" (26, 5–7).[46] The magician's next words subtly appeal to Dymer's earlier efforts to live as an autonomous man when he says, "Your wrong and right / Are also dreams: fetters to bind the weak / Faster to phantom earth and blear the sight" (27, 2–4). The magician's philosophy, that morality is narrow and limiting, recalls Dymer's youthful pride and rebellion. Furthermore, when Dymer, still struggling against the magician's rhetoric, insists he must "undo his sins" and repent, the magician scorns such resolutions: "Throw down your human pity; cast your awe / Behind you; put repentance all away" (28, 3–4). The amorality of the magician is transparent to Dymer, who claims he would happily serve as a slave on earth for anyone, if, at the end of the year, he could see his beloved's face just for a moment and hear her urge him to live with courage for another year. Such virtues the magician mocks, for they are false promises of future reward that restrain autonomous living.

The canto ends conspiratorially, as the magician finally reveals he is not human; he tells Dymer he is ancient and eternal:

I am not mortal. Were I doomed to die
This hour, in this half-hour I interpose
A thousand years of dream: and, those gone by,
As many more, and in the last of those,

> Ten thousand—ever journeying towards a close
> That I shall never reach: for time shall flow,
> Wheel within wheel, interminably slow. (34)

This claim, reflecting an adherence to autonomy like Byron's Manfred before his death, works powerfully upon Dymer. As a consequence, when the magician offers Dymer a drink from his cup that will take him to "the valley of dreams," he is tempted. Moreover, the magician's final argument convinces Dymer to succumb: "Earth is a sinking ship, a house whose wall / Is tottering while you sweep; the roof will fall / Before the work is done. You cannot mend it. / Patch as you will, at last the root must end it" (35, 4–7). Although he does so reluctantly, even admitting suspicions—"Oh, lies, all lies. . . . Why did you kill the lark?" (36, 6)—Dymer drinks deeply of the cup. In effect, Dymer decides to accept the magician's claim that dreams can make a heaven of hell and a hell of heaven.

CANTO VII

Canto VII continues the scene, initially portraying Dymer's dreams as quiet and peaceful. In stark contrast are the magician's dreams. In passages anticipating Weston's demonic possession in *Perelandra* and the mad, chaotic dissolution of Belbury at the conclusion of *That Hideous Strength*, Lewis describes the magician's descent into a personal hell. As the drug from the cup begins to take effect, the magician staggers about, eyes bulging, catching sight, apparently, of "his strange heaven and his far stranger hell, / His secret lust, his soul's dark citadel" (7, 5–7). The magician's reliance on the occult to bolster his dream of autonomy finally catches up to him:

> Old Theomagia, Demonology,
> Cabbala, Chemic Magic, Book of the Dead,
> Damning Hermetic rolls that none may see
> Save the already damned—such grubs are bred
> From minds that lose the Spirit and seek instead
> For spirits in the dust of dead men's error,
> Buying the joys of dreams with dreamland terror.

> This lost soul looked them over one and all,
> Now sickening at the heart's root; for he knew
> This night was one of those when he would fall
> And scream alone (such things they made him do)
> And roll upon the floor. The madness grew
> Wild at his breast, but still his brain was clear
> That he could watch the moment coming near. (8–9)[47]

In the middle of the magician's nightmarish dream sequence, Dymer, groggy with the drug and unaware of his master's descent into madness, calls out for water. He affirms that the dream world of the magician is a lie, telling him: "You did me wrong to send me to that [dream] wood. / I sought a living spirit and found instead / Bogies and wraiths" (12, 3–5). He describes the forest of his dream, noting the many animals, including a bear and beautiful emerald birds. However, even in his dream he is cognizant of what he is doing: "Do you think I could not see / That beasts and wood were nothing else but me? / . . . That I was making everything I saw, / Too sweet, far too well fitted to desire / To be a living thing?" (17, 6–7; 18, 1–3). Dymer calls a place where birds sing beautifully "not for their own delight but for my sake" (18, 7) a world "of sad, cold, heartless stuff, / Like a bought smile, no joy in it" (19, 1–2).

Accordingly, when his dream shows him his beloved, he knows she is "the mirror of my heart, / Such things as boyhood feigns beneath the smart / Of solitude and spring. I was deceived / Almost. In that first moment I believed" (20, 4–7). He describes how "her sweetness drew a veil before my eyes," momentarily causing him to listen to her invitation to live forever in the dream world. Like the femme fatale of Keats's "La Belle Dame Sans Merci," she has a powerful affect upon him:

> She told me I had journeyed home at last
> Into the golden age and the good countrie
> That had been always there. She bade me cast
> My cares behind forever:—on her knee
> Worshipped me, lord and love—oh, I can see
> Her red lips even now! Is it not wrong
> That men's delusions should be made so strong? (23)

The adolescent Dymer could never have reasoned thus, clearly indicating his maturation in the poem. Indeed, in spite of his being "besotted" with this dream of his beloved, he manages to see through the scheme: "She went too fast. Soft to my arms she came. / The robe slipped from her shoulder. The smooth breast / Was bare against my own" (25, 2–4). The eroticism of this passage, much more explicit than anything we saw earlier in the autoerotic sequence at the end of Canto II, ironically does not serve to stimulate Dymer. In point of fact, he sees that his dream of her is simply love of self: "She shone like flame / Before me in the dusk, all love, all shame— / Faugh!—and it was myself" (25, 4–6). Dymer realizes that the great deception in attempting to live an autonomous life is that he is in love with himself; he finally comes to see himself as a self-indulgent narcissist.

This realization, however, is followed by a fierce temptation to return to auto-eroticism: "So the vague joy shrank wilted in my breast / And narrowed to one point, unmasked, confessed; / Fool's paradise was gone: instead was there / King Lust with his black, sudden, serious stare" (26, 4–7). An unbridled orgy of sexual temptation and revelry is then described, a passage Sayer calls "perhaps one of the most powerful in the whole range of English poetry" (109). Like the brown girls of Lewis's *The Pilgrim's Regress,* various figures accost Dymer, singing "we are the lust / That was before the world and still shall be / . . . We are the mother swamp, the primal sea / . . . Old, old are we. / It is but a return . . . it's nothing new, / Easy as slipping on a well-worn shoe" (29, 1–2, 4, 5–7). The most offensive of these is a parody of his beloved, who baldly offers, "I am not beautiful as she, / But I'm the older love; you shall love me / Far more than Beauty's self. You have been ours / Always. We are the world's most ancient powers" (30, 4–7). Although we cannot be sure, Lewis intimates that Dymer resists these autoerotic temptations, since he scorns the magician and turns to leave. However, the magician, hopelessly mad in the deception of his own dreams, pulls out his gun; as with the lark who disturbed his dreams and had to be eliminated, so with Dymer. Besides, the magician cannot afford to have someone leave his autonomous world, since he may become an agent to help pull it down. Dymer tries to avoid the shot, but he is wounded and swoons as the canto ends. In Cantos VI and VII Lewis strips Dymer to yet another layer of understanding; that is, any who attempt to live autonomously, be it literally or via dreams, are certain to be frustrated. Dymer finds himself now unable to rely upon either his physical or imaginative faculties. He is now ready to learn his final lesson and in the process become greater than he might have ever imagined; he has to be humbled before he can be exalted.

CANTO VIII

As we move to the conclusion of *Dymer,* we find in Cantos VIII and IX a description of the redemption of Dymer (recalling that Lewis titled an early version of this story *The Redemption of Ask*). Canto VIII portrays Dymer coming to a full knowledge of himself and his failings, while undergoing a final stripping away of the layers of self-will. Canto IX illustrates how such knowledge equips him for a final denial of self, something he is incapable of in his youthful pride and rebellion. In short, the autonomous man rejects self and dies a sacrificial death for others. Canto VIII opens when Dymer regains consciousness; he has managed to drag himself away from the magician's house and garden, lying by a country lane. Immediately he feels the sharp, terrible pain in his side from the magician's gunshot, perhaps a battlefield detail and certainly one Lewis knew firsthand via his shrapnel wound. Dymer feels the pain cling to him "like a great beast with fastened claws" (VIII, 1, 7), while later it throbs and "raged with power / Fit to convulse the heavens" (3, 5–6). Initially he feels the cold air and earth about him and believes he is alone. Turning on his side, however, he sees a woman standing nearby, "and while he looked the knowledge grew / She was not of the old life but the new" (5, 6–7). What follows is a fascinating dialogue between them, and whether Dymer dreams it, has a vision, or actually experiences it is less important than what he learns about himself. By the ends of their conversation he is a "new" man.

In answer to many questions, she tells Dymer she is "the loved one, the long lost" (6, 1). To his complaint that she should never have permitted him to suffer the pangs of longing and the mental agony of not having her, she shocks him by saying, "You should have asked my name" (6, 7), in effect telling him he was deceived from the very beginning about who she was. This is clarified when he complains that even now she may be a phantom beguiling him with her "harlot smile," and she replies, "I have not smiled" (7, 5). Bitterly, though still not sure who she is, he tells her to leave him, since she does not love him nor understand "human tears and pain / And hoping for the things that cannot be" (8, 3–4). Again she stuns him when she says, "I know them all" (8, 7). She then goes on to reveal that she is one of the gods, "the eternal forms," who lives "in realms beyond the reach of cloud, and skies / Nearest the ends of air. . . . / [Who has] looked into their eyes / Peaceful and filled with pain beyond surmise." As a result, she knows "an ancient woe man cannot reach / One moment though in fire" (9, 2–5 and 6–7). She understands human pain, she implies, because she has watched humans love the beauty of the world rather than the beauty behind the world—the "real beauty" that serves to infuse the beauty men see on earth. Scales fall off Dymer's eyes as he realizes his early love for Nature was misdirected; in effect he loved the creature rather than the creator. He indicates his disgust with himself now by noting, "I called myself their lover—I that was / Less fit for that long service than the least / Dull, workday drudge of men or faithful beast" (10, 5–7).

Yet Dymer still questions her. Why, he asks, do the gods lure spirits like himself, "the weak, the passionate, and the fool of dreams," when stronger men who "never pine / With whisperings at the heart, soul-sickening gleams / Of infinite desire, and joy that seems / The promise of full power" (11, 3–6) are left alone? Why, he presses, has he suffered for mistaking earthly beauty for real beauty? How can this have been sin? Do the gods have no voice to direct men? Must creatures of dust "guess their own way in the dark"? Tersely, she replies, "They must" (12, 7). Dymer's anger grows as he recounts how she came to him in "sweet disguise / Wooing me, lurking for me in my path, / Hid your eternal cold with woman's eyes, / Snared me with shows of love—and all was lies" (13, 2–5). Her surprising response is, "Our kind must come to all / If bidden, but in the shape for which they call" (13, 6–7), and she goes on to add the gods are not at fault if humans shape and mold eternal beauty into earthly forms. Indeed, "with incorruptibles the mortal will / Corrupts itself, and clouded eyes will make / Darkness within from beams they cannot take" (15, 5–7). Her implication is transparent: We fashion our idols according to our own desires. Dymer is momentarily appeased as he considers this and realizes his error in "having seen / Half-beauty, or beauty's fringe, the lowest stair, / The common incantation, [and so] worshipped there" (16, 5–7).

However, his anger flares when he cries out that had he loved a beast, it would have at least responded, "but I have loved a Spirit and loved in vain" (17, 3). Is there no comfort, no human love left for him? She warns him against asking such questions and, instead, tells him he is learning the great truth that life is a process of learning how to die. His own process begins now as he sees the death of his dream of beauty: "Your eyes / First see her dead: and more, the more she dies" (18, 6–7). More important, she finishes her conversation by pointing Dymer toward the truth he must eventually know for himself:

> You are still dreaming, dreams you shall forget
> When you have cast your fetters, far from here.
> Go forth; the journey is not ended yet.
> You have seen Dymer dead and on the bier
> More often than you dream and dropped no tear,
> You have slain him every hour. Think not at all
> Of death lest into death by thought you fall. (19)

Dymer learns that his has been a life of dreams, and that he is to go on from this point, even though terribly wounded, to live. His story is not over, as he has himself to blame for his wounds. He has been his own worst enemy. His death wish, she warns, will be self-fulfilling. After she vanishes, Dymer thinks deeply about her words, leading to the first obvious signs of his renewal: "Link by link the chain / That bound him to the flesh was loosening fast / And the new life breathed in unmoved and vast" (21, 5–7). He remembers the wounded soldier, identifying with him and wondering if he had the same realizations Dymer is just now having; he even blesses him for having revealed the truth of Dymer's deceived nature then.

In doing so, Dymer finally rejects his selfish life and the desire to live as an autonomous being:

> How long have I been moved at heart in vain
> About this Dymer, thinking this was I. . . .
> Why did I follow close his joy and pain
> More than another man's? For he will die,

> The little cloud will vanish and the sky
> Reign as before. The stars remain and earth
> And Man, as in the years before my birth. (23)

This passage is very significant, since we see Dymer for the first time thinking of others rather than himself. In addition, this self-abnegation is followed by the very mature reflection that the universe is not all about Dymer. Indeed, his passing will have little impact upon the great scheme of things. This moment of self-knowledge is the climax of the poem, for now Dymer can move out of himself and his selfish egoism to engage fully in the lives of others. He can turn away from his conceited introspections, autoerotic compulsions, and autonomous yearnings to a new life yet to be discovered:

> There was a Dymer once who worked and played
> About the City; I sloughed him off and ran.
> There was a Dymer in the forest glade
> Ranting alone, skulking the fates of man.
> I cast him also, and a third began
> And he too died. But I am none of those.
> Is there another still to die . . . Who knows? (24)

With these resolutions made, the canto ends, and Dymer struggles to reach a tower he sees nearby. When he reaches it, he sinks down in the grass surrounding it to rest.

CANTO IX

Canto IX provides Dymer the opportunity to complete his redemption through a total giving of himself. As Dymer is lying in the grass, a great wind begins to blow—perhaps a metaphor for his coming renewal—and he is swept up into a vision where "the well-worn fabric of our life / Fell from him," and "himself, one spark of soul, / Swam in unbroken void" (4, 1–2 and 6–7). Echoing the words of Christ on the cross, he cries out, "Why hast Thou forsaken me?" though it appears his question is addressed not to the gods but to earthly beauty: "Was there no world at all, but only I / Dreaming of gods and men?" (5, 1–3). Before he receives an answer, he becomes aware of a sentry, an angelic guardian in his vision. Reminiscent of Gabriel from book 4 of *Paradise Lost*, the sentry explains he watches for a beast who walks "night after night, far scouring from his lair, / Chewing the cud of lusts which are despair / And fill not, while his mouth gapes dry for bliss / That never was" (8, 4–7). Dymer offers to assist the sentry, but he is initially rebuffed since he is "of earth. The flesh is weak." Dymer insists that while he is flesh and weak from his wound, "some deed still [is] waiting to be done" (10, 3 and 5). In fact, Dymer claims that his past wrongs equip him the more to assist: "I am come out of great folly and shame, / The sack of cities, wrongs I must undo" (11, 2–3).

Dymer begs to know more of this beast, and the sentry tells him of a fabulous monster and his parentage. As he listens to the story, Dymer realizes that the monster is the offspring of his sexual encounter with the unknown girl:

> There is a lady in that primal place
> Where I was born, who with her ancient smile
> Made glad the sons of heaven. She loved to chase
> The springtime round the world. To all your race
> She was a sudden quivering in the wood
> Or a new thought springing in solitude.
>
> 'Till, in prodigious hour,[48] one swollen with youth,
> Blind from new-broken prison, knowing not
> Himself nor her, nor how to mate with truth,
> Lay with her in a strange and secret spot,
> Mortal with her immortal, and begot
> This walker-in-the-night. (12, 2–7, and 13, 1–6)

Dymer sees now that his earlier actions have far-reaching consequences, and that it is incumbent upon him to bear the responsibility of resolving the problem he literally begat. With newly found authority, he tells the sentry he must fight the beast, "for either I must slay / This beast or else be slain before the day" (15, 6–7). The sentry, sensing that Dymer's words are true, agrees to his request, even offering Dymer his armor and playing the role of squire in helping Dymer put on the gear. Dymer also has the sentry agree not to intervene in the fight, regardless of the apparent outcome.

The end of the canto is filled with battlefield imagery. For example, while they wait for the beast to appear, the sentry paces impatiently, "humming at first the snatches of some tune / That soldiers sing, but falling silent soon" (21, 6–7). The earth, where the fight is to occur, is stripped and sterile, a vivid evocation of WWI no-man's-land:

> It was a ruinous land. The ragged stumps
> Of broken trees rose out of endless clay
> Naked of flower and grass: the slobbered humps
> Dividing the dead pools. Against the grey
> A shattered village gaped. (24, 1–5)[49]

In the moments before battle and certain death, Dymer bids farewell to earthly beauty and asks to be made part of its greater whole: "Now drink me as the sun drinks up the mist. / This is the hour to cease in, at full flood, / That asks no gift from following years" (26, 1–3). Like Birhtnoth, the brave but foolhardy Anglo-Saxon warrior-king of *The Battle of Maldon,* and the old Beowulf in his doomed fight with the dragon, Dymer is ready to face an overwhelming foe. Indeed, almost instinctively he springs forward, his armor rattling for action, when the "ashen brute wheeled slowly round / Nosing, and set its ear towards the sound, / The pale and heavy brute, rough-ridged behind, / And full of eyes, clinking in scaly rind" (27, 4–7). Dymer throws his spear ineffectually, and his end comes quickly with little elaboration: "A leap—a cry—flurry of steel and claw, / Then silence." All that can be seen beneath the beast are "the ruined limbs of Dymer, killed outright / All in a moment, all his story done" (30, 1–2 and 5–6).

However, the poem builds to an unexpected climax. Immediately upon Dymer's death the sun rises, the sky and landscape are flooded with rich, colorful light, and the earth bursts forth "with dancing flowers / Where flower had never grown; and one by one / The splintered woods, as if from April showers, / Were softening into green" (32, 2–5). Additionally, songbirds trill happily as Dymer's body is surrounded by "crocus and bluebell, primrose, [and] daffodil / Shivering with moisture" (33, 2–3). The air itself grows sweet. All this imagery is furthered enhanced by the astonishing transformation of the beast who becomes "a wing'd and sworded shape, whose foam-like hair / Lay white about its shoulders, and the air / That came from it was burning hot. The whole / Pure body brimmed with life, as a full bowl" (34, 4–7). Dymer's giving of himself, his dying to destroy the monster that his efforts to live autonomously created, transforms that hideous distortion into something beautiful. This explains why Lewis included in the first edition the reference to Odin's High Song from the *Havamal*: "Nine nights I hung myself upon the Tree, wounded with the spear as an offering to Odin, myself sacrificed to myself." Dymer has not *merely died,* a meaningless, insignificant waste. Instead his death has transfused Nature, bringing new life to the scorched, barren wasteland, a fact made clear by the final lines of the poem:

And from the distant corner of day's birth
He [the sentry] heard clear trumpets blowing and bells ring,
A noise of great good coming into earth
And such a music as the dumb would sing
If Balder had led back the blameless spring
With victory, with the voice of charging spears,
And in white lands long-lost Saturnian years. (35)

The allusion to Balder, who was "worshipped as the pure and radiant god of innocence and light," is a fitting conclusion to *Dymer*, a narrative poem rich in Norse imagery and influence (Guerber, 197).

Without question *Dymer* is a difficult poem, requiring careful reading and reflection. As a narrative it is coherent, but Lewis's tendency to shift from one scene to the next without adequate transition is problematic. Given the reluctance of modern readers to read poetry in general, much less complex narrative poetry, it is not surprising that *Dymer* has few admirers. For instance, Richard Hodgens admits to disliking narrative poetry, so we are not surprised to find him saying, "Modern as I am, I cannot adopt a fighting attitude on behalf of Lewis's narrative poems in particular. I must admit that I have not enjoyed reading the poems as much as I have enjoyed reading almost all of his fiction or, in fact, almost all of his prose."[50] Furthermore, Chad Walsh says, "All in all, the various themes twisting through *Dymer* are loosely connected indeed."[51] Yet, it is the highest expression of Lewis's earliest literary aspirations, as both the many years he spent working on it and the various versions it went through illustrate. Barfield recalled, for instance, that the myth of Dymer had long haunted Lewis (Barfield lecture). Accordingly, *Dymer* is worth a careful evaluation, particularly since it shows how his strong affection for poetry consumed his earliest literary efforts. In addition, it is instructive to see how much Lewis improved his narrative technique in subsequent years when he turned to prose fiction. While *Dymer* was not Lewis's final effort to write narrative poetry, it was his longest, most consciously realized effort in the genre. Although flawed, it is a workmanlike poem in which we see him exercise poetic sensibilities that mature in his prose fiction.[52]

CHAPTER FIVE

Narrative Poems: *The Grand Tradition*

.

While *Dymer* received several positive critical reviews,[1] "as far as the general public was concerned it was a failure."[2] Luci Shaw sums up this view when she writes, "*Dymer* deserved to fail. With all its formal intricacies it was unevenly conceived and executed. It is difficult even to describe the theme of *Dymer,* let alone interpret it."[3] Undoubtedly, this cool reception discouraged Lewis from his ambition of achieving acclaim as a poet.[4] Yet he did not stop writing poetry; indeed, he wrote both narrative and lyrical poetry throughout the remainder of his life, although his interest in writing narrative poetry faded by the mid-1930s. Since subsequent chapters will deal with his short lyrical poems, we turn our attention here to an unpublished fragment of a narrative poem as well as to three narrative poems published by Walter Hooper in *Narrative Poems* (1969; hereafter cited as *NP*). In these narrative poems we see Lewis striving to imitate the ancient poets he so admired and sought to emulate.

The narrative fragment, "I Will Write Down," we can reliably date, since it occurred in a letter to Owen Barfield on May 6, 1932.[5] It appears to be another poem by Lewis to chronicle his pursuit of joy and may serve as a prototype for *Surprised by Joy:*

I will write down the portion that I understand
Of twenty years wherein I went from land to land.
At many bays and harbours I put in with joy
Hoping that there I should have built my second Troy
And stayed. But either stealing harpies drove me thence,
Or the trees bled, or oracles, whose[6] airy sense

I could not understand, yet must obey, once more
Sent me to sea to follow the retreating shore
Of this land which I call at last my home, where most
I feared to come; attempting not to find whose coast
I ranged half round the world, with vain design to shun
The last fear whence the last security is won.

    Oh perfect life, unquivering, self-enkindled flame
From which my fading candle first was lit, oh name
Too lightly spoken, therefore left unspoken here,
Terror of burning, nobleness of light, most dear
And comfortable warmth of the world's beating side,
Feed from thy unconsumed what wastes in me, and guide
My soul into the silent places till I make
A good end of this book for after-travellers' sake.

    In times whose faded chronicle lies in the room
That memory cannot turn the key of, they to whom
I owe this mortal body and terrestrial years,
Uttered the Christian story to my dreaming ears.
And I lived then in Paradise, and what I heard
Ran off me like the water from the water-bird;
And what my mortal mother told me in the day
At night my elder mother nature wiped away;
And when I heard them telling of my soul, I turned
Aside to read a different lecture whence I learned
What was to me the stranger and more urgent news,
That I had blood and body now, my own, to use
For tasting and for touching the young world, for leaping
And climbing, running, wearying out the day, and sleeping——[7]

Here Lewis thoughtfully employs classical literary allusions such as "my second Troy," "stealing harpies," the bleeding tree from which Polydorus warns Aeneas to flee Thrace in the *Aeneid* (Book 3), and "trees [that] bled" from the wood of suicides in the "Inferno" (Canto XIII) of *The Divine Comedy*. The allusions to the *Aeneid* are noteworthy, since Lewis links his own halting journey of faith with that of Aeneas, who repeatedly thought he had found his home but was ever spurred onward in his search. Furthermore, we see him ascribe irony to his realization that his search for joy led him to orthodox Christianity, "where most / I feared to come." Yet his prayer is to a God who is decidedly Platonic ("Oh perfect life, unquivering, self-enkindled flame / From which my fading candle first was lit"), and his request is for private, peaceful withdrawal from the world rather than for the public, combative debate for which he later becomes famous ("guide / My soul into the silent places till I make / A good end of this book for after-travellers' sake").

Most telling is the third stanza where we see the influence of Wordsworth's "Tintern Abbey," especially in the final lines of Lewis's fragment: "For nature then / (The coarser pleasures of my boyish days, / And their glad animal movements all gone by) / To me was all in all" (72–75). Had Lewis finished his poem, it is fascinating to speculate whether he would have been influenced further by the climactic lines of "Tintern Abbey":

> That time is past,
> And all its aching joys are now no more,
> And all its dizzy raptures. Not for this
> Faint I . . . .
> . . . . .For I have learned
> To look on nature, not as in the hour
> Of thoughtless youth . . . .
> . . . . .I have felt
> A presence that disturbs me with the joy
> Of elevated thoughts; a sense sublime
> Of something far more deeply interfused,
> Whose dwelling is the light of setting suns,
> And the round ocean and the living air,
> And the blue sky, and in the mind of man:
> A motion and a spirit, that impels
> All thinking things, all objects of all thought,
> And rolls through all things. (83–86, 88–90, 93–102)

Wordsworth's affirmation of the superiority of recollecting memories of nature as an older person over the actual experiences he had as a child in nature is moving, but we cannot help wondering if he protests too much. If this is so, then this passage becomes bittersweet and may have struck Lewis similarly.

As a poem, "I Will Write Down" has uneven merit. The hexameter here is not as clumsy as in earlier poems, the cadence is rapid, and the couplets are easy on the ears. There are effective images ("perfect life, unquivering, self-enkindled flame") mixed with tired ones ("my fading candle" and "the world's beating side"). Furthermore, in a poem conveying something of the spiritual search of his soul, we are not surprised to read, "And when I heard them telling of my soul, I turned / Aside to read a different lecture."[8] Yet this bookishness does not advance his poetic sensibilities; instead, his great learning and literary knowledge inadvertently become the *point* of his poetic efforts. In effect he sacrificed success as a poet because he was not able to escape his literary, academic, and intellectual ethos. Nevertheless, Lewis turned to narrative poetry time and again. Such poetry was in the grand tradition, one he consistently emulated and regularly practiced.

LAUNCELOT

"Launcelot" (Hooper dates as early 1930s)[9] is a narrative fragment of 296 lines in hexameter couplets. The poem, heavily influenced by Lewis's reading of Malory's *Morte D'Arthur* and to a lesser degree Tennyson's *Idylls of the King,* is set within the context of a Sangrail quest by the knights of Arthur's court.[10] Though Gawain is mentioned early, the poem essentially concerns Launcelot's quest, Guinevere's distress while he is gone, her subsequent anger at his delay in coming to her after his return, and the story he tells about his quest. His adventures include meeting a hermit in a dry, sterile land who tells him the land will not be renewed "until there come / The Good Knight who will kneel and see, yet not be dumb, / But ask, the Wasted Country shall be still accursed / And the spell upon the Fisher King be unreversed, / Who now lies sick and languishing and near to death" (157–61). Although this "Good Knight" is Percival in many of the Arthurian versions, Lewis never returns to this subject. After the hermit's unexplained death, Launcelot buries him and rides off on the quest into a rich, fertile country, thinking of Guinevere. Eventually he meets the Queen of Castle Mortal, who invites him into her chapel, where she shows him three stone coffins where "the three best knights of earth shall lie." She reveals that she intends to seduce Sir Lamorake, Tristram, and Launcelot and then kill them: "For endless love of them I mean to make / Their sweetness mine beyond recovery and to take / That joy away from Morgan and from Guinever / And Nimue and Isoud and Elaine" (291–94). Here the poem breaks off.

A critical evaluation of "Launcelot" must begin by noting that in spite of Lewis's knowledge of Malory's and Tennyson's versions of the Arthurian myth, he uses very little from them. For instance, there is no parallel account of Launcelot in either version, Merlin is absent in Lewis's poem, and there is little of court intrigue and deception. As a result, Lewis breaks new ground with this poem, although his success is limited. There are some points of congruence. Both Tennyson's and Lewis's Arthur sense the destructive nature of the Sangrail quest. Arthur, in Tennyson's "The Holy Grail," criticizes his knights for their rash embracing of the quest and predicts hardship for them all:

Go, since your vows are sacred, being made:
Yet—for ye know the cries of all my realm

Pass thro' this hall—how often, O my knights,
Your places being vacant at my side,
The chance of noble deeds will come and go
Unchallenged, while ye follow wandering fires
Lost in the quagmire? Many of you, yea most,
Return no more. (314–21)

Lewis's Arthur has one of his counselors tell him "the Sangrail has betrayed us all," and then we read: "But Arthur, who was daily less / Of speech, through all these winter days, gave answer, 'Yes. / I know it, and I knew it when they rode away'" (24–26). In both instances Arthur has knowledge, but it is ineffectual. Furthermore, all three versions note that Gawain rapidly loses interest in the quest. Malory's Gawain "was departed from his fellowship . . . long without any adventure. For he found not the tenth part of adventure as he was wont to do. For Sir Gawaine rode from Whitsuntide until Michaelmas and found none adventure that pleased him."[11] Tennyson's Gawain freely admits "for I was much a-wearied of the quest, / But found a silk pavilion in a field, / And merry maidens in it" (741–43). In the first two instances, Gawain's disinterest in the quest is eventually associated with his lack of sexual purity. Lewis's Gawain also loses interest in the quest, but we never learn why; instead, we are presented with a sullen, noncommunicative warrior, hardly the image of chivalry:

>   Gawain, first
> Defeat from the long Quest, came riding home, their thirst
> For news he could not or he would not satisfy.
> He was unlike the Gawain they had known, with eye
> Unfrank, and voice ambiguous, and his answers short.
> Gulfs of unknowing lay between him and the court,
> Unbreakable misunderstandings. To the King,
> He answered, No; he had not seen the holy thing.
> And, No; he had heard no news of Launcelot and the rest,
> But, for his own part, he was finished with the Quest. (37–46)

Gawain's attitude infects the entire court, "leaving a hollow-heartedness in every man" (49). As other knights return from the quest, they are similarly affected: "A dim disquiet of defeated men, and all / Like Gawain, changed irrelevant in Arthur's hall, / Strange to their wives, unwelcome to the stripling boys. / Ladies of Britain mourned the losing of their joys" (53–56).

The focus of "Launcelot" quickly moves away from Gawain and the Sangrail quest and onto Guinevere and Launcelot. Lewis's Guinevere is just as querulous as

Malory's and Tennyson's. For example, Malory's Guinevere berates Launcelot for avoiding her: "Launcelot, now I well understand that thou art a false recreant knight and a common lecher, and lovest and holdest other ladies, and by me thou hast disdain and scorn. For wit thou well . . . now I understand thy falsehood, and therefore shall I never love thee no more. And never be thou so hardy to come in my sight; and right here I discharge thee this court, that thou never come within it; and I forfend thee my fellowship" (Malory, 355). Tennyson's Guinevere is perhaps more corrupt in heart than Malory's. This is suggested when she says of Arthur's perfection: "He is all fault who hath no fault at all: / For who loves me must have a touch of earth; / The low sun makes the color. . . . / [Arthur is] a moral child without the craft to rule / Else had he lost not me" ("Launcelot and Elaine," 132–34, 145–46). Lewis's Guinevere, always fearing some break in her relationship with Launcelot, begrudges that he ever leaves her. During the three years the poem describes he is on the quest, she believes he is staying away from her intentionally:

> And the Queen understood it all. And the drab pain,
> Now for two years familiar in her wearied side,
> Stirred like a babe within her. Every nerve woke wide
> To torture, with low-mourning pity of self, with tears
> At dawn, with midnight jealousies; and dancing fears
> Touched with their stabs and quavers and low lingerings. (68–73)

Beyond this, she fears his death:

> And no tidings now could do her good
> Forever; the heart failing in her breast for fear
> —Of Launcelot dead—of Launcelot daily drawing near
> And bringing her the sentence that she knew not of,
> The doom, or the redeeming, or the change of love. (78–82)

All this care, however, turns to rage when she discovers he returns to the city and allows three days to go by before contacting her. When he does come to her, he assuages her fears and anger by the story he tells.

Lewis's Launcelot, like Gawain, has changed: "Not like that Launcelot tangled in the boughs of May / Long since, nor like the Guinever he kissed that day, / But he was pale, with pity in his face writ wide" (105–7). As in the Malory and Tennyson versions, Launcelot's quest includes encounters with hermits, journeys through desolate countries, and some measure of piety, though this is always open to question. For instance, Malory's Launcelot, after achieving his momentary vision of the Holy Grail and subsequently renouncing sin, especially sexual relations with Guinevere, soon succumbs to the flesh: "Sir Launcelot began to resort unto Queen Guinever again, and forgat the promise and the perfection he made in the quest. For . . . had not Sir Launcelot been in his privy thoughts and in his mind so set inwardly to the queen as he was in seeming outward to God, there had no knight passed him in the quest of the Sangreal; but ever his thoughts were privily on the queen, and so they loved together more hotter than they did to-forehand" (Malory, 353). Indeed, Malory's Launcelot is unable to check his sexual urges except in rare circumstances. Tennyson's Launcelot, given his Victorian trappings, appears to be more pious and veils the nature of his sin that keeps him from capturing a vision of the Holy Grail:

> King, my friend, if friend of thine I be,
> Happier are those that welter in their sin,
> Swine in the mud, that cannot see for slime,
> Slime of the ditch; but in me lived a sin
> So strange, of such a kind, that all of pure,
> Noble, and knightly in me twined and clung
> Round that one sin, until the wholesome flower
> And poisonous grew together. . . . Then I spake
> To one most holy saint, who wept and said
> That, save they could be pluck'd asunder, all
> My quest were in vain. ("The Holy Grail," 766–73, 777–80)

Like his literary prototype, he is unable to maintain sexual purity. On the other hand, Lewis's Launcelot engages in pious activities, including burying a hermit who aids him during his sojourn in a desolate country: "And Launcelot alighted there, and in the floor / Of that low house scraped in the dust a shallow grave / And laid the good man in it, praying God to save / His soul: and for himself such grace as may prevail / To come to the King Fisherman and find the Grail" (166–70). In addition to resisting later the seduction of the Queen of the Castle Mortal, Launcelot manages to avoid a sexual encounter with a beautiful woman he meets prior to arriving at Castle Mortal. Since "Launcelot" is a fragment and does not go into what happens between Launcelot and Guinevere after this episode is over, we can only speculate that Lewis would have maintained their illicit relationship.

The Queen of Castle Mortal's attempt to seduce Launcelot is determined. After Launcelot agrees to spend the night in her castle, he is richly clothed (reminiscent of Gawain's welcome in the green castle from *Sir Gawain and the Green Knight*) and attended: "Young servitors enough he found / That kneeled before the lady, and came pressing round; / One took his helm, another took his spear, a third / Led off his horse; and chamberlains and grooms were stirred / To kindle fires and set him at the chimney side" (245–49). Soon everyone leaves them alone in a chamber with hundreds of candles burning where she offers him many cups of strong wine. After a time she takes him to the chapel where she reveals her intentions. In addition to her jealousy of other women, she wants to snare Lamorake, Tristram, and Launcelot, as opposed to other knights, because these are the three "best" knights, at least as recorded by Malory. Like a spider, however, she reveals her intention to lure them into the stone coffins:

> "They shall all be living when they lie
> Within these beds; and then—behold what will be done
> To all, or even to two of them, or even to one,
> Had I such grace." She lifts her hand and turns a pin
> Set on the wall. A bright steel blade drops down within
> The arches, on the coffin-necks, so razor-keen
> That scarce a movement of the spicey dust was seen
> Where the edge sank. (282–89)

She wants their heads so she can "comb their hair and make them lie / Between my breasts and worship them until I die" (295–96).

"Launcelot" in the end is not very satisfying. Although we know Lewis's early interest in and affection for Malory and the Arthurian myths, why he turned to Camelot and away from Norse-inspired subjects for his narrative poetry is a mystery. He gained neither dramatic power nor subject matter from this shift. Even Lewis's attempt to forge a new story did not work. Ostensibly about the search for the holy grail, Lewis fails to develop the quest regarding the Fisher King, normally a key part of the grail tradition; as a result, we seem to be reading a mere travelogue. Also problematic is the flat characterization. Arthur, Gawain, Guinevere, Launcelot, and the Queen of the Castle Mortal are shadowy, undeveloped characters. We never learn what motivates them; they lack psychological complexity. Why should we care about these cardboard representations?[12] Realizing these problems, Lewis abandoned "Launcelot." His ability to judge the poem critically is clear evidence of his maturation as a poet; a maturing craftsman knows when something is not working and puts it aside.

Nevertheless, "Launcelot" is not a complete failure. Lewis handles the hexameter couplets with ease, producing haunting passages like Guinevere's anticipation of Launcelot's return:

> Yet, like a thief surprising her, the moment came
> At last, of his returning. The tormented flame
> Leaned from the candle guttering in the noisy gloom

Of wind and rain, where Guinever amid her room
Stood with scared eyes at midnight on the windy floor,
Thinking, forever thinking. (83–88)

In addition, Lewis's description of Launcelot's moving out on the quest is high-lighted by effective imagery and metaphor:

How Launcelot and his shining horse[13] had gone together
So far that at the last they came to springy weather;
The sharpened buds like lances were on every tree,
The little hills went past him like the waves of the sea,
The white, new castles, blazing on the distant fields
Were clearer than the painting upon new-made shields. (119–24)

Lines like these make "Launcelot" a good read, particularly if spoken aloud. It has imaginative power and evokes the mythic. In the final analysis it is less an imaginative failure than a practical one; that is, for whatever reasons—the press of more important duties, personal commitments, or university demands—Lewis did not or could not give "Launcelot" the same energy and devotion he did *Dymer*. Consequently, "Launcelot" is a poem in process—fraught with possibilities but essentially stillborn.

THE NAMELESS ISLE

On the other hand, "The Nameless Isle" (Hooper dates to August 1930) is a complete narrative poem reflecting Lewis's love of Old English alliterative verse with each line divided into half lines where one sound bridges the halves to connect the whole.[14] For instance, in the opening line of the poem, the first half line "in a spring season" is linked to the second "I sailed away" by the *s* sound that alliterates and creates the bridge; this alliterative pattern is repeated throughout with few exceptions.[15] Its 742 lines of alliterative verse tell a fast-paced story of a shipwrecked mariner and his adventures on a magic isle. Although Lewis did not divide it into cantos, the poem can be broken into four parts. Part 1 covers the first 226 lines and concerns the shipwreck and the mariner's subsequent encounter with a beautiful enchantress, who commissions him to find and release her daughter from the spell of an evil wizard. Part 2, lines 227–373, finds the mariner on his quest where he discovers an abandoned flute and a comically grotesque dwarf who offers to assist him. Part 3, lines 374–593, describes the mariner's meeting with the wizard and the release of the enchantress's daughter. Part 4, lines 594–742, presents the reconciliation of the enchantress and the wizard, as well as the mariner's idyllic voyage back to England. While not perfect, "The Nameless Isle" is well written and imaginative, a more polished narrative than "Launcelot."

Part 1 introduces us to the master mariner and his seventeen shipmates, the fast pace of the alliterative meter paralleling the movement of the story line:

> White-topped the seas
> Rolled, and the rigging rang like music
> While fast and fair the unfettered wind
> Followed . . . Half blind with her speed,
> Foamy-throated, into the flash and salt
> Of the seas rising our ship ran on
> For ten days' time. (5–8, 13–16)

Unfortunately the fine weather gives way to foul, and, in a passage reminiscent of the opening of *The Tempest*, a terrible storm sweeps over them: "Darkness came dripping and the deafening storm / Upon wild water, wet days and long, / Carried us, and caverned clouds immeasurable / Harried and hunted like a hare that ship" (19–22). In their fear, men begin jumping ship, especially as they near rocks, until all except the mariner drown: "Their hearts broke there, / The men I loved. Mad-faced they ran / All ways at once, till the waves swallowed / Many a smart seaman" (36–39). The mariner is literally lifted by a huge wave and thrown unceremoniously onto a flinty shore. He passes out from exhaustion, and when he is in the semiconscious stage between dreaming and wakening, he slowly becomes aware of the rich, sensual environment around him, especially an "unearthly sweet" voice singing a beautiful song:

> Forget the grief upon the great water,
> Card and compass and the cruel rain.
> Leave that labour; lilies in the green wood
> Toil not, toil not. Trouble were to weave them
> Coats that come to them without care or toil.
> Seek not the seas again; safer is the green wood,
> Lilies that live there have labour not at all,
> Spin not, spin not. Spend in vain the trouble were
> Beauty to bring them that better comes by kind. (72–80)

The urging of the singer to forget the seas and be content with the shore recalls Tennyson's "The Lotus-Eaters," but Lewis does not develop this connection. Instead, the mariner becomes aware of a majestic, ancient wood nearby where he sees that the source of the song is a "nobly fashioned" woman: "Her beauty burned in my blood, that, as a fool, / Falling before her at her feet I prayed, / Dreaming of druery, and with many a dear craving / Wooed the woman under the wild forest" (102–5).

When she gently scorns his proffer of love, he, inflamed by passion, rises to ravish her; however, she retreats into the wood, disrobes, and offers her breasts flowing with milk to the animals of the wood: ape, lion, lamb, panther, cat, snake, horse, beaver, bear, rat, and squirrel. Her nursing of the forest links her to the idea of Mother Nature, though this seems too simplistic an association:

> Saw how she suckled at her sweet fountains
> The tribes that go dumb. Teeth she feared not,
> Her nipple was not denied to the nosing worm.
> I thought also that out of the thick foliage
> I saw the branches bend towards her breast, thirsting,
> Creepers climbing and the cups of flowers
> Upward opening—all things that lived,
> As for sap, sucking at her sweet fountains.
> And as the wood milked her, witch-hearted queen,
> I saw that she smiled, softly murmuring
> As if she hushed a child. (128–39)

This fantastic scene is well served by Lewis's alliterative verse, and his description is vivid and memorable. The passage also serves to elevate her above the passionate fantasies of the mariner, as indeed we find she is Queen of the island, mourning her separation from her enchanted daughter. Furthermore, her promise that whoever releases her daughter, "woven in wizardry, wearily she lingers, / Stiller and stiller, with the stone in her heart," shall have her love greatly attracts the mariner: "If he comes again / Bringing that beautiful one, out of bonds redeemed, / He shall win for reward a winsome love" (150–51, 157–59).

The mariner readily agrees to the quest, but he is wary enough to ask about the wizard. She claims the wizard who "is cold at heart" has usurped her rightful rule of the island because of jealousy. Years previous when he had been washed ashore by a fierce storm, she had taken pity on him and given him land upon which to grow food. Over the years he became grasping and has taken more and more of the land, so that now he rules half the island; in addition, he has stolen her magic flute, a powerful instrument:

> Flowers loved it well
> And rose upright at the ripple of the note
> Sound-drenched, as if they drank, after drought, sweet rain.
> Grass was the greener for it, as at grey evening

After the sun's setting of a summer day,
When dusk comes near, and the drooping, crushed
Stalks stand once more in the still twilight.
That reed of delight he ravished away,
Stole it stealthily. In a strange prison
It lies unloved; and of my life one half
With flute followed, and I am faded now,
Mute the music. (201–12)

More cruel than this, however, she says is his enchanting of her daughter: "He has charmed away / My only child out of my own country, / Into the grim garden, and will give her to drink, / Heart-changing draughts. He that tastes of them / Shall stand, a stone" (216–20). Part 1 ends when the Queen gives the mariner a sword and commissions him to strike off the wizard's head, warning him sternly against the wizard's drink and his lying tongue. Never answered is where the flute came from originally nor how it is she continues to rule half the island without it. Is she really as powerless as she suggests, given her fantastic nursing of Nature? Furthermore, what evidence is there the wizard is evil, other than what she says?

These questions and others haunt the mariner as he begins his quest in part 2; in fact, he wonders if he has been in a dream, until he sees the sword she gave him lying at his feet. After eating, he begins his quest in earnest, enjoying the wide open landscape he encounters and setting his goal on the distant hills where he guesses the wizard lives. Unexpectedly, he soon comes across "by a brook's margin a bright thing" in the grass:

As in danger, aside
I swerved in my step: a serpent I thought
Basking its belly in the bright morning
Lay there below me. But when I looked again,
Lo it never moved. Nearer gazing,
I found it was a flute, fashioned delicately,
Purely golden. (264–70)

He picks up the flute and tries to play it, but he can make no music.[16] This so irks him he almost throws the flute back into the grass, but he desists at the last moment and puts it in a pouch he wears. Oddly, he does not consciously connect this flute with the magic flute the Queen has told him about. This lack of reflection, typical of many characters in Lewis's narrative poetry, weakens the drama of the narrative and suggests that the mariner, for all his bravado, is unreflective. This lack of reflection continues when the mariner comes upon a group of stone soldiers, "awful images, as it were an earlier race, / Nearer neighbours of the noble gods, / They were so quiet and cold. Kingly faces / There hushed my heart from its hard knockings" (295–98). Never does he ask himself about these figures nor wonder if they may be the result of the wizard's work.

In the middle of these statues he discovers a misshapen, weeping dwarf. In answer to the mariner's questions, the dwarf tells him he weeps for his lost ship-mates, the very stone statues he sits among who were bewitched by the wizard. Here too, however, there is lack of reflection, since we never hear from him why the men were turned to stone nor why the dwarf was spared. He bemoans what great men they were, powerful and beautiful, noting that their current state, while eternal, comes at a high price: "[The wizard] made them into marble, and of more beauty, / Fairer faces, and their form nobler, / Proud and princely. But the price was death. / They have bought beauty. That broke my heart" (336–39). Beauty, to be permanent, involves a cold, frozen eternity, echoing Keats's "Ode on a Grecian Urn." The mariner pledges to help the dwarf and reveals his quest, carefully omit-ting that his motivation is less hate of the wizard than hope for winning the Queen's daughter. The dwarf, rather than embracing the mariner's help, warns the mariner of the Queen, for she is as ominous as the wizard, being Circe-like in her power:

> She has a wand also, that woman there;
> Whom she chooses to change, she'll choke the voice
> In his throat. Thickly, like a thing without sense,
> Growling and grunting, groveling four-foot,
> He will pad upon paws. Pelt coats him round,
> He is a brute beast then, once her bonds catch him.
> The other half of my shipmates
> She bewitched in her wood. (351–58)

The dwarf, he confesses, lives in great fear between these two powers, hoping one day to find some way to return to "the weald of Kent." This section of the poem concludes with the mariner making "a faltering, faint-hearted guide" of the dwarf. Also, we finally see the mariner reflect on the ambiguous nature of his situation: "Doubts came darkening and all grew dull within, / Cold and clouded with cling-ing dread, / At this new story" (365–67).

Part 3, the climactic core of the poem, is effectively written and compelling as we move quickly to the mariner's encounter with the wizard. Although the jour-ney moves at a rapid pace, the mariner is slowed when he comes upon the statue of the Queen's daughter: "Her beauty made me bow as a brute to the earth. / To have won a word of her winsome mouth, / Scorn or sweetness, salutation, / Bidding or blessing, I would have borne great pain" (393–96). He longs to lay his cheek on the cold smooth stone, even to kiss the figure, but senses the wizard has come up behind him. Tossing aside the pouch containing the flute so he will have free arms to wield his sword, the mariner prepares to fight the wizard. In the wizard, Lewis subtly illustrates the power of words, as he offers the mariner "second counsel," effectively countering the mariner's doubts and fears. He begins by suggesting a life in stone is not so bad, since "marble minds not a man's desire" (417), implying that while stone is cold, it insulates one from the pains and sorrows of living flesh. Furthermore, he reveals that the marble beauty of the Queen's daughter cannot be changed, yet he "can be turned and made / Nearer to her nature; not she to yours" (424–25). He goes on to claim that if the mariner really loves, he will choose to become stone as well: "Only your own changing, / Boy, can bring you, where your bride waits you, / If you are love-learned to so large a deed" (426–28). Listing the many advantages of becoming stone, the wizard argues effectively:

> Left far behind
> Is that race rushing over its roar'd cataracts,
> The murmuring, mixed much thwarted stream
> Of the flesh, flowing with confused noise,
> Perishing perpetually. Had you proved one hour
> Their blessed life whose blood is stilled,
> . . . You would know 'tis small
> Wonder if they will not to wander any more.
> Life has left them, whoso looks without;
> All things are other on their inner side. (442–47, 456–59)

Moreover, he reveals that the Queen's daughter is his daughter as well and that he turned her into stone to save her from "her wild mother, witch-hearted queen" who drew the young girl away to the wood, "a land of dread, / Tangled in torments." The flute, which he had made for his daughter, was stolen by his wife, and when she could not play it, she retreated to the wood, took their daughter, and set up her forest kingdom: "Half this island / Wrongly she has ravished. I am its rightful lord" (478–79). He concludes by saying the flute has been lost, and he asks the mariner to consider his counsel, repeating the line, "All things are other on their inner side."

This refrain, suggesting as it does that we cannot know a thing simply by looking from the outside and that we can only know the truth by risking it all to come to the "inner side," pulls powerfully upon the mariner. Indeed, he raises the wizard's cup to drink, "what for the maiden's love and the man's wisdom" (487), when the dwarf breaks in with a warning. Disregarding the wizard's threat to turn him into peat, the dwarf skips away, pulls out the flute from the mariner's pouch that he has picked up, and begins to play, taunting the wizard with his own refrain: "All things, ogre, have an other side. / I trust even now, by a trick I have learnt, / That I shall drink before I die out of a deep tankard / In the weald of Kent, will you, nill you!" (512–15). The dwarf starts to play the flute beautifully, and its music initiates an amazing transformation, beginning with the dwarf:

> For it sang so well
> First he fluted off his flesh away
> The shaggy hair; and from his shoulders next
> Heaved by harmonies the hump away;
> Then he unbandied, with a burst of beauty, his legs,
> Standing straighter as the strain loudened.
> I saw that the skin was smoother on his face
> Than a five-year boy's. He was the fairest thing
> That ever was on earth. Either shoulder
> Was swept with wings; swan's down they were,
> Elf-bright his eyes. (528–38)

In addition, all the stone statues awaken, and there is much rejoicing as friends are reunited and fellowship restored. As the song continues, the maiden also comes alive:

> The marble maid, under mask of stone,
> Shook and shuddered. As a shadow streams
> Over the wheat waving, over the woman's face
> Life came lingering. Nor was it long after
> Down its blue pathways, blood returning
> Moved, and mounted to her maiden cheek.
> Breathing broadened her breast. Then light
> From her eyes' opening all that beauty
> Worked into woman. (562–70)

This life-infusing event is the culmination of part 3, when the transformed dwarf brings the awakened maiden to the mariner "to hold to her heart my head as I kneeled, / Faint in that ferly: frail, mortal man, / Till I was love-learned both to learn and teach / Love with that lady" (581–84), and when the wizard himself is so affected by the music that he decides to seek his wife: "Long time I've borne / Hate and hungering. Now is harvest come, / Now is the hour striking, the ice melting, / The bond broken, and the bride waiting" (590–93).

Part 4 celebrates the reconciliation of the shipmates who were under the Queen's spell with the newly awakened men of stone and the Queen with the wizard. Love works as a redemptive force:

[Riding a majestic horse] there came, so fair,
The lady of the land, lily-breasted,
Gentle and rejoicing. The magician's love
Made her beauty burn as a bright ruby
Or as a coal on fire, under cool moonlight,
And swam in her eyes till she swooned almost
Bending her body to his back on whom she rode. (631–37)

They then engage in a love duet reminiscent of Adam and Eve in the Bower of Bliss from book 4 of *Paradise Lost* and the lovers in *The Song of Songs;* their words of love are characterized by respect, honor, deference, and harmony. For instance, when the wizard says her "beauty is the free springing / Of the world's welfare from the womb'd ploughland, / The green growing, the great mother-ing, / Her breast smothering with her brood unfurled" (664–67), the Queen re-plies with equal grace: "But my friend's beauty is the form minted / Above heav'n, printed on the holy world" (668–69). This outpouring of love and harmony, per-haps anticipating the loving dialogue between Tor and Tinidril at the conclusion of *Perelandra,* is extended to the mariner, the maiden, and the transformed dwarf, since the wizard soon crafts a ship for them: "Magic helped them, / The boat was built in the blink of an eye, / Long and limber, of line stately, / Fair in fashion" (696–98). Spiders spin sails for the ship, giant stallions pull it into the water, and the three eagerly board it. As it sails away for England, the mariner rejoices in his love, bathed in a glory of rich light and harmony symbolized by the rainbow under which they sail.[17]

"The Nameless Isle" is an interesting narrative poem, but it leaves many un-answered questions. Who are the wizard and Queen supposed to represent at the poem's conclusion? Why do they casually permit their daughter to sail away with the mariner? What is the significance of the dwarf's transformation? What hap-pens to the men of the ship left on the island? How is it the song of the flute is so powerful? These and other provocative questions beg answers, but Lewis pro-vides none. Furthermore, as with "Launcelot," the characters are flat; the lack of reflection is especially disturbing since it makes it difficult for us to enter into their fears, passions, and struggles; we remain always on the outside trying to determine motive as well as meaning. While the love-inspired wizard and Queen are fascinat-ing to overhear, their quick and unexplained reconciliation is not convincing. It is as though Lewis brings their relationship where he wants it to be without showing how such reconciliation actually occurs. This lack of an inside view characterizes much of Lewis's narrative poetry, though in *Dymer*, and as we shall see later in "The Queen of Drum," he worked more deliberately to provide inner views of his characters. Too often Lewis's narrative poems are simple quest stories populated with flat, wooden characters who fail to stimulate our interest beyond the surface; that is, while we may care about them getting to the end of their quest, we hardly see in them fictional representations from whom we can learn about life or the imagination. They are either too far removed from our experiences or dramatically uninteresting. Accordingly, in spite of its metrical niceties, "The Nameless Isle" leaves us unsatisfied.

"The Queen of Drum"

After *Dymer*, "The Queen of Drum" (Hooper dates to 1933–34) is Lewis's most ambitious narrative poem. Though Hooper considers it "Lewis's best poem," John Masefield gets to the heart of the problem with this poem: "I have greatly enjoyed it, and feel an extraordinary beauty in the main theme—the escape of the Queen into Fairyland, . . . [but] at present, I cannot help feeling, that the design is encumbered."[18] Indeed, while the poem contains beautiful lyrical passages, it fails as a compelling work because of its flawed design. This flaw may be stated simply: Lewis focused primarily upon *prosody* at the expense of *plot*. In effect, he writes a number of powerfully evocative passages where metrical structures, rhyme, stanza forms, and so forth dazzle, while at the same time narrative and plot stumble. For example, in the opening canto of "The Queen of Drum," Lewis varies the meter from the opening eight lines of imperfect tetrameter, to lines nine through twenty-six of imperfect pentameter, to lines sixty-two to eighty of regular pentameter. Throughout the poem we also see hexameters and an occasional heptameter; the final canto is almost entirely tetrameter, and its quick pace parallels the events it relates. While this metrical variety makes for a lively and interesting read, in the end we suspect we have read something wonderful, but we wonder what it means.[19] Ironically, this is a problem Lewis solves in his fiction, perhaps because with prose he has fewer "mechanical" restraints to confine his creative imagination.

CANTO I

The poem, written in five cantos, concerns an old, pompous king whose young wife enjoys wandering at night through the realm enjoying visions of faery and transcendent beauty.[20] Recalling similar themes from *Spirits in Bondage*, "The

Queen of Drum" insists that faery exists and intimates a beauty superior to any on earth; in the face of such beauty being denied, the poem argues, it is better to rebel and escape than to obey and acquiesce. Though the Queen is not Dymer, at least in part because she is neither self-obsessed nor malicious, she is strong-willed and resourceful. Canto I immediately introduces us to the Queen's love of faery and beauty. Its unorthodox parenthetical beginning is either literally a conspiratorial rendezvous between her and faery spirits at the end of an evening's wanderings or symbolically her attempt to recall a similar experience in the stage between waking and sleeping:

> (Quick! The last chance! The dawn will find us.
> Look back! How luminous that place
> —We have come from there. The doors behind us
> Swing close and closer, the last trace
> Vanishes. Quick! Let no awaking
> Wash out this memory. Mark my face,
> Know me again—join hands—it's breaking—
> Remember—wait!—know me . . .)
>
>   Remember whom?
> Who is there? Who answered? Empty, the cold gloom
> Before the daybreak, when the moon has set.
> It's over. It was a dream. They will forget. (1–12)

The speaker in the parenthetical portion is one of the faery spirits. Its desire is clearly for the Queen to bond with it in fellowship inspired by memory of the beauty they have just enjoyed together, in spite of her reentry to the workaday world.[21] The Queen is the speaker in the last four lines, and she appears disoriented and unclear in her thinking, characteristic of one awakening from a vivid, intoxicating dream. While we may wonder as to the nature of her experience—real or imagined—she will draw much strength from such memories as she undergoes her ordeals in the remainder of the poem. Indeed, though this beginning is odd, understanding it reveals the pivotal role faery plays in the poem.

As we turn to the other inhabitants of the kingdom, we meet the King, an old, tired, unimaginative, weak-willed ruler. Surrounded by crumbling plaster, peeling wallpaper, and servile flunkies, he is quite a contrast to the Queen. He awakens "blinking like an owl surprised by day, / Rubbing his bleary eyes, muttering between dry gums / 'Gi' me my teeth . . . dead tired . . . my lords—'t all comes / From living in the valley. Too much wood'" (22–25). After he is dressed, he leans on his cane and taps his way down the corridor to the Queen's room. Once there he confronts her about her night wanderings, implying she has been out whoring: "I'll dare to say / You have been abroad by night—not known your bed / More than an hour. Is it true?" (38–40). Her vitality, strength, and tenacity are unmoved by his ignoble charge: "Coldest grey / Those eyes, and sharp of sight from far away: / More bright a little, something steadier than / Man cares to meet with in the face of man / Or woman; alien eyes" (48–52). Cowed by her powerful presence, he leaves with the soft curse that she is a Maenad, a votary of Dionysus given to wild, orgiastic frenzies.

The scene shifts next to a meeting of the Council of state, the rigid, fossilized coterie that advises the King. "The Queen of Drum" is Lewis's most "political" poem, perhaps reminiscent of some of his earliest Boxonian efforts, yet it is not mired in politics per se. Rather, Lewis uses the limited perspective of the Council, intent on protecting its own self-interest, to illustrate the repressive nature of those unaccustomed to the imagination. Instead of opening itself to the possibility of a beautiful reality beyond the walls that enclose them, their diminished senses make them able only to grind their noses into the dirt and grit of a present reality. Their artificial environment is subtly undercut when Lewis describes their chamber as "narrow-windowed" and "lamp-lighted" though it is eleven o'clock in the morning on a June day. As politicians they are a sham: "The oldest of them all play noughts and crosses, / A gambler reckons up his evening losses. / One trims his nails, one spreads his hands and lays / A bright, bald head between them on the baize" (85–88). Three in particular are introduced: The General, with big lips, is seen secretly trying to pick his teeth; the Chancellor is scribbling "angular pigs, straight trees, and armless men"; and the Archbishop has "a rosy face cherubically dimpled." After the King enters the chamber, the political process, in all its leadened glory, drones on without incident until debate turns upon the condition of the state: "What's wrong with Drum?" (114).

Almost predictably the scapegoat is quickly identified when the Queen's name is called out. Responding to this accusation, the Chancellor, in broken, partially incoherent rhetoric, outlines the duty a Queen has to live a respectful, honorable life, above suspicion. He says it is "inhuman" for her to wander the evening exposing "a teeming nation's care / And princes yet unborn, to the damp air / Of middle night, and fogs—the common curse / Of our low land—besides, my lords, what worse / May haunt such place and time" (141–45). Furthermore, he reveals, the people themselves see her haunting the evening, wandering about when respectful folk have been long inside, and scaring the unaware when they see her "like a ghost" flitting through the darkness. Such actions lead to gossip, fear, and anxiety. Accordingly, he calls upon the King "to stamp out the infected thing" by imposing his authority as husband over his wife's indiscreet activities. Even more demanding and demeaning is the recommendation of the General: "Odds my life. / Damn nonsense. Have a wife and rule a wife. / Woman—they say—and dog—and walnut tree— / More you beat'm—better they be" (181–84). The Council then looks for the King to respond, but he is feeble and cowardly; actually, he is saved for the moment because the Queen enters the chamber.

Her defense is bold and spirited. She mocks their silence, and then she makes her most telling point: "What? You—or you, my lord, / Forbid my wandering nights? Are you content / To lose your own? Will you, my lord, be pent / A prisoner every night within the wall?" (211–14). If she is to be bound from her roaming, then all shall be. Moreover, she implies the men before her are hypocrites, since they wander the night with less than pure motives:

> Five hours ago
> Where were you?—and with whom?—how far away?
> Borrowing what wings of speed when break of day
> Recalled you, to be ready, here, to rise
> In the nick of time, and with your formal eyes
> And grave talk, to belie that other face
> And voice you've shown us in a different place? (225–31)

She scorns their self-righteousness and threatens to expose their evening activities if they single her out as an example. In addition, she berates them for their pose of normalcy during the day, their discussions of "Who's dead, / Who's suit is gone awry and whose is sped, / Who's beautiful, and who grows past her prime" (238–40), when all the time their hearts are attending to their evening pastimes. Yet they are adept conspirators and keep silent. If they attempt to stop her, "I have a tongue, and freedom now / To use it. The pact's off. I'll force you yet / To throw down all the cards: and where we met, / By night, and what we were, you shall recall" (251–54). When their silence continues, she functions, she says, like Orpheus and retraces for them the appeal of faery:

> Arise!
> Sea-gold, sea-gems that fill the hollow eyes
> Of admirals dead; out of thy smothering caves
> Where colour is not, up, to where the waves
> Turn emerald and the edge of ocean-cold
> Is yielding, and the fish go slashed with gold,
> Up! 'gainst thy nature, up! Put on again

Colour and form and be to waking men
Things visible. Heave all! Softly . . . it rears
Its dripping head. (283–93)

When no one speaks after her impassioned outburst—in fact the men are puzzled
and scornful—the Queen breaks down, "and scalding came / Tears of deep rage"
(309–10). The canto concludes with an embarrassed king mumbling, "the Queen's
not well today" (313) while the Archbishop helps her out of the room. Does the
silence of the men mean the Queen is simply hysterical, unstable, and mistaken
about the evening wanderings of the men, or are they so able to dissemble that
they maintain their smooth outer demeanors in order to carry on their sham lives?
While no evidence is provided at this point, the Queen's impassioned monologue
is compelling.

CANTO II

Canto II is a dialogue between the King and the Chancellor, over several cups
of wine, in which they explore the question of whether or not faery is real. While
the Queen is being attended to by the Archbishop, the King asks Steenie, the
Chancellor, "what [he] made / This morning of our loving wife's tirade" (32–33).
Ever the diplomat and not wanting to commit himself, Steenie flatters the King
and says he is waiting to be led in his thinking by the King. The key, according
to the King, is to find out if there are "some secret stairs and undiscovered wings /
In the world's house, dark vacancies between / The rooms we know—behind
the public scene / Some inner stage" (52–55). He believes the Archbishop, if anyone, should know the truth; in fact, the King comes very close to admitting there
is faery:

> [The Archbishop] guesses well enough
> That back there on the borderland there's stuff
> Not marked on any map their sermons show
> —They keep one eye shut just because they know—
> Don't we all know?
> At bottom?—that this World in which we draw
> Our salaries, make our bows, and keep the law,
> This legible, plain universe we use
> For waking business, is a thing men choose
> By leaving out . . . well, much; our editing,
> (With expurgations) of some larger thing?
> Well, then, it stands to reason; go behind

> To the archetypal scrawl, and there you'll find
> . . . Well . . . variant readings, eh? And it won't do
> Being over dainty there. (119–33)

As the King presses the Chancellor about the possibility of faery, Steenie, though a sycophant anxious to protect his position, finally engages in serious discussion about faery. He confesses that while the Queen was criticizing them earlier about their own evening wanderings, "I put a bold face on . . . but a knee-cap aching / And a bruised shin kept running in my head. / The devil!—how should knees get knocks in bed?" (152–54). The canto ends with the two of them, now quite drunk, deciding to go down into a dark dungeon in order to bring up one Jesseran, a fortune-teller long ago tried, convicted, and punished for his part in the affairs of faery. This unknowing descent into Hell is one they never return from, though Lewis gives it something of a comic edge as the King sings: "We'll sing charms and ride on brooms / We'll fetch the dead men out of tombs, / We'll get with child the mountain hags / And ride the cruels of the crags. . . . / The King is drunk; long live the King!" (195–98, 208), this last phrase an ominous foreshadowing of the King's approaching fate.

CANTO III

Canto III shifts the action from this descent into Hell to an ascent to heaven, as we move from the dungeon to a high tower within the castle where the Queen is being interviewed by the Archbishop. From her "airy bower" she looks out over

> Meadows and wheeling windmills and meandering brooks
> Five miles towards the mountains of the spacious west.
> The mountains swell towards them like a woman's breast,
> Their winding valleys, bountiful like opened hands
> Spread out their green embracement to the lower lands,
> The pines on the peak'd ridges, like the level hair
> Of racing nymphs are stretched on the clear western air. (6–12)

This landscape recalls Lewis's deep affection for the hills of County Down, so we are not surprised when the Queen looks "towards them and her eyes were brightened, / And her pulse quickened, her brow lightened" (13–14). However, the focus moves rapidly away from the landscape and onto another dialogue, this time between these two sober persons. The Queen initiates the discussions, accusing the Archbishop, who she says knows the truth of her claim about faery, of deliberate dissembling. He uses several tactics to try to dissuade her about the reality of faery. First, he suggests that what we experience while asleep, "waking discourse cannot

reach / The thing we are in dreams" (24–25), and so, while she is no willing de-
ceiver, in the end her stories of faery are lies. At least part of what motivates
his charge against her is his very real concern for her spiritual salvation—"(good
now / On your salvation, never change your brow, / Soft! Softly! Quench those
eyes)" (35–37)—and indeed this becomes the thematic focus of the remainder
of the poem. The Queen, however, easily dismisses this first argument, noting that
if her thoughts about faery are just dreams, how is it that numbers of people in
Drum have seen her wandering the night? Furthermore, she says he knows hers are
not simply dreams, since she has seen him wandering the night as well. He admits,
"Sometimes I think I have, . . . but none / Can tell, being wakened, what the night
has done" (45, 47–48). The Queen scorns this as well: "If you know / Thus little of
the lands to which I go, / How can you call my tale of them untrue? / Give me the
lie who can! so cannot you" (49–52).

His second argument against the reality of her experience is that even if there
is the realm of faery, "We are not native there: we shall not die / Nor live in elfin
country, you and I. / Greatly I fear lest, wilfully refusing / Beauty at hand, you walk
dark roads to find it" (61–64). Unknowingly, the Archbishop anticipates the end of
the poem and the Queen's eventual choice of faery over heaven and hell, but at this
point he is urging the Queen to live for this world, "this sweet form / Of day and
night, the stillness and the storm, / Children, the changing year, the growing god /
That springs, by labour, out of the turn'd sod" (69–72). However, the Queen rejects
this argument, recalling the tone of "*Te Ne Quaesieris*" and other poems from *Spirits in Bondage*:

> I have no child . . . What mockery is this,
> What jailor's pittance offered in the prison of earth,
> To that unbounded appetite for larger bliss
> Not born with me, but older than my mortal birth? . . .
> When shall I be at home? When shall I find my rest?
> . . . .
> And if this threadbare vanity of days, this lean
> And never-ceasing world were all—if I must lose
> The air that breathes across it from the land I've seen,
> About my neck tonight I'd slip the noose
> And end the longing. But it is not so. (73–77, 81–85)

This present world is not enough to satisfy her deepest longings, and the beauty
of this world, rather than meeting her needs, points her to a transcendent reality
she longs to find. Faery is both the promise of and the vehicle for her longings. When she again challenges the Archbishop on these points, he hesitates to

validate her claims, because he genuinely cares for her and for her soul. He cautions her against faery because it may be a deception, since there are "two sorts of the unseen," the one of light that "we do not know" and the other "beneath, where to and fro / Through echoing vaults continually chaos vast / Works in the cellarage of the soul" (109–11). It is to this darker region he fears she is plummeting, one of foolish giants, chimeras, ghosts, and succubi. Her thoughts about faery may be like those of the youthful Dymer, and so he warns the Queen, "Wishing is perilous work" (119).

While the Queen patiently listens to his concerns, she follows up by asking what of the realm of light? Again he hesitates, this time for a longer period as he carefully considers his response. When he speaks, he begins by admitting his fallibility and inconsistency: "God knows I am an old, fat, sleek divine / —Lived easily all my life—far deeper skilled / In nice discrimination of old wine / Than in those things for which God's blood was spilled" (131–34). In effect, his failure to live a pious, godly life negates the spiritual authority and insight he means to offer her, yet he shares with her his honest orthodox belief about the spiritual world:

> I yet believe (if such a word
> Of these soiled lips be not absurd)
> That from the place beyond all ken
> One only Word has come to men,
> And was incarnate and had hands
> And feet and walked in earthly lands
> And died, and rose. And nothing more
> Will come or ever came before
> With certainty. (160–68)

Then he adds that though such truth is hard to accept, it is better to do so than to attempt to pierce "this mortal veil" in search of "some insupportable abyss / Of bodiless light and burning bliss" (172–73). Accordingly, his final answer to her question about faery is staid and conservative: "For my counsel is no other / Than this, now given at bitterest need: / —Go, learn your catechism and creed. / Mark what I say, not how I live" (179–82).

The Queen will have none of this. She calls his orthodox view of reality a "pale, / Numbing, inevitable tale, / The deathbed of desire" (185–87). She rejects his sermon and his advice to renounce faery: "Longsuffering and obedience and salvation! / What is all this to me? Where is my home / Save where the immortals in their exultation, / Moon-led, their holy hills forever roam?" (189–92). His message of Christian orthodoxy is cold and deadly since it stifles the reality of faery she knows experientially:

Not to such purpose was the plucking at my heart
Wherever beauty called me into lonely places,
Where dark Remembrance haunts me with eternal smart,
Remembrance, the unmerciful, the well of love,
Recalling the far dances, the far-distant faces,
Whispering me "What does this—and this—remind you of?"
How can I cease from knocking or forget to watch— (195–201)

Before she can finish her defense of faery and how it overshadows everything else in her experience, they are interrupted by a messenger from the General, now in control of the Council, with the message the King is dead and the edict that she come for an audience with the General. The General, "a Duce," is clearly patterned after the rising group of fascist leaders Lewis saw in the early 1930s, and in him is pictured "a new world" for Drum. The canto ends with the Queen and the Archbishop going off to meet their new leader. In the dialogue between Queen and Archbishop, we see the tension between faery and orthodox religion, one Lewis himself had experienced throughout his early life.[22]

CANTO IV

Canto IV turns on two episodes: the Queen's reaction to the General's offer of marriage and the Archbishop's response to the General's edict that he create a new "Drummian kind of Christianity." As they are being led to the General, each inwardly resolves on their chosen course before knowing what the General wants. The Queen hears "a trumpet in her heart, and smiles; / She is buckling on her byrnie every step they go, / Ready to die or ready to use all her wiles" (6–8). On the other hand, the Archbishop "thinks how his Christendom is all to learn, / His soul to set and harden in the mould that makes / Eternal spirit, his leprosy to heal and turn / Fresh as the skin of childhood" (11–14). Lewis's description of the General as they are brought before him is wonderfully evocative:

The General stood here, so vast,
With legs astride, so planted, that he seemed to bear
The weight of the whole house upon his shoulders square.
His red, full blood grandiloquently in his cheek
Spoke so that you could almost say his body shouted
And was his garish blazon ere his tongue could speak,
Saying, "I am the leader, the event, the undoubted,
All-potent Fact, the firstborn of necessity,
I am Fate, and Force, and Fuhrer, Worship me!" (22–30)

Lewis, atypically for his narrative poetry, gives us something of an inside view of the General as we see him musing on the actions of the Queen earlier that day. We also see him mentally review the details of his coup against the King, and while Lewis provides few details, we learn that the King and the Chancellor were in effect locked in the dungeon after they went down to find the fortune-teller. He had quickly consolidated his power, commanding the servants to become his, ordering large amounts of food ("smacked his lips—large lips, and moist and red"), and sending for Queen and Archbishop.

When the Queen arrives, he informs her of the King's deposition and death, providing no details, immediately turning instead to her new place in his kingdom of Drum. Condescendingly, he tells her, "Politics are not a woman's sphere," and then bluntly reveals his plan for her. Lewis's irony is thick, when we hear the General say "Nobody has anything to fear / From me—provided that I get my way" (96–97), and he informs her he is nice to people who obey him, "specially girls." He promises her an even better life at court than under the King, and explains away the fact he is much older than her by noting he is "young at heart— and our blunt soldiers say / Old fiddles often are the best to play" (105–6). Only one thing he insists upon:

> I'm not a jealous man: I'll leave you free
> Except in one thing only. There must be
> No more night wanderings nor no talk of them:
> All that I most explicitly condemn . . .
> It's nonsense too. Henceforth you must confine
> Your limbs to bed o'night—and that bed mine! (107–12)

That is, while he in principle does not really care whether she wanders about at night, he does wish to exert his power over her. We can only imagine the Queen's thoughts at such pomposity, though the scene recalls the episode in Chaucer's "The Merchant's Tale" when the young wife, May, privately muses that January, her old husband, who fancies himself a lady's man, is really nothing but a fool. We do learn, however, how clever the Queen is, since instead of exploding with anger, she simpers and feigns submission, only asking the General to desist his courting of her at present in front of everyone else. She asks to withdraw to her tower where she will gladly entertain his proposals. The General is delighted and consents to her request, though he is not so naïve as to trust her completely: He sends a guard to watch her safely back to the tower.

In the remainder of the canto, the General turns his attention to the Archbishop. At first he tries to cajole the old priest, claiming, "I'm called to fill / The supreme office, by the people's will / Or, strictly, what the people will discover / To have been their will when all the shouting's over" (164–67). The General has no fear of the church, noting its relative inactivity; in fact, he wants the church to be more active, although with his political agenda in mind rather than a spiritual one:

> Can you contrive a really hot revival,
> A state religion that allows no rival?
> You understand, henceforth it's got to be
> A Drummian kind of Christianity—
> A good old Drummian god who has always some
> Peculiar purpose up His sleeve for Drum,
> Something that makes the increase of our trade
> And territories feel like a Crusade. (180–87)

The General wants his people "in my will to find their peace," not in the will of the God the Archbishop serves. His first task for the Archbishop is to fabricate some explanation for the disappearance of the King. However, much to the General's surprise, the Archbishop, akin to Thomas à Becket's unexpected stance against Henry II, refuses to sell out: "Any man in the world / Has more right to rebuke these words than I. / But I believe—I know you could not know / That I believed—in God. I dare not lie" (200–203). While the Archbishop admits his past life has not indicated his faith, he now affirms it publicly, regardless of the cost.

In face of the old man's religious convictions, the General makes a pragmatic appeal to him, noting he also is religious, "but now we are talking politics" (206). He again urges the priest to make up doctrines for the people that are "easy to digest." Still, the Archbishop affirms, "I cannot tell them more than I believe" (210). His rage rising, the General makes one final offer, one that is baldly an appeal to power and bigotry:

> Have I not made it plain,
> You and your Church have everything to gain?
> Be loyal to the Leader and I'll build
> Cathedrals for you, yes, and see them filled,
> I'll give you a free hand to bait all Jews
> And infidels. (216–21)

To his credit, the old priest resists the pull to create a state religion while empowering and enriching himself. He refuses, "for He of whom I am afraid /

Esteems the gifts that [you] can promise me / Evil, or else of very small account"
(222–24). At this, all the General's pretense of civility evaporates, and he lashes
out at the Archbishop, complaining of his hypocrisy and false religion prior to
this day:

> Why was your other-worldliness so dumb
> When every office went for sale in Drum,
> When half the people had no bread to eat
> Because the Chancellor'd cornered all the wheat,
> When the Queen played her witchery nights, and when
> The old King had his women nine or ten? (233–38)

Although the Archbishop never gets a chance to respond since the General hands
him over to his henchmen for beating, perhaps the old priest "gets religion" in part
because of his encounter with the Queen. That is, if she is willing to suffer and die
for faery, something he does not believe in, should not he be willing to suffer and
die for a God he believes, serves, and fears? Furthermore, Lewis suggests here that
often a crisis becomes the catalyst that sparks to life the smoldering coals of spiritual faith.

Only two additional events occur as the canto closes. First, on the way to the
tower the Queen escapes from her guard by punching him in the mouth, using a
golden arm bracelet as the equivalent of brass knuckles; she then flees toward the
distant hills, the site of her many evening wanderings. Second, the General's thugs
set on the Archbishop with lead pipes and sticks, administering a brutal beating
while laughing and mocking him. The physical details Lewis provides are vivid, as
every "bone breaks or a sinew cracks. / They beat him upon his stomach till its wall
breaks" (288–89). In effect, the old priest becomes a martyr for his faith, and the
imagery at the end clearly connects him with Jesus Christ. In his last moments of
consciousness, this is most obvious: "In his imagination he seems to hang / Upon
a cross and be tormented long, / Not nailed but gripping with his fingers strong"
(290–92). In addition, he calls out to be forgiven by Christ and asks to be taken to
him. His end is gruesome: "Unwearyingly the great strokes are given. / He falls. His
sides and all his ribs are riven, / His guts are scattered and his skull is cloven, / The
man is dead. God has his soul to heaven" (301–4). With amazing foresight, again
assuming this poem was written in the early 1930s, in this canto Lewis captures in
the General and his men the coming brutality of Nazi storm troopers as well as the
danger of uniting political and religious agendas. The Archbishop, weak and hypocritical as he is, nobly resists the temptation to sell out spiritual convictions for
temporal advancement, though he pays the ultimate price.

CANTO V

Canto V is solely concerned with the Queen's escape and the final decision she makes concerning her eternal destiny. The first hundred lines of the canto describe her gradual ascent up the hills she so loves, showing her trying to lose the dogs tracking her by running through streams. Not physically strong, she soon wearies and would have been captured, but she manages to steal some milk from an old miserly hermit's supply, thus reviving and strengthening her. As evening nears, she enters a dark forest where she prays to the moon for help:

> She praised
> The queen whose shafts destroy and bless
> All wild souls of the wilderness,
> Dark Hecate, Diana chaste,
> Virginal dread of woods and waste,
> Titania, shadowy fear and bliss
> Of elf-spun night, great Artemis.
> Deep her idolatry, for all,
> Body and soul, beyond recall
> She offered there. (128–37)

Rejecting the Archbishop's advice, the Queen calls upon mythological goddesses to assist her, now completely identifying with faery and asking to be strengthened in her flight. Her prayer is answered, and she continues on her way until she enters a small valley and comes upon a crossroads (a deliberate spiritual image) with three paths before her. In this section of the canto, Lewis creates an atmosphere appropriate to the gradual encroachment of faery. For instance, the valley is "like a cup / With moonshine to the brim filled up" and the scene in the valley is "night's parody of day" (155–56, 161). In addition, near the crossroads she thinks she sees a silver haze: "She thought there was a giant's head / Pushed from the earth with whiteness spread / Of beard beneath and from its crown / Cataracts of whiteness tumbling down" (171–74). As she moves near this sight, she discovers it is a sweet thornbush in full blossom "that poured sweet smell upon the night" (178).

However, in a slight twist upon Keats's "La Belle Dame Sans Merci" and hearkening back to the Scottish ballad "Thomas Rhymer," Lewis places near the tree an enchanted knight:

> Rich his arms, bewitching
> His air—a wilful, elfin
> Emperor, proud of temper

In mail of eldest moulding
And sword of elven silver,
Smiling to beguile her;
A pale king, come from the unwintered country
Bending to her, befriending her, and offering white
Sweet bread like dew, his handsell at the region's entry,
And honey pale as gold is in the moonlit night. (186–95)

This pale rider advises her to choose the middle way of faery and offers her his bread to eat. He warns her against the road to the right, since it leads to heaven "and the yoke whence I have freed you," and against the road to the left, since it leads "through the world's cleft into that world I name not" (204, 206). Instead, he urges her to keep on the middle road:

Keep, keep the centre! Find the portals
That chosen mortals at the world's edge enter.
Isles untrampled by the warying legions
Of Heaven and Darkness—the unreckoned regions
That only as fable in His world appear
Who seals man's ear as much as He is able

. . . .
[These] woods and land unwounding
The want whereof did haunt you;
Asked for long with anguish,
They open now past hoping
—All you craved, incarnate
Come like dream to Drum-land. (207–12, 215–20)

The pull of his words to choose faery is irresistible, since she longs to realizes her long-held dream: "Warm was the longing, warm as lover's laughter, / Strong, sweet, and stinging, that welled up to drift her / Away to the unwintry country, softer / Than clouds in clearest distance of Atlantic evening" (221–24). Consequently, when she looks away to the right-hand road, there is little that appeals to her; indeed, even the turning of her head to the right causes faery to begin to dissolve, and she feels herself and the world begin to sag, dragged down by the intrusive power of Heaven.

This drag becomes personified when she has a vision of the Archbishop, "she knew it spoke from among the dead" (254), who pleads for her not to choose faery, since it will cost her immortal soul: "Believe not the seducing elf. / Daughter, turn back, have pity yet upon yourself / Go not to the unwintering land where they who dwell / Pay each tenth year the tenth soul of the tribe to Hell" (255–58). Instead, he urges her to choose orthodox faith. She rejects his plea as well as the less appealing pull to Hell, although the strain of this struggle is vividly portrayed by Lewis: "And the fear heightened, / The command tautened; / Between her spirit and soul, dividing, / The razor-edged, ice-brook cold command was gliding" (277–80). The poem's resolution of the Queen's choice is nicely put:

> Nothing now she will ever want again
> But to glide out of all the world of men,
> Nor will she turn to right or left her head,
> But go straight on. She has tasted elven bread.
> And so, the story tells, she passed away
> Out of the world: but if she dreams to-day
> In fairy land, or if she wakes in Hell
> (The chance being one in ten) it doesn't tell. (287–94)

Without question "The Queen of Drum" is Lewis's most successful narrative poem. While it lacks the philosophical depth of *Dymer*, it has well-developed characters and an interesting story line. For instance, the General, for all his cruelty and bluster, is more than a cardboard figure; we understand, though we do not sympathize with, his grasp for power and his pragmatic approach to religion. If it suits his purpose, he will use it; if not, he will toss it aside for some other vehicle toward his goal of consolidating power. The Archbishop, weak, sinful, hypocritical—very human—nonetheless redeems himself to a degree in his stand against the General's demands. As we see him admit his past failures, we sympathize, perhaps even seeing ourselves in his place. Oddly, the Queen, though intended by Lewis to be the character we identify with most, is one we probably understand and sympathize with the least. This is true for two reasons. First, while her defiance of the King and the Council is admirable, even Antigone-like, there is a hardness about her dealings with those she encounters that tempers our ability to identify with her. She is so self-contained and assured that she verges on self-righteousness. Second, few of us understand the pull of faery like she does, so her choice of faery over heaven strikes us as unwise at best and recklessly foolish at worst.

These narrative poems, all in the grand tradition Lewis so wanted to emulate, are important to our comprehensive understanding of Lewis as a writer. "Launcelot," while unfinished, demonstrates both Lewis's commitment to writing a narrative poem focusing upon the Arthurian myth as well as his maturing critical judgment. "The Nameless Isle" celebrates Old English alliterative verse, and the music of the verse complements well the narrative of the mariner and his adventures. Artistically, "The Queen of Drum" surpasses *Dymer*. In these narrative poems, we see Lewis pouring great thought and energy into both the practice of poetry and the making of story. It appears that after the mid-1930s, Lewis ceased writing narrative poetry, turning instead to fiction. At the same time, he continued writing lyrical poems, publishing them frequently until the end of his life. These poems deal with issues important to Lewis when they were written, and in them Lewis explored religious, literary, social, political, personal, and philosophical issues. As a group, they merit our attention in the next several chapters.

CHAPTER SIX

Comic and Satiric Verse

Lewis largely gave up writing narrative poetry by the end of the 1930s. However, he did not give up on poetry. Indeed, he continued to write and to publish poems from 1932 to 1963, and they appeared in journals, periodicals, and anthologies. Fortunately, they are readily accessible, since many were later collected by Walter Hooper and published as *Poems*.[1] They are literally *topical* poems—ones in which he deals with social, political, literary, philosophical, personal, and religious topics. Of the 123 poems, epigrams, and epitaphs appearing in *Poems*, eighty-one were published during his lifetime: sixty-one in various journals, magazines, and *Augury: An Oxford Miscellany of Verse and Prose*; sixteen in *The Pilgrim's Regress;*[2] three in a poetry anthology;[3] and one in *Letters to Malcolm: Chiefly on Prayer*.[4] The other forty-two poems appearing in *Poems* cannot be dated with certainty since they were not published during Lewis's lifetime, although holograph versions of some of them exist in the Bodleian.[5] In addition, Lewis published seven other poems not included in *Poems*.[6]

Several matters need to be noted here. First, if we consider the sheer number of poems Lewis published after *Dymer*, we see a writer consciously exercising his poetic muse. Of the eighty-eight poems published during Lewis's lifetime as noted above, in the 1930s, twenty-seven appeared; in the 1940s, forty; in the 1950s, eighteen; and in the 1960s, three. Obviously Lewis's determined efforts at publishing poetry throughout this period do not indicate someone who had given up on achieving acclaim as a poet, in spite of the fact many of these were published under "N.W.," Lewis's Anglo-Saxon shorthand for *nat whilk*, "[I know] not whom." Second, when we come to study these poems, we encounter a very significant problem: Many printed in *Poems* differ from the original published version. While the differences are sometimes minor—for instance, alternate punctuation or capitalization—others are significant, including rearranged, deleted, or added lines, word changes, and, on occasion, extra stanzas. Until recently, scholars writing on *Poems* either have not known about these variations or have chosen to work with the versions provided in *Poems*.[7] While it is probably true that Lewis tinkered with his poems after they were published, we can never be sure of what his final intention was for any given poem. This study, therefore, cites for discussion only versions of the poems as originally published.[8] Finally, the remaining forty-two poems included in *Poems* not published while Lewis was alive come from papers and notes discovered by Hooper. In many cases several versions of these poems exist; while additional scholarly work needs to be done on these variants, for the purposes of this study Hooper's editorial decisions are accepted and references will be made to the version appearing in *Poems*.[9] One approach to studying these topical poems would be chronological, with an eye toward noting Lewis's continuing maturation as a poet. While there is much to commend this approach, in the end it would be a fragmented, digressive effort. A better approach to these poems is thematic, since they largely fall into three major categories: comic and satiric poems, contemplative poems, and religious poems. We begin here with comic and satiric poems.[10]

Comic Poems

Lewis's comic poems mix lighthearted musings with thoughtful reflections. For instance, "Abecedarium Philosophicum," is nonsense verse and a tour de force. Lewis and Owen Barfield collaborated to write a comic poem in heroic couplets where each line was dedicated to each letter of the alphabet and famous philosophers or philosophical ideas served as the butts of jokes.[11] Representative lines include "H is for Hume who awoke Kant from nappin.' / He said: 'There's no causes for things. They just happen'" and "Z? For poor Zeno who often felt faint, / When he heard you deny that Nonentity ain't." This gentle parody of philosophy is good fun.

"Awake, My Lute" is good-natured playfulness along the lines of "Abecedarium Philosophicum."[12] Utilizing internal rhyme in each odd line and final rhyme in each even line, it appears to consist of incoherent revelries focusing at first upon a boring lecturer: "I stood in the gloom of a spacious room / Where I listened for hours (on and off) / To a terrible bore with a beard like a snore / And a heavy rectangular cough." Unlike Dymer, who murders his boring lecturer, the speaker here finds he has a kinship with the lecturer. Indeed, they are shipmates on the

Ark: "For the Flood had begun and we both had to run / For our place in the queue to the Ark. / Then, I hardly knew how (we were swimming by now), / The sea got all covered with scum." The poem's thematic dissonance continues, as the speaker imagines himself giving insufficient answers on an Oxford examination: "My answer was Yes. But they marked it N.[on] S.[atis], / And a truffle-fish grabbed at my toe, / And dragged me deep down to a bombulous town / Where the traffic was silent and slow." The key to this mishmash of ideas is that they are the disconnected fragments of a dream: "Then a voice out of heaven observed, / 'Quarter past seven!' / And I threw all the waves off my head, / For that voice beyond doubt was the voice of my scout, / And the bed of that sea was my bed."[13] The comedy of the poem is heightened by humorous internal and final rhymes such as *off:cough, croup:soup, baboon:the moon, puns:Donne's,* with *scum:in -um,* and *blurbs:verbs.*

Both "Abecedarium Philosophicum" and "Awake, My Lute" show the influence of Edward Lear and Lewis Carroll, the most famous practitioners of nonsense verse. For instance, Carroll's "Examination Statute," like "Abecedarium Philosophicum," is a comic poem with lines dedicated to each letter of the alphabet; however, instead of dedicating lines to famous philosophers, Carroll dedicated his to well-known Oxford examiners: "A is for [Acland], who'd physic the Masses, / B is for [Brodie], who swears by the gases. / C is for [Conington], constant for Horace. / D is for [Donkin], who integrates for us."[14] In addition, Carroll's "Ode to Damon" uses internal rhyme and a similar meter of "Awake, My Lute": "Oh, do not forget the day when we met / At the fruiterer's shop in the city: / When you *said* I was plain and *excessively* vain, / 'But I knew that *meant* I was pretty'" (emphasis Carroll's).[15] It is not hard to imagine that Lewis was influenced in nonsense poems by the work of Carroll.

Moving from the nonsensical, we turn to "March for Drum, Trumpet, and Twenty-one Giants," a poem where Lewis tries to create an apt rhythm for a procession of giants.[16] The poem opens with giants stomping along in a parade of pride and pomp: "With stumping stride in pomp and pride / We come to bump and floor ye. / We'll tramp your ramparts down like hay / And crumple castles into clay." Throughout the poem Lewis uses internal rhyme, alliteration, monosyllabic words, onomatopoeia, and an iambic meter in order to help us hear this comic procession. Furthermore, this emphasis on sound is reinforced by the progressive refrain at the end of each stanza. Indeed, each refrain (from trumpet to thunder to rumble) is accompanied by a musical direction. The trumpet refrain is to employ crescendo (cresc.), indicating a gradual increase in volume; the thunder refrain is to use fortissimo (ff), indicating it should be the loudest part of the poem; and the rumble refrain is diminuendo (dim.), indicating a softening of the sound. Lewis's use of these musical notations suggests that the poem works like a shaped phrase in music, so that the rise and fall of the sound of music indicates a corresponding rise, climax, and fall in the tension of the poem. This is a comic poem clearly more about sound than meaning. The cumulative effect of these literary and musical devices is percussive, a characteristic shared by many of his satiric poems.[17]

Another percussive comic poem is "The Small Man Orders His Wedding," given from the perspective of a bridegroom on the occasion of arranging details for his wedding.[18] His is to be an elaborate ceremony characterized primarily by a wide variety of sounds. For instance, he plans to have a nuptial parade of dancing maidens playing tambourines, smartly dressed soldiers, and powerful horses drawing the lovers' chariot; in addition, bells will be ringing from the belfries, and trumpets will be blaring to announce the couple's joy. At the wedding feast itself, the boisterous noise of the outer parade will cease, while quieter, gentler sounds of flutes and lutes will serenade the groom's beloved until all withdraw, leaving the two lovers alone, blessed by "Aphrodite's saffron light, / And Jove's monarchal presence bright / And Genius burning through the night / The torch of man's futurity." The poem ends with the happy couple sinking into "dreaming weariness" while the gods appear to bless their union. Written in the tradition of the epithalamium, this piece joyously celebrates wedded love.

Perhaps the most interesting comic poem is "To Mrs. Dyson, Angrie." Penned about the wife of Lewis's long-time friend Hugo Dyson, Margaret Mary Bosworth Robinson, its playful verbal banter suggests the friendly nature of Lewis's relationship with the Dysons and indicates he genuinely enjoyed Mrs. Dyson's company. In a letter to Warren he describes his first meeting with the Dysons: "[Last weekend] I went to spend a night at Reading with a man called Hugo Dyson. . . . We had a grand evening. Rare luck to stay with a friend whose wife is so nice that one *almost* (I can't say quite) *almost* regrets the change when he takes you up to his study for serious smoking and for the real midnight talking" (Nov. 22, 1931).[19] Warren supplements our picture of Mrs. Dyson in several diary entries. The first describes a dinner party hosted by the Dysons: "I arrived at the house about quarter to eight, by taxi, with that sinking feeling which generally accompanies an entry to a strange house, and found J]ack], D[yson], and Mrs. D[yson] in the drawing room—the latter slim and very fair, rather pretty and pleasant, but too anxious to make one at home to be quite successful" (Mar. 18, 1933).[20] Thirteen years later he recalls a similar evening: "We were warmly welcomed and given an excellent dinner—fish salad, sweet, savoury, and hock to wash it down. Mrs. Hugo looking very pretty and attractive, and some pleasant talk" (July 25, 1946).[21] When we consider that Hugo Dyson was one of Lewis's closest friends (he and Tolkien were instrumental in Lewis's conversion to Christianity), especially because Lewis "enjoyed his sort of humour,"[22] it is probable that the poem was a playful apology for an unintended slight or missed appointment such as a dinner engagement:

These inky firmaments and flaws [*sic*] of rain,
The wet weed swaying on the fallows dun,
How falsely our philosophers explain!
These neither spot i' the sun
Nor anticyclone from the western main
Hath made to be. No! with unkindly charm
The mortal *Pearl* such mischief hath us done,
Choosing to "arme
Those lookes, the heav'n of mildnesse with Disdain."
Since, lady, in your face
Daunger the giant hath meek *Pity* slain,
Mist drapes our woods and gusts of anger chace [*sic*]
Leaves (like our hearts) from every rivelled [*sic*] tree.
Yet, sure, in such a gentle heart a place
For mercy too should be.
If but the power were equal to the will,
I would speed hence, a suppliant, to your bowers;
Scarce would I stay to fill
Some pearly chariot with dim Syrian flowers,
To gild for such a progress the pale horns
Of some poor ten or twenty unicorns,
—To harness some thrice happy hippogriff,
—To load with gifts of frankincense the hands
Of seven dusky legions, if—sad if—
(There is no other rhyme for hippogriff)
Power jumped with will. But jealous fate withstands.
So to your queenly self, so to your lord
(If such a style accord
With any mortal; as great Venus' groom,
Anchises old, tho' declined to the tomb
Was honoured for the sea-born goddess sake)
Excuse your slave, for even the humblest take
Free pardon from necessity; and make,
Smiling, our autumn skies put off their gloom.[23]

In brief, the poem argues that the dark, dreary sky with its soggy weather is not the result of climatic conditions. Instead, the bad weather is due to the anger of the noble woman, "the mortal *Pearl*," the poem addresses.[24] Her disdain and anger are the sole source of Nature's discord. As a result, the poet asks that she show mercy and cease her anger. Indeed, if it would help, he says he would race to her home to beg her grace, not even stopping to secure luxurious gifts that might win her sympathy; however, he knows it is best to make a simple appeal to her, for only she can decide when she will be happy again. Once happy, her smiles would even cure the awful autumn weather. The poem lacks a regular meter, is heavy with allusion, and has a bookish tone with its use of allegorical motifs ("*Daunger* the giant hath meek *Pity* slain"). The rhyme scheme is irregular and often comic (*if—sad if: hippogriff*). On the other hand, the humorous comparison of Hugo ("your lord") with old Anchises, the father of Aeneas, was probably a hit with the Dysons, and there is levity in the poem that suggests it was all done in fun.[25]

Satiric Poems: Horatian

Lewis's satiric poems often confront ideas he found destructive to traditional values and civilized life, or they addressed specific individuals with whom he wished to cross swords. Occasionally his satire is Horatian—gentle, smiling, and urbane—as in "Coronation March."[26] The coronation of George VI (May 12, 1937) is the subject of this slightly irreverent commentary where he suggests the glory and heraldry associated with this event is all that is left of England's once-proud stand on the international stage. Pomposity and pretension mark such elaborate ceremonies now:

> Bray the trumpet, rumble tragic
> Drum-beat's magic, sway the logic
> Of legs that march a thousand in a uniform,
> Flags and arches, the lion and the unicorn
> Romp it, rampant, pompous tramping . . .
> Some there are that talk of Alexander
> With a tow-row-row-row-row-row.

The poem's percussive elements place it in the tradition of "March for Drum, Trumpet, and Twenty-one Giants." A similar Horatian satire is the light-hearted "Impenitence," a mock defiance of those who are "too sophisticated" to find in animal stories, including clear references to Homer, E. Nesbit, and Kenneth Grahame, both delightful entertainment and fables of human foibles.[27] The opening stanza takes up arms: "All the world's wiseacres in arms against them / Shan't detach my heart for a single moment / From the man-like beasts of the earthy stories— / Badger or Moly." Lewis confesses he is not "so craz'd as to think the creatures" behave as portrayed in such fictions, yet he argues they "all cry out to be used as symbols, / Masks for Man, cartoons, parodies by Nature / Formed to reveal us / Each to each, not fiercely but in her gentlest / Vein of household laughter."[28] Lacking a rhyme scheme, the poem achieves its poetic effect through its stanza pattern—each quatrain has three lines with eleven syllables and a final line with five syllables.

Lewis's Horatian satire continues in two poems concerning space travel. "Cradle-Song Based on a Theme from Nicolas of Cusa" is a poem about how the heavens draw us, and, as a consequence, we wish we could sail among the stars.[29] Yet if we could travel off the earth, the poem says, we would find not Heaven but only space and stars. Outer space is not so much a place as it is a concept, and we are more likely to find the stuff of life around us here on Earth rather than out there. The title refers to the German cardinal and philosopher (1401–1464) and probably his *De docta ignorantia* ("On Learned Ignorance"), in which he describes the learned man as one who is aware of his own ignorance. Read as a satire critical of science fiction, the poem's middle two stanzas (actually the poem could be read as heptameter tercets with internal rhyme) find nothing remarkable in imagined space travel:

> Suppose it done, Up there, outside,
> Packed in a steel box we ride.
> Gazing out to see the vast
> Heaven-scape rushing past.
> Shall we? All that meets the eye
> Is familiar; stars and sky.
>
> Points of light with black between
> Hang like a painted scene
> Motionless, no nearer there
> Than from the Earth; everywhere
> Equidistant from our ship.
> Heaven has given us the slip.

This view sharply contrasts with Ransom's fascination and wonder as he travels toward Malacandra in *Out of the Silent Planet:*

> The period spent in the space-ship ought to have been one of terror and anxiety for Ransom. . . . The odd thing was it did not very greatly disquiet him. . . . There was an endless night on one side of the ship and an endless day on the other: each was marvellous and he moved from the one to the other at his will, delighted. In the nights . . . Earth's disk was nowhere to be seen; the stars, thick as daisies on an uncut lawn, reigned perpetually with no cloud, no moon, no

sunrise to dispute their sway. There were planets of unbelievable majesty, and constellations undreamed of: there were celestial sapphires, rubies, emeralds and pin-pricks of burning gold; far out on the left of the picture hung a comet, tiny and remote . . . But the days . . . were the best of all. Often he rose after only a few hours' sleep to return, drawn by an irresistible attraction, to the regions of light . . . . There, totally immersed in a bath of pure ethereal colour and of unrelenting though unwounding brightness, . . . he felt his body and mind daily rubbed and scoured and filled with new vitality. (30–32)

"Cradle-Song Based on a Theme from Nicolas of Cusa," published sixteen years after *Out of the Silent Planet*, may reflect Lewis's growing unease with modern man's effort to reduce the numinous to mere scientific calculations; the poem's satire, while subtle, quietly affirms the beauty and mystery of space.

"An Expostulation (against too many writers of science fiction)," written in tetrameter couplets, is another gentle rebuke. This time Lewis complains of science fiction writers who take us to other worlds only to tell the same tired old stories we have on Earth: criminals on the run, conspirators and their schemes, or lovers' triangles.[30] Instead, what Lewis wants is stories that focus on the "otherness" of these worlds. Why, he asks, should he leave this world for stories unless,

> outside its guarded gates,
> Long, long desired, the Unearthly waits,
> Strangeness that moves us more than fear,
> Beauty that stabs with tingling spear,
> Or Wonder, laying on one's heart
> That finger-tip at which we start
> As if some thought too swift and shy
> For reason's grasp had just gone by?

In the essay "On Science Fiction," he makes the same point: "I will now try to divide this species [science fiction] into its sub-species. I shall begin with that sub-species which I think radically bad, in order to get it out of our way. In this sub-species the author leaps forward into an imagined future when planetary, sidereal, or even galactic travel has become common. Against this huge backcloth he then proceeds to develop an ordinary love-story, spy-story, wreck-story, or crime-story. This seems to me tasteless . . . . I am . . . condemning not all books which suppose a future widely different from the present, but those which do so without a good reason, which leap a thousand years to find plots and passions which they could have found at home."[31] For Lewis a major charm of science fiction was the creation of enchanting other worlds where we can imagine experiencing life differently.

"Evolutionary Hymn" is perhaps the funniest of Lewis's Horatian satires.[32] Tongue-in-cheek, this hymn of praise blithely adopts a Darwinian view of the world and assumes the inevitability of human progress:

> Lead us, Evolution, lead us
> Up the future's endless stair:
> Chop us, change us, prod us, weed us.
> For stagnation is despair:
> Groping, guessing, yet progressing,
> Lead us nobody knows where.

Old static norms of good and evil are to be rejected, since new ways and ideas are inherently superior; this notion, what Lewis calls chronological snobbery, is the peculiarly modern notion that the present has more to tell us about the human condition than the past. Thus, "Far too long have sages vainly / Glossed great Nature's simple text; / He who runs can read it plainly, / 'Goodness = what comes next.'" Darwinian utilitarianism is also mocked: "By evolving, Life is solving / All the questions we perplexed." This bit of gentle satire is worth a sing.

Lewis's Horatian satire takes a slight different tack in "The Prodigality of Firdausi."[33] Here Lewis retells a legendary story about Firdausi (Abul Kasim Mansur, 940?–1020?), the poet of the Persian national epic, *Shah Nameh* ("Book of Kings"). Expecting "an elephant's burden of gold" from the Sultan for his poetic efforts, he receives "thirty thousand silver pounds instead, / The price of ten fat vineyards and a fine Circassian girl," brought to him by a churl at a public bathhouse.[34] Rather than accept, Firdausi coolly distributes the money to a bath attendant and a seller of beer, then returns to discussions with his friends: "And instantly their discourse in the baths once more began / On the beauty of horses and women and the brevity of the life of man." The Sultan's disregard for Firdausi's poetry could be a parable of how Lewis saw his own critical valuation as a poet. That is, the poem implies that how critics viewed his poetry was less important to him than his full consideration of the traditional themes and topics of poetry, a notion he returned to nine years later in "*Spartan Nactus*" (discussed below). At the same time, Lewis's use of heptameter as well as odd octameter and decameter lines makes "The Prodigality of Firdausi" a creaky poem indeed, ironically lending support to critics of Lewis's poetry.

On occasion Lewis turned his Horatian pen directly to address other writers, as in "To Mr. Kingsley Amis on His Late Verses."[35] This poem is a witty response to Amis's poetic complaint that the hero of *Beowulf* was not human because we only see him engaged in heroic activities like fighting dragons: "Consider now what this king had not done: / Never was human, never lay with women / (Weak conjugation), never saw quite straight / Children of men or the bright bowl of heaven." Lewis's response is a wry, four-line, epigrammatic criticism: "Why is to fight (if such our fate) / Less 'human' than to copulate, / When Gib the cat, I'll take my oath, / Wins higher marks than you for both?"

Lewis also wrote two satiric pieces addressed to Ignatius Roy Dunnachie Campbell (1901–1957). "To Mr. Roy Campbell" is an attack in heroic couplets on the politics of this South African poet.[36] "Rifles may flower and terrapins may flame," the first line, alludes to Campbell's first long poem, "The Flaming Terrapin" (1924) and his later "Flowering Rifles" (1939). Stylistically, Lewis found in Campbell a kindred spirit, since both were at odds with the modern poetry of Eliot and Auden; politically, however, Campbell's service on the side of the Communists in Spain offended Lewis:

Those Charlies[37] on the Left of whom you write;
No wonder—since it was from them you learned
How white to black by jargon can be turned;
For though your verse outsoars with eagle pride
Their spineless tunes (of which the old cow died),
Yet your bloodthirsty politics and theirs
Are two peas in a single pod, who cares
Which kind of shirt the murdering Party wears?

Lewis ends by appealing to Campbell to repent and to find "some feet of sacred ground" in order to reaffirm the principles of tradition: "There stood your father's house: there you should stand." Lewis's second poem, also in heroic couplets, is "To Mr. Roy Campbell," and it concerns Campbell's literary and political tastes.[38] Specifically, Lewis attacked Campbell's dismissal of English Romanticism, particularly as he mistakenly connected it with Rousseau. Instead the real stream of English Romanticism flows from Sir Walter Scott, who, like Lewis, relied upon "stock responses": "A right branch on the old European tree / Of valour, truth, freedom, and courtesy, / A man (though often slap-dash in his art) / Civilized to the centre of his heart." Lewis goes on to praise Coleridge as well; while admitting Coleridge's weaknesses, Lewis affirms he was "one who restored our faculty for awe, / Who re-discovered the soul's depth and height." Finally, he urges Campbell to embrace Wordsworth for similar reasons. This poem reveals Lewis's deeply held affection for these towering figures of English Romanticism.[39]

Still another Horatian satire directed at an individual, "Lines to Mr. Compton Mackenzie," addresses Edward Montague Compton Mackenzie (1883–1972), prolific Scottish novelist, essayist, and historian. He took a B.A. in history at Magdalen College, Oxford, and eventually moved to the island of Barra in the Outer Hebrides where he helped to found the Scottish Nationalist Party. He is best known for his novels *Carnival* (1912), *Youth's Encounter* (1913; published in England as *Sinister Street*), *Our Street* (1931), and especially *The Four Winds of Love* (1937–41), a fictional chronicle of a middle-class Scottish family in the first forty years of the twentieth century. While widely read during his lifetime (he was even approved of by Henry James early in his career), almost no one reads Mackenzie today. He often reads like a hack writer, cranking out as much prose as he could get paid for:

> Good heavens, Sir, will you condemn us
> To talk of Romulus and Remus
> And Venus—or perhaps Wenoos?
> Each language has its native use,
> And words like Saturn are abom-
> inable here, if not at Rome.
> Man, were you never taught at school
> The genuinely English rule?
> Antepenultimatis with us
> For the most part are shortened. Thus
> *Crime, criminal,* and *rare,* but *rarity*
> (It rhymes in Thomas Hood with *charity*)
> It's English, which you claim to love,
> You're mangling in the interests of
> A long-dead alien form of speech.
> Learn your own tongue before you teach,
> And leave us meanwhile for our share
> "The freedom of oure ain vulgaire."[40]

Unlike the playful banter in his poems to Amis and Campbell, here Lewis is more pedantic and querulous. He is quibbling over Mackenzie's propensity to misuse English, particularly his use of classically correct words and pronunciation; for instance, Lewis has "condemn us" rhyme with "Remus," a gentle satire on insisting that modern English poets retain the ancient pronunciation of Latin or Greek names.[41] Because we do not know which work Lewis has in mind, we can only speculate what prompted this poem. Perhaps Lewis is arguing with Mackenzie's habit of writing odd-sounding dialects or his use of worn-out inflections.[42] What we can see, however, in this eighteen-line poem is Lewis's again using numerous literary allusions, absurd rhymes ("Wenoos" with "native use"), and farcical humor ("*Crime, criminal,* and *rare,* but *rarity* / [It rhymes in Thomas Hood with *charity*]"). In addition, Lewis's forced iambic tetrameter and contrived rhymes poke fun at Mackenzie's odd literary conventions. Lewis's irritation with Mackenzie was real, but this is a gentle rather than a harsh rebuke.

SATIRIC POEMS: JUVENALIAN

If Lewis's Horatian satire is good-natured criticism, his Juvenalian satire is acidic and scathing. For instance, "A Cliché Came Out of its Cage" is a sharp attack upon moderns who believe they are heralds of a return to the "golden age" of paganism.[43] In particular, he mentions F. R. Leavis, whose ideas on literary criticism he disliked, and Bertrand Russell, whose ideas on society, morality, and philosophy he directly opposed: "I saw . . . Leavis with Lord Russell wreathed in flowers, heralded with flutes, / leading white bulls to the cathedral of the solemn Muses / to pay where due the glory of their latest theorem." In fact, Lewis suggests their "scientific" approaches to literature and social mores show that they know little about classical paganism, and that they mistake their pale, insipid, godless modern version for the healthy, robust, theistic paganism of old. Lewis's disregard for these repugnant ideas is mirrored in the ugly unrhymed heptameter of the poem.

Even more bitter is "*Odora Canum Vis* (A defence of certain modern biographers and critics)."[44] The title comes from Virgil's *Aeneid* 4.132 and means "With keen-scented hunting dogs."[45] Biting and barbed, this scathing, ironic defense of writers who churn out works that titillate, glorifying and headlining smut, is an example of what it was like to fall under the wrath of Lewis's unsheathed critical sword:

> Come now, don't be too eager to condemn
> Our little smut-hounds if they wag their tails
> (Or shake like jellies as the tails wag them)
> The moment the least whiff of sex assails
> Their quivering snouts. Such conduct after all,
> Though comic, is in them quite natural.

These writers who are culturally atrophied, Lewis continues, know "neither God, hunger, thought, nor battle, [so] must / Of course hold disproportionate views on lust." In effect, he gives them over to themselves: "So! Cock your ears, my pretties! Play your part! / The dead are all before you, take your pick. / Fetch! Paid for! Slaver, snuff, defile and lick." The virulent tone of this poem shows Lewis the public gladiator, eager to slay the dragons of character assassination.

"Prelude to Space: An Epithalamium" is no comic wedding poem like "The Small Man Orders His Wedding," nor is its satire mild, as in "Cradle-Song Based on a Theme from Nicolas of Cusa" and "An Expostulation (against too many writers of science fiction)."[46] Instead this poem presents the idea that human exploration of space will be characterized by pride, arrogance, and imperialism, themes Lewis explored as well in the Ransom trilogy. The first stanza is a jingoistic parody:

So Man, grown vigorous now,
Holds himself ripe to breed,
Daily devises how
To ejaculate his seed
And boldly fertilize
The black womb of the unconsenting skies.

Lewis's frank use of sexual imagery throughout the poem—he refers to a space ship on the launching pad as "the large, / Steel member grow[n] erect"—is intended to communicate his disgust with human imperialism and its "lust to stamp / Our likeness on the abyss." All that humanity can promise space, he says, are "bombs, gallows, Belsen camp, / Pox, polio, Thais' kiss / Or Judas'" and similar catastrophes. The last stanza asks the rhetorical question of whether humanity should celebrate when the first spaceships head off to explore space: "Shall we, when the grim shape / Roars upward, dance and sing? / Yes: if we honour rape, / If we take pride to fling / So bountiful on space / The sperm of our long woes, our large disgrace." This, no tender bridal poem celebrating man's fathering of himself across the universe; instead, it is an acrid warning of man's probable rape of the cosmos. Such bitter irony marks much of Lewis's writings about space exploration—from the Ransom trilogy to essays like "Religion and Rocketry"—but Lewis is not against progress; instead, he fears the first space explorers will be space exploiters, as portrayed so devastatingly in Weston from *Perelandra*.[47] His poem is a caustic caution against space exploration, but it is not a reactionary prohibition.

Lewis's sober cautions about human pillage through space travel were related to his deep distrust of modern life. For instance, "On a Vulgar Error" is a Juvenalian satire on chronological snobbery.[48] Lewis begins by admitting that new ideas are not always bad: "Was the first pointed arch esteemed a blot / Upon the church? Did anybody say / How modern and how ugly? They did not." That said, he poses the question: "If, then, our present arts, laws, houses, food / All set us hankering after yesterday, / Need this be only an archaising mood?" In reply, he says the answer to this is found in the examples of the man who finds his money drained away by swindlers (he "must compare how he stands with how he stood") and the man who loses a leg: "If a quack doctor's breezy ineptitude / Has cost me a leg, must I forget straightway / All that I can't do now, all that I could?" In other words, newness—ideas, fashions, technology, and so on—are not in themselves bad; again, Lewis is no reactionary. The questions that have to be asked, however, are:

"How does modernity impact on the human condition? Does its manifestations enhance our understanding of who we are, our place in the universe, and our notions of beauty, honor, and virtue? Or does it simply drain away our resources and cut us off at the knees, reducing us to cogs in a mechanistic, naturalistic, meaningless world?" He uses interconnected rhymes in the tercets (*aba aba aba cbc cbc cbc*) to lead up to his ironic concluding couplet (*dd*): "So, when our guides unanimously decry / The backward glance, I think we can guess why."

"*Spartan Nactus*" is Lewis's sharpest attack on modern misuse of language, especially modern poetry.[49] He feigns being a dunce who cannot understand the subtle nuances of contemporary poetic metaphor and imagery, condemned instead only to have stock responses to the figurative language of the past. Tongue in cheek, Lewis uses couplets, a traditional poetic form, and begins with: "I am so coarse, the things the poets see / Are obstinately invisible to me." This opening serves as his platform from which he attacks modern poetry, particularly that of T. S. Eliot, and its absurd metaphors: "For twenty years I've stared my level best / To see if evening—any evening—would suggest / A patient etherized upon a table; / In vain. I simply wasn't able." He ends the poem, still tongue in cheek, taking the pose of a foolish, uneducated person ("I am like that odd man Wordsworth knew, to whom / A primrose was a yellow primrose") who can only appreciate stock responses, those emotional reactions to ideas, objects, and notions intrinsically connected with the past:

> [I am] one whose doom
> Retains him always in the class of dunces,
> Compelled to offer Stock Responses,
> Making the poor best that I can
> Of dull things . . . peacocks, honey, the Great Wall, Aldebaran,
> Silver streams, cowslip wine, wave on the beach, bright gem,
> The shape of trees and women, thunder, Troy, Jerusalem.

While not a poetic manifesto, Lewis was clearly throwing down the gauntlet against modern poetry.

Another Juvenalian satire illustrating Lewis's distrust of human progress is the rhyming alexandrine poem, "Lines During a General Election."[50] Lewis is especially concerned with the false promises of politicians: "Their threats are terrible enough, but we could bear / All that; it is their promises that bring despair." Governments produce "insatiate gadgetry" that will leave "no green, nor growth, nor quietude, no sap at all / In England from The Land's End to the Roman Wall." In particular, he blasts the increasing number of roads, "broad as the road to Hell," since tarmac murders "a million acres that demand the plough." In addition, he fears the shoreline will lose its beauty, marked instead with "cigarette-ends, orange peel, and chewing-gum." He worries further that politicians' "visions are / Global; they mean the desecration of a Star." In such terrestrial imperialism, he envisions a day when the Earth will be left "flickering with sky-signs, gibbering with mechanic mirth, / One huge celestial charabanc" and "will stink and roll / Through patient heaven, subtopianized from pole to pole." Lewis's bitter voice comes through clearly in this percussive satire.

Linked to his distrust of modernity, "The Genuine Article" is a sonnet in hexameter, satirically reflecting upon those who romanticize the idea of loving one's neighbor in the abstract while they are incapable of loving the neighbor next door.[51] If the theme of "Lines During a General Election" casts suspicion upon politicians, this poem scorns political labels and those who avoid the intimacy of caring for others: "You do not love the Bourgeoisie. Of course: for they / Begot you, bore you, paid for you, and punched your head; / You work with them; they're as intimate as board and bed; / How could you love them, meeting them thus every day?" Instead, such people claim to love the Proletariat, "the thin, far-away / Abstraction which resembles any workman fed / On mortal food as closely as the shiny red / Chessknight resembles stallions when they stamp and neigh." Extending this analogy, Lewis says "kicks are dangerous; riding schools are painful . . . / Every way it cost far less / To learn the harmless manage of the wooden horse." To love the real person, he implies, takes hard work: "Who, that can love nonentities, would choose the labour / Of loving the quotidian face and fact, his neighbour?" Real love is costly and cannot be substituted with political jargon.

"Epitaph" is a scathing English sonnet attacking democracy. Lewis suggests that democracy's greatest weakness is the incessant noise its endless discussions and debates cause.[52] Using the constant drone of a wireless (radio) as a symbol for democratic clamoring, the speaker would prefer one quiet spot in Hell for a Heaven filled with such "music." Thus his epitaph: "And therefore, stranger, tiptoe by this grave, / And let posterity record of me, / 'He died both for, and of, democracy.'"[53] "Consolation" is another Juvenalian satire with a political focus. While it ostensibly begins as if celebrating the end of World War II, it concludes with a sharply satirical bite, suggesting postwar England is once again setting on a course of appeasement. This time, however, it is the Soviet Union, not Germany, that is the focus of England's appeasement.[54] The persona is ironically happy, even if "beer is worse and dearer / And milk has got the blues, / Though cash is short and rations / Much shorter than the queues." In spite of the increase in strikes, crime, and business failures, he says "Yet sing like mad that England / Is back to peacetime ways." What, he says, of "butter, eggs, or mutton, / Freedom or spacious days. / All those were non-essentials." The surest test of peace is this: "If we thus caress the Muscovite, / England has turned to rest." The last stanza of the poem uses a historical allusion to further its satire:

> To ease my doubts Appeasement
> Returns. Peace must be here!
> The tune of glorious Munich
> Once more salutes my ear;
> An ancient British melody—
> We heard it first begin
> At the court of shifty Vortigern
> Who let the Heathen in.

Lewis mocks those concessions made to the Soviet Union at the end of World War II as Europe was divided among the Allied forces. To him they sound like the same tune played when the British Prime Minister, Neville Chamberlain, went to Munich and acquiesced to Hitler in 1939, believing such appeasement would prevent large-scale conflict. In fact, such appeasement, he says, is "an ancient British melody," first evident in the actions of Vortigern whose commitment to compromise led to the destruction of his empire by the Saxon invaders he thought he could appease.[55]

Lewis's comic and satiric verse is not his best poetry. While his exuberant playfulness with meter and sound in the comic pieces is engaging, the nonsense verse is second rate. On the other hand, when he turns to satire, he is querulous, pedantic, and brittle. The percussive characteristics of the comic and satiric poetry, while sometimes effective in creating rhythm and cadence, more often than not lead to poor verse. It is hard to take these poems seriously because they are either inane or venomous; in neither instance do we find the subtle beauty and powerful nuance of language illustrated in his more effective poems. Lewis achieved greater success when he wrote contemplative verse.

CHAPTER SEVEN

Contemplative Verse

Lewis's contemplative poems are reflective pieces denoting personal and public concerns he felt compelled to consider in verse. In general, Lewis wrote contemplative poems that fall into two broad categories. The first group consists of poems that deal with the shallowness of modern life. By and large these poems muse upon the vacuity of life in large cities, the destructive encroachment of civilization on the English countryside, and the deconstruction of language, meaning, and objective truth. The second group consists of poems that reflect upon the human condition and focus upon both the positive and negative realities of existence. Accordingly, he wrote poems on the one hand dealing with joy and on the other hand dealing with uncertainty, obsessive love, despair, loss, and death. If the poems dealing with the shallowness of modern life may be thought of as public analysis and social criticism, those dealing with the human condition may be thought of as personal reflections and private ruminations.

Contemplative Poems on the Shallowness of Modern Life

In "Finchley Avenue" Lewis reflects at length upon the quiet unease he connects with those who live in large English cities such as London.[1] Although the poem, written in alexandrine couplets, begins "We are proud of Finchley Avenue" and goes on to chronicle its attributes—its quietness, good views of London, copper beeches, beautiful stands of laurel and rhododendron, banks of lush grass, finely manicured driveways, and stately homes—we sense hollowness and emptiness.

The Tudor homes, once a symbol of bourgeois success, are now ironic commentaries on the vacuity of modern life. The only laudatory aspects of the homes are the gardens: "That garden lawn / Is the primordial fountain out of which was drawn / All you have since imagined of the lawn where stood / Eve's apple tree, or of the lands before the flood." The nostalgia of "Leaving For Ever the Home of One's Youth" is also captured:

> In that suburban attic with its gurgling sound
> Of water pipes, in such a quiet house, you found
> In early days the relics of still earlier days,
> Forgotten trumpery worn to act forgotten plays,
> Old books, then first remembered, calling up the past
> Which then, as now, was infinitely sweet and vast.
> There first you felt the wonder of deep time, the joy
> And dread of Schliemann standing on the grave of Troy.[2]

Human activity on the avenue is limited to the rush of the owners of the houses to get to work and tradesmen making their daily rounds; by one o'clock in the afternoon the street sinks "to the dead silence of the afternoon." Lewis emphasizes the loneliness of such streets:

> No countryside can offer so much solitude.
> I have known the world less lonely in a winter wood,
> For there you hear the striking of a village clock
> Each hour, or the faint crowing of a distant cock.
> But here is nothing. Nobody goes past. No feet
> But mine. I doubt if anyone has used this seat,
> Here in the shade, save only me. And here I sit
> And drink the unbroken silence and reflect on it.

The poem concludes with the speaker wondering about the families living in these homes. He assumes most of the children are grown and gone, leaving for the most part only the wives of the men who own the homes: "The whole long avenue exhales the sense / Of absent husbands, housework done, uncharted hours."[3] He wonders if this gives the wives "painful emptiness" or "a blessed state / Of truancy wherein they darkly celebrate / Rites of some *Bona Dea* which no man may see?" Regardless, while he affirms that the wives of this street may be virtuous, he feels it is "an eerie rashness to possess a wife / And house that go on living with their different life, / For ever inaccessible to us, all day." The last lines reflect a final musing: "For as we knew in childhood, if the fathers stay / At home by chance, that

whole day takes a different tone, / Better, or worse, it may be; but unlike its own."
The poem suggests that suburban life serves to drive apart a husband and a wife—
he to a life of work and activity outside the home and she to a dull, if settled, life
of housework. For neither is there vital, meaningful living. This sober meditation
on the shallowness of modern life may not be his best poetry, but it reveals his concern with the social constructs of his day that he found disturbing.

"The Future of Forestry" is the first of three poems in which Lewis extended
his social critique of contemporary life beyond the limits of the modern city; the
concern in these poems is the encroachment of the modern world upon the English countryside.[4] The poem asks, when all the trees are gone, sacrificed to roads
and shops, who will tell the children what trees were: "What was a chestnut? /
Say what it means to climb a Beanstalk? / Tell me, grandfather, what an elm is. /
What was Autumn? They never taught us." He insists that some remnants of the
existence of trees will be passed down, "creatures of lower nature / Able to live
and die, though neither / Beast nor man." Actually he extends the poem beyond the natural world to include questionings about the "future" of faery, returning to central themes of *Spirits in Bondage* and "The Queen of Drum." For instance, rumors of "trees as men walking," goblins, and the pale faces of birchgirls
will never cease: "So shall a homeless time, though dimly / Catch from afar (for
soul is watchful) / A sight of tree-delighted Eden."[5] For Lewis there is always more
to reality than just the natural world; faery is always there, hidden only by the veil
of our own blindness.

The second poem concerning the violation of the English countryside, "Under
Sentence," appeared seven year later. It is written from the perspective of the wild
animals of England, and it more directly considers the destruction of the landscape and its creatures.[6] Instinctively the animals shrink from human progress:
"Do not blame us too much if we, being woodland folk, / Cannot swell the rejoicing at this new world you make; / We, hedge-hogged as Johnson, we unused to the
yoke / As Landor, surly as Cobbett (that badger), birdlike as Blake." In this deft
touch, Lewis connects the wildlife of England with notable writers whose animal-
like personalities celebrated the English countryside.[7] Furthermore, the animals'
suspicions are linked to their sense that the modern advancement into the landscape spells their destruction: "A new scent troubles the air—friendly to you
perhaps— / But we with animal wisdom understand that smell. / To all our kind
its message is guns, ferrets, traps, / And a Ministry gassing the little holes in which
we dwell." This ominous tone identifies the poem as a verse introduction to the
same theme considered more fully in *That Hideous Strength*.[8]

Related to "The Future of Forestry" and "Under Sentence" is "Pan's Purge," an
apocalyptic dream vision of the revolt of Nature against mankind.[9] The poem
opens with man finalizing his plans for neutering Nature:

I dreamt that all the planning of peremptory humanity
Had crushed Nature finally beneath the foot of Man;
Birth-control and merriment, Earth completely sterilized,
Bungalow and fun-fair, had fulfilled our Plan,
But the lion and the unicorn were sighing at the funeral,
Crying at the funeral,
Sobbing at the funeral of the god Pan.

However, unlike the passive animals in "Under Sentence," the animals here are awakened: "But dangerously, suddenly, a strange ecstatic shuddering, / A change that set me shuddering / Through all the wailful noises of the beasts ran." Inspired by Pan and his "ringing scimitar," they lash back:

Towering and cloven-hoofed, the power of Pan came over us,
Stamped, bit, tore, broke. It was the end of Man,
Except where saints and savages were kept from his ravaging,
And crept out when the ravaging
Was ended, on an empty earth. The new world began.

Only these newly instructed men ("a small race") are permitted a place on the liberated earth, and the poem ends with the promise of harmony between man and Nature. In spite of its mixed meter, this is Lewis's most powerful poem attacking man's destruction and violation of the natural world, a theme he dealt with two years earlier in *That Hideous Strength* (1945), particularly when the bear, Mr. Bultitude, and his companions overwhelm N.I.C.E. Lewis's poem argues that man's shallow focus upon modernity, progress, and advancement is like cutting off one's nose to spite one's face; by destroying the countryside, he alienates himself from his natural origins. In a deft juxtaposition of rhyme, Lewis underscores this irony: *Man:Plan:Pan; ran:began:ran; Pan:Pan:Man; Man:Man:began; Man:ran:Man.*

"The Country of the Blind" shifts Lewis's concern about the shallowness of modernity to the disconnect between language and meaning.[10] He pictures a race of people who think they can see, but who are actually blind: "Hard light bathed them—a whole nation of eyeless men, / Dark bipeds not aware how they were maimed." While the disconnect between language and meaning has occurred gradually, moderns are now blind to what words really mean: "Whose blind mouths would abuse words that belonged to their / Great grandsires, unabashed, talking of *light* [Lewis's emphasis] in some / Eunuch'd, etiolated, / Fungoid sense, as a symbol of / Abstract thoughts." As a result of this, no objective truth can be conveyed through words:

> If a man, one that had eyes, a poor
> Misfit, spoke of the grey dawn or the stars or green-
>   Sloped sea waves, or admired how
>   Warm tints change in a lady's cheek,
>
> None complained he had used words from an alien tongue,
> None question'd. It was worse. All would agree. "Of course,"
>   Came their answer. "We've all felt
>   Just like that."

Such mawkish woolly-headedness has resulted in jargon: "The words— / Sold, raped, flung to the dogs—now could avail no more; / Hence silence. But the mouldwarps, / With glib confidence, easily / Showed how tricks of the phrase, sheer metaphors could set / Fools concocting a myth, taking words for things." To prove his point, he invites readers to speak with others about the old, vital truths: "Attempt speech on the truths that once, / Opaque, carved in divine forms, irremovable, / Dread but dear as a mountain- / Mass, stood plain to the inward eye." Sadly, Lewis intimates, all one will receive in response is the blank stare of the blind. Philosophically, this is one of Lewis's most profound poems, a thoughtful antidote to attempts to strip meaning from language.[11]

"Re-Adjustment" amplifies Lewis's concern that modern man has lost the ability to connect words with meaning.[12] The poem, an unrhymed "sonnet," begins with the speaker confessing he had hoped old age would bring comfort: "I thought there would be a grave beauty, a sunset splendour / In being the last of one's kind: a topmost moment as one watched / The huge wave curving over Atlantis, the shrouded barge / Turning away with wounded Arthur, or Ilium burning." This persona is an example of what Lewis terms Old Western Man in his inaugural address, *De Descriptione Temporum*, delivered upon his assuming the chair of Medieval and Renaissance English literature at Cambridge in 1955, and this poem has obvious affinities with the address.[13] The speaker says he had assumed the next generation would look on the cultural accomplishments of the past with gratitude, gentleness, and understanding. However, he realizes this will not be, since language and meaning are under attack: "Between the new *Hominidae* and us who are dying, already / There rises a barrier across which no voice can ever carry, / For devils are unmaking language." The next generation has cut itself off from the old core values of civilized life, desiring instead to find purpose and direction in modernity: "Uproot your loves, one by one, with care, from the future, / And trusting to no future, receive the massive thrust / And surge of the many-dimensional timeless rays converging / On this small, significant dew drop, the present that mirrors all."[14] This ironic conclusion suggests not only his own "re-adjustment," but one many will have to make because of the future that will result from shallow modernity. Although Lewis never lived to encounter deconstruction as a literary theory, his poem anticipates its approach to language and the possibility (or impossibility) of meaning.

CONTEMPLATIVE POEMS ON THE HUMAN CONDITION

"Sweet Desire" is about joy from the perspective of one who has been so often disappointed in experiencing joy that he is tentative, even fearful, about giving himself over completely to the pursuit of joy.[15] In alliterative half lines, the speaker addresses God and says he is being haunted by faint hints of "*sweet stabbing*" joy "*coming from your country*" reminding him of past experiences.[16] This disturbs him, and he compares himself to a man in a dungeon who has heard in past "the *hinge* on the *hook turning / Often. Always that opened door / Let new tormentors* in." As the door to joy appears to be opening again, he retreats into a corner of his cell, like a jaded prisoner, rather than risk a disappointing attempt at escape: "So, fearing, I / *Taste* not but with *trembling. I was tricked before.*"[17] In his past disappointments with joy, he has mistaken imitations of joy for the real thing, and so he is wary of yet another cheat. But he cannot resist:

> But what's the *use?* For *y*ield I must
> Though *l*ong de*l*ayed, at *l*ast must dare
> To give *o*ver, to be *e*ased of my *i*ron casing,
> *M*olten at thy *m*elody, as *m*en of snow
> In the *s*olar *s*mile. *S*low-paced I come,
> *Y*ielding by inches. And *y*et, oh *L*ord, and *y*et,
> —Oh *L*ord, *l*et not *l*ikeness fool me again.

This alliterative admission exposes the speaker's passion for joy and reflects Lewis's own persistent pursuit of joy.[18]

Lewis penchant in his verse to use topics inspired by literature is seen in the next poem on joy. "The Landing" reflects Lewis's debt to classical literature, as it recalls Heracles' labor to retrieve one of the golden apples from the Garden of Hesperides.[19] However, Heracles is not its subject. Instead the poem concerns a speaker who is delighted to be landing finally at the Garden of Hesperides, a place he had seen previously only from afar at the Helicon: "All, then, was true! Such lands in solid verity / Dapple the last sea that laps against the sky; / Apple-gold, the headlands of the singing Hesperides / On glass-clear water lie." Inspired, he and his companions journey forth to satisfy this final longing: "Up from the shore then, benumbed with hope, we went upon / Danceable lawns and under gum-sweet wood, / Glancing ever up to where a green hill at the centre of / The hush'd island stood." However, they do not find golden apples. Instead they look through a golden telescope pointed to the West and see "true" Hesperides: "There for the second time I saw, remote and perilous— / Bliss to behold it in the circle of the lens, / And this time surely the true one—the Hesperides' / Country which is not men's." This vision so encourages them, they determine to sail off "to find / That genuine and utter West. Far astern to East of us / The false hope sank behind."[20] The poem has obvious connections to Lewis's pursuit of joy and also recalls the conclusions of *The Voyage of the Dawn Treader* and *The Last Battle*.

"The Day with the White Mark" suggests how joy comes unexpected, unexplained, and unsolicited.[21] In a boisterous opening, we find that joy invades every action of the speaker's day: "All day I have been tossed and whirled in a preposterous happiness." Oddly, however, the speaker's reality shouts that all is bleak and grim: "Reason kept telling me all day my mood was out of season. / It was too; all ahead is dark or splashed with hideous light. / My garden's spoiled; my holidays are cancelled; the omens harden; / The plann'd and the unplann'd miseries deepen; the knots draw tight." But joy sweeps reason aside so that he "could have kissed the very scullery taps." He says "the colour of / My day was like a peacock's chest." Joy washes reason away:

> In at each sense there stole
> Ripplings and dewy sprinkles of delight that with them drew
> Fine threads of memory through the vibrant thickness of the soul.
>
> As though there were transparent earths and luminous trees should grow there,
> And glimmering roots were visibly at work below one's feet,
> So everything, the tick of the clock, the cock crowing in the yard,
> Probing my soil, woke diverse buried hearts of mine to beat,
>
> Recalling either adolescent heights and the inaccessible
> Longings, the ice-keen joys that shook my body and turned me pale.

The unpredictability of joy leads him to wonder, "Who knows if ever it will come again, now the day closes?"[22] He ends by noting that joy is never predictable: "I question if the angel himself / Has power to choose when sudden heaven for me begins or ends." Lewis's "sudden heaven" recalls his affirmation in *Surprised by Joy* that joy cannot be actively sought: "Only when your whole attention and desire are fixed on something else—whether a distant mountain, or the past, or the gods of Asgard—does the 'thrill' arise. It is a by-product. Its very existence presupposes that you desire not it but something other and outer. . . . Often I frightened it away by my greedy impatience to snare it, and, even when it came, instantly destroyed it by introspection, and at all times vulgarized it by my false assumption about its nature" (168–69). "The Day with the White Mark," published six years before *Surprised by Joy*, affirms that joy comes as a surprise in the human experience.

"As One Oldster to Another" offers another reflection on joy, this time noting its rejuvenating power. The poem opens by admitting the physical hardship of growing old: "Well, yes. The old bones ache. There were easier / Beds thirty years back. Sleep, then importunate, / Now with reserve doles out her favours. / Food disagrees. There are draughts in houses."[23] Lewis then employs the metaphor of a train moving through various stations to suggest the rapid passing of the last years of life: "Headlong, the down night train rushes on with us, / Screams through the stations. . . . How many more? Is it / Time soon to think of taking down one's / Case from the rack? Are we nearly there now?" However, rather than turn to nostalgic self-pity, the poem notes how aging is tempered by joy's surprise, catching him unawares and breathing moments of unspeakable delight and inarticulate desire: "Still beauty calls as once in the mazes of / Boyhood. The bird-like soul quivers. Into her / Flash darts of unfulfill'd desire and / Pierce with a bright, unabated anguish." These lines are Lewis at his best and lead him to claim that joy mitigates the journey toward death: "Armed so with anguish, Joy met us even in / Youth—who forgets? This side of the terminus, / Then, now, and always, thus and only / Thus were the doors of delight set open." The delights of joy, always surprising him, were palpable in the midst of the certainty of growing old and offered him an anodyne.

While Lewis's contemplative poems on joy are primarily positive, his reflections upon other sobering issues that confront humanity tend to be introspective, often communicating an uncertain, tentative perspective about the human condition. For instance, three poems initially published anonymously from the anthology *Fear No More: A Book of Poems for the Present Time by Living English Poets* are very introspective.[24] "Essence" is an internal musing on thought and will and their relationship to the essence of self.[25] While the speaker frankly admits his reluctance to speak about the inner world ("Thoughts that go through my mind, / I dare not tell them"), he rejects the bifurcation of *Spirits in Bondage*. Instead, he seeks an integration of thought and will in defining the essence of self: "That essence must have been / Which still I call / My self, since—thus unclean— / It dies not at all." In the second poem, "Break, Sun, my Crusted Earth," Lewis uses a mining metaphor and invites light to pierce his unconscious self as shafts of sun penetrate and expose the hidden depths of caves.[26] As work in mines goes on in secret, so goes the work of his unknown self, "where blind, immortal metals have their birth /

And crystals firm begin." The speaker calls upon the sun to expose his secret life the same way it reveals metals in the earth: "To limbs and loins and heart / Search with thy chemic beam, / Strike where the self I know not lives apart / Beneath the surface dream."[27] The bifurcation between his conscious and unconscious selves is not resolved as the poem concludes: "For Life in secret goes / About his work. In gloom, / The mother helping not nor hindering, grows / The man inside the womb."

The third poem in this sequence, "The World is Round," has the exiled Adam attempting to recall the delights of the Garden of Eden:

Naked apples, wooly-coated peaches
Swelled on that garden wall. Unbounded
Spicey odour of unmoving trees
Surrounded me, lying on the sacred turf,
Sweetened the sheltered air. The forest of trees,
Buoyed up in air like weeds in ocean
Grew without motion. I was the pearl,
Mother-of-pearl my nest.[28]

However, he cannot completely recapture his memory: "I do not really remember that garden; / I remember the remembering, when first waking / I heard the golden gates behind me / Shut fast upon it."[29] Consequently, he finds some solace in remembering the rich odors and brilliant images of a garden, an attractive alternative to the dull, weary journey he is currently experiencing: "On a flinty road, / With east-wind blowing over the black frost, / I found my feet. Forth on a journey / Gathering thin garment over aching bones, / I went." His final resolution suggests a perhaps foolish musing: "I wander still. But the world is round." That is, he appears to hope he can wander his way completely around the world until he finds the gates to reenter Eden. The tentative nature of these poems, their lack of certainty, and their honest admission of two levels of consciousness are unusual for Lewis. He rarely focused upon introspection in his literary work, so these three poems are notable in that we see a persona reviewing the buried life.

"Pilgrim's Problem" continues this kind of introspection, and its conclusions are tentative as well, since it challenges the notion that age brings wisdom and settled peace.[30] A walker, late in the day, relies on his map and assumes he is nearing a restful end to his journey. The poem becomes symbolic when we read of how he looks forward to charity, humility, contemplation, fortitude, temperance, and chastity. In fact, he realizes none of these: "I can see nothing like all this." He wonders rhetorically whether it is the map or he that is flawed: "Maps can be wrong. But the experienced walker knows / That the other explanation is more often true."[31] Ironically, he implies it must be he rather than the map that is flawed. "Leaving For Ever the Home of One's Youth" dates to 1930 and is a personal reflection upon leaving Little Lea for the last time after Lewis and his brother settle their father's estate.[32] Accordingly, it is very nostalgic, and Lewis writes about "the old, disconsolate / Familiar pangs [he has] felt as in the past." Written as if he is at the moment driving away from the house and down the driveway, he tells himself to harden his gaze ahead, even though "grey memories drop and dreams thick-dusted lie / beneath" the trees on either side. He recalls how this place has been a haven from the turmoil of war in France and a blissful retreat from their early school days: "And think of some divine first day / In holidays from school." Yet he goes even further back in his memory as he regards the enduring power of this home: "Always from further back breathes the thin scent, / As of cold Eden wakenings on wet lawns; / And eldest hours had elder to lament / And dreamed of irrecoverable dawns." In spite of such powerful memories, however, he urges himself to look forward, not back. For, indeed, "the past you mourn for, when it was in flight, / Lived, like the present, in continual death."

Perhaps the most disturbing poem questioning the significance of the human condition is "The Salamander."[33] Sitting before a fire, the speaker gazes mindlessly into burning coals where "blue waves / Of shuddering heat . . . r[i]se and f[a]ll, / And blazing ships and blinding caves, / Canyons and streets and hills of hell." However, this familiar atmosphere is suddenly changed, when "amidst it all / I saw a living creature crawl." From this point on the fiery salamander gives a soliloquy about what he "sees" outside the fire; his melancholic reflections are compared to ones men make, since he looks with "sad eyes . . . as men [look] out upon the skies." Gazing into the dark room, the salamander says "this is the end," the place "where all life dies," the universe of "blank silence, distances untold / Of unimaginable cold." The lights from the room he can see only dimly, since they "are but reflections cast from here, / There is no other fire but this. / This speck of life, this fading spark / Existed amid the boundless dark." The creature intimates, therefore, that the real world, the world of meaning, is found only within the fire; outside there is isolation, estrangement, and alienation.[34] Because he can see only what is physically in front of him, the only world he is willing to accept is the tangible one. That there could be an invisible or spiritual realm beyond his fiery world is unthinkable. And, of course, by implication mankind has a similar mind set; rather than face boldly the prospect of another dimension, we, like the salamander, deny anything we cannot perceive as a part of the material world about us. He ends with a nihilistic credo, one suggesting that even values are hollow:

Blind Nature's measureless rebuke
To all we value, I received
Long since (though wishes bait the hook

With tales our ancestors believed)
And now can face with fearless eye
Negation's final sovereignty.

Yet, he confronts such nihilism courageously "with fearless eye, / Negation's final sovereignty." The salamander's affirmation of nihilism implies, if we make the invited comparison between the salamander and the human condition, that men often make a similar discovery and affirmation about their own existence. Life may be without meaning, yet man's task is to face that reality courageously. This is a very different voice of Lewis, a distant voice, contrasting dramatically with the confident, buoyant voice of so much of his prose.[35]

A variation on this distant voice occurs in "Infatuation," unique for Lewis since it considers the obsessive nature of romantic love.[36] One of Lewis's longest poems, it is a poignant internal monologue a man has concerning both the character of the woman he loves and his inability to control his thoughts about her. His dilemma is expressed succinctly in the opening lines: "Body and soul most fit for love can best / Withstand it. I am ill, and cannot rest, / Therefore I'm caught." Echoing themes from Shakespeare's sonnets, Lewis expands the analogy between sickness and love: "Disease is amorous, health / At love's door has the pass both in and out." Most frustrating to the persona is his complete incapacity to block her out of his mind. When he strains with every fiber to keep her out, "then in she comes by stealth."[37] This is compounded by the fact she is not worth his obsession: "Her brain's a bubble, / Her soul, a traveller's tale." Yet time and again she "comes between / My thoughts and me." He tries to force himself to read a book, but this does not help. In fact, it drives him to delve ever deeper into his soul in an effort to understand his obsession. He confesses, "I do not love her, like her, wish her well," yet he says he is not driven by lust either. As he reflects back over their relationship, he realizes he has fallen in love with the idea of love:

She stood, an image lost as soon as seen,
Like beauty in a vision half-caught between
Two aimless and long-lumbering dreams of night.
The thing I seek for was not anywhere
At any time on earth.

Sadly, when he finds she cannot live up to his idea of love, he finds himself still driven to want her; the visceral rules the cerebral. Consequently, he considers trying to teach her love through an exercise of charity toward her, but he knows this will not work: "She can never learn; / And what am I, whose voice should wake the dead?" Such honest self-revelation on his part saves the poem from being self-righteous invective.

As he analyzes her character more, he notes she is really a product of what she thinks men want, and she is ever ready to play "the rapt disciple," to flatter whichever man she happens to be with at the moment. She is beautiful on the outside, but empty on the inside:

Her holiest moods are gaudy desecrations
Of poor half holy things: her exaltations
Are frothed from music, moonlight, wine and dances;
Love is to her a dream of bridal dresses,
Friendship, a tittering hour of girl's caresses,
Virtue, a steady purpose to advance,
Honoured, and safe, by the well-proven roads,
No loophole left to passion or to chance.

Recalling a party they attended together the previous evening, he remembers how he longed to tell her the truth about herself. But she, enjoying her triumph as men buzzed about her and other women envied her, would never have listened. Even he was momentarily deflected from his purpose: "Could she have looked so noble, and no seed / Of spirit in her at all?" Eventually, however, he knows that "Venus infernal taught such voice and eyes / To bear themselves abroad for merchandise."[38]

The poem ends with him, in spite of his obsession with her, being relieved that "she'd never have me," for he imagines how awful a life with her would be. Yet, in his obsession he believes he learns something about the human condition: "For each one of us, down below / The caldron brews in the dark. We do not know / By whom, or on what fields, wc are reined and ridden. / There are not acts; spectators of ourselves / We wait and watch the event, the cause hidden." Whatever confidence we have in ourselves—our good name, our native abilities—is vanity. The truth is darker: "The motion / That moves us is not ours, but in the ocean / Of hunger and bleak fear, like buoys we ride, / And seem to move ourselves, and in the waves / Lifting and falling take our shame and pride." The speaker ends by affirming the essential impotence of human intention. Even if we think we have some ability to control our fortunes, the truth is we ride upon the waves of time and providence, and, like buoys, we ride rather than direct our destinies. "Infatuation" is among Lewis's most thoughtful poems, as he dealt frankly and openly with the subtleties of human obsession. Indeed, Lewis managed a poem that well illustrates the eternal war between the mind and the will, the spirit and the flesh, reason and passion. Avoiding "pat" answers about the human experience, Lewis demonstrated here a mind fully awake to the danger of human choice and will.

"Reason" continues Lewis's focus upon the human condition and the inner conflicts noted above in "Infatuation."[39] This time, however, the conflict is between reason and the imagination.[40] He personifies reason as "a virgin, arm'd, commercing with celestial light" and claims the absolute necessity of joining with her. Yet he equally argues the necessity of uniting with imagination, "warm, dark, obscure and infinite, daughter of Night." The poem turns upon discovering some way to reconcile these two and "make imagination's dim exploring touch / Ever report the same as intellectual sight." If he can ever discover a way to bring these two together, "then could I truly say, and not deceive, / Then wholly say, that I BELIEVE" (Lewis's emphasis). The poem itself never achieves such reconciliation, but instead it reveals how important these two concepts are to Lewis's creative and intellectual process. Perhaps the most impressive work where Lewis achieves such reconciliation is *Perelandra*. There we see his rich and powerfully evocative imagination illustrated in his lush physical descriptions of that world as well as the dialectic of reason in the lengthy, closely argued debate among the Green Lady, Weston, and Ransom.

Lewis's "Five Sonnets" is a sequence dealing with despair and extends our insights into his musings on the human condition.[41] Sonnet "1" is in many ways antithetical to many of the poems in *Spirits in Bondage* that exhibit a young man's immature anger at the world and at a God he denies yet blames.[42] In "1" an older speaker defends himself and others who do not "shake / [their] fists at God when youth and bravery die." Actually the young have an advantage over older people like him, since they "have what sorrow always longs to find, / Someone to blame." The anger of youth is an "anaesthetic of the mind," as "it does men good, it fumes away their grief." Like them, older men feel the pain of life, but experience has shown them the ultimate futility of anger; accordingly, not hating, they strive "to want, and then (perhaps) to win / A high, unearthly comfort, angel's food, / That seems at first mockery to flesh and blood." Perseverance in the face of life's disappointment and grief comes only with age, a notion clearly informed by Lewis's biblical understanding of the human condition.[43]

Sonnet "2" shifts the focus slightly when the persona admits there is something "good" about despair: "There's a repose, a safety (even a taste / Of something like revenge?) in fixed despair / Which we're forbidden." However, the antidote to despair is "to rise with haste" and avoid wallowing in it; consolation comes—only after "the dreadful process has unrolled"—that is, when we realize "one bereavement makes us more bereft." In other words, hitting rock bottom and coming through it is our "consolation": "It asks for all we have, to the last shred." Lewis then alludes to Dante and the *Divine Comedy* by way of illustration. Dante has to journey through Hell before he reaches Paradise:

Read Dante, who had known its best and worst—
He was bereaved and he was comforted

—No one denies it, comforted—but first
Down to the frozen centre, up the vast
Mountain of pain, from world to world, he passed.

As Dante journeys through Hell, anguished both for his desire to see Beatrice and for the damned whom he has seen writhing in torment, his last act is momentous: He must climb on the hairy body of Satan, who is frozen waist deep in the very center of Hell, in order to "climb" out the other side to begin his final pilgrimage up the mountain of Purgatory and on, eventually, to Paradise. Dante, therefore, has to journey to despair personified in the figure of Satan, embrace it, and only then begin the upward journey from darkness. What "2" recommends is essentially the same thing: Embrace the worst, as Dante did, since there can be only movement upward from there.

Sonnet "3" comments further upon the idea of consolation and echoes a passage from *A Grief Observed*. In brief, this sonnet posits one certainty: that heaven's door is no place to find earthly comfort. Even the knocking can deceive since "You'll begin / To fancy that those echoes (hope can play / Pitiful tricks) are answers from within." Make no mistake, however: "Far better to turn, grimly sane away. / Heaven cannot thus, Earth cannot ever, give / The thing we want." In *A Grief Observed* Lewis puts it this way: "Talk to me about the truth of religion and I'll gladly listen. Talk to me about the duty of religion and I'll listen submissively. But don't come talking to me about the consolations of religion or I shall suspect that you don't understand" (28). In the poem, he adds that our asking for consolation from heaven only ends up heightening our suffering, since "by our asking [we] water and make live / That very part of love which must despair / And die and go down cold into the earth." Only after we die to the hope of consolation can we move to "talk of springtime and re-birth."

Sonnet "4" begins with an ironic invitation to "pitch your demands heaven-high and they'll be meet." But then the sonnet turns upon the incredibly difficult task this necessitates, since at every turn despair looms again: "The silence of one voice upon our ears / Beats like the waves; the coloured morning seems / A lying brag; the face we loved appears / Fainter each night, or ghastlier, in our dreams." In a return to Dante, Nature then whispers that Dante's way "was meant / For mighty saints and mystics not for me." Nature, "red in tooth in claw," suggests we indulge in self-pity, a powerful temptation in the face of despair. The poem ends with a wonderfully apt metaphor denoting the futility of such thinking: "Yet if we once assent / To Nature's voice, we shall be like the bee / That booms against the window-pane for hours / Thinking that way to reach the laden flowers."

Sonnet "5" continues this metaphor and imagines someone being able to speak to the bee, pointing out the vanity of its efforts. More than likely, however, the bee would reply, in a tone reminiscent of "The Salamander": "Let queens and mystics and religious bees / Talk of such inconceivables as glass; / The blunt lay worker flies at what he sees." If the speaker then captures the bee and releases her to the outside, she will "gaily" fly to "where quivering flowers stand thick in summer air, / To drink their hearts." The poem's ending completes the sonnet sequence's focus upon despair: "Left to her own will / She would have died upon the window-sill." Lewis's thoughtful sonnet sequence is instructive. For the most part he reflects a biblical understanding of the way to deal with despair; eschewing either casual, flippant dismissal or self-indulgent introspection, he suggests facing it fully and working through it to the other side. This is a telling study of how despair is fundamental to the human condition, and the poem is a mature, reasoned response.

Not surprisingly, among the most moving of Lewis's poems dealing with the human condition are those considering loss and death. For instance, "To G. M." contrasts the goodness of the deceased with the selfishness of the speaker and ponders the impact of the death of the deceased.[44] As people recall the life of the deceased, they recall a positive one, fertile and inspiring to others: "From your rich soil what life will spring, / What flower-unfolding paradise, / Through what green walks what birds shall sing; / What med'cinable gums, what spice." In contrast, the speaker admits his reaction to the death is one of "fear [that] assails me for myself." Comparing himself to the moon, he says "the noon / That nourishes earth, can only sear / And scald the unresponding moon." In the end he is caustic, bitter, and sterile, filled with "long despair." We cannot with certainty connect this poem with the death of a specific person Lewis knew, but clearly Lewis expressed here a profound sense of loss, surpassed in emotional intensity only by his later poems on his wife's suffering and death.

One of Lewis's most poignant treatments of death appears in "On the Death of Charles Williams." This poem records the shock of losing a friend and how it throws one's view of the human condition into a tailspin: "I can't see the old contours; the slant alters. It's a bolder world / Than I once thought. I wince, caught in the shrill winds that dance on this ridge. / Is it the first sting of a world's waning, the great Winter? Or the cold of Spring?"[45] The old comfortable thought that human life had meaning is challenged by death. Indeed, the knowledge that life is fragile causes him to "wince" and question whether or not such a loss is just the tip of the iceberg. Although he allows that he may be overreacting, he never answers the question, and we are left with the impression that the loss of a friend challenges well-worn assurances about life having ultimate meaning and purpose. Ironically, Lewis notes that it would only be with Williams that he could hope to talk through and make sense of this death: "I have lost now the one only friend wise enough to advise, / To touch deftly such problems. I am left asking. Concerning your death / With what friend now would it help much to spend words, unless it were you?" Like other poems Lewis wrote lamenting the loss of friends, this poignant piece indicates the presence of the distant voice of dissonance and disorientation.

While "Lines Written in a Copy of Milton's Works" hints subtly at Lewis's literary indebtedness to both Marvell and Milton, the poem concerns the personal isolation one feels as the result of lost friendship.[46] It begins with a persona noting how natural creatures blithely carry on in harmony with one another: "Alas, the happy beasts at pasture play / All, all alike; all of one mind are they." Not only are the animals in harmony, but also they easily change companions and are blessed with disinterested friendship: "None loves a special friend beyond the rest." Indeed, even if a sparrow loses a friend to a bird of prey or to a hunter's arrow, "with a new friend next day, content, he wings his flight." The persona then contrasts this Wordsworthian ethos with the dissonant relationships between human beings. Man, the persona suggests, cannot unthinkingly and casually find the easy friend since he "in his fellows finds / (Hard fate) discordant souls and alien minds!" Actually, in the effort to find even one close friend, "one heart amidst a thousand like his own," he will encounter a good deal of difficulty. And, ironically, even if he does eventually find such a friend, it will be only temporary:

> Or if, at last relenting, fate shall send
> In answer to his prayer, the authentic friend,
> Him in some unsuspected hour, some day
> He never dreaded, Death will snatch away
> And leave behind a loss that time can ne'er allay.

Once bereft of that friend, he is left without a companion to "charm to rest each eating care," to share "the secrets of my bosom," or to "while away with delight / Of his discourse the livelong winter night." The last stanza begins with an emphasis upon the persona's sense of isolation: "Alone I walk the fields and plains, alone / The dark vales with dense branches overgrown." In his solitude he feels confined and aimless. In addition, the imagery of the last two lines of the poem indicates an overwhelming sense of estrangement: "Here, as day fades, I wait, and all around / I hear the rain that falls with sullen sound." The cold dampness of the fading day suggests a pathetic fallacy, especially as the rain falls with "sullen sound." The melancholy tone of this poem links it with "To G. M." and "On the Death of Charles Williams."

The final three poems are deeply emotional sonnets concentrating upon loss.[47] "Joys That Sting" is almost certainly a melancholic reverie about a terminated romantic friendship.[48] The persona is saddened "to take the old walks alone, or not at all, / To order one pint where I ordered two, / To think of, and then not to make, the small / Time–honoured joke (senseless to all but you)." That he now only orders "one pint where I ordered two" indicates an erotic if not marital connection, since two male friends would probably have ordered separately; on the other hand, a husband would normally order for his wife.[49] He goes on to underscore his estrangement and comments that his life is now little more than show:

> To laugh (oh, one'll laugh), to talk upon
> Themes that we talked upon when you were there,
> To make some poor pretence of going on,
> Be kind to one's old friends, and seem to care,
> While no one (O God) through the years will say
> The simplest, common word in just your way.

The grief this poem expresses over the loss of the beloved is both simple and profound: "It is the joys once shared that have the stings."

"Old Poets Remembered" is more about suffering than lost friendship, although the speaker clearly senses impending loss.[50] As he watches his friend suffer with dignity, he is initially buoyed, yet when he sees his friend's pain, "down through a waste world of slag and sewers / And hammering and loud wheels once more I go." The only hint the friend might be a woman occurs in the third stanza: "Thus, what old poets told me about love / (Tristram's obedience, Isoud's sovereignty . . .) / Turns true in a dread mode I dreamed not of, / What once I studied, now I learn to be." Lewis, the scholar who writes *The Allegory of Love*, a scholastic treatise on medieval courtly love, communicates in this poem something of the emptiness of academic knowledge about romantic love when compared to the actual experience of love, especially when the beloved is suffering painfully.

The third poem, "As the Ruin Falls," is actually about the anticipated loss of eros.[51] In the poem, the persona rebukes himself with bitter honesty: "All this is flashy rhetoric about loving you. / I never had a selfless thought since I was born. / I am mercenary and self-seeking through and through: / I want God, you, all friends, merely to serve my turn." His confession about his egocentricity continues as he admits that he "cannot crawl one inch outside my proper skin"; he has spoken of love in the past, but he recognizes that his has not been a giving love: "Self-imprisoned, [I] always end where I begin." The beloved, however, has taught the persona, by example, both what loving means (giving) and how his has been self-centered: "Only that now you have taught me (but how late) my lack." But there is an added dimension; the beloved appears to be leaving him, whether because of circumstance or death we cannot be sure: "I see the chasm. And everything you are was making / My heart into a bridge by which I might get back / From exile, and grow man. And now the bridge is breaking." To the beloved he credits his own faltering steps toward a love that is giving; indeed, the beloved has given him the capacity to be less selfish—she has made his heart a bridge—and less isolated— she has helped to end his "exile, and grow man." His comment that the bridge is now breaking almost certainly refers to his anticipated loss of her. And so he blesses her: "For this I bless you as the ruin falls. The pains / You give me are more precious than all other gains." Given the intensely emotional nature of these last three poems, it is not surprising that some critics have assumed they deal explicitly with Lewis's relationship with Joy Davidman.[52] Because all three poems exist only in holographs and are not dated, there is no way to establish definitively this connection. Regardless, they are powerful witnesses to Lewis's ability to mine the depths of the human condition.

Lewis's contemplative poems illustrate deep and seasoned reflection. While the ones concerned with the shallowness of modern life tend to be public, perhaps even being offered as social criticism, they lack the biting, acerbic tone of his satirical poems; instead they are measured soundings illustrating a profoundly nostalgic sensibility. In most cases, they lament the erosion of core values important to civilized life. Tracing these values back to the Greek and Roman writers he so admired—Homer, Virgil, and Ovid—as well as the towering figures of Western literature—Dante, Chaucer, Shakespeare, Milton, Wordsworth, Shelley, Keats, and Yeats—Lewis's contemplative poems are framed by his conviction that honor, courage, bravery, honesty, charity, respect, and related values infuse human existence with purpose and meaning. At the same time, his contemplative poems considering the commonalities of human existence—doubt, obsession, loss, death, grief—offer compelling evidence that he was fully human. While the tone of these poems may disturb some who believe Lewis was always the confident, buoyant Christian apologist, they actually make his corpus complete. That Lewis endured the shifting sands of life like everyone else makes his work "ring" true. His contemplative poems lead naturally to his religious verse, perhaps the finest body of poetry he produced.

CHAPTER EIGHT

The Religious Verse

That there has yet to be a study of Lewis's religious poetry is ironic, since for many his reputation rests upon his work as a Christian writer. Of special interest is how such a study illustrates Lewis's journey of faith from atheism to Christianity. For instance, we have already noted that Owen Barfield says, "[his early poetry, *Dymer* in particular] is practically the only place where the voice of the earlier Lewis [pre-conversion to Christ] . . . is heard speaking not through the memory of the later Lewis but one could say in his own person."[1] After Lewis's conversion, however, many of his poems deal with religious themes; in fact, of his more than two hundred poems, over fifty (or one quarter of all his poems) may be classed as religious. These poems focus upon the character of God; biblical themes, events, or motifs; and the Christian life, including prayer, the nature of love, joy in Christ, spiritual pride, the incarnation, the resurrection, angels, thanksgiving, grief, doubt, Heaven, Hell, and temptation.[2] Lewis's religious verse begins with his youthful, jaundiced perception of God as found in *Spirits in Bondage*, where, as we have seen, he portrays God as cruel and malicious. However, a radical shift in his understanding of God is revealed in the poetry of *The Pilgrim's Regress;* these poems reflect Lewis's conversion to Christ and his initial growth as a believer. Later religious poems offer mature ruminations on life in Christ. In total, Lewis's religious verse provides us valuable insights into his efficacy as a communicator of Christian truth while powerfully supplementing his work as a prose apologist.

The Poetry of *The Pilgrim's Regress*

By the time Lewis published *The Pilgrim's Regress* (hereafter *PR*) in 1933, fourteen years after *Spirits in Bondage* and two years after his conversion to Christ, his view of God had undergone profound changes. He no longer viewed God as malicious, arbitrary, and cruel, and many passages in *Surprised by Joy* chronicle this change. The culmination of Lewis's evolving view of God is revealed where he writes of his conversion from atheism to theism:

> You must picture me alone in that room in Magdalen, night after night, feeling, whenever my mind lifted even for a second from my work, the steady, unrelenting approach of Him whom I so earnestly desired not to meet. That which I greatly feared had at last come upon me. In the Trinity Term of 1929 I gave in, and admitted that God was God, and knelt and prayed: perhaps, that night, the most dejected and reluctant convert in all England. I did not then see what is now the most shining and obvious thing; the Divine humility which will accept a convert even on such terms. The Prodigal Son at least walked home on his own feet. But who can duly adore that Love which will open the high gates to a prodigal who is brought in kicking, struggling, resentful, and darting his eyes in every direction for a chance of escape? The words *compelle intrare,* compel them to come in, have been so abused by wicked men that we shudder at them; but, properly understood, they plumb the depth of the Divine mercy. The hardness of God is kinder than the softness of men, and His compulsion is our liberation.[3]

Not surprisingly, his religious verse reflects these views. *The Pilgrim's Regress* contains sixteen poems that focus primarily upon the spiritual life; as a group they rank among the best of Lewis's poems, perhaps in part because they so intimately and immediately reflect aspects of Lewis's life in Christ.[4]

The first poem, "He Whom I Bow To" (144–45),[5] sonnet-like although written in alexandrine couplets, does not appear until three-quarters of the way through *The Pilgrim's Regress.* This late appearance suggests that as John, the hero of the book, awakens to the beauty of poetry, he correspondingly awakens to the truth of his broken spiritual condition and need for God's grace.[6] The speaker confesses that language used to address God is so inadequate that "prayers always, taken at their word, blaspheme" and "all men are idolaters, crying unheard / To senseless idols, if thou take them at their word." Accordingly, anticipating the later "Legion," the poem ends with the prayer, "Take not, oh Lord, our literal sense, but in thy great, / Unbroken speech our halting metaphor translate."

Among the most powerful poems in *The Pilgrim's Regress* is "You Rest Upon Me All My Days" (147–48),[7] reflecting a tone similar to poems in *Spirits in Bondage* which confront the cruel, malicious God; the difference here is that God, while demanding and jealous, loves rather than hates the speaker. The speaker grapples with a fierce omnipotence, much as a dog strains at the leash of an unyielding master. He feels like a person trapped in a burning desert bathed by unrelenting, suffocating light and heat. God, like the sun, is the "inevitable Eye" that confines a desert traveler in smothering tents and "hammers the rocks with light." He is an unyielding, unrelenting, uncompromising force. In desperation the speaker longs for "one cool breath in seven / One air from northern climes / The changing and the castle–clouded heaven / Of my old Pagan times." These lines recall Lewis's affection for Norse myth and literature in terms of both its religious and metaphorical influences on his youth and young adulthood. In addition, these lines suggest a powerful longing for freedom from the "heat" of God's eye; he is ready to retreat from the demands of an unyielding God toward the comfortable fixed certainty of his pagan days. Such an option, however, is denied him: "But you have seized all in your rage / Of Oneness. Round about / Beating my wings, all ways, within your cage, / I flutter, but not out." Here God is pictured as possessive, jealous, and demanding, and the speaker pictures himself as a bird trapped in a cage, straining earnestly though in vain to wing his way out.

The poem leaves two distinct impressions. The first is of a "convert" who yearns for his preconversion days where, rightly or wrongly, he believes that life held more freedom, more satisfaction. Indeed, the tone is similar to George Herbert's "The Collar," where the speaker advises himself to "leave thy cold dispute / Of what is fit and not. Forsake thy cage, / Thy ropes of sands, / Which petty thoughts have made." As in Herbert's poem, Lewis's speaker is frustrated ("beating my wings") yet thwarted ("I flutter, but not out"). The second is that God is an all–encompassing, smothering, demanding deity, unyielding in His jealous possession of a follower. Such a God seizes "all in [His] rage / Of Oneness." These impressions combine to highlight the speaker in "You Rest Upon Me All My Days" as one who regards with nostalgia his preconversion lifestyle, yet he also has grudging appreciation for this jealous God. He senses it is now Yahweh, not Odin, that he serves.

Since "You Rest Upon Me All My Days" partially resolves the question of God's real character, Lewis's religious verse in *The Pilgrim's Regress* turns to consider what it means to live as a Christian. For example, "My Heart Is Empty" (162),[8] with its alternating alexandrines and trimeters, examines the contradiction between living the expected "abundant life" and the cold reality of spiritual torpor. It is a candid admission that the speaker's spiritual life is a dry, arid wasteland: "All the fountains that should run / With longing, are in me / Dried up. In all my countryside there is not one / That drips to find the sea." What is worse, he has no desire to experience God's love, except as it serves to lessen his own pain. Yet the speaker avoids despair by calling out to the one "who didst take / All care for Lazarus in the careless tomb." The vigor of his faith in Christ is seen in his belief that, if God will intervene in his own Lazarus-like life, he may survive for later rebirth, much as a seed "which grows / Through winter ripe for birth." Just as the dormant seed avoids the chilling winter wind, so he will endure this winter of his life: "Because, while it forgets, the heaven remembering throws / Sweet influence still on earth, / —Because the heaven, moved moth-like by thy beauty, goes / Still turning round the earth." The pleading tone of Lewis's poem is similar to many of Herbert's. For instance, "Dullness" from *The Temple* begins, "Why do I languish thus, drooping and dull, / As if I were all earth? / O give me quickness, that I may with mirth / Praise the brim-full!"[9]

The next three poems in *The Pilgrim's Regress* anticipate material that Lewis returns to in *The Screwtape Letters* and *The Great Divorce.* The rhyming alexandrines of "Thou Only Art Alternative to God" (177)[10] baldly posit that we either serve God or Satan; there is no other choice: "God is: thou art: / The rest illusion." The speaker notes he can either serve the pure "white light without flame" of God or the "infernal starving in the strength of fire" of Satan. It ends with the speaker noting fearfully, "Lord, open not too often my weak eyes to this!" The poem's portrayal of a malicious Satan borrows heavily from "Satan Speaks" (I) and "Satan Speaks" (XIII) of *Spirits in Bondage.* Furthermore, the poem contains the kernal of Screwtape's counsel to Wormword about keeping his patient from engaging in dialectic thinking, encouraging him instead to promote muddle-headedness and hazy logic. The focus upon Hell continues in Lewis's triolet, "God in His Mercy" (180),[11] a terse, pithy, epigrammatic observation about why God created Hell. Framed around the refrain, "God in his mercy made / The fixed pains of Hell," the poem says God actually limits misery by creating Hell as a fixed area for the suffering of those within. That is, God's creation of Hell is not cruel, but merciful, since God limits the place and thus the extent of suffering for those who reject him. He could have just as easily permitted Hell to be boundless, limitless, and formless. By carving out a limited sphere for those who choose Hell, God is being kind, echoing the line from *Surprised by Joy,* "the hardness of God is kinder than the softness of man."[12]

In the third poem about Hell, "Nearly They Stood Who Fall" (181–82),[13] Lewis, reflecting the pervasive influence of Milton, considers both the angels who fell and those who did not. He imagines those who fell looking back and seeing "the one false step" they took, realizing the "lightest swerve / Of foot not yet enslaved" could have meant they "might have been saved." However, such insight is not limited to the fallen angels, since Lewis notes that the unfallen angels know similarly how easily they could have fallen, "and with cold after fear / Look back to mark how near / They grazed the Sirens' land / . . . The choice of ways so small, the event so great." The poem ends by urging onlookers to consider how angelic examples speak to us, warning us of "the road that seems so clear" and reminding us "which, being once crossed forever unawares, / Denies return." Almost certainly Lewis had in mind Satan's speech at the beginning of book 4 of *Paradise Lost* where he says:

> Oh had his powerful Destiny ordain'd
> Me some inferior Angel, I had stood
> Then happy; no unbounded hope had rais'd
> Ambition. Yet why not? some other Power
> As great might have aspir'd, and me though mean
> Drawn to his part; but other Powers as great
> Fell not, but stand unshak'n, from within
> Or from without, to all temptations arm'd.
> Hadst thou the same free Will and Power to stand?
> Thou hadst.[14]

Playing off Satan's realization that he could have chosen not to fall, Lewis affirms in "Nearly They Stood Who Fall" that human choices and their consequences are critically important; they are deadly serious and connect us to a spiritual reality that exists whether we recognize it or not. The three poems on Hell in *The Pilgrim's Regress* are sober reflections on the nature of man's spiritual adversary, the extent of God's mercy, and the spiritual significance of human responsibility.

The next two poems concern spiritual pride, what Lewis calls the "great" sin in *Mere Christianity*, and already noted as something he struggled with throughout his life.[15] The first poem, "I Have Scraped Clean the Plateau" (183),[16] centers its alexandrines on the ugliness of self-righteous pride. The female persona, echoing the autonomy of Dymer, rejects both the earth—filthy, unchaste, a "sluttish helot"—and man—"filthy flesh," embracing instead a hard, flinty asceticism: "I have made my soul (once filthy) a hard, pure, bright / Mirror of steel . . . / I have a mineral soul." Her rejection and isolation are attempts to live only for self, unsullied by aspects of human life that might shake her belief in her own superiority: "So I, borrowing nothing and repaying / Nothing, neither growing nor decaying, / Myself am to myself, a mortal God, a self-contained / Unwindowed monad, unindebted and unstained." These lines anticipate Orual's self-righteousness and self-sufficiency through part I of *Till We Have Faces* and the initial self-absorbed pride of Jane Studdock in *That Hideous Strength*.

"Because of Endless Pride" (184–85),[17] treats spiritual pride from an opposite perspective, as the persona recognizes that in every hour of his life he looks "upon my secret mirror / Trying all postures there / To make my image fair."[18] Instead of delighting in the luscious, rich grapes God gives him for nourishment, he admires the "white hand" holding them. Though he catches himself admiring himself in the mirror of his soul, he is sensitive enough to know "who made the glass, whose light makes dark, whose fair / Makes foul, my shadowy form reflected there / That Self-Love, brought to bed of Love may die and bear / Her sweet son in despair." The answer to spiritual pride, therefore, is humility, and recognizing it is God, not self, who rules human life and the natural world. Lewis may have been influenced in part by Herbert's "The Bunch of Grapes" that ends:

> But can he want the grape, who hath the wine?
>   I have their fruit and more.
> Blessed be God, who prosper'd Noah's vine,
>   And made it bring forth grapes good store.
>   But much more him I must adore,
> Who of the laws sowre juice sweet wine did make,
> Ev'n God himself, being pressed for my sake.[19]

Moving from poems focusing upon spiritual pride, "Iron Will Eat the World's Old Beauty Up" (187)[20] is a direct commentary on the modern world as Lewis sees it, employing themes from *Spirits in Bondage* and echoing his distrust of human progress when it occurs at the expense of beauty and truth. He imagines the industrial revolution, particularly the new machines of his own day, involved in the destruction of Nature; as the new cities and buildings emerge (the "iron forests"), they will block out Nature so there will be "no green or growth." In addition, the growing popularity of sensational journalism—"the printing presses with their clapping wings"—shall drown out the wisdom of the past: "Harpy wings, / Filling your minds all day with foolish things, / Will tame the eagle Thought: till she sings / Parrot-like in her cage to please dark kings."[21] The poem also reflects Lewis's disgust with chronological snobbery by parodying it in the last stanza: "The new age, the new art, the new ethic and thought, / And fools crying, Because it has begun / It will continue as it has begun!" Indeed, the inevitability of human progress is undercut throughout the poem, since each stanza ends with a parenthetical portion noting God's continued presence and rule of the world, regardless of human pride and arrogance. The last parenthetical sentence is an apt way to finish the poem: "(Though they [man] lay flat the mountains and dry up the sea, / Wilt thou yet change, as though God were a god?)."

Lewis follows this up with two poems emphasizing the relationship between the spiritual life and sexual temptation.[22] In both, he is frank without being prurient. The three sonnet-like quatrains of "Quick!" (189),[23] recalling portions of *Dymer,* almost certainly deal with autoeroticism, particularly as the speaker emphasizes his struggles when "old festering fire begins to play / Once more within" and he wrenches his "hands the other way." To his credit, the speaker, with the passion of John Donne in his "Holy Sonnet: Batter My Heart," appeals to God to overpower his perverse desire and to replace it with a heavenly one: "Quick, Lord! Before new scorpions bring / New venom—ere fiends blow the fire / A second time—quick, show me that sweet thing / Which, 'spite of all, more deeply I desire."[24] Donne puts it this way: "Batter my heart, three person'd God; for, you / As yet but knocke, breathe, shine, and seeke to mend; / That I may rise, and stand, o'erthrow mee, and bend / Your force, to breake, blowe, burn and make me new."[25] The heat of unbridled lust is continued in "When Lilith Means to Draw Me" (190–91),[26] a poem that suggests there is something ultimately unfulfilling, even emptying, when one reaches the end of repeated sexual gratification. The persona freely confesses that Lilith, symbolizing sexual temptation, "does not overawe me / With beauty's pomp and power." As a matter of fact, he sees the cup (sexual gratification) she offers as unable to satisfy: "Her cup, whereof who taste, / (She promises no better) thirst far more." In spite of this, he ponders why he returns again and again to her cup. His realization is that her offerings, while insipid and sterile, *appear* more satisfying than the dry, arid reality in which he moves and lives: "The witch's wine, / Though promising nothing, seems / In that land of no streams, / To promise best—the unrelished anodyne." These two poems, as well as the sexually explicit portions of *Dymer*, reveal that, like most human beings, Lewis knew the powerful pull of sexual temptation.

"Once the Worm-laid Egg Broke in the Wood" (192–93)[27] is an almost humorous poem in blank verse given from the point of view of an old, lonely dragon; full of self-pity over his isolation, he cannot bring himself to give up his golden hoard in exchange for fellowship with others. Actually, he has even eaten his mate, since "worm grows not to dragon till he eat worm." In particular, he fears men who plot "in the towns to steal my gold," whispering of him, "laying plans, / Merciless men." He prays that God will give him peace, yet it is a hollow request since he wants such peace on his terms: "But ask not that I should give up the gold, / Nor move, nor die; others would get the gold. / Kill, rather, Lord, the men and the other dragons / That I may sleep, go when I will to drink." "Soul's ease," serving God on our terms, praying, like King Claudius in *Hamlet* without truly repenting for the murder of his brother—"My words fly up, my thoughts remain below: / Words without thoughts never to heaven go" (III, iii, 69–70)—these sophisticated spiritual dodges are specious, revealing the bankruptcy of our souls.[28] In addition, the poem implies that many human beings are like the dragon—preferring material things over vital engagement with others. The second dragon poem focuses upon a dragon-slayer rather than a dragon.[29] In "I Have Come Back with Victory Got," the tercets reveal a warrior returning from killing a dragon (195–96).[30] The warrior is filled with joy for having defeated his greatest foe and is prepared to fight even greater battles. After describing the details of his victory, he claims that when he bit into the heart of his vanquished enemy, "I felt a pulse within me start / As though my breast would break apart." Flushed with victory, he feels invincible: "Behemoth is my serving man! / Before the conquered hosts of Pan / Riding tamed Leviathan."[31] Still in celebration, he sings: "RESVRGAM and IO PAEAN, / IO, IO, IO, PAEAN!!"[32] He realizes his conquest of the dragon has been a rite of passage, signifying his bravery, courage, and honor: "Now I know the stake I played for, / Now I know what a worm's made for!" Avoiding pride, the warrior delights in experiencing his victory.[33]

The last three poems of *The Pilgrim's Regress* concern God's authority, man's dignity, and angel's wonder. In "I Am not One that Easily Flits Past in Thought" the speaker considers the authority of God, especially over death and time (197).[34] The rhyming alexandrines express the paradox that God both makes and unmakes: "Therefore among the riddles that no man has read / I put thy paradox, Who liveth and was dead. / As Thou hast made substantially, thou wilt unmake / In earnest and for everlasting." While we might wish to recall those who have died, such musings are really futile:

Whom Thy great *Exit* banishes, no after age
Of epilogue leads back upon the lighted stage.
Where is Prince Hamlet when the curtain's down?
    Where fled
Dreams at the dawn, or colours when the light is sped?
We are thy colours, fugitive, never restored,
Never repeated again. Thou only art the Lord,
Thou only art holy.

In this, the most theocentric poem in *The Pilgrim's Regress*, Lewis affirms God's sovereign rule over time and ends by recalling lines from Psalm 139: "Thou art Lord of the unbreathable transmortal air / Where mortal thinking fails: night's nuptial darkness, where / All lost embraces intermingle and are bless'd, / And all die, but all are, while Thou continuest."[35] This paradoxical ending, that although all die they nonetheless "live" under the eternal authority of God, echoes lines from the *Te Deum*: "When Thou hadst overcome the sharpness of death, / Thou didst open the Kingdom of Heaven to all believers."

"Passing To-day by a Cottage, I Shed Tears" shifts the focus to how God lends us the dignity of being created in His image, replete with both the positive and negative this encompasses (198).[36] For instance, as humans we can know the pain of loss: "Passing to-day by a cottage, I shed tears / When I remembered how once I had dwelled there / With my mortal friends who are dead." Nor does time heal such losses: "I, fool, believed / I had outgrown the local, unique sting, / I had transmuted away (I was deceived) / Into love universal the lov'd thing." That is, God created us, unlike angels, with "the tether and pang of the particular"; because we are created in His image, we can know experientially the heights of pleasure but also the depths of pain. This profound dignity means that while we share His nature, we also enter into His knowledge, one involving responsibility and consequence. Accordingly, though we are small compared to Him, we "quiver with fire's same / Substantial form as Thou—nor reflect merely, / As lunar angel, back to thee, cold flame. / Gods we are, Thou hast said: and we pay dearly." Entering into the divine image means entering into divine suffering, but such price is worth the anguish. The last poem in *The Pilgrim's Regress*, "I Know Not, I" (198–99),[37] plays off the previous poem, as it presents an angel pondering over what it must be like to be a man: "I know not, I, / What the men together say, / How lovers, lovers die / And youth pass away." He has no understanding of romantic love, aging, love of country, and especially human grief: "Why at grave [do] they grieve / For one voice and face, / And not, and not receive / Another in its place." Yet, while the angel has in the past appeared satisfied with his temperate, emotionally balanced existence, the poem's conclusion belies this: "Sorrow it is they call / This cup: whence my lip, / Woe's me, never in all / My endless days must sip." Paradoxically, the angel's sorrow is his regret that he cannot experience the pang of the particular reserved only for human beings.[38]

The sixteen poems in *The Pilgrim's Regress* are Lewis's most moving, unified, and deliberate attempt at sustained religious verse. Although the poems appear within the text of this prose allegory, and thus rightly must be read as commentary on the story of John, the poems also exist outside the text,[39] offering us insight into Lewis's own spiritual and poetic maturation.[40] In them, we see him striving to come to grips with what his new faith in Christ means to his intellectual, sexual, and spiritual life. Lewis never again clusters this many poems around such a unified theme, and so the poems of *The Pilgrim's Regress* testify to the artistic and spiritual progress of his poetic pilgrimage.

POEMS ON PRAYER

As Lewis matured in Christ, he continued to write religious verse, from pieces on the incarnation and the resurrection to ones on the seven deadly sins and the life of the soul. A favorite topic was prayer. He discusses it in disparate prose works such as *The Screwtape Letters* and *Letters to Malcolm*, while petitionary prayer is the subject of the essay, "The Efficacy of Prayer," where he ponders over the following questions: If God is sovereign and omniscient, of what value is prayer? That is, if He knows already what is going to happen, why bother to ask Him to change His mind? Can our petitions to God *really* change His will?[41] In the poems on prayer, Lewis does not offer a systematic theology of prayer, but rather snapshots of his thinking about prayer. For instance, in "Sonnet," Lewis connects the defeat of the cruel Assyrian conqueror, Sennacherib, recorded in 2 Kings 19 and by the historian Herodotus, to the relationship between prayer and divine action.[42] The biblical account suggests that angels intervene to save Israel, while Herodotus ascribes the reason for Sennacherib's defeat to mice "innumerably nibbling all one night . . . to eat his bowstrings piecemeal as warm wind eats ice." This English sonnet in alexandrines melds the two accounts, suggesting that the defeat occurred when angels worked through mice. Lewis does not find this odd, but instead sees in it a glimpse of God working through human prayer: "No stranger that omnipotence should choose to need / Small helps than great—no stranger if His action lingers / Till men have prayed, and suffers their weak prayers indeed / To move as very muscles His delaying fingers." Lewis suggests that the divine masks itself in order to work through the weak, thus lending the latter a dignity not its own: "Who, in His longanimity and love for our / Small dignities, enfeebles, for a time, His power."

More often than not, however, Lewis's poems dealing with prayer do not focus upon the nature of prayer; instead, they *are* prayers. Sometimes they are powerful pleas for God's intercession. The Italian sonnet "Legion" is such a poem. Akin to "Quick" from *The Pilgrim's Regress* and Donne's "Batter My Heart," "Legion" implores God to see the *real* character of the speaker. The real man is the one who desperately turns to Him at the very moment of the poem's composition: "Lord, hear my voice; this present voice, I mean, / Not that which may be speaking an hour hence / When pride or pity of self or craving sense / Blunt the mind's edge, now momentarily clear."[43] He implores God not to consider the myriad of other selves within him that in only a few minutes will feign to be the real him. While he knows God will not override his free will, he beseeches Him to see his real will in this present moment; if not, his warring selves may cancel God's work in him: "Hold me to this. Oh strain / A point; use legal fictions. For, if all / My quarreling selves must bear an equal voice, / Farewell—thou hast created me in vain." The desperate tone suggests the state of the soul familiar to many Christians who struggle with the internal war between the flesh and the spirit. Like Lewis, many have despaired of self and longed for Christ to overrule their wills. This is a poignant prayer for God's grace.

Rather than being an intercession for grace, "They Tell Me, Lord" is a poem in which a speaker comes to a surprising conclusion about the dialogue of prayer.[44] He notes that some think prayer a futile exercise, "since but one voice is heard, it's all dream, / One talker aping two." He admits there is but one voice, but with this twist: The voice is not his, but God's: "Seeing me empty, you forsake / The listener's role and through / My dumb lips breathe and into utterance wake / The thoughts I never knew." Since, therefore, it is God speaking to him through prayer, God has no need to reply to Himself: "While we seem / Two talkers, thou are One forever, and I / No dreamer, but thy dream."[45] Lewis's deeply penetrating spiritual insight about prayer—that when we are empty, then God can speak through and to us—rivals similar ones in *The Problem of Pain* and *Mere Christianity*.

Other poems are prayerful meditations. For instance, Lewis's "No Beauty We Could Desire" is about how one who seeks joy eventually finds it in Christ.[46] The poem begins almost with a sigh as the speaker admits, "Yes, you are everywhere," but then goes on to say he "could never bring the noble Hart to bay." When he tried to track what he longed for, he was thwarted by confusing scents: "Nowhere sometimes, then again everywhere. / Other scents, too, seemed to them almost the same." As a result, he stopped the search for joy through things (including poetry) and made himself available instead to be found by the source of the joy: "Not in Nature, not even in Man, but in one / Particular Man, with a date, so tall, weighing / So much, talking Aramaic, having learned a trade." This realization was the fulcrum leveraging his understanding that in Christ there is a beauty beyond any earthly one: "Not in all food, not in all bread and wine / (Not, I mean, as my littleness requires) / But this wine, this bread . . . no beauty we could desire." In the person of Christ there was no greater beauty for him to desire, and the Eucharist became a visible symbol of this beauty. The joy he found in Christ surpassed all earthly joys, and this poem becomes a measure of Lewis's personal devotion.

Another prayerful meditation is "Arise my Body," a sonnet-like poem written in rhyming alexandrines about experiencing God's forgiveness: "Arise my body, my small body, we have striven / Enough, and He is merciful: we are forgiven."[47] In addition, it recalls how, when one is spent through weary struggles with God and life, the best course is to rest, patiently enduring all that is sent one's way. Lewis uses several effective metaphors to suggest such spent struggles: "A meadow whipt flat under heavy rain, a cup / Emptied and clean, a garment washed and folded up, / Faded in colour, thinned almost to raggedness / By dirt and by the washing of that dirtiness." Although such passivity is not especially pleasant, it is superior to the certain coming of pain involved in everyday living: "Lie cold; consent / To weariness and pardon's watery element. / Drink all the bitter water and the chilly death; / Soon enough comes the riot of warm blood and breath." In this meditation Lewis may be faintly echoing Milton's admonition in his sonnet "When I Consider":

> God doth not need
> Either man's work or his own gifts; who best
> Bear his mild yoke, they serve him best; his State

Is Kingly. Thousands at his bidding speed
And post oe'r Land and Ocean without rest:
They also serve who only stand and wait.

Still another prayerful meditation is "Epitaph," a poem that finds the dead person it commemorates both a microcosm of the universe and a promise of future life in Lenten lands.[48] Its opening lines effectively suggest the vastness of the universe summed up in this person's life: "Here lies the whole world after one / Peculiar mode; a buried sun, / Stars and immensities of sky / And cities here discarded lie."[49] "Epitaph for Helen Joy Davidman" is a later powerful reworking of this epitaph. Lewis concentrates his imagery more intensely in the opening lines of the revision: "Here the whole world (stars, water, air, / And field, and forest, as they were / Reflected in a single mind)." In addition, the revision contains Christian motifs, culminating in the promise of resurrection: "Like cast off clothes was left behind / In ashes yet with hope that she, / Reborn from holy poverty, / In lenten lands, hereafter may / Resume them on her Easter Day."[50]

In addition to prayers of intercession and meditation, several of Lewis's religious poems are confession-like prayers. For example, "Evensong" is a plea one might make before falling asleep.[51] The speaker commits his body and mind to God as "Nature for a season / Conquers our defences." Furthermore, he offers his soul to God, "trusting Thou wilt tend her / Through the deathlike hours, / And all night remake her / To Thy likeness sweetly." The ending is more ominous as he considers death, "slumber's less uncertain Brother," but he transfers the confidence he has in God's watching over his sleep to a similar confidence in his jurisdiction over death: "And, as Thou hast risen, / Raise us in Thy dawn." A confessional prayer with a tone similar to "Legion" is "The Apologist's Evening Prayer," written in heroic couplets.[52] The speaker, famous for his brilliant defenses of the faith, his "cleverness shot forth on Thy behalf / At which, while angels weep, the audience laugh," pauses and asks to be delivered from his own high opinion of himself: "Let me not trust, instead / Of Thee, their thin-worn image of Thy head." As he approaches sleep, he prays to be delivered from all thoughts, even his thoughts of God, and especially from his thoughts of self: "Lord of the narrow gate and the needle's eye, / Take from me all my trumpery lest I die." This frank admission of the danger of spiritual pride in the life of one who defends God is consistent with Lewis's other writings on spiritual pride. He knows well that regardless of his best intentions, an outwardly successful apologist can seek self-glory rather than God's. This prayer is a sober reminder against self-promotion.

The Italian sonnet "Prayer for My Brother" is still another confessional prayer and dates from World War II.[53] It is an apology to God for praying as if his prayer could ever overrule God's intended good for his brother: "How can I ask thee,

Father, to defend / In peril of war my dearest friend to-day, / As though I knew, better than Thou, the way, / Or with more love than thine desired the end?" Yet, Lewis reasons, God has given man prayer to lend him the dignity of agreeing with Him: "But prayer / Thou givest to man, not man to thee: thy laws / Suffering our mortal wish that way to share / The eternal will; at taste of whose air / Man's word becomes, by miracle, a cause." Whether intercession, meditation, or confession, Lewis's poems on prayer are among his best and indicate the central role of prayer in his life.

Other Religious Poems

Lewis rarely wrote poems directly connected to a biblical narrative, perhaps in part because he saw little need to plow well-tilled ground. However, in the instances where he plays off of biblical narratives, the results are engaging. For example, "The Sailing of the Ark" is loosely based on the Old Testament story of Noah and the flood.[54] In one of his most rhythmic and speculative poems, he imagines Ham, the youngest son of Noah, denying entry to one last animal as the rains begin.[55] Ham is shown to be a shirker when one last animal is heard knocking at the door of the Ark. He warns his brothers not to answer because it will awaken their father: "Once he comes to see / What's at the door it's sure to mean more work for you and me."[56] Awakening finally to the pounding on the ark's door, Noah is horrified to discover that the forsaken animal is the unicorn. When it turns away, Noah curses his son: "Now all the world, O Ham, may curse the hour that you were born— / Because of you the Ark must sail without the Unicorn." Despite this somewhat somber theme, the lively musical rhythm of the lines makes this seriocomic poem a must to read aloud.

"Stephen to Lazarus" melds two biblical narratives, as the poem imagines St. Stephen, the first Christian martyr as described in Acts 6:8–7:60, reflecting upon the resurrection of Lazarus found in John 11.[57] In an interesting twist, Stephen wonders if Lazarus was not in fact the first martyr; he reasons this way by noting that while Stephen "gave up no more than life," Lazarus gave up death and its peace. That is, while Stephen left this life and its vale of tears for the peace of death in Christ, Lazarus had to give up the peace of death and "put out a second time to sea / Well knowing that [his] death (in vain / Died once) must be all died again?" Stephen implies, therefore, that Lazarus's resurrection to the pain of life is a more noble martyrdom than his to the peace of death.

While poems linked to a biblical narrative are rare, those connected to biblical themes appear frequently. For example, in addition to "Sonnet" mentioned above, where angels and mice work together to accomplish the defeat of Sennacherib, several poems focus upon angels. In "On Being Human," Lewis notes that while angels have some real advantages over mankind, they are also limited.[58] Although the poem admits angels have direct knowledge of spiritual and philosophical truth denied to mankind, it subtly underscores that they lack the five senses God gave to mankind. Lewis uses humor to show that while angels understand the Platonic eternal forms of earthly realities, they lack rich, sensuous understanding of earthly experience:

> The lavish pinks, the new-mown field, the ravishing
> Sea-smell, the wood-fire smoke that whispers *Rest;*
> The tremor on the rippled pool of memory
> Which from each scent in widening circle goes,
> The pleasure and the pang—can angels measure it?
> An angel has no nose.[59]

Lewis's point, therefore, is that in some ways it is better to be human than angelic. The playfulness of this poem is characteristic of many others, and its theme is an insightful gloss to the angelic *eldila* of the Ransom space trilogy. There Lewis describes angels as "white and semi-transparent—rather like ice" with "inorganic" voices speaking syllables sounding "more as if they were played on an instrument than as if they were spoken . . . as if rock or crystal or light had spoken."[60]

Two religious poems deal with the biblical theme of Christ's nativity. "The Turn of the Tide" is finely crafted; for instance, Lewis uses internal rhyme in each odd line and final rhyme in each even line. In this poem Lewis focuses upon the very moment of Christ's birth and how this marks a universal turn of the tide: from the certitude of death for all to the promise of new life for all.[61] Profoundly influenced by Milton's "On the Morning of Christ's Nativity," Lewis, in a slow and deliberate fashion, chronicles how the spiritual impact of Christ's birth quietly yet inexorably sweeps over the world, invigorating and bringing to life a dead, silent planet.[62] For instance, at the moment just before Christ's birth, Lewis pictures a world on the verge of its dying moment: "Breathless was the air over Bethlehem; black and bare / The fields; hard as granite were the clods; / Hedges stiff with ice; the sedge, in the vice / Of the ponds, like little iron rods. / The deathly stillness spread from Bethlehem." By comparing the frozen, dead landscape to the adamantine spiritual torpor of mankind before Christ's birth, Lewis effectively highlights the world's spiritual ebb tide. He vividly portrays this deadly pallor by noting various notions connected with Christ's nativity, beginning with Caesar and the Palatine and culminating in great Galactic lords asking:

> "Is this perhaps the last
> Of our story and the glories of our crown?—

The entropy worked out?—the central redoubt
   Abandoned?—The world-spring running down?"
Then they could speak no more. Weakness overbore
   Even them; they were as flies in a web,
In lethargy stone-dumb. The death had almost come,
   And the tide lay motionless at ebb.

Yet at this critical juncture in the history of the universe, Lewis likens Christ's birth to a stabbing "shock / Of returning life, the start, the burning pang at heart, / Setting galaxies to tingle and rock." This event promises "rumor and noise of resuming joys / Along the nerves of the universe."

Symbolic of this renewal is "a music infinitely small," yet clear, loud, and deep: "Such a note as neither Throne nor Potentate had known / Since the Word created the abyss." At this universal sound, "Heaven danced," "revel, mirth and shout / Descended to" earth, and the frozen universe began to thaw: "Saturn laughed and lost his latter age's frost / And his beard, Niagara-like, unfroze." The reviving universe reaches its fever pitch of rebirth in the reigniting of the Phoenix, which, as we will see below in "The Phoenix," functions as a metaphor for Christ:[63]

A shiver of re-birth and deliverance round the Earth
   Went gliding; her bonds were released;
Into broken light the breeze once more awoke the seas,
   In the forest it wakened every beast;
Capripods fell to dance from Taproban to France,
   Leprechauns from Down to Labrador;
In his green Asian dell the Phoenix from his shell
   Burst forth and was the Phoenix once more.

In spite of the universal significance and magnitude of this paradoxical rebirth—the condemned cosmos revived by God's incarnation—Lewis manages to treat it with great tenderness and poignancy: "So Death lay in arrest. But at Bethlehem the bless'd / Nothing greater could be heard / Than sighing wind in the thorn, the cry of One new-born, / And cattle in stable as they stirred." Omnipotent God—Author, Creator, and Sustainer of all that was, is, and will be—contracted into a little child lying seemingly unnoticed in this most humble of birth places. Furthermore, in these last lines Lewis alludes to Christ's crown of thorns and crucifixion by noting the ominous thorns through which the wind sighs. In his deft handling of the theme, images, and language in "The Turn of the Tide," we experience one of Lewis's most powerful poems.

"The Nativity" continues Lewis's interest in God's physical incarnation, but here he focuses instead upon the animals present at the nativity and links them to human parallels.[64] Specifically, Lewis personifies three animals and attributes we associate with them to the state of the speaker's spiritual condition. First, he says he is slow like an ox, but he sees "glory in the stable grow" so that "with the ox's dullness" he eventually might gain "an ox's strength." Second, he says he is stubborn as an ass, but he sees "my Saviour where I looked for hay" so that through his ass-like folly he may learn "the patience of a beast." Finally, he is like a straying sheep watching "the manger where my Lord is laid" so that his "baa-ing nature" (repentance) would someday win "some woolly innocence!" The spiritual condition of the speaker—from being as slow and dull as an ox, to as stubborn and hard as an ass, to as broken and contrite as an erring sheep—is nicely encapsulated in this brief reflection.

Still other religious poems concern God's glory, as does the Italian sonnet "Noon's Intensity."[65] Utilizing the light of the sun as a metaphor for God's glory, the octet identifies God's "alchemic beams [that] turn all to gold." The speaker then describes how sunlight, and by extension God's glory, is spread over all the earth: "From the night / You will not yet withdraw her silver light, / And often with Saturnian tints the cold / Atlantic swells at morning shall enfold / The Cornish cliffs burnished with copper bright." The poem goes on to suggest our sight may one day be "trained by slow degrees" until "we have such sight / As dares the pure projection to behold." Biblical allusions come into focus in the sestet. For instance, the lines "When Sol comes ascendant, it may be / More perfectly in him our eyes shall see / All baser virtues," recall Moses' encounter with God in Exodus 33:18–19a: "Then Moses said, 'I pray Thee, show me Thy glory!' And He said, 'I Myself will make all My goodness pass before you, and will proclaim the name of the Lord before you.'"[66] The speaker delights in the fact that now he can "hear you [God] talking / And yet not die." He adds that until he is given the opportunity "the pure projection to behold," God has "left free, / Unscorched by your own noon's intensity / One cool and evening hour for garden walking." The final line alludes to a pre-lapsarian state and the immediate fellowship the speaker has with God when they would walk together in "the cool of the day" (Genesis 3:8). This ending also echoes the descent of Perelandra-Venus, a reflection of God's glory and love, at the conclusion of *That Hideous Strength*: "And now it came. It was fiery, sharp, bright and ruthless, ready to kill, ready to die, outspeeding light: it was Charity, not as mortals imagine it, not even as it has been humanised for them since the Incarnation of the Word, but the translunary virtue, fallen upon them direct from the Third Heaven, unmitigated. They were blinded, scorched, deafened. They thought it would burn their bones. They could not bear that it should continue. They could not bear that it should cease. So Perelandra, triumphant among planets, whom men call Venus, came and was with them in the room."[67] "Noon's Intensity" similarly celebrates God's glory and his compelling love for man.

A related poem is "The Phoenix," in which Christ's glory is considered.[68] To do this, Lewis employs the Egyptian myth of the fabulous bird that is reborn every five hundred years as a metaphor for Christ's glory. After consuming itself in fire, the phoenix rises renewed from the ashes to begin another long life. For this reason it is often seen as an emblem of immortality. In the poem, the bird flies into the speaker's garden, its brilliant flame lighting up the entire landscape. With great delight, the speaker shouts out and praises its glory, and he is overheard by a passing "dark girl." Together they approach the "Wonder," but, ironically, when they reach the bird, he sees her eyes focused on him, "not on the Bird." The speaker then warns her against looking in him for what she should find in the Bird: "Make not of your spoon your meat, for silver / . . . contains no nourishment." The speaker warns the dark girl against hoping to find in him purpose and meaning (via romantic love) instead of finding them in the glory of Bird: "I will be all things, any thing, to you, save only that. / Break not our hearts by telling me you never saw / The Phoenix, that my trumpery silhouette, thrusting between, / Made an eclipse." In effect, the Bird is Christ. This becomes evident when he tells her he dreams of catching for the Bird "a silver, shining fish such as He loves" as an offering: "Having little of my own to offer Him, / [I] was building much on this miraculous draught." That is, rather than giving himself, he dreams he can give Christ "shining fish"—worldly efforts, spiritual practices, material tokens, or similar substitutes—rather than that which is required: himself and his thoughts, passions, ideas, and addictions. What needs to happen is for his resurrection to be grafted upon Christ's glory. That the speaker has yet to realize this is apparent in the irony of the poem's concluding lines: "If the line breaks, / Oh with what empty hands you [the girl] send me back to Him!"

Several poems are introspective considerations of the spiritual life. For example, "On Another Theme from Nicolas of Cusa"[69] with its tetrameter couplets is gem-like, a second poem inspired by Lewis's reading of Nicolas of Cusa, particularly his writings on plant growth where he cleverly contrasts the different ways body and soul are affected by food. The poem explores first the chemistry of how the body takes in food, changes it, and uses it to produce energy: "Firmness of apple, fluted shape / Of celery, or the bloom of grape / I grind and mangle as I eat. / Then in dark, salt, internal heat / Obliterate their natures by / The mastering act that makes them I." But next the poem considers the paradox of what happens to the soul when it consumes its food (good and truth): "But when the soul partakes of good / Or truth, which are her savoury food, / By a far subtler chemistry / It is not they that change but she, / Who lets them enter with the state / Of conquerors her surrendered gate, / Or mirror-like digests their ray / By turning luminous as they." While the body consumes food in order to change it for its use, the soul consumes "food" and is changed by it. This paradoxical spiritual insight is as profound as many appearing in *Mere Christianity* or *The Problem of Pain*.

A different kind of spiritual insight occurs in "Deadly Sins," where Lewis reflects upon the all-pervasive nature of the seven deadly sins in human life.[70] The history of the seven deadly sins in the church, especially the development of a list of seven, is somewhat problematic. Early church fathers, including Hermas, Tertullian, and Augustine, while never actually listing specific "deadly" sins, did suggest that some sins were worse than others, perhaps with 1 John 5:16–17 in mind: "If anyone sees his brother committing a sin not leading to death, he shall ask and God will for him give life to those who commit sin not leading to death. There is a sin leading to death; I do not say that he should make request for this. All unrighteousness is sin, and there is a sin not leading to death." What eventually resulted, therefore, were numerous lists of especially harmful sins. However, the list that came to be most influential in the church was the one developed by Gregory the Great (540–605) characterized by its Latin acronym, *saligia: superbia* (pride), *avaritia* (greed), *luxuria* (luxury, later lust), *invidia* (envy), *gula* (gluttony), *ira* (anger), and *acedia* (sloth).[71]

Lewis was no stranger to the literary life of these sins, since they appear in works he knew well, including William Langland's *Piers Plowman*, Dante's *Divine Comedy*, Chaucer's "The Parson's Tale," and Spenser's *Faerie Queene*. Furthermore, Lewis writes about them himself in *The Allegory of Love*. For example, while commenting on Langland, Lewis says that his "excellent satiric comedy, as displayed in the behavior of the seven Deadly Sins belongs to a tradition as old as the *Ancren Riwle*."[72] In addition, in other works he refers to specific sins on the list. For instance, in *Mere Christianity* he saves an entire chapter for pride ("the great sin"); in *Screwtape Letters* he devotes letters to lust (IX, XVII) and pride (XXIV); and in *The Great Divorce* he pictures sinners unable to choose heaven because of greed, sloth, and envy. Accordingly, it is no surprise he writes a poem centered on the seven deadly sins.[73]

He begins by noting how all of them "through our lives [their] meshes run / Deft as spiders' catenation, / Crossed and crossed again and spun / Finer than the fiend's temptation." He then devotes a four-line stanza to each. Sloth, "deadly" according to the church fathers because it deadened one to vigorous spiritual life, Lewis portrays in like manner: "Sloth that would find out a bed / Blind to morning, deaf to waking, / Shuffling shall at last be led / To the peace that knows no breaking." In *Piers Plowman*, Langland shows Sloth similarly: "I've never visited the sick, or prisoners in their cells. And I'd much rather hear a filthy story or watch a shoemakers' farce in summer, or laugh at a lot of lying scandal about my neighbours, than listen to all that Gospel stuff—Matthew and Mark and Luke and John. As for vigils and fast-days, I give all that a miss; and in Lent I lie in bed with my girl in my arms till mass and matins are well and truly over. I then make off for the friars' church, and if I get to the place before the priest's 'go, mass is finished,' I feel I've done my bit. Sometimes I never get to confession even once in a year, unless a bout of sickness scares me into it; and then I produce some confused mishmash or other."[74] About greed, Lewis writes: "Avarice, while she finds an end, / Counts but small the largest treasure. / Whimperingly at last she'll bend / To take free what has no measure." Lewis uses a clever sexual pun to illustrate the pull of lust: "Lechery, that feels sharp lust / Sharper from each promised staying, / Goes at long last— go she must— / Where alone is sure allaying." In each case, the particular sin leads eventually to God, because the sin repeated does not ultimately satisfy: "So inexorably thou / On thy shattered foes pursuing / Never a respite dost allow / Save what works their own undoing." Ironically, deadly sins both consume and feed our fractured experience.

In spite of sin's very real presence in our lives, Lewis's most powerful religious poem, "Love's as Warm as Tears," is not about sin; instead it is about love.[75] In four brief stanzas, Lewis helps us see that love exists in at least four forms reminiscent of his *The Four Loves*. The loves are often in striking contrast to one another. For instance, the first stanza focuses upon affectionate love, or what he calls *storge:* "Love's as warm as tears, / Love is tears: / Pressure within the brain / Tension at the throat." This is familiar, weeping, tender, emotional love common to those who know each other well. Yet in the second stanza, he considers bold, passionate, burning love: "Love's as fierce as fire, / Love is fire: / All sorts—infernal heat / Clinkered with greed and pride." This is what he calls *eros;* it is the consuming, painful, possessive, sexual love known best to lovers. In the third stanza he writes of love that is anticipated: "Love's as fresh as spring, / Love is spring: / Bird-song hung in the air, / Cool smells in a wood." Such love is expectant, exciting, and encouraging.

The final stanza tells us of sacrificial, selfless, unconditional love; it is a hard love born of total giving, what he calls *agape:*

> Love's as hard as nails,
>   Love is nails:
> Blunt, thick, hammered through
> The medial nerves of One
> Who, having made us, knew
> The thing He had done,
> Seeing (with all that is)
> Our cross, and His.

The tone of this stanza is unexpected, and the abrupt shift to the cross and Christ's suffering catches us by surprise; we can feel the pounding of the hammer and the nails piercing flesh. At the same time, this refocus is entirely appropriate and raises the poem from being just another poem about human love to a moving testimony about the depth and breadth of divine love. In order to secure man for Himself, God, who spans the universe with his outstretched hands, contracts Himself onto the cross and willingly takes our place of suffering. This is certain, costly, compassionate love. "Love's as Warm as Tears" is without doubt Lewis's finest religious poem.

"Hermione in the House of Paulina" has thematic connections to "Love's as Warm as Tears." The poem is a lovely consideration of Hermione from Shakespeare's *The Winter's Tale,* spurned wife of the insanely jealous Leontes, King of Sicilia.[76] Falsely accused of infidelity, Hermione is brutally treated by Leontes, and everyone believes she dies of a broken heart. Actually she is secretly cared for by her lady-in-waiting, Paulina, for sixteen years (Lewis says fifteen years) in an isolated chapel before she is dramatically reunited with Leontes and her family. This poignant poem captures the still, quiet beauty of her years in the chapel: "How soft it rains, how nourishingly warm and green / Is grown the hush'd solemnity of this low house / . . . Oh how the quiet cures / My pain and sucks the burning from my breast." Whatever bitterness she may have initially had has been replaced by the peace she achieves through suffering: "It [the quiet] sucked out all the poison of my will and drew / All hot rebellions from me." However, Hermione's great insight is her finding in the dedicated love of Paulina the incarnate love of God: "Pardon, that when you brought me here, / Still drowned in bitter passions, drugged with life, / I did not know . . . in faith, I thought you were / Paulina, old Antigonus' young wife." This is a moving poem, transparently commemorating God's love acted out through other people.[77]

Lewis's religious verse reveals him moving from the cruel, malicious deity of *Spirits in Bondage,* to the possessive, jealous Yahweh of *The Pilgrim's Regress,* to the sacrificial savior of "Love's as Warm as Tears."[78] In addition, the religious poems reveal Lewis as using poetry to reflect deeply about life in Christ while avoiding self-conscious navel-gazing or self-righteous posturing. Perhaps most noticeable is the absence of mawkish, maudlin emotion, too often a detrimental characteristic of religious verse. While Lewis's religious poems as a whole are not as effective as those of George Herbert and John Donne—the two poets who combined most winsomely their faith in Christ with their craft as lyric poets—Lewis's religious poetry offers powerful testimony to the role that faith and verse played in his imaginative life.

In reviewing Lewis's comical, satirical, contemplative, and religious poems, several points should be noted. First, the poems of the 1930s are split between the theologically introspective pieces of *The Pilgrim's Regress* and eleven others, the majority with literary or environmental themes. Second, Lewis's production of these poems peaked in the 1940s, suggesting this was the decade where he reached his imaginative pinnacle. This is supported when we note that this was also the decade when he wrote *The Problem of Pain, The Screwtape Letters, The Abolition of Man, Perelandra, The Great Divorce, That Hideous Strength, Miracles,* and *The Lion, the Witch and the Wardrobe.* Moreover, during this same time period he delivered the BBC radio broadcasts that later resulted in *Mere Christianity.* It is tempting, therefore, to think of Lewis during the 1940s as a literary dynamo. Third, the number of poems he published in the 1950s dropped significantly, ranging from pointed satires to dark prophecies to mature musings. While there is no way to determine why he published fewer poems, given the passing of Mrs. Moore and his ever-growing responsibilities, including the start of his friendship with Joy and his shift from Oxford to Cambridge, the simple demands upon his time may have precluded opportunities to work on poems. Finally, Lewis's "public" poetry—poems that are primarily comic and satiric—is often witty, combative, percussive, shrill, and rhetorical. When he turns to social commentary, he is critical of the contemporary, favoring traditional core values and "stock responses." On the other hand, his "private" poetry—poems that are contemplative and religious—is personal, subjective, reflective, and poignant. As he considers issues central to the human condition, he engages in analysis and frequently is tentative, open ended, searching, and questioning. Throughout all, Lewis employed the topical poems to give voice to his muted but never abandoned poetic sensibilities.

CHAPTER NINE

Poetic Prose: Lewis's Poetic Legacy

Notwithstanding Lewis's desire to achieve acclaim as a poet, he never did. Although he consciously considered himself a poet when writing *Spirits in Bondage*, *Dymer*, and many of his topical poems, he wrote his best "poetry" in prose. That is, Lewis's poetic legacy is seen most clearly in his prose, where poetic qualities abound— rich lyrical passages, vivid description; striking similes, metaphors, and analogies; careful diction; and concern for the sound of words. In addition, the fact that Lewis saw himself early in life primarily as a poet begs that we take a new approach in our understanding of his mature prose, both nonfiction and fiction. Lewis's prose needs to be explored from the perspective of his being an earnest if minor poet. Jerry Daniel points the way here when he notes that Lewis has "the soul of a poet . . . [and] all works were 'poetry' to him in the sense that the 'feel' or 'taste' was primary."[1] In light of this, Lewis's prose poetry throughout the Ransom trilogy is noteworthy, and this chapter emphasizes how much of his prose in *Perelandra* "works" like poetry. Furthermore, critical scrutiny of the rhythm and cadence of his prose reflects his deeply felt poetic sensibility, and the prose imagery of *A Grief Observed* suggests that it was inspired by his deeply felt poetic imagination.

The Poetry of Prose: C. S. Lewis, Ruth Pitter, and *Perelandra*

An examination of the correspondence from C. S. Lewis to Ruth Pitter (1897–1992) and her journal recollections of the same (with one exception, her letters to Lewis have not survived) reveal that the two shared a deep love for poetry. Pitter, a poet of no small stature, received copious notes from Lewis about her poetry. Likewise,

Lewis often asked Pitter's advice about his own verse, admiring her native ability and appreciating her critical insights. In effect, Pitter became Lewis's mentor as a poet. While Pitter was the better poet, she found much to admire in Lewis's verse; ironically, however, it was in the prose of *Perelandra,* the second book of the Ransom trilogy, that she discovered Lewis's most effective poetry. Accordingly, in order to explore thoroughly the poetic elements of *Perelandra,* we will first survey the lively discussions Pitter and Lewis had about poetry. Second, we will note specific poetic qualities of *Perelandra.* Third, we will investigate Pitter's request to transcribe into verse portions of the end of *Perelandra,* including an examination of portions of her transcription.

While Lewis struggled unsuccessfully to gain recognition as a poet, Pitter had extensive poetic credentials.[2] In total she produced eighteen volumes of verse.[3] Her *A Trophy of Arms* (1936) won the Hawthornden Prize for Poetry in 1937. In 1954 she won the William Heinemann Foundation Award, in 1955 she became the first woman to receive the Queen's Gold Medal for Poetry, and she appeared regularly on the BBC program *The Brain Trust.* The Royal Society of Literature elected her to its highest honor, a Companion of Literature, in 1974, and she was appointed Commander of the British Empire in 1979. For all this, she remained connected to her country roots. Her poetry offers penetrating observations of the natural world she lovingly celebrates, while often moving toward mystical religious themes in the tradition of Thomas Traherne.[4] For instance, "Sudden Heaven" from *A Trophy of Arms* (1936) combines a clipped, terse style with an incisive eye to create a poem of striking power:

All was as it had ever been—
The worn familiar book,
The oak beyond the hawthorn seen,
The misty woodland's look:

The starling perched upon the tree
With his long tress of straw—
When suddenly heaven blazed on me,
And suddenly I saw:

Saw all as it would ever be,
In bliss too great to tell;
For ever safe, for ever free,
All bright with miracle:

Saw as in heaven the thorn arrayed,
The tree beside the door;

And I must die—but O my shade
Shall dwell there evermore.[5]

"Sudden Heaven" is filled with rich natural images, including "misty woodland's look," "starling perched upon the tree," and "long tress of straw." Yet its real power comes through Pitter's subtle infusion of biblical images, motifs, and allusions such as "suddenly heaven blazed on me," "bliss too great to tell," "bright with miracle," and "the thorn arrayed." Most impressive is her deft use of the tree as an image both of Nature, where the starling perches, and the divine, where we envision Christ and his crown of thorns.

However, while she was brought up in a religious family, her own faith became energized only after listening to Lewis's radio broadcast talks (later published as *Mere Christianity*) near the end of World War II. Depressed after a hard workday in a wartime crucible factory, she wondered if she could go on: "I stopped in the middle of Battersea Bridge one dreadful March night, when it was cold and the wind was howling over the bridge, and it was dark as the pit; and I leaned over the parapet and thought: Like this I cannot go on. I must find somebody or something. Like this I cannot go on" (cited by Russell in Cecil's *Homage*, 28). She claimed the broadcast talks did much to deliver her from the despair she felt about to consume her as the war was coming to an end.[6] Consequently, out of a sense of gratitude she began to write Lewis shortly after the war was over.

Journal entries show that Pitter writes in early July 1946 asking to meet Lewis. In his response to her first letter, he expresses surprise that she is hesitant in asking for the meeting: "But what you should be 'trepidant' about in calling on a middle aged don I can't imagine" (July 13, 1946, *RP*, 001). The connection between them is poetry, since she recalls that her friend Herbert Palmer "at that time was determined to 'bring out' Lewis as a poet."[7] A visit to Lewis followed shortly afterwards, as her letter to Lewis recalling the visit indicates: "I have hunted these out [her *The Spirit Watches* (1939), *A Mad Lady's Garland* (1934), and *The Bridge* (1945)] wishing you to see something more recent than the 'Trophy' [*A Trophy of Arms* (1936)], and particularly that you should see 'A Mad Lady's Garland', which though only grotesque & satirical . . . I think is my best & most original. . . . My visit to you has discountenanced all the gypsy's warnings of people who say 'never meet your favourite authors. They are so disappointing'" (July 17, 1946).[8] Pitter's delight in their meeting is evidenced by her closing remark, but even though they had gotten on so well in their visit,[9] she could not have been prepared for Lewis's high praise for her poetry in his next letter: "*Trophy of Arms* is enough for one letter for it has most deeply delighted me. I was prepared for the more definitely mystical poems, but not for this cool, classical quality. You do it time after time—create a silence and vacancy and awe all round the poem. If the Lady in *Comus* had written poetry one imagines it wd. have been rather like this." About some lines Lewis is ecstatic: "'Cadaverous in Storm' is marvellous and 'then alleluia all my gashes cry' [from "Solemn Meditations"] just takes one up into regions poetry hasn't visited for nearly a hundred years." Her poetry is so good that Lewis is dissuaded from sharing his with her: "I meant to send you something of mine but I shan't. It all sounds like a brass band after yours. . . . Why wasn't I told you were as good as this?" (July 19, 1946, *RP*, 002–003).

The high praise of this letter sets the tone of Lewis's correspondence to Pitter. Time and again he is powerfully affected by her poetry, and he lavishes praise on her verse. At the same time, however, he is critical as well. For instance, about one of her longer poems, he says: "As a rule, the bigger a thing is physically the less it works in literature. One ghost is always more disquieting than ten; no good fight in a story can have more than a dozen or so combatants: the death of a million men is less tragic than that of one." Also, he cautions her against coming under the influence of modern poetry: "'Funeral Wreaths' [from *The Bridge*]. No, no, no. The Moderns have got at you. Don't *you* of all people, be taken in by the silly idea that by simply mentioning dull or sordid facts in sub-poetical rhythms you can make a poem. The effect is certain, but it's not worth getting. You know far better than that" (July 24, 1946, *RP*, 005). More often than not, however, Lewis can only offer compliments, sometimes spiced with characteristic humor. Upon receiving a copy of Pitter's *The Rude Potato* (1941), he writes: "Thanks for the book. I look forward to finding out how rude a potato can be. All the ones I meet are civil enough" (July 21, 1947, *RP*, 030). And, after rereading *The Bridge*, he writes, "A lot of it is stunning good, you know" (Aug. 24, 1949, *RP*, 041).

His greatest praise comes in a letter after he has read *The Ermine: Poems 1942–1952*:

Dear Miss Pitter, or (to speak more accurately) Bright Angel! I'm in a sea of glory! Of course I haven't had time to read it [*The Ermine*] properly, and there'll be another, more sober, letter presently. This is just a line to be going on with, and to assure you at once that the new volume is an absolute CORKER. I had feared that you might be one of those who, like Wordsworth, leave their talent behind at conversion: and now—oh glory—you come up shining out of the frost [a writer's block she had endured] far better than you were before. 'Man's despair is like the Arabian sun' [a line from "The World Is Hollow"]—I seriously doubt if there's any religious lyric between that one and [George] Herbert on the same level. And then my eye strays to the opposite page and gets the "dying-dolphin green" [a phrase from "The Captive Bird of Paradise"]. And "What we merit—A silence like a sword" [a line from "The Other"]. I wonder have you yourself any notion how good some of these are? But, as you see,

I'm drunk on them at this present. Glory be! Blessings on you! As sweet as sin and as innocent as milk. Thanks forever, Yours in great excitement, C. S. Lewis. (May 12, 1953, *RP,* 060–061)

Several days later he still is overwhelmed by *The Ermine:* "The brightness does not fade: appealing from Lewis drunk to Lewis sober, I still find this an exquisite collection. When I start picking out my favourites, I find I am picking out nearly all. . . . I do congratulate you again and again. I hope you are as happy about the poems as you ought to be" (May 15, 1953, *RP,* 062–063).

On a different occasion, Lewis chides Pitter for waiting so long to send her remarks on poems he has sent her: "On a railway platform this morning (I am just back from Malvern) I made a resolution. I said 'I will no longer be deterred by the fear of seeming to press for an opinion about my poems from writing to find out whether R. P. is dead, ill, in prison, emigrated, or simply never got my letter.' So it was with great pleasure that I found yours awaiting me" (Aug. 31, 1948, *RP,* 032). In her letter she apparently offered sharp criticism about his recent poems, so a month later he writes her, still musing on her remarks: "I was silent about yr. criticism because I was still chewing it and have been early taught not to speak with my mouth full. And I'm still chewing and can't really quite eat it. a. Because of a deep suspicion that . . . [your criticism] is really only a rationalisation of a deep and inarticulate (and prob. correct) feeling that mine isn't really poetry after all—a feeling repressed by your kindness and liking for my prose work and coming out in this form. b. By an understanding of the charge (supposing it not to be a rationalisation) wh. is still v. imperfect. But I'll try some more on you anon, and we may hammer it out" (Sept. 29, 1948, *RP,* 034). Pitter's journal recollection of this incident provides the most detailed account of her personal evaluation of Lewis as a poet:

> Now, I wonder. *Is* his poetry after all not? About how many poets or poems would readers agree 100% or even 50%? "The peaks of poetry are shiftingly veiled, and different readers catch different glimpses of the transcendental." I should like to know more about the actual process of conception in his case. Did his great learning, a really staggering skill in verse inhibit the poetry? Did he ever (like most of us) catch some floating bit of emotional thistledown & go on from that, or did he plan on a subject like an architect? (Producing perhaps short epics?) He had a great stock of the makings of a poet: strong visual memory, strong recollections of childhood: desperately strong yearnings for lost Paradise & hoped Heaven ("sweet desire"): not least a strong primitive intuition of the diabolical (not merely the horrific). In fact his whole life was oriented & motivated by an almost uniquely-persisting *child's* sense of glory and

of nightmare. The adult events were received into a medium still as pliable as wax, wide open to the glory, and equally vulnerable, with a man's strength to feel it all, and a great scholar's & writer's skills to express and to interpret. It is almost as though the adult disciplines, notably the technique of his verse, had largely inhibited his poetry, which is perhaps, after all, most evident in his prose. I think he wanted to be a poet more than anything. Time will show. But if it was *magic* he was after, he achieved this sufficiently elsewhere.[10] (Sept. 29, 1948)

While clearly sympathetic to Lewis's poetry, Pitter knows it is in his prose where he makes "magic," an assessment shared by many. Specifically, she finds his most moving poetry in the prose ending of *Perelandra*.[11]

Before turning to the transcriptions, a brief examination of *Perelandra* confirms that it contains some the most attractive passages of sustained poetic prose Lewis ever wrote.[12] While the majority of the book is prose narrative, approximately one quarter of the novel may be deemed poetic.[13] Thomas Peters claims, "*Perelandra* reads like poetry," and Kath Filmer argues that Lewis's frequent use of metaphor in his poetry is readily transferred to his prose, noting his "fiction has that imaginative, 'magical' quality that he failed to express in his poetry."[14] In explaining what stimulated his writing the story, Lewis characteristically connects it with his poetic impulse of conceiving images: "The starting point for my second novel, *Perelandra*, was my mental pictures of floating islands. The whole of the rest of my labours in a sense consisted in building up a world in which floating islands could exist."[15] Walter Hooper argues the novel may have had its genesis in poetic form, citing the only surviving fragment:

> The floating islands, the flat golden sky
> At noon, the peacock sunset: tepid waves
> With the land sliding over them like a skin:
> The alien Eve, green-bodied, stepping forth
> To meet my hero from her forest home,
> Proud, courteous, unafraid; no thought infirm
> Alters her cheek.[16]

In addition, in recalling all he saw on Perelandra, Ransom corrects Lewis (the character in the novel) for assuming "It's all too vague for you to put in words": "On the contrary, it is words that are vague. The reason why the thing can't be expressed is that it's too definite for language."[17] Indeed, chapter 3 in its entirety and much of chapter 4 can be cited as evidence of this, as in them Lewis creates lavish verbal pictures of the idyllic, paradisal environment Ransom enjoys. What he writes is a lyrical shower unprecedented in his fiction and characterized by a cloudburst of figurative language, including effusive metaphors, similes, and symbols.[18]

For example, after Ransom realizes he is floating and then swimming in the ocean of Perelandra, he tastes the water and is delighted by the first of a series of unanticipated sensuous pleasures: "Though he had not been aware of thirst till now, his drink gave him a quite astonishing pleasure. It was almost like meeting Pleasure itself for the first time. He buried his flushed face in the green translucence, and when he withdrew it, found himself once more on the top of a wave" (35). Naked and awash in the water, Ransom is completely open to experiencing his senses in a unique, primeval fashion. He sees "a rich, varied world in which nothing, for the moment, seemed palpable. . . . [Eventually looking at the sky, he sees] the golden roof of that world quivering with a rapid variation of paler lights as a ceiling quivers at the reflected sunlight from the bath-water when you step into your bath on a summer morning" (34–35). He describes his first sight of the floating islands as "variegated in colours like a patch-work quilt—flame-colour, ultramarine, crimson, orange, gamboge, and violet" (36). Lewis balances his numerous lengthy visual descriptions with ones highlighting smell, as when Ransom first walks through a forest: "The smells in the forest were beyond all that he had ever conceived. To say that they made him feel hungry and thirsty would be misleading; almost, they created a new kind of hunger and thirst, a longing that seemed to flow over from the body into the soul and which was a heaven to feel" (41). Ransom also notes the utter silence, yet "the sense of his solitude became intense without becoming at all painful—only adding, as it were, a last touch of wildness to the unearthly pleasures that surrounded him" (42).

However, Ransom's heightened taste buds may be the most memorable episode in this riot of the senses. As he moves through a forest "where great globes of yellow fruit hung from the trees—clustered as toy-balloons are clustered on the back of the balloon-man and about the same size," he picks one. Inadvertently, he punctures a rind and places the opening to his lips: "He had meant to extract the smallest, experimental sip, but the first taste put his caution to flight. It was, of course, a taste, just as his thirst and hunger had been thirst and hunger. But then it was so different from every other taste that it seemed mere pedantry to call it a taste at all. It was like the discovery of a totally new *genus* of pleasures, something unheard of among men, out of all reckoning, beyond all covenant. For one draught of this on earth wars would be fought and nations betrayed. It could not be classified. He could never tell us, when he came back to the world of men, whether it was sharp or sweet, savoury or voluptuous, creamy or piercing" (42). As his first day comes to a close, Ransom looks across the ocean and the sunset: "The sea, far calmer now than he had yet seen it, smoked towards heaven in huge dolomites and elephants of blue and purple vapour, and a light wind, full of sweet-ness, lifted the hair on his forehead. The day was burning to death" (43). All these overwhelming sensuous experiences are linked by feelings of excessive pleasure untainted by guilt, as if old earthly prohibitions against enjoying oneself too much are foreign to this world: "The strange sense of excessive pleasure . . . seemed somehow to be communicated to him through all his senses at once . . . [and] there was an exuberance or prodigality of sweetness about the mere act of living which our race finds it difficult not to associate with forbidden and extravagant actions" (37). The next day Ransom's sensuous feast continues, as he encounters wonder-fully soothing bubble trees that shower him with a refreshingly cool and intense aromatic liquid, yellow gourds with a flavor, while not as exotic as the fruit of the previous day, that hint at protein-like heartiness, and a small, friendly dragon who becomes his first companion on Perelandra.

After this, Ransom meets the Green Lady, and the poetic prose, while never entirely absent, retires into the background. The rhetorical debates among Wes-ton, the Green Lady, and Ransom dominate chapters 7–14, culminating in the death of Weston and Ransom's descent into Hell and subsequent emergence from the cave in chapter 15. He recovers from his ordeal by being "breast-fed by the planet Venus herself," enjoying sustenance from a grape-like fruit that always seemed to be hanging near his tired, battered body, the "endless sound of rejoicing water," and a reviving song: "Now high in air above him, now welling up as if from glens and valleys far below, it floated through his sleep and was the first sound at every waking. It was formless as the song of a bird, yet it was not a bird's voice. As a bird's voice is to a flute, so this was to a cello: low and ripe and tender, full-bellied, rich and golden brown: passionate too, but not with the passions of men" (185). Regaining his strength, he moves down the mountain and enjoys deep blue streamer bushes with "soft, almost impalpable, caresses of the long thin leaves on his flesh," thickets of flowers that shower his head and cover his sides with pollen, and especially the song of a shy, horse-like creature (189–91).

When Ransom eventually meets Malacandra (Mars) and Perelandra (Venus), passages of poetic prose begin to cascade one upon the other. In describing their bodies, Lewis writes that while they are white, "a flush of diverse colours began at about the shoulders and streamed up the necks and flickered over face and head and stood out around the head like plumage or a halo" (199). As the animals gather to witness the enthronement of the King and the Queen (the Green Lady), Ran-som sees a wondrous menagerie: "They came mostly in pairs, male and female together, fawning upon one another, climbing over one another, diving under one another's bellies, perching upon one another's backs. Flaming plumage, gilded beaks, glossy flanks, liquid eyes, great red caverns of whinneying or of bleating mouths, and thickets of switching tails, surrounded him on every side" (203).

However, the most compelling piece of poetic prose occurs as the King and Queen approach. Ransom notes how the entire atmosphere seems bathed in pure daylight coming from no apparent source, connects this light with holy things, and describes it as reaching perfection on the mountain top "like a lord upon a throne or like wine in a bowl." The light then reveals "Paradise itself in its two Persons, Paradise walking hand in hand, its two bodies shining in the light like emeralds yet not themselves too bright to look at" (204).

Chapter 17, the final chapter of the novel, provides the richest passages of poetic prose. Pitter's transcription actually covers the dialogue in this chapter between several voices regarding the Great Dance—a celebration of both God's loving majesty and the promise of his eventual reconciliation with fallen creation—and consists of twenty-three Spenserian stanzas. As early as April 1947 Pitter tells Lewis she is so impressed with the prose ending of *Perelandra* that she wants to put some of it into Spenserian stanzas. Lewis readily agrees although he is surprised she wants to spend her time doing this: "I'm rather shocked your wasting *your* verse on *my* prose. But I hope it'll only be the irritant to start your real activity [she had confided earlier that she was experiencing writer's block]" (Apr. 16, 1947, *RP,* 023). A month later he asks: "When am I to see the Spenserians? They'll do me good in a way you probably hadn't thought of. In my job one is always ferreting out the 'Sources' of the great poets. Now (serve me right) I shall be a source myself" (May 25, 1947, 024). Pitter reveals in her journal why she felt compelled to turn Lewis's Perelandran prose into verse: "I had been transcribing the paean of praise towards the end of *Perelandra* into irregular Spenserian stanzas simply as a mnemonic: I wished so much to have these enormous transcendental ideas in a form I could memorise & use wherever I happened to be" (July 6, 1947).[19]

Pitter's transcriptions, faithful to the source, suggest the underlying poetic nature of Lewis's prose in *Perelandra*.[20] When Lewis receives her verses, he writes: "I like them—and you manage to be closer to the original in verse than some of my continental translators seem to get in prose. I think that XXI probably wd. be taken in a pantheistic sense by a reader who did not start with the doctrine of the Trinity in mind, but so wd. the original. I think XXIII *has* high eloquence—but of course it is hard for me to judge. IX is specially good" (July 6, 1947, *RP,* 028). Somewhat later, apparently in response to her asking if he would object to her publishing her transcriptions, he writes: "I should be delighted if you used your Spenserians for that purpose, and don't really see why you should need my permission" (Nov. 17, 1949, 043).

A comparison of Pitter's transcriptions with the corresponding passages from *Perelandra* offers several insights. First, Pitter's verse often sharpens and clarifies Lewis's prose. For example, the second speech about the Great Dance in *Perelandra* is: "Never did He make two things the same; never did He utter one word twice.

After earths, not better earths but beasts; after beasts, not better beasts, but spirits. After a failing, not a recovery but a new creation. Out of the new creation, not a third but the mode of change itself is changed for ever. Blessed is He!" (214). Pitter's "II" closely follows this:

> He who has never made two things the same,
> He who has never uttered one word twice,
> First made the earths, and after them there came
> Not better earths but beasts: then there arise
> Not nobler beasts but spirits: then He dies
> Their death to save the fallen: but these shall be
> Not mended, but clothed on in Paradise
> With new creation fashioned gloriously:
> So change itself is changed for ever.
>   Blest be He!

Her last four lines, assuming they reflect Lewis's meaning—nowhere does he contradict her—clarify the meaning of his original. For instance, Lewis's somewhat vague "after a failing, not a recovery but a new creation" is made more concrete by Pitter's "then He dies / Their death to save the fallen." Similarly, his "out of the new creation, not a third" is considerably sharpened by her expansion: "But these shall be / Not mended, but clothed on in Paradise / With a new creation fashioned gloriously." Moreover, her rhyme scheme, while dependent upon eye rhyme, is an effective enhancement of Lewis's prose.

In a like manner, Pitter's "XVI" is powerful poetry communicating the boundless love, mercy, and compassion of God while at the same time sharpening the meaning of Lewis's original. The passage in *Perelandra* reads: "Each thing was made for Him. He is the centre. Because we are with Him, each of us is at the centre. It is not as in a city of the Darkened World where they say that each must live for all. In His city all things are made for each. When He died in the Wounded World He died not for men, but for each man. If each man had been the only man made, He would have done no less" (216–17). Pitter's transcription is:

> He is the Centre, and each thing was made
> For Him, and in Him each for ever dwells:
> Not, as in cities of the dark is said,
> Each one for all: but utter love compels
> All to the service of each one. So tells
> The story of the wounded World: He came
> For each man, not for men. His miracles

Of strongest mercy would have been the same
If but one living soul had dwelt there in that flame.

While Pitter's version loses the power of Lewis's line, "Because we are with Him, each of us is at the centre," she considerably clarifies his "He died not for men, but for each man. If each man had been the only man made, He would have done no less" in her expansion: "He came for each man, not for men. His miracles / Of strongest mercy would have been the same / If but one living soul had dwelt there in that flame."

Second, Pitter's verse makes concrete some of Lewis's more abstract imagery, albeit with somewhat limited success. Lewis, as noted above, gives Pitter's "IX" special praise:

The Tree was planted in that world, but here
The ripened fruit hangs in the heaven high:
Both blood and life run from the Fountain there,
Here it runs Life alone. We have passed by
The first strong rapids: the deep waters ply
On a new course toward the distant sea.
Till now, all has but waited. In the sky
There hangs the promised star, and piercingly
The trumpet sounds: the army marches. Blest be He!

The passage in the original reads: "The Tree was planted in that world but the fruit has ripened in this. The fountain that sprang with mingled blood and life in the Dark World, flows here with life only. We have passed the first cataracts, and from here onward the stream flows deep and turns in the direction of the sea. This is the Morning Star which He promised to those who conquer; this is the centre of worlds. Till now all has waited. But now the trumpet has sounded and the army is on the move. Blessed be He!" (215). Why Lewis thought this stanza merited special praise is problematic, although it may be he thought Pitter's concrete transcription heightened his subtle allusions to both the Garden of Eden (the tree of life) and to Calvary by his use of the Tree.[21] On the other hand, her "Till now, all has but waited. In the sky / There hangs the promised star, and piercingly / The trumpet sounds: the army marches" is perhaps too terse an alternative to Lewis's "This is the Morning Star which He promised to those who conquer; this is the centre of worlds. Till now all has waited. But now the trumpet has sounded and the army is on the move." In particular, her "the promised star" forfeits the specificity of "the Morning Star," a clear reference to Venus; also, by dropping "conquer," Pitter loses Lewis's allusion to Revelation 2:28: "And I will give him the morning star." Finally, by omitting "this is the centre of worlds," Pitter obscures an important parallelism that interconnects many of Lewis's paragraphs.[22]

Third, Pitter's transcriptions sometimes blur Lewis's original meaning. For instance, Lewis was concerned that her "XXI" "probably wd. be taken in a pantheistic sense by a reader who did not start with the doctrine of the Trinity in mind, but so wd. the original." A comparison of Pitter's transcription with Lewis's original prose supports his concern. The passage in *Perelandra* is: "All things are by Him and for Him. He utters Himself also for His own delight and sees that He is good. He is His own begotten and what proceeds from Him is Himself. Blessed be He!" (217). Pitter's transcription, adding the concrete image of a tree to powerful effect, is:

> He made all things, and for Him all was made.
> Himself He utters too for His delight,
> And sees that it is good. Under the shade
> Of His own branches does He sit, and bright
> He shines upon Himself: by His own might
> Begets Himself from all eternity,
> And what proceeds from Him is His by right,
> Himself eternally coming to be;
> Surely He is His own begotten. Blest be He!

In Pitter's line three ("and sees that *it* is good"), her substitution of "it" for "He" (Lewis's "and sees that *He* is good") tends to identify the Creator overmuch with the creation.[23] Furthermore, in line eight, "Himself eternally coming to be" oddly suggests God continually evolves into what He will become. On the other hand, Pitter's transcription effectively echoes the opening chapter of the book of Colossians where St. Paul emphasizes the "all" sufficiency of Christ: "For by him all things were created: things in heaven and on earth, visible and invisible, whether thrones or powers or rulers or authorities; all things were created by him and for him" (Col. 1:16).[24]

Finally, Pitter's transcriptions reconfigure Lewis's prose into poetic language and cadence, at times making his original more eloquent. For instance, Pitter's transcription of Lewis's third paragraph offers several improvements. His "it is loaded with justice as a tree bows down with fruit" becomes "like a fair tree with bounteous fruit bowed down." Pitter's inclusion of *fair* and *bounteous* heightens the impact of Lewis's line. In like fashion, his "as when stones support and are supported in an arch" is made more eloquent by Pitter's "for not as stones on ground, but bonded tight / Into the living arch." The impact of Lewis's *supported* and *arch* are heightened by Pitter's *bonded tight* and *living arch*. However, Lewis singled out Pitter's "XXIII" for its "high eloquence":

> Yet seeming also is the cause and end
> For which Time is so long, and Heaven deep:
> Lest if we never met the roads that tend
> Nowhere, nor darkness, where the answers sleep
> To questions silence must for ever keep:
> Nothing could image in our mind that Sea,
> That Gulf and that Abyss, the Father. Leap
> Into that depth, O thoughts: only to be
> Sunk drowned and echoless for ever. Blest be He!

Lewis's original is: "Yet this seeming also is the end and final cause for which He spreads out Time so long and Heaven so deep; lest, if we never met the dark, and the road that leads nowhither, and the question to which no answer is imaginable, we should have in our minds no likeness of the Abyss of the Father, into which if a creature drop down his thoughts for ever he shall hear no echo return to him. Blessed, blessed, blessed be He!" (218). At least part of Pitter's success in making this passage more eloquent is her turning Lewis's difficult "the question to which no answer is imaginable" into the memorable "where the answers sleep / To questions silence must for ever keep." Furthermore, Lewis's ambiguous "Abyss of the Father" is helped by the synonyms "Sea" and "Gulf."

Lest we think Pitter's efforts were so much presumptuous self-indulgence, consider the criticism leveled at Lewis when the novel was first published: "Bravely as Mr. Lewis has assaulted the high and mighty symbols of human hope, serious and imaginative as is his purpose, the things he intends . . . cannot be done at the pace and within the structure of narrative prose. It is a subject for verse, and verse at its most immense." The reviewer, Kate O'Brien, added later that "Passages in this book which tremble near the absurd because they have to be so much explained, might well have been majestic and beyond question in the simple, inevitable dress of poetry."[25] Pitter's transcriptions suggest both the underlying poetic nature of Lewis's prose in *Perelandra* and how he might have turned it into verse.[26]

Ruth Pitter was a trusted confidant for Lewis the poet. In other letters to her, he expounds at length upon different kinds of poetry, the role of the individual poet, his deep love of Milton, his "experiments" in verse, encouragement that she will overcome her writer's block, the novel experience of having in his "old age" a poem rejected by the *Spectator* ("Very tonic: I'd forgotten the taste of that little printed slip"; Jan. 4, 1947, *RP*, 016), the "hard" subjects for poetry, and his favorite meters.

Undoubtedly Pitter was grateful to be a sounding board, thankful she could in some small way repay Lewis for the broadcast talks that had helped her avoid the "slough of despond" she felt herself slipping into as World War II came to a close. Even after his death, she paid him poetic compliment by alluding to *Perelandra* in her *Still by Choice* (1966). "Angels" speculates about the real character of an angel ("terrible, tender, or severe?"), and she tacitly refers to Lewis's *eldila*: "Or likelier, now we dream of space, Lewis's dread sublime / Pillars of light, no limbs, no face, / Sickening our space and time?"[27] While some might wish to make more of the personal relationship between these two poets than the evidence merits, all we can say with certainty is that they did meet on a number of occasions, but generally in the company of others and always in the context of discussing books, writers, literature, and poetry in particular.[28] Lewis deeply valued the strength and beauty of Pitter's poetry, while she found Lewis's greatest poetry in the prose of *Perelandra*.[29]

A GRIEF OBSERVED

A Grief Observed (hereafter *AGO*), first published in 1961, is an unsettling book.[30] So disturbing is the tone that some argue it is not about Lewis's anguish over Joy's death but instead a fictional account of grief. Mary Borhek summarizes the position of those who hold this view: "The only reasons I can see for believing the book to be a fictionalized account are a desire to distance oneself from the extreme discomfort of confronting naked agony and an unwillingness to grant a revered spiritual leader and teacher permission to be a real, fallible, intensely real human being."[31] Others object to Lewis's candid expressions of anger at God, suggesting the book demonstrates Lewis's loss of faith: "There is no case for Christianity in this book. Gone are the persuasive arguments and the witty analogies. Gone, too, are the confidence and urbanity evident in *The Problem of Pain*. . . . The fundamental crisis of the book is a crisis of *meaning*, a crisis of such paralyzing magnitude that Lewis tries to distance himself from it in every possible way."[32] Still others find the book, while a deeply moving account of loss, overly introspective and emotional, verging on the maudlin. Yet Lewis avoids bathos, at least in part because of a clipped, prose style characterized by short, simple sentences and brief, almost snapshot-like paragraphs. These stylistic devices prevent his wallowing in excessive self-pity; in effect, he becomes a surgeon analyzing a patient's medical chart. Ironically, of course, he is at the same time both surgeon and patient.

A closer consideration of the prose style of *A Grief Observed* suggests the book may be read as *vers libre* or free verse, poetry relying not upon a regular metrical pattern but instead upon pace or cadence. Furthermore, whereas conventional poetry places a premium upon the foot and the line, free verse finds its rhythm in the stanza. Accordingly, the short paragraphs of *A Grief Observed* function as stanzas linking it with other ostensible prose works such as *Psalms* and the *Song of Songs*. If we read *A Grief Observed* this way, we find that while Lewis's focus upon traditional poetic conventions in his consciously conceived poetry actually restrains his poetic impulse—that is, his concern with prosody overshadows his poetic sensibilities—the release he experiences unconsciously in free verse liberates his poetic impulse, so that *A Grief Observed* becomes his greatest poem. Basic to this study, therefore, will be a discussion of word, sentence, and paragraph/stanza patterns; in addition, recurring metaphors serving to link paragraph/stanzas will be examined. Finally, we will consider the book's markedly negative view of God as reminiscent of many poems in *Spirits in Bondage*.

As we explore Lewis's use of words, it quickly becomes apparent that he relies heavily upon monosyllabic ones. This pattern is established in the first paragraph/stanza: "No one ever told me that grief felt so like fear. I am not afraid, but the sensation is like being afraid. The same fluttering in the stomach, the same restlessness, the yawning. I keep swallowing" (*AGO*, 7). Of the thirty-seven words, twenty-seven are monosyllabic. Similarly, in the second paragraph/stanza, sixty-one of seventy-six words are monosyllabic. Such a heavy reliance upon monosyllabics is consistent throughout, perhaps climaxing in the final paragraph/stanza where of forty words, thirty-five are single syllable. In effect, these monosyllabic words create a terse, quantitative cadence giving the entire work a chopped, clipped rhythm. When we move to the sentence level, this staccato style is repeated. The recurring syntax is the simple sentence—that is, a single, short clause with a simple subject and simple predicate. For example, in an early musing upon God, Lewis writes: "Sometimes it is hard not to say 'God forgive God.' Sometimes it is hard to say so much. But if our faith is true, He didn't. He crucified Him" (25). Three of the four sentences are simple, and the one complex sentence ("But if our faith is true, He didn't") is terse and abbreviated. Lewis frequently uses syntax to create cadence as in the following three compound sentences: "Talk to me about the truth of religion and I'll listen gladly. Talk to me about the duty of religion and I'll listen submissively. But don't come talking to me about the consolations of religion or I shall suspect that you don't understand" (23). The final thing to notice at the sentence level is that, while Lewis is not intent upon establishing a regular meter, often sentences employ trochees; in particular, he frequently uses individual words with trochaic rhythms. Examples include "cancer, and cancer, and cancer" (14); "What reason have we, except our own desperate wishes, to believe that God is, by any standard we can conceive, 'good'?" (26);[33] and "feeling, and feelings, and feelings" (31). This stress pattern is often referred to as a "falling meter" and is an apt one, since it parallels the book's emotional tone.

At the paragraph/stanza level we see the clipped, abbreviated cadence continued. For instance, in part 1, of thirty-one paragraph/stanzas, twelve contain five or fewer sentences, while only one has fifteen or more sentences; in part 2, of thirty-three paragraph/stanzas, ten contain five or fewer sentences, while four have fifteen or more sentences; in part 3, of forty-eight paragraph/stanzas, nineteen contain five or fewer sentences while four have fifteen or more sentences; and in part 4, of forty paragraph/stanzas, nineteen contain five or fewer sentences while four have fifteen or more sentences. The cumulative impact of monosyllabic words, simple sentences, and brief paragraph/stanzas is poetic prose filled with emotion, but not emotional. That is, the clipped, terse, abbreviated cadence of *A Grief Observed* reveals Lewis's pained sensibilities; rather than the reasoned reflection he offers in *The Problem of Pain*, here he is a wounded creature shrinking from pain. He is in a state of spiritual shock. All he can manage are quick, truncated jottings—raw reactions to pain. The short paragraph/stanzas, therefore, are akin to the brief lyrics of Tennyson's *In Memoriam*, another personal and literary response to grief and obviously a poem influencing Lewis's poetic prose. In fact, "Lyric 7" from *In Memoriam* could serve as the preface to *A Grief Observed:*

> I sometimes hold it half a sin
> To put in words the grief I feel;
> For words, like Nature, half reveal
> And half conceal the Soul within.
>
> But, for the unquiet heart and brain,
> A use in measured language lies;
> The sad mechanic exercise,
> Like dull narcotics, numbing pain.
>
> In words, like weeds, I'll wrap me o'er
> Like coarsest clothes against the cold;
> But that large grief which these enfold
> Is given in outline and no more.[34]

A writer all his life, Lewis's characteristic response to crisis is the "sad mechanic exercise" of putting on paper the "unquiet" of his heart, and, as he works through his grief, his brain.[35] For while *A Grief Observed* contains the ravings of a wounded creature, it also moves at its end toward the thoughtful, if numbed, reflections of a rational mind.

The frequent similes and metaphors dealing with grief; reality; his wife, Joy; himself; and Heaven/God also illustrate this movement. Grief, he writes, is like fear and being drunk or concussed. It is marked by suspense and waiting and is a downward spiral or a festering wound. Employing a war simile, he says it is like preparing for a falling bomb. It is "the monotonous, tread-mill march of the mind round one subject" (12), and "like a long valley, a winding valley where any bend may reveal a totally new landscape" (47). Grief, he says, has a way of showing us the reality of human existence, undercutting our fantasies about significance, purpose, and meaning with its "red-hot jabs." Reality reveals we are living "under the harrow [a heavy plough made of spikes or sharp-edged disks used to break up and level ground] and can't escape" (25). In addition, he says reality is like a knot that comes unraveled when it is pulled by grief. He notes in several places how grief makes him feel like a rat in a trap, eventually introducing a recurring metaphor: "I am more afraid that we are really rats in a trap. Or, worse still, rats in a laboratory. Someone said, I believe, 'God always geometrizes.' Supposing the truth were 'God always vivisects?'" (26). When he remembers the love he and Joy shared, he recalls it being as fierce as a thunderstorm and as soft as slippers; life together had been an open road, but now it is a cul-de-sac. Love cut short is like a dance stopped mid-step or a blossom prematurely snapped off. Perhaps his most poignant analogy is linked to the sea: "One flesh. Or, if you prefer, one ship. The starboard engine has gone. I, the port engine, must chug along somehow till we make harbour. Or rather, till the journey ends. How can I assume a harbour?" (29).

His figurative language about Joy is rich though brief. She had a mind like a leopard, "lithe and quick and muscular . . . [able to scent] the first whiff of cant or slush; then [it] sprang, and knocked you over before you knew what was happening" (8). In one sustained passage, he catalogs all she was to him: daughter, mother, pupil, teacher, subject, sovereign, trusty comrade, best friend, shipmate, fellow-soldier, mistress, sister, and brother. The most striking simile he uses about Joy occurs when he writes that she was "a splendid thing; a soul straight, bright, and tempered like a sword" (35). Later he imagines that God "grasps the hilt; weighs the new weapon; makes lightnings with it in the air. 'A right Jerusalem blade'" (50). Lewis's relatively sparse use of figurative language about Joy is due in part to his overemphasis upon himself, a fault he confesses: "The notes have been about myself, and about H., and about God. In that order. The order and the proportions exactly what they ought not to have been" (49).[36] Regardless, he describes himself as a widower greeted by friends and acquaintances as if he were a dentist or leper; some regard him as a death's-head. When he thinks of himself, he is like an empty house, a snail out of its shell, or a drowning man. His grief eats away at him, so he wonders, "Didn't the eagle find a fresh liver to tear in Prometheus every time it dined?" (46).

As he considers the nature of his faith, he calls it a frayed rope, broken at the first real crisis in his life when he puts his full weight upon it. An even stronger simile appears when he repeatedly emphasizes that his faith was like a house of cards. Initially he believes Joy's death and his grief knock this flimsy house to pieces, seeing some benefit in this: "The sooner it was knocked down the better" (32). Still, he does not trust whatever "new" house of faith he might build, since he knows himself too well: "However often the house of cards falls, shall I set about rebuilding it?" (32). In the end, he sees it was not Joy's death nor his grief that knocked down his house of cards, but instead it was God who "always knew that my temple was a house of cards. His only way of making me realize the fact was to knock it down" (42–43). His faith has also been like a card game with no money riding on the outcome: "Apparently it's like that. Your bid—for God or no God, for a good God or the Cosmic Sadist, for eternal life or nonentity—will not be serious if nothing much is staked on it. And you will never discover how serious it was until the stakes are raised horribly high; until you find that you are playing not for counters or for sixpence but for every penny you have in the world" (32). The most powerful and memorable metaphor Lewis uses is a surgical one: He is an amputee. He contrasts a patient who has had a relatively minor operation for appendicitis with one who has had his leg cut off. The man with appendicitis will soon recover, none the worse for wear. Not so the amputee. While the stump will gradually heal and the pain abate, he will never "get over it." He "will always be a one-legged man" (43). In his every waking moment he will know his handicap: "His whole way of life will be changed. All sorts of pleasures and activities that he once took for granted will have to be simply written off. Duties too. At present I am learning to get about on crutches. Perhaps I shall presently be given a wooden leg. But I shall never be a biped again" (43). Later, in noting how quickly grief can well up unexpectedly, he says "the same leg cut off time after time. The first plunge of the knife into the flesh is felt again and again" (46). In fact, his crippled nature constantly surprises him: "I was wrong to say the stump was recovering from the pain of amputation. I was deceived because it has so many ways to hurt me that I discover them only one by one" (48). While we can read to the conclusion of *A Grief Observed* and sense that Lewis has reconciled his anger with God, he never steps back from this view of himself as an amputee; he is maimed for the rest of his life.

Lewis's metaphorical language about Heaven is highly critical. Heaven is an iron curtain, a vacuum, absolute zero. While he once thought it a refuge, now he says it is no harbor: "A lee shore, more likely, a black night, a deafening gale, breakers ahead—and any lights shown from the land probably being waved by wreckers" (29). His most memorable simile posits Heaven as an uninhabited house with locked doors: "Go to Him when your need is desperate, when all other help is vain, and what do you find? A door slammed in your face, and a sound of bolting and double bolting on the inside. After that, silence. You may as well turn away.

The longer you wait, the more emphatic the silence will become. There are no lights in the windows. It might be an empty house. Was it ever inhabited?" (9). He ameliorates his view later, noting, "I have gradually been coming to feel that the door is no longer shut and bolted. Was it my own frantic need that slammed it in my face? . . . Perhaps [my] own reiterated cries deafen [me] to the voice [I] hoped to hear" (38). Still later, he adds, "My mind no longer meets that locked door" (49). The last time he refers to the door, he seems reconciled to the lack of an answer: "[It is] a rather special sort of 'No answer.' It is not the locked door. It is more like a silent, certainly not uncompassionate, gaze. As though He shook His head not in refusal but waiving the question. Like, 'Peace, child; you don't understand'" (54–55).

While Lewis's view of Heaven is critical, his view of God is bitter, verging upon the blasphemous.[37] He sees God as a cruel clown, a practical joker, a spiteful imbecile, a spiteful potentate, an interfering hostess or teacher, a denier, an experimenter, and a celestial killjoy. One running metaphor is God as surgeon or dentist. He is the doctor who cuts off the leg or removes the cancer; he is the oral surgeon who removes the cavity by drilling deeply into the nerve. He even sees a grim humor in this: "What do people mean when they say 'I am not afraid of God because I know He is good?' Have they never even been to a dentist?" (36). More often than not, however, Lewis cannot see his situation in light of doctor and patient; rather, he returns to the trapped animal metaphor, viewing God a torturer or Cosmic Sadist at worst or a vivisector at best. As he so succinctly puts it in the shortest paragraph/stanza in the book, "Either way, we're for it" (36). Actually, it is Lewis's metaphors concerning the character of God that are the most disturbing elements in A Grief Observed. He sees his loss in terms of torture that God must inflict because "only torture will bring out the truth [about the nature of Lewis's faith]. Only under torture does [a man] discover [the character of his faith] himself" (32). Nor does God come out any better as a vivisector, since Lewis posits that Christ's last words upon the cross may have been a similar realization: "He had found that the Being He called Father was horribly and infinitely different from what He had supposed. The trap, so long and carefully prepared and so subtly baited, was at last sprung, on the cross. The vile practical joke had succeeded" (26).

Before leaving Lewis's metaphorical conceptions of God, it is worth noting how his bitter views of God in A Grief Observed echo his earlier view in Spirits in Bondage. For example, in "Satan Speaks" (I) Lewis's cruel God says, "I am the fact and the crushing reason / To thwart your fantasy's new-born treason" (SB, 3). "Ode to New Year's Day" has its "red God" who appears to delight in the human pain:

And what should the great Lord know of it [the idea of goodness]
Who tosses the dust of chaos and gives the suns their parts?
Hither and thither he moves them; for an hour we see the show of it:
Only a little hour, and the life of the race is done.
And here he builds a nebula, and there he slays a sun
And works his own fierce pleasure. All things he shall fulfill,
And O, my poor Despoina, do you think he ever hears
The wail of hearts he has broken, the sound of human ill?
He cares not for our virtues, our little hopes and fears,
And how could it all go on, love, if he knew of laughter and tears? (15)

It is the "rankling hate" of such a God he mocks in "De Profundis": "Laugh then and slay. Shatter all things of worth, / Heap torment still on torment for thy mirth— / Thou art not Lord while there are Men on earth" (21). Finally, "Dungeon Grates" expresses well Lewis's sense of desolation in *A Grief Observed:*

So piteously the lonely soul of man
Shudders before this universal plan,
So grievous is the burden and the pain,
So heavy weighs the long, material chain
From cause to cause, too merciless for hate,
The nightmare march of unrelenting fate,
I think that he must die thereof ... (25)

Happily, Lewis's dark view of God lifts a bit toward the end of *A Grief Observed* so that he is able to suggest He may be a gardener—so careful of his plants that he prunes them when necessary—or a smith—so expert with the anvil and hammer that he beats the raw metal into perfect shapes. This view is best seen when Lewis comes to see God as "the great iconoclast," since he is nothing like what metaphors intimate: "Not my idea of God, but God. Not my idea of H., but H. Yes, and also not my idea of my neighbour, but my neighbour. For don't we often make this mistake as regards people who are still alive—who are with us in the same room? Talking and acting not to the man himself but to the picture—almost the *precis*— we've made of him in our own minds? And he has to depart from it pretty widely before we even notice the fact. In real life—that's one way it differs from novels— his words and acts are, if we observe closely, hardly ever quite 'in character,' that is, in what we call his character. There's always a card in his hand we didn't know about" (*AGO*, 53). As the book ends, Lewis moves away from considering the character of God. Instead, he focuses again upon Joy. The final paragraph/stanza underscores the poetic nature of his elegy for her: "How wicked it would be, if we could, to call the dead back! She said not to me but to the chaplain, 'I am at peace with God.' She smiled, but not at me. *Poi si torno all, eterna fontana*" (60). Here Lewis lovingly compares Joy with Dante's Beatrice; the line is translated "Then she turned herself back toward the eternal fountain" (from *The Divine Comedy*, "Paradiso," Canto XXXI, 30). Beatrice's last words to Dante had been in the preceding canto, and the line just before the one Lewis quotes is, "And she, however far away she seemed, smiled, and looked at me." In *A Grief Observed*, Lewis works through his grief to a new understanding and a renewed faith; it is his free verse lament for Joy, himself, and his understanding of God.

Perelandra and *A Grief Observed* suggest Lewis's propensity toward poetic prose. Other of Lewis's prose works, including *Mere Christianity, The Problem of Pain, The Screwtape Letters, The Great Divorce, The Chronicles of Narnia*, as well as others, demonstrate similar poetic elements, though not as extended nor marked as these. Additional scholarly work in this area will yield a rich harvest and help propel Lewis studies further in the direction of his accomplishments as an artist, as a crafter of words, as a writer per se. Such study will not stand in opposition to his prose apologetics or polemics, but will instead complement and enlarge our understanding and appreciation of them and his prose in general. In a letter Lewis writes in 1954 to the Milton Society of America, he thanks them for bestowing upon him an honor: "[In all my books] there is a guiding thread. The imaginative man in me is older, more continuously operative, and in that sense more basic than either the religious writer or the critic. It was he who made me first attempt (with little success) to be a poet. It was he who, in response to the poetry of others, made me a critic, and, in defence of that response, sometimes a critical controversialist. It was he who after my conversion led me to embody my religious belief in symbolical or mythopoeic forms, ranging from *Screwtape* to a kind of theologised science-fiction. And it was of course he who has brought me, in the last few years, to write the series of Narnian stories for children" (*LL,* 444). Lewis's imaginative side, his poetic sensibility, bears additional critical scrutiny. As his letters, journal and diary entries, and early poems demonstrate, he longed to walk with Homer, Virgil, and the other ancient poets. To this end, he devoted much of his early literary life and was forever marked by the experience. Though he never achieved the kind of acclaim he desired as a poet, he achieved an even greater acclaim for his prose. The legacy of Lewis's poetic impulse, therefore, finds its richest expression in his prose. By "making the poor best of dull things" in his prose, Lewis realized his poetic aspirations. The world is undoubtedly richer because this would-be poet found expression for his poetic sensibilities in prose.

The Unpublished Narrative Poetry of C. S. Lewis and Ruth Pitter's Spenserian Transcriptions of Passages from Perelandra

I. "Descend to Earth, Descend, Celestial Nine" (from *LP*, 3:321–36)

I

Descend to earth, descend, celestial Nine
And sing the ancient legend of the Rhine:
What races first upon the world did dwell
In earliest days, descend Oh Muse and tell.
Who did the mighty hills inhabit, who
The earth's deep clefts: narrate the story true.
Upon the mountain tops in happy light
Abode the gods with majesty and might,
Whom Wotan ruled as chief. The sluggish Rhine
Rhine maidens sheltered, nymphs of form divine,
Who for their sire a noted treasure held,
The Rhinegold, and in watch of this they dwelled.
Beneath the river's bed a hollow cave
To Nibelungen welcome shelter gave,
A stunted race who never see the light,
Of hideous visage and of puny height:
Abide they thus in corners dark and deep,
Like ants which through a tunell'd city creep.
And cunning they, and full of vicious greed
Live that they may their base ambitions feed.
Their king, a petty despot, Alberich

With bloodshot eyes and beard of volume which
The razor ne'er had known and to his feet
Reached almost, and the cave's smooth floor did meet,
One day ascended by a shaft whose mouth
Through the green Rhinebed rose and pointed south:
He stood: and through the water's shimmery sheen
The three fair maidens swimming could be seen.
Their beauty wakened in him base desire,
And kindled in his eyes an ugly fire,
And as they dive and circle in the dance
They hold the dwarf who stands as in a trance.
Their eyes, as through the ripples smooth they roam
Light on the ugly, rapt, and gazing gnome.
They see the purpose in his face and mock,
Laughing down on him from a lofty rock:
"Does Alberich indulge in dreams of love
And steer his mind through thoughts of his state above?"
The words the passion in him urge on more,
And darts he forward from the pumice shore,
With arms outstretched to catch the laughing forms,
Who with fresh mirth elude his passion storms.
Then love gave place to anger. With a cry
He rushes forth; they to the surface fly.
Then for a moment mirth gives place to fear
And laughter changes to the frightened tear.
This mood prevails for but a little while
And soon return the scorn and mocking smile.
They tantalize with dance the tiny king,
The waters wide with wanton laughter ring.
Then darts the ugly imp with wanton eyes,
They dive and swim and to the surface rise:
As now he almost seems to grasp the maids,
And merrily they fly before his raids.
Anon the nymphs, made frail by easy life,
Grow faint and weary of the heated strife:
Alberich glories in his sinews strong
And knows he may maintain the chase for long:
For as they whirl and circle, laughter dies
And joy from weary countenances flies,
In vain they seek by wiles the dwarf t'elude

Nor longer can resist his sallies rude.
To one, as in despair the maidens swim,
A scheme suggests itself by which the whim
Of Alberich the base they may evade:
Above them in a cleft the treasure laid
Would tantalize the dwarf far more than they.
And with this thought she upwards wends her way
And, drawing back the curtain which obscures
The Rhinegold, by a call the dwarf allures,
Who, glancing upward through the water cold,
With greedy eyes espied the glint of gold.
As eagerly he sees the metal shine
No more he heeds the maids of form divine.
The glimmer and the gold his senses please
And up he dashes, arms outstretched to seize
The hoard. But like a dreamer in his sleep
He sinks repulsed and floundering in the deep
By force invisible, and does not reach
The gold. The nymphs with loud unguarded speech
Thus to each other: "Knows he not the key
By which alone the hoard his own may be?
Knows he not as he tries to grasp in vain
The treasure, that who would the Rhinegold gain
Must first curse love before his hands may hold
The glistening and so much desired gold.
And he, should he but gain the pile he wants
(If there be truth in legendary vaunts)
If to a RING he forge it by the art
Of goldsmith, then to rule shall be his part;
Whoe'er the treasure keeps and wears the RING
Shall rule the world, and everlasting king.
But Alberich, the basest slave of sense
Will never frame the destined curse: and hence
The treasure ne'er will gain." The greedy gnome
As eagerly he through the waves did roam,
To hear the maidens voice did not appear
And yet their every word his open ear
Drank in: And with a cry of triumph fierce
He upwards strove the tepid waves to pierce.
Then cursed he love; nor did the force this time

Repulse the squalid king of Nibelheim.
He clutched the pile, and with a mournful cry
The maids beheld their hope of safety die.
And with lugubrious strokes, no longer quick,
They swim away. The darkness gathers thick,
And Alberich with gait of triumph proud
Approaches through the soft and sedgy shroud,
And at the tunnel's mouth he stops and calls
Down to th'infernal kingdom of the trolls.
"Come up ye dwarfs, come up and greet your king;
For he has gained the Rhinegold and the ring."
The Nibelungs come up, an ugly throng
With tattered garb and muscles coarse and strong.
The darkness thickens at the dwarfs approach
And noxious fumes upon the light encroach.
With joy they gather round like busy ants
And bear the treasure to their secret haunts;
Beneath the rolling Rhine the pile they lay
In jet black caves, far from the light of day.

II

The darkest hour it was before the light
Of dawn had burst upon the silent night;
The mountain of the gods enveloped stood,
Surrounded by the dense, mysterious shroud.
Then rose the sun upon the fertile hill,
Which beareth fruit although no ploughman till,
And touched with fire, Valhalla's stately hall,
Tinging each buttress and each turret wall:
Reared by the hands of giants was the place
Fit home for members of th'immortal race.
For Wotan, chief of all the gods, desired
A hold of strength, and Logie him inspired
(The god of fire, who Wotan most advised
And by his cunning many a scheme devised)
To compact with the mighty giants twain
Fasolt and Fafnir, monsters of the plain
To rear a hall. And as their price they claim
The goddess fair of love, to whom the name
Was Freia. Wotan gave a sad consent

To sacrifice which he had never meant;
And trusted Logie's wisdom to regain
The captive from the giants of the plain.
Thus, as the dawn was breaking, lay the god
Before the castle on the verdant sod;
The light caressed with gentle touch his form,
His noble visage, free from passion's storm,
His golden beard, and arms and limbs divine.
As on the herbage lay the god supine
Closed were his eyes, and sweet, refreshing sleep
The mighty king in soft embrace did keep.
Some paces off another form reclined
Of tender beauty like a mountain hind,
'Twas Frika, Wotan's everlasting spouse.
Then Wotan did himself from dreams arouse,
And, rising, turned and viewed his noble home,
Let his dark eye o'er every cornice roam.
Then with majestic anthem greets the hall:
"Fit shelter for the lord and king of all!
Valhall! My home! Oh be thou strong and blessed,
Standing so firmly by the light caressed
See! How vermilion grows each stony point.
How flames like fire each wooden beam and joint:
Yet grim foreboding in my heart prevails,
Whispering, fearful, half unuttered tales."
Then turning to the goddess, Wotan cried:
"Awake, Oh Frika: wake my holy bride.
Come: let us enter our new built abode.
And taste the fruits which Logie's wit hath sowed
In Walhall's hall we'll dwell in peace and for aye."
And Frika waking, said: "I know not why,
The name seems strange: and unaccustomed fears
Rise in my heart and urge the burning tears.
Can all be well, if Logie you inspires
To sell a goddess for your own desires?
Freia, bring Friea back, with her departs
Our happiness from faint and sickened hearts."
To whom the god with gravity replies:
"Ah, wipe the sorrow from those streaming eyes;
I did not wish the goddess fair to sell

But power of Logie's speech thou knowest well.
Advised by him—and let this bring you cheer—
I somehow hope to save our Freia dear.
By counsels smooth and words we will regain
The loved one from the monsters of the plain."
He spoke. And at that moment from below,
With those quick steps which terror's anguish shew
Freia herself came with dishevelled hair
And bloodless cheeks, and all her visage fair
Was strained with fear as o'er the turf she trod,
Full eagerly: and now she eyed the god.
"False traitor! Thou should'st my protection be
Oh save me from the monster's grasp." Thus she.
And even as she spoke, with heavy tread
Approached the cumbrous objects of her dread.
With slow and awkward gait the giants move,
And slowly dog the goddess fair of love.
First comes Fasolt, the kindlier of the two,
Armed with a mighty tree like weapon, who
For her own sake the goddess sad desires:
But Fafnir a far different plan inspires,
Reflects he thus as up his way he wends:
"Tis Freia who the golden apples tends,
Of which the gods immortal eat and live.
Were she not there the duteous care to give,
The gods must some day pass in death away,
I, with Fasolt, will hold unbounded sway
O'er all the world." As thus the giant thought,
Him one more pace before great Wotan brought.
Thus halting near the god the monster stands
Towering o'er him with his spread out hands.
Then thus with voice of thunder he addressed
The god: "Oh mighty lord of Valhall blessed.
We come the bargained price you owe to claim,
Fulfill your vows or yield t'eternal shame."
The troubled thoughts on Wotan's brain encroach,
For he expects the god of fire's approach,
By whose aid only can he hope to gain
A triumph o'er the monsters of the plain.
He glances round and falters in his speech,

Retreating with a step from Fafnir's reach.
The giant sees the step, and on his brow
The anger grows. Then: "Dost remember how
I reared for you Valhalla's stately hall
And likewise could remove your home, your all?"
Said he. The prudent god, composed, replies:
"Fafnir! Suspect me not of ugly lies.
While I the woeful news to Freia tell,
I'll send you two of those who round me dwell,
Immortal gods, with converse to beguile
The space of time." He speaketh such things while
The molten glow of anger in the eyes
Of Fafnir quickened as he heard the lies.
Then leading Freia, Wotan inward goes.
To twain of the immortal gods he shows
His plans, and tells them how with words to cheat
The giants while he waits the god of heat.
The two were Froh, the laughing god of joy,
And Donner, god of thunder. They employ
The time with oily words and counsels fair.
Fasolt, the lover, scarce delay can bear.
Thus the four great ones grouped together stood,
The giants' anger boiling in their blood:
Opposed to Fafnir stood the god of joy,
A laughing, fair, and well appointed boy.
And Donner stood and wielded in his hand
A mighty mallet which might crush a land,
With louder rhetoric and clumsier speech
To Fasolt patience he desires to teach:
In whose blue eyes the fire flames fiercer still,
Nor can he more control his yearning will,
His conversation flags and terser grow
His short replies: his twitching fingers shew
How tense his longing. Then at last he cries:
"No more of this. Arise, Oh Fafnir, rise.
And let us take the goddess in our hands
And bear her off from Walhall's wordy lands."
Thus speaking, both the giants think t'advance,
And Donner sees their harsh and meaning glance;
The god of thunder did no more delay

But sought to check their onslaught by a way
Of reasoning so sure, that none could stand
Against its power—the mallet in his hand.
Ah! Ne'er the giant had aris'n again
Did but that blow descend with stunning pain;
But as the god for his fierce stroke drew back,
And in the effort every bone did crack,
Valhalla's door with creaking groanings oped,
And Wotan brought the friend for whom he'd hoped;
For by the hand he led a slender god,
In burning robe, in burning sandals shod:
His frame was thin, nor was his stature great,
His raven eyes with varied thoughts dilate.
He counts and counts again his every wile,
And whispers in his master's ear the while.
Then Wotan sees the mallet raised to strike
And rushes in between th'opponents like
A flash of lightening. Grasps he Donner's arm,
And stays the blow and rectifies the harm.
Then turns the god to Loge and enquires:
"Where have you been? What thought your brain inspires?"
To whom Red Fire replying, forward stands:
"Obedient have I been to your commands.
And scoured the stretching earth from end to end
To find what might our sorry bargain mend
And love replace: but useless was the task,
I could not find the substitute you ask.
Nor found I any mortal high or low
Who Freia's gentle favour would forgo.
But while I searched for one decided thing,
I many others found of moment, King.
One thing there was; which threatened all the earth
With downfall dire; and this new power's birth
I will relate. In yonder wand'ring Rhine,
Three maidens dwelled, you know, of form divine;
Who in their keeping held a hoard of gold,
Which they have guarded from the days of old.
But this mysterious virtue has the thing:
Whoe'er shall forge the metal to a ring
All earth shall rule—aye, gods as well as men.

How would it fare with mighty Walhall then?
But all was well. The nymphs dreamed not of power,
Nor pondered aught beyond the fleeting hour.
Thus far 'twas well: but only for a time,
Until the king of hollow Nibelheim
Ascending, stole the treasure from the maids:
They, helpless victims, fell before his rage.
I pitied them and—pray forgive me king—
I did therein an uncommanded thing,
Exceeding thy high mandates: I did swear
Valhall assistance to their cause would bear."
Thus did narrate th'intriguing god of fire,
And did a thought great Fafnir's brain inspire.
Forward he dashed, and cried: "I beg thee, stay.
And hear my words." And Wotan answered: "Say
Fafnir what things you wish. Our ears are oped."
Fasolt thus hotly: "I had fondly hoped
Freia to gain: But since you do not choose
To give her up, I will not therefore lose
My whole reward. Freia to thee I'll give,
(So may she always in Valhalla live).
Give me that treasure which the god of fire
Hath told us of: for that I most desire."
"The treasure," answered Wotan, "Is not mine;
The greedy dwarfs who stole it from the Rhine
Will doubtless hold it dearer than their lives.
And if a god with Nibelungen strives
Who shall prevail? Although our mighty arms
And pow'r divine secure us from alarms
Of martial foes: the cunning gnomes may snare
Our person by their wiles, did we but dare
Their noisome caverns where in gloom they dwell;
I fear their hidden, untried depths of hell."
Then answered Loge with a hidden sneer:
"Tis not alone to face the regions drear
Of Nibelheim, descending from above
Is needful. But the hero must curse love
To gain the gold." Then Wotan stood aghast
Although the passion of his youth was past,
And doted he on power, he could not make

His lips the curse to frame and love forsake.
So casts he on the ground a troubled eye:
The giants see he fears to make reply
"Accept you not the liberal terms we make?
So be it. Freia then we justly take."
So Fafnir spoke; but Wotan, plunged in thought
Scarce heard the words, nor saw what sense they brought.
Then the two giants can restrain no more
Their purpose, but they open wide the door
Of Valhall: and bring forth the goddess sad.
Oh Freia, thou who once more glad than all
In freedom roamed, nor did one care appall
Thy gentle breast, what sorrow now you bear!
Nor do the giants in their haste forbear
To one of Asgard's great immortal race
To offer sacrilege and durance base:
Freia they lead away: with mournful tread,
Herself she sadly suffers to be led,
Nor strives with petty strength the fates to move,
Resigned, descending from the realms above.
Then Logie to his master turned and said:
"A gloomy day for Asgard dawns ahead:
Think not with impious words that I would strive
The righteous sorrow from your heart to drive,
I know your grief—indeed I share your pain.
But if Valhalla ere would raise again
Her haughty head above the hated clouds,
And cleanse her from the woe which now enshrouds
Her stately halls, we must to warfare turn,
Nor let the sorrow more our spirits burn.
For think of this: she is not here to tend
The golden apples. Who the want may mend?
By these alone the gods immortal live."
He spoke. And Wotan studious ear did give.
And all the gods who stood around did quake,
And frigid fear their every bone did shake;
Should Wotan not the goddess fair regain,
No more the gods immortal, free from pain,
Could hope to dwell: and thus on every hand
In speechless agony th'immortals stand.

And as they stand, a deathlike mist descends,
And with these words the god his thoughts now ends:
"No more of this: we do but waste the time.
Let us descend to tunnelled Nibelheim:
There may we gain the treasure and the RING
The one will gain our Freia, one a king
Of all the world for aye myself will make,
If I but love will curse and love forsake."

III

Guide me, my muse, down yonder sloping way,
Far lead me from the happy light of day.
Let us descend by clefts, where fathoms deep
The Nibelungs their hollow city keep.
Here, in the regions of eternal night,
By pumice rocks enclosed: where never light
With shining radiance spreads its warming ray,
Nor morning dawns, nor differs night from day:
And hidden from the winds and waves and storms,
There dwells the race, of small ungainly forms,
More hideous far than fancy can devise.
And in all cunning knowledge are they wise:
Ready to plot and scheme for others harm.
And here they dwell secure from all alarm:
Dark is the cave, suffused with ruddy glow,
And rocky arches propped on pillars low
Support its roof of clay. And in the light
Of some red furnace gleaming through the night,
A goldsmith's forge of tiny size is seen,
The glare returning with a brighter sheen
From every burnished point. And heated air
Resounds with wild mysterious whispers there,
And taps of naked feet on earthy floors,
And creaking of the hinges and the doors
Of dark and unknown side apartments few
Would dare to penetrate. And waters blue
With phosphorescent glare, in one weird coin
Rush down the world's internal lake to join.
Then in the firelight's ruddy glow appeared
A tiny dwarf of visage dark and weird:

'Twas Alberich, the king of Nibelheim,
And by the ear he dragged another—Mime,
A larger dwarf of uglier visage yet,
And in his eyes the tears of rage were wet;
Nor was his chin adorned by flowing beard
Like that of Alberich at whom he leered
—Now spitefully, by hidden hatred shook,
Now with a cringing and submissive look.
To him with rage began the angry king:
"You idle dog! You worse than useless thing!
Have you not learned my mandates to obey,
And execute my words without delay?
Nor idly sit, yourself with peace to gorge:
Where is the headgear that I bade you forge,
The cap, the Tarnhelm from the stolen gold?
Hast thou forgot the crafts thou knew of old?"
Then Mime's shrill voice through all the caverns rang:
"Tis wrong that you should bitterly harangue
Your most obedient slave. The cap you bade
The cunning smith to forge, that cap is made.
Nor does the work disgrace my stablished art:
Full well have I fulfilled my humble part."
Thus, honey in his mouth, but in his brain
Hatred, the fruit of long endured pain,
The smith stooped down towards the pumice floor
And picked a bundle from amongst the store
Of instruments that to the forging trade
Pertain: the pack was in rich cloth arrayed,
And tenderly he did unfold the wrap;
Then in the firelight gleamed the golden cap.
"Behold," he cried, "the work is here to see:
Which willingly, my king, I give to thee."
Then Alberich, with eager hands acquired
The trinket which his heart so much desired:
His eyes with secret triumph glistened while
He placed it on his head and with a smile
The goldsmith gnome surveyed. But not alone
The fact that such a headgear was his own,
So finely wrought, so well with gems arrayed,
And to the proper form so fitly made

That with such joy inspired him, but he knew,
That if the legend of the Rhine were true,
Which for the Tarnhelm—so the cap was named
This virtue for the golden helmet claim;
Whoe'er the headgear wore, at any time
What form he wished could take. And therefore Mime,
Who thought the cap must hold some power divine
Was loath to forge the metal of the Rhine
To that which would his hated king endow
With powers new. The other gladly now,
The cap upon its head, its virtue tried:
As standing by his cunning servant's side
One instant he was seen, the next the air
Was empty: to the loathing smith's despair
A scourge unseen his trembling limbs did greet,
And empty air upon his back did beat.
In vain he falls in terror on the ground,
And pity begs with noisy wailing sound:
Then, still invisible, the cruel king
Through the dark cave his unseen path did wing,
And leaves the smith in tears upon the floor.
Then opened from behind the cavern's door—
Ye gods! What light, what radiancy divine,
Fails to recite this earthly pen of mine,
Which that dark cavern flooded as the forms
Of two fair gods appeared. Their presence warms
The cavern with a glow it n'er had known;
Leaps out the furnace then to meet its own,
(For Logie and his master, Wotan, came
The gold they wished by stealth or arms to claim).
That furnace which before with ruddy beams
Had lit the place, now over feeble seems
Compared with that great, more than mortal light
Which from th'immortal places broke the night.
And like as when a housewife with a lamp,
Invades some cellar full of stores, and damp
The rats with evil patterings haste away,
Recoiling from the glare in wild dismay:
So crowds of Nibelungen, right and left,
To hidden caves rush off. Alone, bereft

Of terror by his pain, the smith lies prone,
His wounds and sad existence does bemoan.
Then Wotan, drawing nearer, kindly says:
"Explain, good dwarf, what grief your soul dismays."
And eagerly the moaning dwarf returned,
"Long has the wish for fitting vengeance burned
In this poor soul of mine. Didst thou but know
What tyranny I daily undergo
From Alberich's hand, the hateful king,
The owner of the thrice accursed ring,
Then would your hearts be moved. I pray you hear
My tale of woe. Nor spurn the crushed out tear.
I daily live in terror of my lord,
Alternate blows receive of scourge and sword."
So spoke he weeping; then the god of fire
Said: "If you, dwarf, deliverance desire
From your tormentor, listen to my words:
We come to conquer wealth, but not with swords.
By cunning shifts and wiles we seek to gain
The Rhinegold. And if you to cruel pain
Would bid farewell to aye and free become,
Help us to gain the treasure of your home."
As Mime, the cunning smith, would make reply
The caverns shudder with a painful cry,
And from the darkest corners of the place,
The members of the Nibelungen race,
Rush wearily with cries and tears of woe:
The lights of fire and gods their driver show,
The squalid king approaches; whip in hand,
Before him drives a Nibelungen band.
Then holds he high above his head the ring,
And yearns for all the triumph it will bring:
And mighty schemes revolves his tiny breast,
A swelling heart in narrow body pressed;
And all his being trembles with delight,
Grasping the gold, with golden headgear dight.
As thus he stands in rapt and joyous pose,
The gods their presence in these words disclose:
"Hail, mighty king. We know your stirling worth,
Nor, being wise, despise your dwarfish birth.

We come our due respect as brother kings
To pay. Valhalla worthy homage brings."
And Alberich in scorn does make reply:
"Tis false, ye gods: and hast thou thought that I
Like some young child, by honeyed words deceived
Imagine I have homage true received.
Ye lying race of gods. I loathe ye all,
As you despise my body dark and small
And puny height, so I a fiercer shame
Impute to Asgard's oft repeated name.
What virtue have you in your godly pow'r,
What though Valhalla's mountains dimly tower
O'er all the ages? Didst thou by thine own
Unaided power this gain? No: 'tis well known,
The dark unknowable which men call fate
Set up the immortal objects of our hate:
Supplied them with dominion undeserved,
With immortality their throne preserved;
Thus tyrants helped by destiny, a blind
Unthinking power, they left all woes behind,
And lived forever in their haughty home.
Now of these tyrants lying, twain have come
To offer homage as they say. Do gods
Descend the dark and unfrequented roads
That lead to my dark realm, respects to pay
To Alberich? Or leave the glowing day
To seek the caverns of a king they hate?
Or doth the eagle with the beetle mate?
Am I a child that I should thus believe
Ye come love-laden spirits to relieve
With kindly words? Nay: never was there yet
A god but did all misery beget
With lofty schemes. The price of Asgard's good
Is running rivulets of human blood.
To better your estate ye gladly slay
Crowds of the bad: the good alike dismay.
Through all the ages war has been between
Thy race and mine. And do th'immortals mean
These words of homage as an ill timed jest,
Or do the dotards really strive their best

My spirit to deceive? Which're it be,
I care not!! Get ye gone from mine and me,
But stay. Before the hated schemers go,
To them their coming ruin I would show:
Although devoid of power my person seems,
The golden pile that in yon crevice gleams
Hath made me lord of all. Nay, start not so,
Ye did not deem a prince to meet below.
The ring this Nibelungen finger wears,
The Tarnhelm which this wrinkled forehead bears
My kingdom they set up. Ah! what a jest.
The power fate, which once of all its best
Gifts to Valhalla's gave, that very same
Fate hath prepared its downfall and its shame:
The ring hath made me monarch of ye all,
Valhalla's stately realms I will enthrall:
From harms I always easily escape,
The Tarnhelm gives me power to change my shape.
And when the world's broad kingdom is my joy,
Schemes for your torture will my brain employ:
I once to gain this ring sweet love did curse,
Now I will not than Asgard's race be worse:
Your doom, mendacious tyrant, learn and hear,
Ye also shall curse love." And at this jeer
The rage swelled up in Wotan's godly heart;
Forgets the god to play his subtler part,
And, like as when the hounds with barking stand
About the antlered deer, on either hand,
And vex the mighty monarch of the glades
Who, for a time, resists their paltry raids
With only lazy strength. Then rears his head
Above the throng, the meadow swims with red
And curdling gore as charges he the throng,
Invaded their ribs with cruel horns and strong:
Not otherwise than this Valhalla's king
Rages upon the owner of the ring.
And as he rushes forward to the blow,
And gleaming eyes their owner's passion shew,
And upwards Wotan did his weapon raise,
Loge the prudent, Loge far more wise,

Seizes his masters [*sic*] arm and softly says:
"Reserve your anger king, for other days,"
But, turning to the dwarf, he gaily sneers:
"No doubt to thee, your scheme sublime appears;
You taunted us with deeming you a child
When we our homage on your spirit piled;
Accept you then, who are in wisdom great,
That we believe the legend you dictate?
Prove you the power you say the Tarnhelm grants,
Change thou thy shape. Fulfill your empty vaunts."
The crafty Niblung raised his hoary head,
And answered with a look of hate and dread,
"Still rave the dotard gods? And think ye, friends,
I do not know your avaricious ends:
Shall I a small and feeble beast become,
That you my bear the treasure from my home?"
The baffled Wotan raised his haughty eyes,
And faltered twixt his fury and surprise;
But Loge, speaking calmly, said: "My friend,
If this in truth be of your power the end,
Lying were those who told us of your might,
You are not than mere men in better plight.
So fare thee well. We go to Walhall's hall."
Then in a trice the cunning, crafty Troll
Forgot his plans, and as a mortal will
When moved by pride, performed his office ill.
Stung to the quick by Loge's taunting words,
He answers, "Think not dazzling pomp and swords
And gleaming halls and tesselated [*sic*] courts
And armour bright and giant reared forts
Alone mean power. Nay, in this gloomy cave
Lies more concealed than Asgard's host would brave.
Credit ye not my words? Then I will give
A sign by which your quavering faith may live."
And with this bitter word once more he set
The Tarnhelm on his head. His fingers met
And clasped each other till the flesh grew white
About the knuckles, trying that he might
Compress his willing spirit, every thought,
Into the wish the golden Tarnhelm brought.

Ha! Wild, unprecedented, weird event
That through the godlike forms a shiver sent;
For looked they once, and in the ruddy glow
The furnace cast across that cavern low,
Saw they the uncouth Niblung's figure stand,
Solid in form and breathing close at hand;
Then looked again—Oh! horror that they saw!
E'en as the snow before the sun doth thaw
And leaveth streams where stood the solid mass,
E'en so the gods beheld their victim pass.
Slow into air dissolved the dwarfish flesh,
Melted the bones and teeth to take afresh
A body new. And in the troubled air
Hovered the spirit like a mass of fair
Yet fetid vapour, and alone the eyes
Dissolved not in the common mass. Surprise
Seized hold upon the gods when once again
With groanings like some animal in pain
The members in the glow ferment around
Those steadfast orbs of light, and all is bound
Into one solid whole. Fear Wotan rocks,
When stands where stood the dwarf a vicious fox.
And thrice he oped his lips and thrice surprise
The Father's speech did bar. The gleaming eyes
That did the fox's evil face adorn
Upon great Wotan flashed with Haughty scorn,
But Loge of the cool foreknowing brain
Renewed the smile which on his lips had lain
Before the dark event, and said, "Oh king
I now believe the power of your ring.
Forgive my foolish words, my scornful smiles,
These were to hide my awe transparent wiles;
I pay, oh mighty Niblung just, to you
The reverend homage which is all your due.
The warriors which Valhalla's chambers hold ·
Do not such marvels of your power behold:
A novel joy, this rapturous, trembling fear,
Unknown delights that Nibelheim doth bear!!
Show us again, great dwarf, your wondrous might,
And let us taste again this fierce delight."

Once more the ruddy fox's limbs convulsed
In effort of desire. The sight repulsed
The watching gods who knew what was to come
Knew the dread secrets of the Niblung home;
Drank they with greedy eyes the wondrous sight
And pondered on it in the ruddy light
Revealed the coming change. Once more the mass
Of snowy fog before the dwarf did pass
Into which melted slowly every part,
The shining claws, the palpitating heart.
And still the ugly spirit hovered o'er
The shifting whirlwind, gathering more and more
Its specks of dust together, and the eyes
Above the ruin of the form arise.
Great golden orbs of light with lustrous sheen,
And where the dwarf in form of fox had been
There writhed a slimy toad upon the floor.
Then Wotan darted forward with a roar
Of triumph, and his garment gathered round
His godly waist. And to the pumice ground
He pinned the fragile reptile with his foot.
Again the effort of desire did shoot
Through Alberich's frame—it was too late!
The Tarnhelm on his brows no longer sate:
For Loge—scheming god.—had seized the toy,
And god a god embraced in solemn joy.
Ah! sight of pleasure and of woe!—The cave
In deepest gloom was wrapped and hidden save
The scarlet oblong which the furnace cast
Across the earthen floor, and with its last
Expiring rays by distance dimmed alit
The farthest corners of the squalid pit.
And in the light two godly forms embraced
Each other, and each other gladly faced,
And Wotan's golden locks seemed brighter yet
As every hair the gleaming firelight met,
And Loge, skillful, fair and slight withal
Enraptured stood before his master tall.
Beneath the other's foot, in dismal plight,
—A contrast to the other pleasant sight—

The reptile sought its bleeding limbs to tear
From under that proud foot that crushed them there.
Then turned the mighty gods and Loge grasped
The toad in his strong hand and up they passed:
Up winding clefts the rocks had rent apart
In deep convulsions of the earth's deep heart,
Up tunnels long, down which the freshening breeze
Odourous with the scent of lands and seas
Unnumbered, swept to choking Nibelheim.
The gods laughed loud, for, having been a time
In that foul den whose secrets few would dare
Rejoiced once more to breathe the upper air.

IV

To that dim shadow land of unknown space
Where twilit dwells the great immortal race—
I speak of Asgard, that mysterious hall
Which is the home of gods: that mountain tall
On which it stands, I speak of—to that shore
The gods their toad-formed victim gladly bore.
And as they neared the godly place on high
A thousand voices filled the azure sky:
Across its depth a thousand wondrous things
Floated at ease or hastened with their wings;—
The flying steeds that bear the Valkyrie maids
And mighty serve them at their bloody raids.
As through the twilight winged the gods their way
In the last light of the departing day.
Out flew the warrior maidens bravely armed,
And music shrill the listening ear alarmed
—The music of the storm: the failing light
Revealed the lovely forms in armour dight.
And first of all that eerie cavalcade,
Whom every Valk'rie duteously obeyed,
Great Wotan's daughter rode, Brunhilda named,
Whose beauty would the fair of earth have shamed.
Then clashed a thousand spears. A joyous shout
Through and above the storms wild song rang out,
The multitude of Valk'ries joyous cheer,
As sound of joy to gods; no man may hear

That cry and live: thus sing they when they bear
The bravest warriors from the battle sore
To live in Asgard's bliss for evermore.
So, with this mede, the flying train drew nigh
Through the resounding fathoms of the sky
Sweet in the twilight. And the gates of gold
Upon the well poised hinges open rolled
And gave admittance to the gods. They went
Onwards and upwards with the eyes intent
Of all the gods and heroes on their path,
And on the reptile which in frenzied wrath
Quaked in their iron grasp, and as they neared
The hall of Clouds, a radiant form appeared—
Fricka—great Wotan's spouse—she comes and leaves
The hall where cloudy fates she softly weaves.
Her stance is sad, her eyes betray her woe:
But Wotan loudly calls to her ....
(caetera desunt)

II. *Loki Bound* (from *LP*, 4:217–20)

Warren Lewis writes (he places this immediately after the letter to Arthur Greeves dated October 6, 1914; this is letter 3 in *They Stand Together*, 50–53): "Whether Arthur Greeves ever attempted any part of his share in this music drama is not known; Clive completed his part, which we have before us. It occupies thirty-two pages of a folio note book, and is elaborately written, in black ink, with the characters names, episode headings etc. in red. The volume bears for title, 'LOKI BOUND and other poems' by C. S. Lewis. The stage directions for this tragedy read as follows:—"The scene of this tragedy is laid in a wild, volcanic valley, surrounded by mountains of the most precipitous description. In the background is a vast mountain on the top of which stands a very beautiful and mysterious city, from whose gate a bridge in the form of a rainbow leads down to the neighbouring hills. The left of the stage is supposed to lead off to this bridge. Therefore the gods and the chorus make their entrance through it. The right, whence Fasholt enters, leads to Jottumheim. The scene is the same throughout, and action begins in the evening. In the foreground must stand an altar, a lake, or some such mark, to serve as a centre for the grouping of the chorus."

   Warren Lewis continues: "Loki's opening speech, for which 'sombre and eerie' music is required, reads thus:—"

This is the awful city of the gods,
Founded on high to overlook the world;
And yonder gabled hall, whose golden roof
Returns the sinking sun's red glare again
With twofold force, is Valhall. Yonder throne
That crowns th'eternal city's highest peak
Is Odin's throne, whence once the impious Frey
With ill-starred passion eyed the demon maid.
Fair is the city while the mellow light
Caresses every bulwark, while the cliffs,
Some, standing forth, with borrowed splendour shine,
Whilst others in the purple shade retire.
Aye surely, too, it seems impregnable,
Perched high above all fiends and monsters dire
Out of their reach—yet if my soul speak sooth,
Not long shall she be fair, not long have peace.
For soon the red birds cry at Ragnavik
Shall muster all the sons of night for war,
And the fierce brood from Surtur sprung shall come
And plant their grisly hosts about her walls.
And I shall shed no tear at Asgard's fall:
Nay rather will I join the demon band,
And with my monster children at my back
Defy my erstwhile masters. For know this,
All mortals, that tho' I enjoy the name,
The glory, and the hollow, hollow pomp,
The worship and the common reverence paid
To gods, yet I have never been of them.
For, in the dawn of all, ere time began,
Or haughty Asgard overlooked the world
Or men had come to being, and when still
Great Ymer's corpse lay wallowing in the gulf,
I walked with Odin through the shapeless void.
Ah! We were brothers then, and then we pledged
Eternal friendship in those earlier times
—Fool that I was! But as we looked around,
And viewed the wild chaotic waste, the sun
The moon, the stars, all ignorant of their tasks,
Knowing not each his place, then Odin told
How he would build a world a home for man,

And lay the Ocean round it like a cloke;
Confining to its utmost marge the vast
Uncomely giants and the monsters fell;
And over all that lived create the gods
Companions to himself, and he proposed
To make the conjuring dwarfs and beasts and men,
Building for each its habitation meet.
But even in that early age I saw
The awful error and injustice dread.
Then, knowing what I knew, addressed the god.
"Odin! And who art thou to make a soul
And force it into being? Who art thou
To bring forth men to suffer in the world
Without their own desire? Remember this,
In all the universe the harshest law,
No souls must ever die: it can but change
Its form and thro' the myriad years
Must still drag on for aye its weary course,
Enduring dreadful things for thy caprice."
He answered darkly, with uncertain words
Hiding his thoughts. And when I would have called
The new made universe to sleep again,
Me he forbade, and with his magic power
Bound as his slave, bound me to work for him.
Thus, therefore have I lived thro'all these years,
Forced to obey the mighty criminal,
The father of injustice, he who makes
Sorrow and pain on earth, in heaven strife.
But not for ever shall his rule endure,
And even now in plans unknown to him
I set on foot destruction for the gods.
In Asgard, stone on stone shall not be left
And all the gods shall perish—haste that day.
Let all of them such pains as they have caused
Soon taste in full and learn what sorrow is!!
Curse them, the light-souled gods! Yea, curses on them!!
What form is this that glistens up aloft,
Athwart the gathering darkness? What that cry
Echoing wild across the riven clouds?
Lo! The bald ravens flutter down to earth:

'Tis Odin that I see. The cloud grey steed
Flies through the storm clouds, and upon his back
The grim creator of the world is borne.

Warren Lewis writes: "The entry of Fasholt, for which 'bluff, swinging' music is
asked, is handled thus:—"

FA. "Hail strangers! Who are ye that sit alone
Thus brooding in the cruel winter night?
Nay, answer not; for I perceive myself,
Ye are the high gods' kinsfolk, and ye wait
Doubtless to watch the building of my wall.
Well, rest assured of this: it shall be done,
For I am bent on gaining that dear prize,
To cheer my lonely home in Jottumheim."

Warren Lewis writes: "Then follows the episode of the maddened horse and
Fasholt's exit, after which succeeds the following song for the chorus which is obviously the 'dawn music' referred to:—"

Yonder, over the hill, the pale precursor of Billing
Paints with a ghostly line of white that corner of heaven:
Down in the silent woods, to the Westward, buried in shadow,
Tho' it be still dark night, yet every bird hath awoken.

Borne on the chill night breeze, a restless whisper ariseth,
Where they are stirring below, chattering down in the thickets.
Now, with a ruddier tint, the roofs of adorable mansions
Gleam in the city above, high in impregnable Asgard.

Lo! He is coming at last, the sun, and wherever he touches
Mountain or wall with his rays, with his life giving breath he ignites it.
Now from the vale and the hill, from the throat of many a songster
Poureth the song of the dawn, the song that is old as the mountain.

Gone is the night of our fear: let us greet the day with rejoicing.
Praising, each from her heart, the Norns that have pitied our sorrow.
Who cometh hither in haste, so wild and so eager for tidings?
Surely over the brow of the mountain Loki appeareth.

Warren Lewis writes: "The drama closes with Loki's rejection of Odin's proffered pardon and friendship, and a short final speech by Odin, for which Clive asks 'some inexpressibly sad, yearning little theme':—"

OD. "So be it then. The day
Of doom at last has fallen. Wo is me,
Never again as in the days of yore,
To clasp thy hands in friendship, or to walk
Together through the chaos, as of old
Ere yet the worlds were builded! Thou alone
Couldest be my friend, or understand. For these—
Gods, men, or beasts, what are they but my self,
Mirrored again in myriad forms? Alas,
How weary is my soul ....
                  But let us come,
Oh, maidens, and repair to heaven's halls."
(Exeunt Odin and Chorus.)
                THE END.

Lewis also quotes Loki in the following line from the poem in *Surprised by Joy:* "I pay respect to wisdom not to strength" (115).

III. "On Cupid and Psyche" (from *LP,* 8:163–67)

Warren Lewis writes: "It will perhaps be remembered that in this year [1923] Clive describes himself as being very full of the idea of re-writing the story of Cupid and Psyche. To what state of completion the scheme was brought is not known, but I have found the following draft in one of his note books:—"

The tale of Psyche is unjustly told
And half the truth concealed by all who hold
With Apuleius. Famous poets sing
That once upon a time there lived a king
Whose daughter was so fair that from the sky
Venus beheld her with an evil eye;
And afterwards, for Venus' hate, they say
By singing priests the girl was led away
And left upon the hills in fetters where
An old, big sacred serpent kept his lair
Among grey rocks. So far they tell it right:

Only—it was no fabled Venus' spite
That drove them to this thing; but summer rains
Withheld and harvest withering on the plains.
The streams were low, and in the starving tribe
Ran murmurs that of old a dearer bribe
Had charmed the rain. Forgotten customs then
Stirred in their sleep below the hearts of men
Thrusting up evil heads. The priests began
To feed their god, the sacred snake, with man,
—Prisoners at first, then slaves. But this was vain
They must give more, give all, to get the rain,
Give the land's best and first—give anything—
Even to the royal blood. Now let the king
Deny them, and within the hour he's dead.
"What. Shall the king be spared? Our sons have bled
To build his throne. His turn has come today.
Children are dying. Lead the girl away."
—I think it was like that.
                              What follows next
I take for truth; but who can read the text?
In the worst hour, close to the serpent's den,
At twilight and in chains, and when the men
Had left her (and they went in haste, to leave
The silent place)—that moment I believe
When fear had done his worst in the girl's heart
That some strange helper came and took her part.
They talk of the wind spirit opening wide
His cloudy arms—and on the mountain side
Palaces rising—music in the air—
The bed in the dark room—the lover there
Whose face must not be seen. Amidst it all
Something is lost, but not without recall,
Blurred in the tale, yet somehow told enough.
But what comes after this is poorer stuff
And slander; for across the tale, they bring
Two ugly elder daughters of the king,
Two Cinderella's sisters, who must come
To visit Psyche in her secret home
And envy it: and for no other cause
Tempt her to break that fairy country's laws

—Which leads to her undoing. But all this
Is weighted on one side and told amiss.
It's like the work of some poetic youth,
Angry, and far too certain of the truth,
Mad from the gleams of vision that claim to find
Bye ways to something missed by all mankind.
He thinks that only envy or dull eyes
Keep all men from believing in the prize
He holds in secret. In revenge he drew
—For portrait of us all—the sisters two,
Misunderstanding them: and poets since
Have followed.
                    Now I say there was a prince
Twin brother to this Psyche, fair as she,
And prettier than a boy would choose to be,
His name was Jardis. Older far than these
Was Caspian who had rocked them on her knees,
The child of the first marriage of the king.
****

Warren Lewis writes: "(Another version of the last six lines:—)"

                              But when I rest my eyes
Upon that house, I see far otherwise.
First it is weeping shapes: then these begin
To come apart. And here is Psyche's twin,
A brother, not a sister, fair as she
And prettier than a boy would choose to be,
Reading his book, self pleased in hazy thought.
Now, on my life, I'll guess it's he that taught
The story, as we have it, to the world.
****

Warren Lewis writes: "This note book contains six or seven other drafts of the first thirty odd lines of the poem."

IV. "The Silence of the Night" (from *LP*, 8:164–67)

Warren Lewis writes: "Here we have another fragment which appears to have been written about the same period [1923]:—"

The silence of the night upon the stroke
Of midnight like a bubble snapt and broke
Into ten thousand clamours. Forests wide
With leagues of oaks whipt over to one side
Came roaring out of slumber, scattering birds
Like dead leaves up the sky. Half spoken words
Snatched from the lips of shepherds that lay out
Rose wheeling and became a giant's shout
Over six counties. In his turret room
Hippolytus woke shrieking in a gloom
That staggered like a ship: the clothes were blown
Out of his clutching hand. With ocean tone
The seven-mile-crested waves of air were hurled
Against his walls. The doors of half the world
Seemed banging in his ears. The hollow halls
Echoed like caves beneath him. On the walls
His hanging helmet clanged and on the floor
He heard the carpets flap. Then more and more
Came other noises through the wuthering wind,
Cat calls that raised the hair and drums that dinned,
Struck cymbals, screaming voices and the sounds
Of divine beasts at mort and gaining hounds
Baying their thirst, that nearer, nearer rang
Now in the street, now at the door. He sprang
Naked from rest, quivering from heel to head
Dry mouthed. The dogs that slept about his bed
Crouched whimpering at the door with fangs laid bare
In foam, and on their backs the roughening hair
Rose stiff. With fingers fumbling round about
The straining latch he loosened and thrust out
The chamber door into the wind, hard pressed,
Labouring with shoulder weight and panting breast
Choked like a fish upstream, then, for a space
Dizzied with moonlight stabbing his flushed face,
Then—forward, where the dogs before him went
Flat eared and nosing on a fiercer scent
Than earthly quarry had. In haste he passed
Blind labyrinths of the house and came at last
Forth on the street. None stirred. As clear as noon
Showed every stone and tile. That night the moon

Had slipt her moorings and with one huge eye
Through headlong clouds flooded the ruined sky
Low blazing to the earth. Immense and blind,
As if at dawn his shadow lurched behind,
A monstrous escort up the empty street,
Measuring uneven strides. And now his feet
Fell on cool grass; wide fields before him lay,
Hedgerows with flowers shut up and ghostly may
A faintest perfume fluttering the dim air.
The great hill-voice was calling everywhere
Breathing sharp strength upon him. Now each limb
Ran riot, charge with god. Through coverts dim,
Up slopes where the uncounted daisies sleep,
Slant woods and the high tracks of wandering sheep,
Up winding glen, riven gulley, cragg'd ascent,
—The wild goat's path—bleeding and mired he went
Up to the hills, away.
                              Then suddenly
Running beside the prince there seemed to be
Innumerable hordes of beast and man.
Under his feet the little foxes ran:
Wings smote upon his temples. Often he felt
The hoarse breathed mountain bear with shaggy pelt
Brushing his thighs. Women with skirts caught up
And revellers fresh crowned from the full cup
And maudlin pipe, ancients with silver head,
Young children, priests, merchants, and maids unwed
Ran there with labouring breath, wide gaping mouth,
Some naked, wounded some, all parched with drouth
In the burning throat; but fiercer burned the fire
In heart and bloodshot eye, the insane desire
Fixed towards the cloven passes and the bare
Storm-fostering heights. Around them everywhere
The houseless hills made carnival; the trees
Strained with the mimic noise of raging seas
In orgy to the wind. Green boulders torn
From mossy rest down the full streams were borne
Breaking the greenwood. Break. Break everything,
Break the old world for life is on the wing
To strange adventures. Dian's out tonight.

Brothers, how fair you are. See, red and white,
See, the ghost hounds before us in the dales,
The moon dogs. Onward now. The spirit fails,
The brain cracks. Earth reels under us. Faster yet,
Lead, Goddess, lead. The bracken dewy wet
Gleams diamonds and the white enormous moon
Dazzles the eyes and fills the heavens. Now soon
She will be here herself, the Cold-of-the-Air
The freezing Chastity, the haggard fair;
Mania is in her feet, and in her face
The hopes of the long dead. We of the chase
See but her shoulders. Lead. Lead on the pack.
Brothers, I have grown hound. I smell the track
I am all nose—Look. Look; with flanks of snow
See where the quarry flies—it is a doe—
It is a lion—it's a man—
****

Warren Lewis writes: "In the same note book is what appears to be another beginning of the same poem; in this version however 'Hippolytus' becomes 'The King of
Drum.' The storm and the hero's awaking are told in much the same, often the
same language as in the version above, but the poem is in a lighter vein. After the
hero's entry into the moonlit street it continues:—"

                    But soon his feet
Ran in the singing grass, by leaping hedges
That flogged the entangled stars, by reeds' and sedges'
Dry treble in steep glens: upward to where
On the higher slopes the huge ninth wave of air
Caught him behind the knees. Holm oak like bows
Bends double. The leaves race. Among them goes
Head-over-heels the king—one pace in thirty
Touching the earth by luck—through clean and dirty
A king of the dead leaves. Oh night, be dumb,
Cover his shame. Whisper it not in Drum
How Majesty scuds breechless, blown away
Like washing from the line: up past the grey
And niggard grass of the heights, further than sheep
Climb furtherest, through the pines and heathery steep
Up to the moon, straight on.

                                            There suddenly
Crowding the nine leagues ridge, the king could see
Innumerable hordes—beast, woman, man.
Nuzzling his feet, tongues out, the foxes ran.
Wings lashed him in the face. Often he felt
The wheezy mountain bear with icy pelt
Brushing his side. But the men—alas for Drum.
Why should my lord Archbishop home hither come
Showing his teeth so yellow, and except
His mitre, bare as an egg? And now he has leapt
The chasm ***********************"

Warren Lewis writes: "Another fragment of the 'Drum' version:—"

The rough breathed mountain bear with icy pelt
Brushing him. Then came whinney and drumm'd hoof
And over his head a momentary roof
Of darkness: and he ducked: and square between
The vast moon and his eyes, one moment seen,
Dead black the alighting horse appeared—a shape
Well known—his horse—how should the brute escape?
Was he not stalled—are the grooms mad? And now
Flicking irreverent hoofs at our dread brow.
Oats are the devil.
                                    The men—alas for Drum.
Why should my lord Archbishop hither have come,
Showing his teeth so tawny, bare except
His mitre and soft beard? And now he's leapt
The crevase (eighty years upon his shoulder)
Laughing, amid young lads, and no lad bolder,
Nor, by the Lord, none fairer. Who'd have thought it?
What has alighted on his limbs? He caught it
Out of the moon. He spread both hands and dipped
****

V. A Passage from *Perelandra* by C. S. Lewis done into irregular Spenserian stanzas by Ruth Pitter.[1] From a holographic notebook beginning: "*Transcribed 1970.* All published [poems], and of widely varying dates." "Passages from 'Perelandra'" is given first and covers over eleven pages. MSS Verse Pitter, box 28, 1–11, Bodeleian Library.

1st. Spirit.   I

    We do not wait till you are gathered in,
    You of the little inward earths and low:
    We speak not, we, of when it will begin.
    Before forever and the long ago,
    Before the stream of time began to flow,
    We dance before His face rejoicingly.
    We at the centre ever praise Him so:
    For the great Dance have all things come to be,
    And all was made that we might praise Him.
                      Blest be He!

2nd. Spirit.   II

    He who has never made two things the same,
    He who has never uttered one word twice,
    First made the earths, and after them there came
    Not better earths but beasts: then there arise
    Not nobler beasts but spirits: then He dies
    Their death to save the fallen: but these shall be
    Not mended, but clothed on in Paradise
    With new creation fashioned gloriously:
    So change itself is changed for ever.
                      Blest be He!

3rd. Spirit.   III

    Like a fair tree with bounteous fruit bowed down
    All is filled full of justice and of right:
    It is all righteousness: it is His own,
    And no two things are equal in His sight,
    For not as stones on ground, but bonded tight
    Into the living arch, so crown and key
    Are all things to each other: rule and might
    Fulfilled by answering humility:
    The heat descends, the life leaps up:
                      blessed be He!

Another Voice   IV

    Not in the tale of years, the length of days,
    Not in the measured miles, uncounted spheres,
    His greatness is. They do not sing His praise,
    To approach His majesty shall not be theirs
    That make account of them. No endless years,

And no eternity the sun shall see,
No, nor the heavens. Rather the small seed bears
Him in itself, and all eternity
Contained with Himself at ease.

Blessed be He!

V

Each thing is part of a most unlike thing,
To which it bears no semblance. Point to line,
And line to shape, and shape to body bring
Their lesser natures, and to one divine,
One Absolute, the unutterable Trine:
As the bare circle to the globe shall be
The unfallen to the world redeemed: in fine,
As point to line redeemed felicity
To the far fruit of its redeeming:

blessed be He!

VI

Yet is the perfect circle not less round
Than the round sphere, which in itself doth hold
Circles uncounted, fatherland and ground
And home of circles infinite, untold:
Which if they spoke (so one, so manifold)
Would say, "For us, unnumbered as the sea,
Were spheres created," nor be overbold:
Let no mouth open to gainsay them: free
Are they to speak in truth and beauty.

Blest be He!

VII

The sinless peoples who have seen no shame,
The peoples of the ancient world, are those
For whom those worlds were made: He never came
To them: for though the healing of the woes,
The bearing of the sins of all who rose
Against Him, makes new harmonies to be,
Changes the mode of glory, yet He knows
He made them to be whole unchangingly:
Good was not made to be corrupted. Blest be He!

VIII

All which is not in the great Dance was made
That he might there come down and enter in.
That world which fell, and its own light betrayed,
He visited embodied, so to win
The dust unto His glory: and the sin
That caused this is called Fortunate: and we
Know that this deed of entire love, wherein
Abides and is expressed all majesty,
Is end and cause of all creating. Blest be He!

IX

The Tree was planted in that world, but here
The ripened fruit hangs in the heaven high:
Both blood and life run from the Fountain there,
Here it runs Life alone. We have passed by
The first strong rapids: the deep waters ply
On a new course toward the distant sea.
Till now, all has but waited. In the sky
There hangs the promised star, and piercingly
The trumpet sounds: the army marches. Blest be He!

X

The worlds are for themselves, though men may rule
Or angels: desert seas, the fruit unknown,
The secret caves, the fire impassable,
Though, when you come, obedient as your own,
Are perfect in their nature all alone:
Times without number, long before your time,
Have I about the fields of Heaven gone,
And they were not a desert. The sublime
Was centred there, and I heard all those voices chime.

XI

Be comforted, immortal creatures small:
Be comforted, for you are not the voice
That all things utter, nor does silence fall
In regions where you weep not, nor rejoice:
No feet have walked upon the globe of ice,
No eyes looked up from where eyes cannot be,

Beneath the Ring: and chaste and empty lies
The plain of naked iron: yet ceaselessly
The gods still walk the fields of Heaven. Blest be He!

XII

That Dust itself, scattered so thin and rare
In heaven, of which the peopled worlds are made,
And bodies other than the worlds, is there,
There at the centre, needing not the aid
Of eyes to see it, hands upon it laid,
To be His strength and splendour. Of its all,
The least part of that Dust has ever paid
Service to any living thing, or shall:
Yet it still renders service, praise perpetual.

XIII

Before they came, and after they have gone,
And where they never come, the Dust still sings,
Uttering the heart of the most holy one,
Though furthest from him of created things,
And nearest, for from every grain he brings
The unmixed image of his energy,
So that each mote of wide Heaven's winnowings
Might say, "The whole was made only for me."
Let no mouth open to gainsay it. Blest be He!

XIV

Each grain is at the centre, and the Dust,
And all the worlds, and each created beast,
The ancient peoples, and the race that must
Be bought by death divine, within whose breast
Was Pride engendered against heaven's behest:
And these the fair, the sinless creatures free,
And august spirits that for ever rest
In Him, yet move in Him unceasingly,
Pervading the great deep of Heaven. Blest be He!

XV

The centre is the place where He abides
And all of Him abides in every place:

Not here one part, and there another hides,
But everywhere the whole. No mind can trace
A path to any things hid from His face,
For smallness beyond thought, the atomy
Contains Him too: no refuge from that grace,
Save in the hellish will that seeks to be
Outside Him, and finds only Nothing.
                              Blest be He!

XVI

He is the Centre, and each thing was made
For Him, and in Him each for ever dwells:
Not, as in cities of the dark is said,
Each one for all: but utter love compels
All to the service of each one. So tells
The story of the wounded World: He came
For each man, not for men. His miracles
Of strongest mercy would have been the same
If but one living soul had dwelt there in that flame.

XVII

If each had been the only fallen soul,
One man mankind, He would have done no less.
Each thing is cause and purpose of the whole
Creation, and the grains of dust confess
His glory with the mighty ones who dress
Their rays in His: for both were made to be
Clear mirrors of bright everlastingness,
Receiving and reflecting faithfully;
Where His beam rests, and whence returns.
                              Blessed be He!

XVIII

Innumerable within the master-plan
Of the Great Dance the lesser plans are twined,
Each being in its season, for its span,
The flower for which the whole has been designed,
Thus all are at the centre, yet none find
Their equal; but in reciprocity
They give and take their places each in kind;

Thus, and thus only, small and great agree,
All linked in kneeling to their Love. Blessed be He!

XIX

As a strong river ever flowing full,
That fills each cranny and each little bay,
Brimming alike the channel and the pool,
All full, but all unequal, and when they
Must overflow, will take another way,
And makes[2] another outlet to the sea,
He has all use for all. Love me, I say,
All need and all delight bind you to me,
Made as we were for one another. Blest be He!

XX

And yet He has no need: strong angels are
Needful to Him no more than grains of sand:
The peopled star than the unpeopled star,
All the magnificence that He has planned[3]
Needless, and all that springs at His command
Needless to us: all superfluity,
A bounty undeserved, as from His hand,
Shall be the love uniting you to me:
Like His own Love, a pure largesse. Blessed be He!

XXI

He made all things, and for Him all was made.
Himself He utters too for His delight,
And sees that it is good. Under the shade
Of His own branches does He sit, and bright
He shines upon Himself: by His own might
Begets Himself from all eternity,
And what proceeds from Him is His by right,
Himself eternally coming to be;
Surely He is His own begotten. Blest be He!

XXII

All that is made seems planless to the mind,
The darkened mind, for there is so much more
Plan than the mind can see: as when we find

So fine a turf upon some island shore
It looks all one, for eyes cannot explore
The weaving, nor the fine threads severally,
So with the Dance. Each figure seems the core,
And a true seeming: centre nor plan you see
Because it is all plan, all centre. Blessed be He!

XXIII

Yet seeming also is the cause and end
For which Time is so long, and Heaven deep:
Lest if we never met the roads that tend
Nowhere, nor darkness, where the answers sleep
To questions silence must for ever keep:
Nothing could image in our mind that Sea,
That Gulf and that Abyss, the Father. Leap
Into that depth, O thoughts: only to be
Sunk drowned and echoless for ever. Blest be He!

The Ten Short Poems Previously Published Only in Don King, "Glints of Light: The Unpublished Short Poetry of C. S. Lewis," SEVEN: An Anglo-American Literary Review 15 (1998): 73–96

1. "'Carpe diem' after Horace" (From *LP*, 4:88.)

When, in haughty exultation, thou durst laugh in
    Fortune's face,
Or when thou hast sunk down weary, trampled in
    The ceaseless race,
Dellius, think on this I pray thee—but the
    Twinkling of an eye,
May endure thy pain or pleasure; for thou knowest
    Thou shalt die
Whether on some breeze-kissed upland, with a
    Flask of mellow wine,
Thou hast all the world forgotten, stretched be-
    Neath the friendly pine,
Or, in foolish toil consuming all the springtime
    Of thy life,
Thou hast worked for useless silver and endured
    The bitter strife
Still unchanged thy doom remaineth. Thou art
    Set towards thy goal,
Out into the empty breezes soon shall flicker
    Forth thy soul,
Here then by the plashing streamlet fill the
    Tinkling glass I pray

Bring the short lived rosy garlands, and be
Happy—FOR TODAY.

2. "In Winter When the Frosty Nights Are Long" (From *LP,* 4:121.)

In winter when the frosty nights are long
And sedge is stiff about the frozen meres,
One night above a volume of old song
Of legendary loves and magic fears
Sweetened by long elapse of slumbering years,
I nodded in the frosty firelight beam
And fell on sleep and straightway dreamed a dream.

I thought it was a luminous summer night,
And in the star-flecked welkin overhead
A fading sickle of soft golden light
Its wonder over all the landscape spread,
While fleecy clouds athwart its paleness sped:
Ten thousand thousand points of light did peep
Out of the boundless heaven's velvet deep.

Meseemed I stood upon a goodly plain
Full of soft streams and meadows deep in corn,
While the far thunder of a foaming main
Across the calm, delicious air was born.
Beyond the plain, a mountain waste forlorn
Clear seen beneath the trembling silver light,
Rose, and yet rose with height still piled on height.

Higher than mountains seemed, than Alpine peaks
Or fabled mountains spied from the moon,
And tortured into grim fantastic freaks
Of rock: o'erhanging cliffs that seemed to swoon
Towards me, ready with vast ruin soon
To fall and whelm the plain, and vallies steep
Engulphed with icy torrents swift and deep.

The eye could hardly reach, and senses failed
In gazing on those unimagined . . .

3. "Ovid's 'Par estis pauci'" (From *LP*, 4:191–92.)

Of the host whom I NAMED
As friends, ye alone
Dear few!, were ashamed
In troubles unknown
To leave me deserted; but boldly ye cherished my cause as your own.

My thanks shall endure
—The poor tribute I paid
To a faith that was pure—
Till my ashes be laid
In the urn; and the Stygian boatman I seek, an impalpable shade.

But nay! For the days
Of a mortal are few;
Shall they limit your praise
Nay rather to you
Each new generation shall offer—if aught be remembered—your due.

For the lofty frame
That my VERSES ENFOLD,
Men still shall acclaim
Thro' ages untold:
And still shall they speak of your virtue; your honour they still shall uphold.

4. "Heart-Breaking School" (From *LP*, 3:41–42.)

Heart-breaking school
Received me , where an ogre hearted man held rule,
Secret and irresponsible, out of the call
Of men's reproach, like Cyclops in his savage hall:
For at his gate no neighbour went in, nor his own
Three fading daughters easily won out alone,
Nor if they did, dared wag their tongues, but, in a trice
Their errand done, whisked home again, three pattering mice,
Pale, busy meek: more pitiable far than we
From whom he ground the bread of his adversity,
Himself a theme for pity: for within him boiled

The spirit of Genghis Khan or Timur, ever foiled
And force back to the dogs-eared Virgil and the desk
To earn his food: ridiculous, old, poor, grotesque,
A man to be forgiven. Here let him pass, by me
Forgiven: and let the memory pass. Let me not see
Under the curled moustaches on the likerous, red,
Moist lips, the flat Assyrian smile we used to dread
When in the death-still room the weeping of one boy
Gave the starved dragon inklings of ancestral joy,
Antediluvian taste of blood.

5. "And After this They Sent Me" (From *LP,* 3:262–63.)

And after this they sent me to another place,
New miseries, another school. But I retrace
Only the good which there I found; one master dear,
At thought of whom the bird of memory sings. More clear
And dulcet grows the firmament of the world within.
Mediterranean metres at my ear begin
And at my veins with Dionysiac drum to knock,
Like goat foot dancers thudding on the thin soiled rock
Of blue volcanic country, where the hammered hills
Grow hot like metal, and metallic sunshine fills
The basin of the burning sky till the blue is dark,
And the small insects' shadow is as deep and stark
As the jagg'd rocks: and from on high the Olympians throw
The thunderbolt, and quakings from the gods below
Trouble the earth: and gods in the leaf shaking mountains
Cluster, and in cold water glens and sacred fountains
Gods and half gods and sons of gods, and all the crew
Of Maenads in the mountain tread the bloodied dew
In honour of the beautiful and beastlike son
Of Semele—Then cold Platonic forms: the One
Arching forever above all height; the long process
From lovely, up through lovelier things, to Loveliness
Herself, and in herself, abstract, alone, complete—
Then Sabine woods and worshipped river heads and neat
Virgilian farms, and cattle, and the care of bees,
The old pieties of temperate Numa's time. All these,
An old man with a honey-sweet and singing voice

Led me among; an innocent old man whose choice
Once made to dwell with beauty and melodious thought,
Unchanged, from early youth to sad old age, had brought
The spirit gently ripening onward to the place
Where courage droops. "Mý Joízv μετ' àμουσίας!
Gentlemen (for he chose to call us urchins so)
Let us not rest save where the springs of beauty flow."
Therefore the ancient beauty brought him clear delight
Each day, and all day long, and in the wakeful night
Forgetfulness of the unhappy thousand things
Age thinks of, making equal to the wealth of Kings
His poverty. Oh Master, may the earth be green
Above thy grave! Far hidden in the lands unseen,
Far off now, and mature among the ghosts, yet fare
Well and thrice well forevermore and everywhere.

6. "Old Kirk, Like Father Time Himself" (From *LP*, 4:64–65.)

Old Kirk, like father Time himself, was coming after,
With clouds of cheap tobacco smoke, with claps of laughter,
My third and greatest teacher who of old had taught
My father; then my brother; and now I was brought
A solitary pupil where he lived alone
With few books and no friends, and in his garden, sown
Up to the gates with green utilitarian kale,
Laboured all day, a tall, gnarled shape, hirsute and hale
As Charon: crude antiquity: a leathery, lean
Northeaster of a man whose seventy years had seen,
Unflinching, many hopes destroyed. He drew his blood
From the brave, bitter Presbyterian race who stood
For Calvin to the gallow's foot. But Kirk allowed
No God in the world, nor spirit in man. He did not shroud
That unbelief in pious frauds, as teachers love.
He thought the reverence owed to boys was Truth. He drove
With lance in rest and loud Have-at-thee on the foe,
Hammer of priests and kings, true lineage of Rousseau
Hume and Voltaire. And all the enlightenment's gay din
Of onset rang about his veteran ears, and in
And out of season (Covenanter still) he preached
The word of death.

But mark this well: his daring reached
Never so far as to forbid each seventh day
A Presbyterian shift of suits from rusty grey
To rusty black. He gardened differently clad
On Sundays. Such peculiar praise the Mighty had
One day in seven from this redoubtable, whose boast
Of reason meant to shake the Throne. On the iron coast
Of such a man, with noise of yeasty waves, the young
Spring-swellings of my uncorrected mind were flung
So often that even now I see him as he spoke
Fling up his arm, and hear him from the cloud of smoke
Break in. "I hear you well enough. Stop there! I hear!
Have you read this—and that—and the other?—Hah! I fear
You've got no facts. Give me the FACTS!" Repeated shame
Silenced my babbling: months wore on, and I became
Aware how the discourse of men (what none before
Of all my teachers showed me), asks for something more
Than lungs and lips. Across my landscape, like the dawn,
Some image of the sovranty of truth was drawn,
And how to have believed an unproved thing by will
Pollutes the mind's virginity; how reasons kill
Beloved supposals: day makes tawdry lesser lights,
And mountain air is med'cinal. Oh Attic nights
And rigour of debate! Shrewd blows. Parry and thrust.
No quarter. And above us like a battle dust
Fine particles of poets and philosophers
Went flying in the midnight room. I had my spurs
Of intellectual knighthood in that bannered field
From Kirk's strong hand. He first hung on my maiden shield
Who now is dead, and died without hope, like a beast.
Let tongue and pen betray me if I break the least
Of the oaths he then administered, the glittering laws
Of battle; blameless champion of a pitiful cause.

7. "The Carpet Rises in the Draught" (From *LP*, 11:251.)

The carpet rises in the draught. The little scarlet leaf,
That's blown in from the window sill, is wicked past belief:
That old face in the picture there is bad as bad can be,
And thro' its chromolithic eyes it says strange things to me.

Beyond this room, if I went out, there's thirty feet or more
Of passage thro' the empty house and many an open door
And many an empty room that's full of breeze and sunless light
With empty beds for visitors all neat and cold and white.
And sometimes now a door will bang and then at other whiles
A little bit of wind gets lost—strays in beneath the tiles
And among beams and water pipes it makes a fretting sound
Behind the walls, between the laths it wheezes round around,
There's so much room about a house . . . .

8. "I Will Write Down" (From a letter to Owen Barfield, May 6, 1932, *OB*, vol. 2
(1932–1940), cat. no. 26–50, index no. 0065, Wade Center.)

I will write down the portion that I understand
Of twenty years wherein I went from land to land.
At many bays and harbours I put in with joy
Hoping that there I should have built my second Troy
And stayed. But either stealing harpies drove me thence,
Or the trees bled, or oracles, whose airy sense
I could not understand, yet must obey, once more
Sent me to sea to follow the retreating shore
Of this land which I call at last my home, where most
I feared to come; attempting not to find whose coast
I ranged half round the world, with fain design to shun
The last fear whence the last security is won.
        Oh perfect life, unquivering, self-enkindled flame
From which my fading candle first was lit, oh name
Too lightly spoken, therefore left unspoken here,
Terror of burning, nobleness of light, most dear
And comfortable warmth of the world's beating side,
Feed from thy unconsumed what wastes in me, and guide
My soul into the silent places till I make
A good end of this book for after-travellers' sake.
        In times whose faded chronicle lies in the room
That memory cannot turn the key of, they to whom
I owe this mortal body and terrestrial years,
Uttered the Christian story to my dreaming ears.
And I lived then in Paradise, and what I heard
Ran off me like the water from the water-bird;
And what my mortal mother told me in the day

At night my elder mother nature wiped away;
And when I heard them telling of my soul, I turned
Aside to read a different lecture whence I learned
What was to me the stranger and more urgent news,
That I had blood and body now, my own, to use
For tasting and for touching the young world, for leaping
And climbing, running, wearying out the day, and sleeping—

9. "To Mrs. Dyson, Angrie" (From MS. Eng. lett. c. 220/7, fols. 1–3, Bodleian
Library.)

These inky firmaments and flaws [*sic*] of rain,
The wet weed swaying on the fallows dun,
How falsely our philosophers explain!
These neither spot I' the sun
Nor anticyclone from the western main
Hath made to be. No! with unkindly charm
The mortal *Pearl* such mischief hath us done,
Choosing to "arme
Those lookes, the heav'n of mildnesse with Disdain."
Since, lady, in your face
Daunger the giant hath meek *Pity* slain,
Mist drapes our woods and gusts of anger chace [*sic*]
Leaves (like our hearts) from every rivelled [*sic*] tree.
Yet, sure, in such a gentle heart or place
For mercy too should be.
If but the power were equal to the will,
I would speed hence, a suppliant, to your bowers;
Scarce would I stay to fill
Some pearly chariot with dim Syrian flowers,
To gild for such a progress the pale horns
Of some poor ten or twenty unicorns,
—To harvest some thrice happy hippogriff,
—To load with gifts of frankincense the hands
Of seven dusky legions, if—sad if—
(There is no other rhyme for hippogriff)
Power jumped with will. But jealous fate withstands.
So to your queenly self, so to your lord
(If such a style accord
With any mortal; as great Venus' groom,

Anchises old, tho' declined to the tomb
Was honoured for the sea-born goddess sake)
Excuse your slave, for even the humblest take
Free pardon from necessity; and make,
Smiling, our autumn skies put off their gloom.

10. "Lines to Mr. Compton Mackenzie" (From MS. Eng. lett. c. 861, fol. 69,
    Bodleian Library.)

Good heavens, Sir, will you condemn us
To talk of Romulus and Remus
And Venus—or perhaps Wenoos?
Each language has its native use,
And words like Saturn [?] are abom-
inable here, if not at Rome.
Man, were you never taught at school
The genuinely English rule?
Antepenultimatis with us
For the most part are shortened. Thus
Crime, criminal, and *rare,* but *rarity*
(It rhymes in Thomas Hood with *charity*)
It's English, which you claim to love,
You're mangling in the interests of
A long-dead alien form of speech.
Learn your own tongue before you teach,
And leave us meanwhile for our share
"The freedom of oure ain vulgaire."

Eleven Previously Unpublished Short Poems
by C. S. Lewis

1. From *OB* and the notebook "Including author manuscripts of poems undated," Wade Center.

> Laertes to Napoleon

> Oh all day long wave out the banner.
>   My ears are full of roaring guns,
> The culverin cracks the eldritch spanners
>   And both are tight—are these the ones

> That later, when night turns the heaven
>   Sweep far out from the shore? Then lo,
> The corslet eased, unstrapped the sweven*,
>   And the aftermath one lubric glow.

> *Sweven is here used to mean a knapsack [Lewis's note].

2. From *OB* and the notebook "Including author manuscripts of poems undated," Wade Center.

> YAH!

> From a paper
> "When Banquo saw the witches he remarked,

"What rhubarb, senna, or purgative drug
has spoiled my reason?"

You will laugh when I tell you that I
read yours *twice,* much mystified, before
I saw what it was.

3. From *OB* and the notebook "Including author manuscripts of poems
undated," Wade Center.

But in all dialects save wersex
Long E*A's, mutated, turned to E*'s: ex-
amples, wersex HIERAN : HERAN
Elsewhere: instead of CIERAN, CERAN.

*Note: both E's in this line have accent marks over them [Lewis's note].

4. From *Letters of CSL to Owen Barfield*, vol. 1, 0021: 8a–T (no date).

The Hedgehog Moralised

Hedgehog hase ane sturne rynde
uppon his bak wha sall it se
bot wambe and brest after his kynde
bathe is softe as silk harde.
þat ane signifyeþ to my mynde
fortitude al witerle
þat oþer as man iwriten finde
þe noble vertue of charitee

Whan þat he is idrad of fas
intill ane bal then torneþ he
what mister beste ojeins him gas
can nat gar him grue ne dee
his heued he ligges untill his tas
þat lowest to þat heizest sal bee
quhilk signifyeþ as in this cas
guid skeltrom is in humilitee.

EXPLICIT

5. From *OB*, vol. 1, 0036: 15T (June 26, 192[9]?). Lewis prefaces this with: "What do you [Barfield] think of the following alliterative lines—as metre: the matter is unintelligible out of its context (After that you are pretty well bound to find something in it?)."

> Artless and ignorant is Andvari
> As a kneaded clod, if never he heard
> Where is gold growing, the glory of Rhine!
>   A second sun, under still water
> (Can it be Odin's eye?) that upward shoots
> Answering that other (or, from under earth,
> Balder bringing the buried good?)
>   Who knows the nature of that noble kind
> Would not laugh lightly at the lover of it;
> It holds inherent in it the heritage of nine worlds.
>   None shall reave it from Rhine, nor to ring twist it
> Till he unlearn the law whereby Love made him
> And spill himself for the sake of the gold.
>   Ignorant and artless is Andvari—
> Never dwarf but was dull, daring only in greed.

6. From *OB*, vol. 1, 0044: 21T (Spring 1930?).

> Long at lectures
> On Monday morning
> I work till one! Hoike!!
> Piddling pupils
> I in taking am engaged!!
> Can your car
> So swiftly over
> Earth's back wander
> From Oxford to London between one and 5:45?
> Walawei? Hoo-ruddy-rah!!!!
> Ho-hei!!!!!
> !!
> ?!!!!
> If so, to call
> For me at Magdalen
> Were wisest rune
> On Monday at one!

If you lie
On Teusday [*sic*] night
In Magdalen's ancient College
You will meet Dyson
Dining with me
Of men the justest!!
(The whole scene explodes)

7. From *OB*, vol. 2, 0077: 38T (Apr. 5, 1935). Lewis prefaces this with: "I hope to
   arrive at Rudyard (wh. on nearer acquaintance wth. guidebooks turns out to
   be Rudyard Lake) at 3.13 on Monday."

Where reservoys ripple
And sun-shadows stipple
    The beard of the corn,
We'll meet and we'll kipple
We'll carp and then kipple
At Rudyard we'll Kipple
    From evening to morn.

And then we'll set off, yus!
Discussing your Orpheus
    His meaning and myth,
Till fettered by Morpheus,
The leaden-maced Morpheus,
Inaccurate Morpheus
At Chapel-en-le-Frith.

8. From *Letters of CSL to Miscellaneous Correspondents*, Wade Center, 881, to
   Kathleen Raine (Apr. 11, 1956). In a reply about her poetry, Lewis writes: "They
   are like a combined bathe and drink (you know—all pores and mouth open at
   once) that I once had on a walk in the Highlands: cold, bright, and yet with a
   dash of the dark earth-taste in them. I congratulate you. Philosophically
   (as you will guess) I am in much disagreement, which I've twisted into the
   enclosed—an exercise in usprezza . . . you know, Della Scala in thingummy's
   book on Milton's sonnets, and all that."

Who knows if the isolation, the compact, the firm-shaped,
    Dividual selving and peculium of the blood and breath
    (Oh skull-roofed thought, oh rib-caged love!) can be escaped

By such an old, simple expedient as death?
How if this were the arena, not the prison? If here,
Focus'd at last, hence conquerable, hand to hand
That retiarius meets us with his net and spear,
And now's our chance to kill him, on this hot, dry sand?

Here he takes form; elsewhere he's a pervasive poison.
Mosses complete; each flower is militant; the trees,
Lacking eyes, cannot cool their souls on the horizon;
Sap is dark will that works and neither loves nor sees;

And the grave, though not a fine, is a most private, place;
Two bodies can't (all souls could) occupy one space.

9. From The Dorothy L. Sayers Letters, Wade Center, 94/72.
At the very top of the page Lewis wrote: "Libellous! Or too nasty! C.S.L."

D.H. Lawrence, Sigmund Freud,
Taught by you we now avoid,
All restraints that once destroyed
Wholly earthly Luv.

Money-making calls for brains,
And of all our hard-won gains
After taxes what remains?
     No one taxes Luv.

Whisky, port, or gin-and-It
Harm the liver, rap the wit;
We can take (and yet keep fit)
     Lots and lots of Luv.

All the outdoor games we play
Fail us as years pass away;
Even the very old, they say,
     Still can manage Luv.

Even when toothless, blind, and hoar,
Able to perform no more,
Still in thought we fumble o'er
     Dreams and dreams of Luv.

Therefore let each film and book,
Every dinner that we cook,
Every tonic, garment, look,
Nudge us on to Luv.

10. From the deposit Hooper made to the Bodleian Library, Fall 1997, containing
the manuscript of "Young King Cole."

If with posterity good fame
I cannot have, then let my name
Become at least a friendly joke
That where men congregate to smoke
My bathos and my rimes absurd
With laughter may be sometime heard
But with a friendly feeling still
For where they laugh they'll think no ill.
With Bozzy, Bavius, Blackmore be
Room for the Vorticists and me.
For tho long dead I'll love the earth
And have no shame to mend their mirth.

11. From the deposit Hooper made to the Bodleian Library, Fall 1997, containing
the manuscript of "Young King Cole."

That was an ugly age. There was a wind rising
Black enough to blow out all the lamps of the world,
Loud enough to roar down both the dance tune and the hymn.
Goths were coming. It was the beginning of the end.
They pulled Rome out from the castle of cards
Which history had been building. The whole thing collapsed,
Athens, ?????, Mycenae, immemorial Khan
Ur and Babylon. It was the very end.

Young King Cole and Other Pieces *and Holographs*
of Other Lewis Poems, Bodleian Library

Here are the contents of Hooper's deposit to the Bodleian in Fall 1997.

1. A letter by Walter Hooper to Dr. Judith Priestman explaining why he is depositing the materials. It reads in part:

    I wonder if I may deposit these holograph poems under deposit in the Bodleian? There are still a few more to come. This, however, is the major collection of Lewis's poems. At the time of his death he was working on a volume of verse to be called *Young King Cole and Other Pieces,* and he had written an Introduction (which I include) to go with it [this introduction has been published in *CP*]. Lewis almost never stopped revising his poems, and that explains why some of these later versions are quite different from some of those he published years before. If Lewis had lived longer, I'm sure he would have made a thorough search of his files for missing items. However, he did not get the chance, and it was left for me to chase down all the poems I could find amongst his papers.

Unless otherwise noted, the following appear in both holograph and typescript versions.

2. A title page: "Young King Cole and other Pieces by C. S. Lewis, Fellow of Magdalen College, Oxford."
3. A note page thanking various magazines for permission to publish already published poems.
4. An introduction Hooper has published in *Collected Poems* (hereafter *CP*); unlike most of the poems that follow, it is written on lined paper. There are

numerous corrections; however, it appears to be Lewis's handwriting. In holograph only.

5. "What the Bird Said Early in the Year." There are slight variations between the holograph and the typescript. A version is published as *"Chanson D'Aventure,"* *The Oxford Magazine* 56 (May 19, 1938): 638 (under the pseudonym Nat Whilk, hereafter N.W.). Revised and retitled as "What the Bird Said Early in the Year" in *Poems* (hereafter *P*) and *CP*.

6. Epigrams and epitaphs. The typescript and holograph versions have in common ten epigrams and epitaphs; there are slight variations between the holograph and the typescript versions. Number one (two holograph versions appear) is published as "Epitaph 1" in *P* and *CP*. Number two is published as "Epitaph 2" in *P* and *CP*. Number three is published as "Epitaph 5" in *P* and *CP*. Number four is published as "On Receiving Bad News," *Time and Tide* 26 (Dec. 29, 1945): 1093, and as "Epitaph 12" in *P* and *CP*. Number five is published as "Epitaph 6" in *P* and *CP*. Number six is published as "Epitaph," *The Month* 2 (July 1949): 8, and "Epitaph 17" in *P* and *CP*. Number seven (two holograph versions appear) is published as "Epitaph," *Time and Tide* 23 (June 6, 1942): 460, and as "Epitaph 11" in *P* and *CP*. Number eight is published as "Epitaph," *The Spectator* 181 (July 30, 1948): 142, and as "Epitaph 14" in *P* and *CP*. Number nine (two holograph versions appear) is published as "Epitaph 10" in *P* and *CP*. Number ten is published as "Epitaph in a Village Churchyard," *Time and Tide* 30 (Mar. 19, 1949): 272, and "Epitaph 16" in *P* and *CP* (two other holograph fragments of this epitaph also appear here). Four other epigrams and epitaphs in Lewis's handwriting are added to the typescript. Number eleven is published as "Epitaph 8" in *P* and *CP*. Number twelve is published as "Epitaph 13" in *P* and *CP* (number twelve also exists as two other holograph versions below). Number thirteen is published as "Epanorthosis (for the end of Goethe's *Faust*)," *The Cambridge Review* 77 (May 26, 1956): 610, and as "Epitaph 15" in *P* and *CP*. Number fourteen is published as "Epitaph 9" in *P* and *CP*.

Within the holograph version, an original number three ("You call them Fascists: so the rabbit, / Regardless of their varying merits, / Thinks all who share the simple habit / Of eating rabbit-pie [meat] are ferrets") has been struck through. Also the original number eleven has been struck through and is not readable.

7. "The Adam Unparadised"; in the holograph, the title "Footnote to Pre-History" has been struck through; there are slight variations between the holograph and the typescript. A version is published as "A Footnote to Pre-History," *Punch* 217 (Sept. 14, 1949): 304 (N.W.). Revised and retitled "The Adam Unparadised" in *P* and *CP*.

8. "*Vitrea Circe.*" There are two different holographs versions, and there are slight variations between both holograph versions and the typescript version. A version is published as "*Vitrea Circe,*" *Punch* 214 (June 23, 1948): 543 (N.W.). Revised and reprinted in *P* and *CP.*

9. "Late Summer." A version is published in *P* and *CP.*

10. "The Late Passenger." There are two different holograph versions; the first version matches the typescript. The second holograph version has lightly penciled notes above some of the lines. A version is published as "The Sailing of the Ark," *Punch* 215 (Aug. 11, 1948): 124 (N.W.). Revised and retitled "The Late Passenger" in *P* and *CP.*

11. "Five Sonnets." There are two different holograph versions; the first version matches the typescript. A version is published in *P* and *CP.*

12. "Pattern" ("Some Believe the Slumber"). A version is published as "Experiment," *The Spectator* 161 (Dec. 9, 1938): 998. The poem is also found in *Augury: An Oxford Miscellany of Verse and Prose,* edited by A. M. Hardie and K. C. Douglas, Oxford: Blackwell, 1940, p. 28. There it is a slightly different version called "Metrical Experiment." Still another version appears as "Pattern" in *P* and *CP.*

13. "The Last of the Wine." A version is published as "The End of the Wine," *Punch* 213 (Dec. 3, 1947): 538 (N.W.). Revised and retitled "The Last of the Wine" in *P* and *CP.*

14. "Le Roi S'Amuse." There are slight variations between the holograph and the typescript. A version is published as "Le Roi S'Amuse," *Punch* 213 (Oct. 1, 1947): 324 (N.W.). Revised and reprinted in *P* and *CP.*

15. "The Turn of the Tide." There are slight variations between the holograph and the typescript. A version is published as "The Turn of the Tide," *Punch:* Almanac 215 (Nov. 1, 1948): n.p. (N.W.). Revised in *P* and *CP.*

16. "Donkey's Delight." A version is published as "Donkey's Delight," *Punch* 213 (Nov. 5, 1947): 442 (N.W.). Revised and reprinted in *P* and *CP.*

17. "Nearly They Stood." A version is published in *The Pilgrim's Regress* as "Nearly They Stood Who Fall." Revised and retitled "Nearly They Stood" in *P* and *CP.*

18. "Scazons." A version is published in *The Pilgrim's Regress* as "Passing To-day by a Cottage, I Shed Tears." Revised and retitled "Scazons" in *P* and *CP.*

19. "Footnote to All Prayers." A version is published in *The Pilgrim's Regress* as "He Whom I Bow To." Revised and retitled "Footnote to All Prayers" in *P* and *CP.*

20. "Solomon." There also appear to be holograph fragments of early versions. A version is published as "Solomon," *Punch* 211 (Aug. 14, 1946): 136 (N.W.). Revised and reprinted in *P* and *CP.*

21. "To a Friend." There are slight variations between the holograph and the typescript. A version is published as "To G. M.," *The Spectator* 169 (Oct. 9, 1942): 335. Revised and retitled "To a Friend" in *P* and *CP*.

22. "The Condemned." A version is published as "Under Sentence," *The Spectator* 175 (Sept. 7, 1945): 219. Revised and retitled "The Condemned" in *P* and *CP*.

23. "Man is a Lumpe Where All Beasts Kneaded Be." A version is published as "The Shortest Way Home," *The Oxford Magazine* 52 (May 10, 1934): 665 (N.W.). Revised and retitled "Man is a Lumpe Where All Beasts Kneaded Be" in *P* and *CP*.

24. "Pindar Sang." There are slight variations between the holograph and the typescript. A version is published as "Arrangement of Pindar," *Mandrake* 1, no. 6 (1949): 43–45. Revised and retitled "Pindar Sang" in *P* and *CP*.

25. "As One Oldster to Another." A version is published as "As One Oldster to Another," *Punch* 218 (Mar. 15, 1950): 294–95 (N.W.). Revised and reprinted in *P* and *CP*.

26. "The Apologist's Evening Prayer." A version is published in *P* and *CP*.

27. "The Birth of Language." There are slight variations between the holograph and the typescript. A version is published as "The Birth of Language," *Punch* 210 (Jan. 9, 1946): 32 (N.W.). Revised and reprinted in *P* and *CP*.

28. "On a Picture by Chirico." A version is published as "On a Picture by Chirico," *The Spectator* 182 (May 6, 1949): 607. Revised and reprinted in *P* and *CP*.

29. "On Being Human." A version is published as "On Being Human," *Punch* 210 (May 8, 1946): 402 (N.W.). Revised and reprinted in *P* and *CP*.

30. "The Landing." There are two different holograph versions; the first version matches the typescript. A version is published as "The Landing," *Punch* 215 (Sept. 15, 1948): 237 (N.W.). Revised and reprinted in *P* and *CP*.

31. "The Adam at Night." There are slight variations between the holograph and the typescript. A version is published as "Adam at Night," *Punch* 216 (May 11, 1949): 510 (N.W.). Revised and retitled "The Adam at Night" in *P* and *CP*.

32. "The Dragon Speaks." A version is published in *The Pilgrim's Regress* as "Once the Worm-laid Egg Broke in the Wood." Revised and retitled "The Dragon Speaks" in *P* and *CP*.

33. "The Day with a White Mark." A version is published as "The Day with a White Mark," *Punch* 217 (Aug. 17, 1949): 170 (N.W.). Revised and reprinted in *P* and *CP*.

34. "The Saboteuse." A version is published in *P* and *CP*.

35. "Angel's Song." A version is published in *The Pilgrim's Regress* as "I Know Not, I." Revised and retitled "Angel's Song" in *P* and *CP*.

36. "The Small Man Orders His Wedding." A version is published as "The Small Man Orders His Wedding" in *P* and *CP*. (Another holograph in the Bodleian, "A Wedding has been Arranged," is a slightly different version. A third holograph version is in the Bodleian, MS. Eng. c. 2724, fol. 55; it has the title "An Epithalamium for John Wain feigned to be spoken in his person giving orders for his wedding" signed C.S.L., June 1947; there also appear to be other draft fragments of this version.)

37. "Hermione in the House of Paulina." There are slight variations between the holograph and the typescript. A version is published as "Hermione in the House of Paulina," *Augury: An Oxford Miscellany of Verse and Poetry*, edited by A. M. Hardie and K. C. Douglas, Oxford: Blackwell, 1940, p. 28. Revised and reprinted in *P* and *CP*.

38. "Young King Cole." There are slight variations between the holograph and the typescript. There is a separate holograph with the final three stanzas repeated. A version is published as "Dangerous Oversight," *Punch* 212 (May 21, 1947): 434 (N.W.). Revised and retitled "Young King Cole" in *P* and *CP*.

39. "The Ecstasy." There are slight variations between the holograph and the typescript. A version is published in *P* and *CP*.

40. "The Magician and the Dryad." The holograph is titled "Conversation Piece: The Magician and the Dryad." A version is published as "Conversation Piece: The Magician and the Dryad," *Punch* 217 (July 20, 1949): 71 (N.W.). Revised and retitled "The Magician and the Dryad" in *P* and *CP*.

41. "A Cliché Came out of its Cage." There are slight variations between the holograph and the typescript. A version is published as "A Cliché Came Out of its Cage," *Nine: A Magazine of Poetry and Criticism* 2 (May 1950): 114. Revised (a second stanza is added) and reprinted in *P* and *CP*.

42. "Re-adjustment." There are slight variations between the holograph and the typescript. A version is published as "Re-Adjustment," *Fifty-Two: A Journal of Books and Authors* [from Geoffrey Bles] no. 14 (Autumn 1964): 4. Reprinted in *P* and *CP*.

43. "To Charles Williams." A version is published as "On the Death of Charles Williams," *Britain Today* no. 112 (Aug. 1945): 14. Revised and retitled "To Charles Williams" in *P* and *CP*.

44. "The Prudent Jailer." In the holograph the title "The Wise Jailer" has been changed to "The Prudent Jailer." There are substantial differences between the two versions, including the reversal of stanzas two and three. A version is published as "The Romantics," *The New English Weekly* 30 (Jan. 16, 1947): 130. Revised and retitled "The Prudent Jailer" in *P* and *CP*.

45. "The Prodigality of Firdausi." In typescript only. A version is published as "The Prodigality of Firdausi," *Punch* 215 (Dec. 1, 1948): 510 (N.W.). Revised and reprinted in *P* and *CP*.

46. "After Aristotle." In typescript only, and because the typescript is different, this poem was probably not intended to be a part of *Young King Cole and Other Pieces*. A version is published as "After Aristotle," *The Oxford Magazine* 74 (Feb. 23, 1956): 296 (N.W.). Reprinted in *P* and *CP*.

47. "Aubade (Eight Strokes Sound from Within)." The typescript is signed "C. S. Lewis, Magdalene College, Cambridge." Because the typescript is different, this poem was probably not intended to be a part of *Young King Cole and Other Pieces*. A version is published in *P* and *CP*.

The following appear in holograph only.

1. "A Confession." Two versions. A version is published as *"Spartan Nactus,"* *Punch* 227 (Dec. 1, 1954): 685 (N.W.). Revised and retitled "A Confession" in *P* and *CP*.

2. "Lord, Hear My Voice, This Present Voice I Mean." Three versions. A version is published as "Legion," *The Month* 13 (Apr. 1955): 210. Revised and reprinted in *P* and *CP*.

3. "Two Kinds of Memory." Three versions. A version is published as "Two Kinds of Memory," *Time and Tide* 28 (Aug. 7, 1947): 859. Revised and reprinted in *P* and *CP*.

4. "On a Vulgar Error." Two versions. A version is published in *P* and *CP*.

5. "Narnian Suite." Four versions (with varying titles) including a separate "March for Trumpet, Drum, and Twenty-one Giants." A version is published as "Narnian Suite" in *P* and *CP*. In addition, a version of "March for Trumpet, Drum, and Twenty-one Giants" is published as "March for Drum, Trumpet, and Twenty-one Giants," *Punch* 225 (Nov. 4, 1953): 553. A bit of this poem, called "an old Narnian marching song," appears midway through *The Last Battle*.

6. "Science-Fiction Cradlesong." A version is published in *P* and *CP*.

7. "Cradle-song Based on a Theme from Nicolas of Cusa." Three versions. A version is published as "Cradle-Song Based on a Theme from Nicolas of Cusa," *The Times Literary Supplement* (June 11, 1954): 375. Revised and reprinted in *P* and *CP*.

8. "On a Theme from Nicolas of Cusa." A version is published as "On Another Theme from Nicolas of Cusa," *The Times Literary Supplement* (Jan. 21, 1955): 43. Revised and retitled "On a Theme from Nicolas of Cusa" in *P* and *CP*.

9. "Government." Two versions. One is titled "Lines During a General Election." A version with the latter title is published in *P* and *CP*.

10. "A Wedding has been Arranged." This is a slightly different version of "The Small Man Orders His Wedding" published in *P* and *CP*. Also, another version is in the Bodleian, MS. Eng. c. 2724, fol. 55; it has the title "An Epithala-

mium for John Wain feigned to be spoken in his person giving orders for his wedding" signed C.S.L., June 1947. There also are holograph fragments of early versions of this poem.

11. "I Dream't That All the Planning." A version is published as "Pan's Purge" in *P* and *CP*.

12. "Vowels and Sirens." Two versions. A version is published as "Vowels and Sirens," *The Times Literary Supplement,* Special Autumn Issue (Aug. 29, 1954): xiv. Revised and reprinted in *P* and *CP*.

13. "The Nativity." A version is published in *P* and *CP*.

14. "Love's As Warm As Tears." Two versions. One is titled "Song"; since it is written on the back of paper with a Cambridge letterhead, it may have been written after Lewis's move to Cambridge. A version is published in *P* and *CP*.

15. An epitaph, "Here Lies One So Kind of Speech." Two versions. A third version appears as number twelve in the *Young King Cole and Other Pieces* typescript mentioned above. A version is published as "Epitaph 13" in *P* and *CP*.

16. An epitaph, "Here Lies the Whole World after One." Two versions. A third version appears as number 6 in the *Young King Cole and Other Pieces* typescript mentioned above. A version is published as in "Epitaph 17" in *P* and *CP*.

17. "Stephen to Lazarus." A version is published in *P* and *CP*.

18. "One Happier Look on Your Kind, Suffering Face." A version is published as "Old Poets Remembered" in *P* and *CP*.

19. "Prelude to Space (An Epithalamium)." A version is published in *P* and *CP*.

20. "Yes, You Are Always Everywhere." Two versions. A version is published as "No Beauty We Could Desire" in *P* and *CP*.

21. "You, Beneath Scraping Branches." A version is published as "Leaving For Ever the Home of One's Youth" in *CP*.

22. "Among the Hills." An expanded version is published as "The Meteorite" in *P* and *CP*.

23. "To the Author of *Flowering Rifles.*" Signed by Lewis, Magdalen College, Oxford. A version is published as "To Mr. Roy Campbell," *The Cherwell* 56 (May 6, 1939): 35 (N.W.). Revised and retitled "The Author of *Flowering Rifle*" in *P* and *CP*.

24. "Dear Roy—Why Should each Wowzer on the List." A version is published as "To Roy Campbell" in *P* and *CP*.

25. "The Phoenix Flew into My Garden." A version is published as "The Phoenix" in *P* and *CP*.

26. "Consolation." A note from Lewis at the bottom of the page reads "And—in quite a different vein—what about this?" A version is published in *CP*.

27. "Now that Night Is Creeping." A version is published as "Evensong" in *P* and *CP*.

28. "I Have Scraped the Rock Clean." Two versions. A third version is published as "I Have Scraped Clean the Plateau from the Filthy Earth" in *The Pilgrim's Regress* (reprinted as "Virtue's Independence" in *P* and *CP*).

29. "All This Is Flashy Rhetoric." Three versions. One version is published as "As the Ruin Falls" in *P* and *CP*.

30. "Oh Do Not Die." Three versions. One version (with a slight variation) is published as "Joys That Sting" in *P* and *CP*.

31. "Who Knows if the Isolation, the Compact, Firm-shaped"; another holograph version appears in Letters of CSL to Miscellaneous Correspondents, Wade Center, 881, to Kathleen Raine (Apr. 11, 1956). This poem has not been published.

32. "Aubade (Somehow It's Strange)." This poem has not been published.

33. There are also five holograph poems I have never seen or heard of elsewhere. Most are very hard to read; sometimes only the first line or two is decipherable and the rest is impossible to read. Until additional evidence can be gathered, the authorship of these poems must be viewed as doubtful: "Oh My Forbidden Tree, [Forbidden Imp?]"; "If with Posterity Good Fame"; "God Why (Call? Carve?Cart?) Me for an Ogre's Heart?"; "That was an ugly age" (two versions); "Through chink and cranny sinking."

The Holograph Contents of "Half Hours with Hamilton" by C. S. Lewis

Available at The Wade Center, *OB*, Poems.
"Half Hours with Hamilton or Quiet Moments."

There is a note by Lewis that prefaces the poems: "It is hoped that this little selection from my works, from which all objectionable matter has been carefully excluded, will be found specially suitable for Sunday and family reading, and also to the higher forms of secondary schools."

1. "I woke from a fool's dream to find all spent." Published as "Epitaphs and Epigrams 3" in *P* and *CP*.
2. "He whom I bow to only knows to whom I bow." Published in *The Pilgrim's Regress* as "He Whom I Bow To." Revised and retitled "Footnote to All Prayers" in *P* and *CP*.
3. "You rest upon me all my days." Published in *The Pilgrim's Regress* as "You Rest Upon Me All My Days." Revised and retitled "Caught" in *P* and *CP*.
4. "Is this your duty? Never lay your ear." Published as "The Shortest Way Home," *The Oxford Magazine* 52 (May 10, 1934): 665 (N.W.). Revised and retitled "Man is a Lumpe Where All Beasts Kneaded Be" in *P* and *CP*.
5. "Nearly they stood who fall." Published in *The Pilgrim's Regress* as "Nearly They Stood Who Fall." Revised and retitled "Nearly They Stood" in *P* and *CP*.
6. "When Lilith means to draw me." Published in *The Pilgrim's Regress* as "When Lilith Means to Draw Me." Revised and retitled "Lilith" in *P* and *CP*.
7. "Thoughts that go through my mind." Published as "Essence," in *Fear No More: A Book of Poems for the Present Time by Living English Poets*. Cambridge:

Cambridge University Press, 1940, p. 4. All the poems in this volume are published anonymously; however, six copies contain an additional leaf giving the names of the authors of the poems; one of these is in the Bodleian Library, Oxford. Reprinted in *CP*.

8. "Better go on and leave me. I must go back." Revised and published as "Epitaphs and Epigrams 6" in *P* and *CP*.

9. "See, Lord, the sulphurous, never-quenched." Published in *The Pilgrim's Regress* as "Quick!" Revised and retitled "Forbidden Pleasure" in *P* and *CP*.

10. "I have come back with victory got." Published in *The Pilgrim's Regress* as "I Have Come Back with Victory Got." Revised and retitled "Dragon-Slayer" in *P* and *CP*.

11. "Once the worm-laid egg broke in the wood." Published in *The Pilgrim's Regress* as "Once the Worm-laid Egg Broke in the Wood." Revised and retitled "The Dragon Speaks" in *P* and *CP*.

12. "Because of endless pride." Published in *The Pilgrim's Regress* as "Because of Endless Pride." Revised and retitled "Posturing" in *P* and *CP*.

13. "They tell me, Sir, that when I seem." Published as "They tell me, Lord" in *Letters to Malcolm: Chiefly on Prayer*. London: Geoffrey Bles, 1964. Revised and retitled "Prayer" in *P* and *CP*.

14. "I am not one that easily flits past in thought." Published in *The Pilgrim's Regress* as "I Am not One that Easily Flits Past in Thought." Revised and retitled "When the Curtain's Down" in *P* and *CP*.

15. "Walking to day by the river I shed tears." Published in *The Pilgrim's Regress* as "Passing To-day by a Cottage, I Shed Tears." Revised and retitled "Scazons" in *P* and *CP*.

The Holograph Contents of Lewis's Earliest Poems, In the Handwriting of Arthur Greeves

Available at the Wade Center, "Early Poems." While these poems are most probably by Lewis, his authorship cannot be verified with absolute certainty at this time; I offer a speculation here. In the Lewis Family Papers, Warren Lewis writes: "In the two years intervening between Easter 1915 and Easter 1917, he [his brother] wrote fifty-two poems which he copied carefully into an old . . . notebook. The whole is entitled 'The Metrical Meditations of a Cod'" (4:306). As noted below, the Table of Contents of this notebook lists fifty-two poems; numbers fifty-three (which is missing) through fifty-eight were obviously added to the notebook at some later point. Accordingly, I surmise this notebook is a somewhat later and annotated version of "The Metrical Meditations of a Cod."

The title page reads: "English Verses Made By—Clive Staples Lewis:—and Copied by His Friend: —Joseph Arthur Greeves:—Belfast in the Year 1917."

Table of Contents
1. My Western Garden (Easter 1915)
2. A Death Song (Easter 1915)
3. The Hills of Down (Easter 1915)
4. Against Potpourri (Summer 1915)
5. To the Gods of Old Time (Summer 1915)
6. The Town of Gold (Summer 1915)
7. The Wood Desolate (Summer 1915)
8. Anamnesis (Summer 1915)
9. A Prelude (Summer 1915)
10. Ballade of a Winter Morning (Christmas 1915)

11. Sonnet—to John Keats (Christmas 1915)
12. Yet more of the Wood Desolate (Christmas 1915)
13. The Wind (Christmas 1915)
14. Sonnet (Christmas 1915)
15. New Year's Eve (Christmas 1915)
16. Noon (Christmas 1915)
17. Night (Easter 1916)
18. Ad Astra (Easter 1916); early version of "Victory"
19. A Hymn (Easter 1916); early version of "To Sleep"
20. The Roads (Easter 1916)
21. Laus Mortis (Easter 1916)
22. In His own Image (Easter 1916)
23. Sonnet (Easter 1916)
24. Loneliness (Easter 1916)
25. The Little Golden Statuette (Easter 1916)
26. Sonnet (Summer 1916); to poesy
27. The Satyr (Summer 1916)
28. The Star Bath (Summer 1916)
29. Sonnet—to Sir Philip Sydney (Summer 1916)
30. Lullaby (Summer 1916)
31. Exercise on an old Theme (Summer 1916)
32. The Autumn Morning (Summer 1916)
33. Of Ships (Christmas 1916)
34. Couplets (Christmas 1916)
35. Hylas (Christmas 1916)
36. The Ocean Strand (Christmas 1916)
37. Hesperus (Christmas 1916)
38. How I saw Angus the God (Christmas 1916)
39. Decadence (Christmas 1916)
40. Milton Read Again (Easter 1917)
41. Ballade Mystical (Easter 1917); early version of "Ballade Mystique"
42. L'Apprenti Sorcier (Easter 1917)
43. MHÄEN ATAN (Easter 1917)
44. Irish Nocturne (Easter 1917)
45. Ballade on a certain pious gentleman (Easter 1917); this poem is referred to in Heinemann's letter of October 8, 1914 to Lewis (see chapter 2, n. 45).
46. Circe—a fragment (Easter 1917)
47. Song of the Pilgrims (Easter 1917)
48. Exercise (Easter 1917)
49. The Philosopher (Easter 1917)

50. Ode; early version of "Ode for New Year's Day"
51. Venite; early versions of stanzas from to "De Profundis" and "Apology"
52. My Own Death Song; early version of "Death in Battle"

The following poems are in the notebook, but not listed in the Table of Contents:

53. ??MISSING??
54. Lullaby! Lullaby!; early version of "Lullaby"
55. Tho' its truth they tell, Despoina; early version of stanzas from "Ode for New Year's Day"
56. If men should ask; early version of "Apology"
57. Oh there is a castle built; early version of "World's Desire"
58. Despoina, bear with me

Also available at the Wade Center in a separate notebook entitled "Poems" are four additional unpublished poems:

1. Go litel tugge upon thes watres shene
2. As long as rolling wheels rotate
3. Tu silentia perosus
4. Of this great suit who dares forsee the end?

Notes

1. C. S. Lewis, Poet

1. Don King, "Glints of Light: The Unpublished Short Poetry of C. S. Lewis," *seven: An Anglo-American Literary Review* 15 (1998): 73–96. These poems also appear in appendix 2. In addition, there are another eleven unpublished short poems that appear in appendix 3.

2. Thomas Howard, "*Poems*: A Review," *Christianity Today* 9 (June 18, 1965): 30.

3. Chad Walsh, *The Literary Legacy of C. S. Lewis* (New York: Harcourt Brace Jovanovich, 1979), 35.

4. Dabney Hart, "Editor's Comment," *Studies in Literary Imagination* 22 (Fall 1989): 128.

5. Charles Huttar, "A Lifelong Love Affair with Language: C. S. Lewis' Poetry," in *Word and Story in C. S. Lewis*, ed. Peter Schakel and Charles Huttar (Columbia: U of Missouri P, 1991), 86.

6. George Sayer, "C. S. Lewis's *Dymer*," *seven: An Anglo-American Literary Review* 1 (1980): 113.

7. W. W. Robson, "The Poetry of C. S. Lewis," *The Chesterton Review* 17 (3–4) (Aug.–Nov 1991): 437.

8. Luci Shaw, "Looking Back to Eden: The Poetry of C. S. Lewis," *Bulletin of the New York C. S. Lewis Society* 23 (Feb. 1992): 3.

9. Owen Barfield, address given at Wheaton College, Wheaton, Ill., Oct. 16, 1964, Marion E. Wade Center, Wheaton College, Wheaton, Ill.

10. Lewis's shorthand allusion to Bergen-Belsen, German Nazi concentration camp near the villages of Bergen and Belsen, about ten miles northwest of Celle, then in Prussian Hanover, Germany. Anne Frank died at Bergen-Belsen in March 1945.

11. *Surprised by Joy: The Shape of My Early Life* (New York: Harcourt, Brace and World, 1955), 25 (hereafter cited as *SJ*). Lewis has a poem fragment in which he provides further information about his recollection of Capron. This is discussed in detail in chapter 4.

12. See Warren Lewis's "C. S. Lewis: A Biography," unpublished manuscript, Marion E. Wade Center, 21.

13. Before Lewis enters Cherbourg House, he spends a short time at home which he thoroughly enjoys: "Curiously enough it is at this time, not in earlier childhood, that I chiefly remember delighting in fairy tales. I fell deeply under the spells of Dwarfs—the old bright-hooded, snowy-bearded dwarves. . . . I visualized them so intensely that I came to the very frontiers of hallucination; once, walking in the garden, I was for a second not quite sure that a little man had not run past me into the shrubbery. I was faintly alarmed, but it was not like my night fears. A fear that guarded Faerie was one I could face" (*SJ*,

54–55). This intense love for faery is a key theme in many poems in *Spirits in Bondage* and the narrative poem "The Queen of Drum."

14. Lewis goes on in this passage to connect the experience with his rediscovery of the role of joy in his life.

15. Copies of the magazine, *The Soundbox,* from this time period (1911–12) appear not to have survived. In checking the significant holdings of libraries in both Ireland and England, I have been unable to find surviving copies.

16. This 794-line fragment I have entitled "Descend to Earth, Descend, Celestial Nine" has survived, is discussed in detail in chapter 2, and the complete text is published in appendix 1.

17. The idea that he tried to write poetry rather than allowing it to flow from his pen is one that recurs many times; it may explain why he never achieved the poetic acclaim he desired.

18. Lewis has a poem fragment in which he provides further information about his recollection of Smith. This is discussed in detail in chapter 4.

19. Lewis has a poem fragment in which he provides further information about his recollection of Kirkpatrick. This is discussed in detail in chapter 4.

20. Fewer than 120 lines in four fragments of *Loki Bound* have survived. They are discussed in detail in chapter 2, and the complete text is published in appendix 1.

21. A complete scheme for an opera version of the poem is found in C. S. Lewis, *They Stand Together: The Letters of C. S. Lewis to Arthur Greeves (1914–1963),* edited by Walter Hooper (New York: Macmillan, 1979), 50–53.

22. Hearing and reading poetry aloud was always an important principle, indicated as he writes to his brother eighteen years later: "By the way, I most fully agree with you about 'the lips being invited to share the banquet' in poetry, and always 'mouth' it while I read. . . . I look upon this 'mouthing' as an infallible mark of those who really like poetry" (Apr. 8, 1932, *LL,* 303).

23. Lewis includes "Milton Read Again" in *Spirits in Bondage,* a tribute to his deep affection for the blind poet. His lifelong admiration for Milton is later reflected in his *A Preface to Paradise Lost* (London: Oxford UP, 1942).

24. Later, in a telling letter to his brother on August 2, 1928, he does admit that the thrill of discovering a great new poem in English is over: "There is no longer any chance of discovering a new long poem in English which will turn out to be just what I want and which can be added to the *Faerie Queen, The Prelude, Paradise Lost, The Ring and the Book,* the *Earthly Paradise,* and a few others—because there aren't anymore. . . . In that sense I have come to the end of English poetry—as you may be said to have come to the end of a wood, not where you have actually walked every inch of it, but when you have walked about in it enough to know where all the boundaries are and to feel the end near even when you can't see it; when there is no longer any hope (as there was in the first few days) that the next turn of the path might bring you to an unsuspected lake or cave or clearing on the edge of a new valley" (*LL,* 259). Clearly there is in this letter sadness and a longing for the old thrill of discovering a new poem; Lewis's tone here recalls Wordsworth's "Tintern Abbey": "That time is past, / And all its aching joys are now no more, / And all its dizzy raptures."

25. While "The Quest of Bleheris" is a prose romance and not a poem (see the Bodleian Library, Oxford, MS. Eng. lett. c. 220/5. fols. 5–43, dated 1916), it is not far from poetry. It is

a fascinating piece of writing, very much in the school of Arthurian romance/allegory. One interesting point is that the old, ugly hag who thwarts Bleheris may be the prototype for the hag who similarly thwarts Dymer. A very long and involved effort, it was never finished. For recent scholarship on "Bleheris," see David C. Downing, "'The Dungeon of his Soul': Lewis's Unfinished 'Quest of Bleheris,'" *SEVEN: An Anglo-American Literary Review* 15 (1998): 37–54 and my "C. S. Lewis's 'The Quest of Bleheris' as Prose Poetry," *The Lamp-Post of the Southern California C. S. Lewis Society* 23, no. 1 (Spring 1999): 3–15.

26. The quote means "to be praised by a man who is [himself] praised."

27. *LKB*, 0087.

28. Such critical self-assessment foreshadows an even more penetrating episode several years later (discussed below); this weakness also may be related to Lewis's lifelong search for joy and his repeated realization that when he actively sought joy he never found it.

29. While this focus linked him with the ancient poets he so admired (for example, he placed great emphasis upon meter, even writing several poems expressly to experiment with various meters that fascinated him), in another way it cut him off from them. For Homer and Virgil, poetry was their natural form of expression. Yet Odysseus and Aeneas live on, less because of verse per se, and more because of their characters and the narratives about them. Lewis, lacking an Odysseus or Aeneas (although later he almost adopted Wotan/Odin), focused too much on the *form* of poetry rather than on the *creation* of a story, whether original or borrowed. Happily, Lewis's prose is not encumbered by a similar focus.

30. Lewis writes Greeves on December 2, 1918, about this prose version: "I have just finished a short narrative, which is a verse version of our old friend 'Dymer', greatly reduced & altered to my new ideas. The main idea is that of development by self-destruction, both of individuals & species. . . . The background proceeds on the old assumption of good *outside & opposed to* [Lewis's emphasis] the cosmic order. It is written in the metre of [Shakespeare's] Venus and Adonis: 'Dymer' is changed to 'Ask' (you remember Ask and Embla in the Norse myths) & it is in the 3rd person under the title of 'The Redemption of Ask'"(*TST*, 239).

31. Lewis offers his own chronology for the development of *Dymer* in "The Lewis Papers: Memoirs of the Lewis Family, 1850–1930," 11 vols., Wade Center, 9:129–30.

32. *All My Road Before Me: The Diary of C. S. Lewis 1922–1927*, edited by Walter Hooper (New York: Harcourt Brace Jovanovich, 1991), 20–21.

33. See *The Beacon* 3, no. 31 (May 1924): 444–45. This poem is discussed in chapter 4.

34. Unfortunately, only the opening eight-line stanza has survived. It is discussed briefly in chapter 2.

35. Though a poem by this title has not survived, I believe "The Carpet Rises in the Draught" is in fact the fragment referred to here. This fragment is discussed in detail in chapter 4.

36. "Foster" has not survived.

37. In a footnote on this same page, Walter Hooper says: "The first version of this sonnet sequence survives in the same notebook as the last portion of the Diary. A revised version of it, entitled 'Infatuation,' is found in Lewis's *Poems* (1964)."

38. "Wild Hunt" has not survived, though its relationship to "The King of Drum" will be discussed in chapter 4. "Sigrid" has not survived. A fragment of a poem on Cupid and

Psyche has survived, will be discussed in detail in chapter 4, and the complete text is in appendix 1. Of course, Lewis's fullest realization of this theme appears in *Till We Have Faces: A Myth Retold* (London: Geoffrey Bles, 1956).

39. These included the fact that Heinemann had already published *Spirits in Bondage* and that Lewis had hoped to make a profit, desired personal fame, desired that the poem itself achieve a place in literary history, and desired that his poem validate his poetic ability.

40. This letter contains the diary entry for March 6, 1926, cited above.

41. Hooper collects both the published poems and others he discovers after Lewis's death in *Poems* (New York: Harcourt Brace Jovanovich, 1964) and later *The Collected Poems of C. S. Lewis* (London: Fount, 1994). As noted earlier, my "Glints of Light: The Unpublished Short Poetry of C. S. Lewis" includes ten more poems previously unpublished; they are reprinted in appendix 2.

42. *OB,* March 16, 1932, 0054.

43. Lewis addressed this topic as early as March 30, 1930, in a paper he read to the literary group, the Marlets. Entitled "The Personal Heresy in Poetics," the paper introduced themes Lewis expanded upon in his debate with Tillyard in *The Personal Heresy* (London: Oxford UP, 1939) (hereafter *PH*). In *C. S. Lewis: A Biography* (New York: Harcourt Brace Jovanovich, 1974), Roger L. Green and Walter Hooper note that the paper "attacked the notion that poetry is the 'expression of personality' and is useful for putting us into contact with the 'poet's soul': in short, that a poet's 'Life' and 'Works' are two diverse expressions of a single quiddity" (125).

44. *The Personal Heresy,* 4.

45. Later, in *An Experiment in Criticism* (Cambridge: Cambridge UP, 1961), Lewis makes a similar point: "[Literature is valuable] not only nor chiefly in order to see what [the authors] are like but [because] . . . we see what they see [and] occupy, for a while, their seat in the great theatre, [and] use their spectacles and [are] made free of whatever insights, joys, terrors, wonders or merriment those spectacles reveal" (139).

46. Interestingly, Lewis appears here to be endorsing something similar to T. S. Eliot's "objective correlative," in spite of the fact that elsewhere he disagrees with Eliot's literary perspective. Joe R. Christopher says, "I'm not certain that Lewis really meant what he was saying [here]" (e-mail to author, Nov. 18, 1997). At the same time, Lewis's claim here is tied to his frequent celebration of the core values of civilized life, what he terms "stock responses." Tracing these back to the Greek and Roman writers he so admired—Homer, Virgil, and Ovid—as well as the towering figures of Western literature—Dante, Chaucer, Shakespeare, Milton, Wordsworth, Shelley, Keats, and Yeats—Lewis infuses his work with passages promoting honor, courage, bravery, honesty, charity, respect, and related values.

47. *RP,* 0008.

48. Lewis to Rhona Bodle, Miscellaneous Letters, June 24, 1949, 0192–0193, Wade Center. Jerry Daniel in his "The Taste of the Pineapple: A Basis for Literary Criticism" (in *The Taste of the Pineapple: Essays on C. S. Lewis as Reader, Critic, and Imaginative Writer,* ed. Bruce L. Edwards [Bowling Green, Oh.: Bowling Green State U Popular P, 1988]) emphasizes how wonderfully effective Lewis is in describing the "essence of things." Calling this focus an "emphasis on the quiddity of things" (10), Daniel offers thoughtful commentary and numerous examples from Lewis's work to sustain his argument. As a reader, Lewis, according to Daniel, "immersed himself in the quality of a story or a poem he was reading,"

and "whether prose or verse, all works were 'poetry' to him in the sense that the 'feel' or 'taste' was primary" (10–11). Indeed, Daniel uses throughout the image of the "taste" of a poem as a way of describing Lewis's acquisition of poetry. In addition, Daniel applies this same rubric to Lewis as literary critic and imaginative writer. He finds Lewis's love of stock responses in poetry a connection to his desire for the essence of things: "Lewis felt . . . that literature *ought* to produce stock responses: if a story presents a scene of cruelty, we ought to respond with horror; if a poem describes a mother's love for her child we ought to respond with warm satisfaction. Since he, as an artist, was attempting to impart a vision, he was attempting to elicit a response to that vision; and, believing in absolute values, he preferred to elicit a stock response. . . . [Lewis forces] us to attend to the great reality of the poetry, the vision, inherent in so many works written by so many different persons in different ages of our history" (25). Daniel's essay is must reading for anyone interested in Lewis's use of poetic language.

49. Lewis to Martyn Skinner, Miscellaneous Letters, Oct. 11, 1950, 942, Wade Center.

50. Lewis to Dom Bede Griffiths, Letters of CSL to Dom Bede Griffiths, Vol. 2, Apr. 22, 1954, 0070, Wade Center.

51. Introduction to *Collected Poems*, xv–xvi.

52. This poetic fragment is discussed in chapter 5.

53. Lewis's correspondence with Pitter and their shared interest in poetry is discussed more fully in chapter 9.

54. Feb. 2, 1947; MS. Eng. lett. c. 220/3, fol. 38, Bodleian Library.

55. July 6, 1947; MS. Eng. lett. c. 220/3, fol. 52, Bodleian Library.

56. According to Hooper, Lewis even revised poems after they had been published. Until recently it has been difficult to verify this contention. This task is somewhat easier now because, in the fall of 1997, Hooper deposited in the Bodleian Library the typescript of *Young King Cole and Other Pieces* as well as holographs of many other Lewis poems. Still problematic, however, is verifying whether the changes to or various versions of a poem occurred *before* or *after* the published version, since in most cases neither the typescript of *Young King Cole and Other Pieces* nor the holographs are dated. In appendix 4, I provide a complete list of the contents of this deposit as well the publication history of each poem.

57. This poem (and its possible connections to Lewis's wife, Joy) is discussed in detail in chapter 7.

58. The holographs are available in Hooper's 1997 deposit to the Bodleian Library. See the bibliography for a complete listing of holographs.

59. This is the version Hooper published in *Poems*.

60. Charles Huttar's, "A Lifelong Love Affair with Language: C. S. Lewis's Poetry," is the best piece of criticism available on Lewis's prosody. Huttar focuses upon both Lewis's love of language and his technical expertise as poet. While relegating Lewis to the role of minor poet, Huttar finds Lewis's "attitudes toward language [include] a respect for its illusive and elusive nature and at the same time an overflowing enjoyment of it" (87). Among the chief characteristics of Lewis's poetry is his "sheer love of the sounds of words . . . [often revealed] in his virtuoso deployment in poem after poem of intricate patterns of exact or slant rhyme, both final and internal" (87). Another notable characteristic of his poetry "is semantic change, specifically the alteration of meaning which may disrupt communication

between members of a speech community" (92). Huttar then cites poems revealing Lewis's use of semantics as a tool for critiquing contemporary culture, and he comments upon the way that "Lewis examines language as a fundamental human attribute, one that reveals both our greatness and our limitations" (103). Huttar reviews several poems that celebrate the birth of language, human reason and dominion, and freedom of the will. In addition, he cites letters showing Lewis's admission of the inadequacy of language to communicate anything effectively. Huttar believes Lewis's poems on God best demonstrate the shortcoming of language, and he offers from "Footnote to All Prayers" the following as an example: "To 'attempt the ineffable Name' . . . is to risk worshipping an 'idol' shaped by one's 'own unquiet thought;' the language of prayer references only 'frail images' in the speaker's mind, 'which cannot be the thing Thou art' . . . 'Take not, oh Lord, our literal sense. Lord, in Thy great, / Unbroken speech our limping metaphor translate'" (106). Huttar's work in this essay is thorough and keen; his critical focus upon Lewis's use of language in his poetry is essential reading.

61. *Selected Literary Essays* (Cambridge: Cambridge UP, 1969), 15. Originally published as "A Metrical Suggestion," *Lysistrata* 2 (May 1935): 13–24.

62. *Selected Literary Essays,* 46. Originally published in *Essays and Studies by Members of the English Association* 26 (1939): 28–41.

63. *Selected Literary Essays,* 280–85. Originally published in *A Review of English Literature* 1 (Jan. 1960): 45–50.

64. These poems are discussed at length in chapter 2.

65. These ten poems appear in the "Miscellany" from *Collected Poems.* The poems are "The Hills of Down," "Against Potpourri," "A Prelude," "Ballade of a Winter's Morning," "Laus Mortis," "Sonnet—To Philip Sydney," "Of Ships," "Couplets," "Circe—A Fragment," and "Exercise." All date from 1915–17.

66. Gleeson White from his *Ballades and Rondeaus* (1893) cited in Raymond Mac-Donald Alden, ed., *English Verse: Specimens Illustrating Its Principles and History* (1929; reprint, New York, AMS, 1970), 360.

67. "The Approach to English," *Light on C. S. Lewis,* ed. Jocelyn Gibb (New York: Harcourt Brace Jovanovich, 1965), 53.

68. Joe R. Christopher offers this insight: "I'd say that Lewis wanted to be a Romantic poet and he actually was (most often) a classical epigrammist—he wanted to be John Keats and he was actually Ben Jonson" (e-mail to author, Nov. 18, 1997).

2. Early Poems, 1908–1919

1. With the amount of scholarly interest in Lewis's poetry having recently increased, it is not surprising the *Collected Poems* have come under intense critical scrutiny, especially the "Miscellany." Kathryn Lindskoog has written at length in *The Lewis Legacy* about her concerns; see especially "Here We Go Again: Two New Lewis Forgeries," *The Lewis Legacy* 64 (Spring 1995): 1. See also 65 (Summer 1995), in a series of short notes, beginning with "Laureate Richard Wilbur Critiques 'Finchley Ave,'" (1) through "Fear No More: C. S. Lewis and Laureate Masefield" (8).

2. Actually, there is some confusion regarding the title. While the title page says *The Collected Poems of C. S. Lewis,* the cover of the book says *Poems.* In a letter Hooper explains

this error: "After deciding to re-print the earlier *Poems* (1964), the publishers rushed to get the cover ready. However, I saw this as an opportunity to include many poems which were either out of print, such as *Spirits in Bondage,* or had never been published. In the end, the publishers used the cover they had already printed, and so the cover gives one title and the title-page another" (letter to the author, Mar. 24, 1996). Further adding to the confusion is that none of the narrative poems appear in *Collected Poems.*

3. See chapter 1, n. 1. See also appendixes 1, 2, and 3.

4. Ten in the *Collected Poems* "Miscellany," four in various journals, and four in Don King, "Glints of Light."

5. Luci Shaw says, "Though there are some gleams of vision, some powerful images, and some felicitous phrases, they are clearly inferior, to my mind, to the poems collected and published by Hooper" (letter to the author, May 7, 1997). I argue that while the unpublished poems are not fully polished works, they are glints of light illuminating Lewis's early aspirations to achieve acclaim as a poet.

6. "The Old Grey Mare," first published in R. L. Green's "C. S. Lewis," *Puffin Post* 4, no. 1 (1970): 14–15.

7. See *LP,* 3:321–36.

8. The book title Lewis saw was *Siegfried & the Twilight of the Gods,* trans. Margaret Armour, illus. Arthur Rackham (London: Heinemann, 1911). This is the second of two volumes, the first being *The Rhinegold and The Valkyrie.* Eventually a one-volume edition was published, *The Ring of the Nibelung,* trans. Margaret Armour, illus. Arthur Rackham (New York: Doubleday, 1923).

9. This unfamiliarity explains why his poem has minor differences when compared with published translations of the *The Ring of the Nibelung.*

10. The entire text in published in appendix 1.

11. Though Lewis leaves them unnamed, the Rhine maidens in Wagner are Woglinde, Wellgunde, and Flosshilde.

12. Wagner's Alberich is shown cursing love; we do not see Lewis's Alberich curse love, but the implication is that he does.

13. Lewis's Wotan and Frika are more sympathetically drawn than Wagner's arrogant husband and shrewish wife; indeed, all Lewis's characterizations are more human and less one dimensional than Wagner's.

14. This recalls the scene in Dante's *Inferno,* Canto IX, when the appearance of the heavenly messenger causes the damned "as frogs, spying the foeman snake, / Go squattering over the pond, and dive, and sit / Huddled in the mud" (*The Divine Comedy,* trans. Dorothy L. Sayers [London: Penguin, 1949], 76–78). Lewis was probably reading Dante in Italian while studying with Kirkpatrick, but he recommended that Greeves read the translation by H. F. Cary, *The Vision; or Hell, Purgatory and Paradise of Dante* (1814), noting "that Cary's version in blank verse is supposed to be the best piece of verse-translation ever written" (Oct. 15, 1918, *TST,* 236, n. 2).

15. Wagner's version has Alberich a serpent; why Lewis does not is puzzling. Later, of course, in Letter XXII of his *Screwtape Letters* he uses a serpent transformation episode, even referring to the *Paradise Lost* story.

16. This follows Wagner's version.

17. *Cherbourg School Magazine* (July 1913). Reprinted in *LP,* 4:51–52; there it is dated July 29, 1913.

18. Lewis writes about Smith in *Surprised by Joy* and devotes part of an unpublished narrative poem to him; see chapter 4 and appendix 2.

19. King, "Glints of Light," 74, and reprinted in appendix 2. Warren Lewis quotes W. T. Kirkpatrick's comment on this poem after receiving a copy of it from Albert Lewis: "The verse translation takes my breath away. It is an amazing performance for a boy of his age—indeed for a boy of any age" (*WLB*, 29). Although Lewis artificially presents the poem as if it has twenty-four lines, it is actually only twelve lines of eight-stressed meter, each one wrapped over to a second line typographically, but metrically the break comes at random. A slightly different version in holograph without this artificial typography appears in Douglas Gilbert and Clyde Kilby's *C. S. Lewis: Images of His World* (Grand Rapids, Mich.: Eerdmans, 1973), 113.

20. Latin text is found in C. E. Bennett, ed., *Horace: The Odes and Epodes* (Cambridge: U of Massachusetts P, 1914), 114. The translation follows:

> One bourne constrains us all; for all
> The lots are shaken in the urn,
> Whence, soon or late, will fall our turn
> Of exile's barge without recall.

Translated by J. H. Deazeley, in *The Complete Works of Horace*, ed. Caspar Kraemer, Jr. (New York: Modern Library, 1936), 186.

21. King, "Glints of Light," 75, and reprinted in appendix 2.

22. In a letter to Arthur Greeves, Lewis writes, "You will perhaps be surprised to hear that I am reading 'The Prelude' by way of graduating in Wordsworth-ism. What's even funnier, I rather like it! I'm coming to the conclusion that there are two orders of poetry—real poetry and the sort you read while smoking a pipe. 'The Prelude' is nearly always on the second level but very comfortable and interesting all the same. . . . You read it, didn't you? I expect like me you recognized lots of the early parts from recollections of your own childhood. I fancy the first Book the best" (Sept. 18, 1919, *TST*, 261). A month later he adds, "I finished the Prelude and liked it. It is about as bad as a poem could be in some ways but one considers the great passages not too dearly bought at the price of the rest" (Oct. 18, 1919, 263). Five years later his appreciation of the poem is even greater: "I brought Wordsworth out to the garden and there in the delicious coolness I read Book 1 of 'The Prelude.' This poem is really beginning to replace *Paradise Lost* as my literary metropolis" (June 14, 1924, *DCSL*, 333).

23. Luci Shaw also faults it for cliché expressions such as "slumbering years," "luminous summer night," "fleecy clouds," "heaven's velvet deep," "foaming main," "mountain waste," and "icy torrents" (letter to the author, May 7, 1997).

24. Other poems reflecting this include "The Satyr" (5), "The Autumn Morning" (34), "The Ass" (51), "How He Saw Angus the God" (61), and "The Roads" (63).

25. The title comes from Ovid's *Ex Ponto* 3.2.25. The complete phrase is *pars estis pauci melior* and means "you few are a better group," referring to several loyal friends who remained dedicated to and supportive of him during his exile. Stanzas one and three appear in the Green and Hooper biography, 38.

26. The phrase probably refers to the requirement to write in a verse form with many rhymes.

27. King, "Glints of Light," 77–78, and reprinted in appendix 2.

28. "From the Latin of Milton's *De Idea Platonica Quemadmodum Aristoteles Intellexit,*" (a translation), *English* 5, no. 30 (1945): 195. Milton's poem essentially asks the Muses to answer this Platonic riddle: "Who was the first being who served as the archetype for the creation of mankind?" In the headnote to his translation, Lewis says he hopes his translation, poor as it is, will send others off to explore Milton's "exquisite grotesque."

29. "Arrangement of Pindar," *Mandrake* 1, no. 6 (1949): 43–45. Pindar (518?–438? B.C.), was the greatest lyric poet of ancient Greece, the master of epinicia. He is pictured with his chorus, dancing, while he somberly speaks of the demands on an artist. Pindar argues that an artist is born, not made; hard work is necessary, but if the gods do not give genius and blessing, the best effort will achieve but silence. Hymn-like, the poem follows loosely the epinicia pattern: praise of the gods, reference to myth, and aphoristic moralizing. Lewis also translated passages from *The Romance of the Rose* into Middle English octosyllabic couplets in *The Allegory of Love: A Study in Medieval Tradition* (Oxford: Oxford UP, 1936).

30. Other poems of this sort include "After Kirby's *Kalevala*" (a translation), *The Oxford Magazine* 55 (May 13, 1937): 595; "*Vitrea Circe,*" *Punch* 214 (June 23, 1948): 543; "The Prodigality of Firdausi," *Punch* 215 (Dec. 1, 1948): 510; and "Vowels and Sirens," *Times Literary Supplement,* Special Autumn Issue (Aug. 29, 1954): xiv.

31. The entire text is published in appendix 1. Lewis was undoubtedly influenced by Aeschylus's *Prometheus Bound* and Shelley's *Prometheus Unbound.*

32. This is letter 3 in *TST,* 50–53; it contains an elaborate summary of Lewis's plan for his "would-be" tragedy.

33. Sadly, the thirty-two pages Warren mentions have not survived. The parts of the text saved by Warren Lewis are reproduced in appendix 1. Two additional lines appear in an October 14, 1914, letter to Greeves, *TST,* 54: "The moon already with her silvery glance,— / The horned moon that bids the high gods dance."

34. Lewis's spelling of this name in "Descend to Earth" had not been consistent, alternating between Loge and Logie.

35. In the preface to *Narrative Poems* (New York: Harcourt Brace Jovanovich, 1969), Hooper published only seven of the first eight lines, omitting line four: "Returns the sinking sun's red glare again."

36. Hooper reproduced all but the first line of this passage in his Preface to *Spirits in Bondage: A Cycle of Lyrics* (1919; reprint, New York: Harcourt Brace Jovanovich, 1984), xvi.

37. The rest of the passage follows: "The main contrast in my play was between the sad wisdom of Loki and the brutal orthodoxy of Thor [Donner from 'Descend']. Odin was partly sympathetic; he could at least see what Loki meant and there had been old friendship between those two before cosmic politics forced them apart. Thor was the real villain, Thor with his hammer and his threats, who was always egging Odin on against Loki and always complaining that Loki did not sufficiently respect the major gods; to which Loki replied: 'I pay respect to wisdom not to strength.' Thor was, in fact, the symbol of the Bloods [the stronger older boys at school who preyed on the younger, less athletic ones]. . . . Loki was a projection of myself; he voiced that sense of priggish superiority whereby I was, unfortunately, beginning to compensate myself for my unhappiness" (*SJ,* 115).

38. In *They Stand Together* Lewis indicated this scene is a part of the "Prologos." See *TST,* 50.

39. The song appears to have been intended for "Episode II." See *TST,* 51.

40. The female fates of Norse mythology.

41. In the introduction to the *Collected Poems,* Hooper says these are "the ten poems from the youthful 'Metrical Meditations of a Cod'" (xvii). There is a full discussion of "The Metrical Meditations of a Cod" in chapter 3, note 8. Many of these were probably written while Lewis was studying under Kirkpatrick.

42. Also *They Stand Together* is filled with references to Lewis's love of faery. See *TST,* 62, 68, 101, 187, 196.

43. This same love of literature was reflected in Lewis's first visit to the house of the Master of Oxford University; he was overwhelmed by the books he saw. To Greeves he writes, "But what pleased me most was the masses upon masses of books in his house: among which I saw, tho' of course I couldn't look at it properly, a volume of that glorious new Malory. . . . So you may imagine I left the Univ. very much relieved and delighted." Later in the same letter he described his wonder at the numerous booksellers in Oxford, admitting "so you see dear Oxford in a dangerous place for a book lover. Every second shop has something you want," *TST,* 158, 159 (Jan. 28, 1917).

44. Lewis returned to his interest in Hades later with two poems in *Spirits in Bondage,* "Apology" and "Ode for New Year's Day." However, his focus in these poems is upon Hades' Queen, Despoina.

45. In *LP,* 5:122, Warren Lewis writes, after a letter from Lewis to Greeves dated September 18, 1916, "During the holidays which are now nearly at an end, Clive, in spite of a visit with his friend Arthur to Donegal, had found time to add seven poems to his 'Metrical meditations' [an early collection of Lewis's poetry that has not survived]. Of these two were subsequently published, one as it stands in the MS., and another with some alteration. The first of these, the Star Bath [a version appears in *Spirits in Bondage*], had possibly been suggested by Arthur Greeves' account of the lakes near Port Salon, which town he had apparently visited in the previous year, and we reproduce it, both for its intrinsic worth, and for the sake of the author's reference. My other selection from this holiday's harvest was probably drafted at Bookham while he was reading Sydney's 'Arcadia'" (122). Apparently this poem was originally submitted by Lewis for publication in *Spirits in Bondage* but was taken out, at least in part because of an objection by the publisher, William Heinemann. Heinemann wrote Lewis on September 3, 1918: "I have read with pleasure your little volume of poems you were good enough to send me, and shall be pleased to make an arrangement with you for publication . . . . I think it will be advisable for you to reconsider the inclusion in the volume of some of the pieces which are not perhaps quite on the level of your best work" (*LP,* 6:31). Lewis revised the manuscript. In a letter dated October 8, 1918, Heinemann writes:

Dear Mr. Lewis,

I have read through your "Spirits in Prison" again, in its revised form, and suggest that the following numbers might with advantage be ommitted [*sic*], partly because they do not strengthen the book as a whole, partly because they are less original perhaps than the bulk of your work:

5.) To Sir Philip Sydney

7.) Ballade on a certain pious gentleman.

14.) Sonnet.

22.) Retreat.

24.) In Venusberg. (Oct. 8, 1918, *LP,* 6:49)

Although there is a "Sonnet" in *Spirits in Bondage,* there is no way to know if this is the one referred to by Heinemann above. Also, poems entitled "Ballade on a certain pious gentleman," "Retreat," and "In Venusberg" do not appear in *Spirits in Bondage,* though he may have renamed them. A poem entitled "Ballade on a certain pious gentleman" is found in "Early Poems." See note 53 below and appendix 6.

46. Walter Hooper reprints lines 21–28 of this poem, entitles it "*To the memory of* Arthur Greeves," and places it as a kind of dedication to *They Stand Together,* 5.

47. These lines also appear in the Green and Hooper biography, 49.

48. The bracketed line is inexplicably omitted in the *Collected Poems.*

49. Joe R. Christopher notes that this reference to floating islands, while not associated with Circe's island in Greek myth, may be "an early imaginative version of Tinidril on Perelandra" (e-mail to author, Dec. 3, 1997). Charles Huttar, however, notes an allusion to *The Faerie Queen* 2.12.10–11 and points out Spenser's Acrasia is a Circe figure (see stanzas 26, 56 ["excesse"], and 86) (Huttar, "Lifelong Love Affair with Language").

50. *Punch* 214 (June 23, 1948): 543.

51. This eight-line first stanza of "Nimue" is the only portion of the poem to survive and appears in Lewis's letter of September 18, 1919. In Malory's *Le Morte D'Arthur* (London: The Medici Society, 1920), Merlin is pictured as aggressively pursuing Nimue, one of the ladies of the lake; indeed, he is "assotted [besotted] upon her, that he might not be from her." Eventually she tires of him and tricks him into going beneath a stone to find out the wonders there; once there "she wrought so there for him that he came never out for all the craft he could do" (Book 4, chapter 1). Tennyson's "Merlin and Vivien" from *The Idylls of the King* (1888) updates Malory with Nimue transformed into the cultured but crass seductress, Vivien.

52. I believe this is the blank verse version he refers to in a diary entry of July 4, 1923; see *DCSL,* 253.

53. The Marion E. Wade Center at Wheaton College in Wheaton, Illinois, contains a curious holograph work purported to be in the hand of Arthur Greeves. The title page of the notebook, "Early Poems," holding the holographs reads: "English Verses Made By— Clive Staples Lewis: —and Copied by His Friend—Joseph Arthur Greeves: —Belfast in the Year 1917." Fifty-two poems are listed in the "Table of Contents." However, the notebook actually holds five more poems, numbered fifty-four through fifty-eight; I have not been able to discover why the poem that would have been numbered fifty-three is missing. Appendix 6 contains a complete listing of these poems by first line. The most interesting to this study is "Sonnet" (no. 26):

I have not bowed in any other shrine
From babyhood, nor sought another god
To worship and with faithless footsteps trod
In any flower-strown path, save only thine
Dear poesy. Not Pallas' love divine
Nor red Lyaeus with his ivied rod
Nor Ares with his stern feet brazen-shod

To crush, no Aphrodite's maddening wine
Have turned me back from following after thee
And sueing[?] still thy flying tracks of song,
If but for some curt season thou mayest be
Gracious of heart to him that wooed thee long.
    And grant the lowliest burden of my cry,
    —To make one worthy song before I die.

While this poem is additional evidence of Lewis's early devotion to poetry, the fact it is not in his hand, nor is it referred to anywhere else in his letters or diaires or in any of Warren Lewis's writings, leads me to treat it with caution. I believe similar caution should be used with the other poems in this notebook, in spite of the fact that many appear to be versions of poems later appearing in *Spirits in Bondage* and *Collected Poems*.

3. SPIRITS IN BONDAGE: FRUSTRATED DUALIST AT WAR

1. Chad Walsh's "The Almost Poet" in his *The Literary Legacy of C. S. Lewis* is the first serious attempt to consider Lewis as poet. About *Spirits in Bondage*, Walsh acknowledges Housman, Hardy, Yeats, and Keats as Lewis's poetic inspirations. He argues that "the poems are usually direct and easy to understand; they demand no excessive psychologizing" (36). Furthermore, Walsh claims these poems may be broadly categorized in the Romantic tradition with an occasional reference to World War I pulling them into the twentieth century. Walsh is helpful in summarizing the major themes of *Spirits in Bondage;* for example, he rightly shows these poems as reflecting Lewis's youthful struggles with "great religious and metaphysical questions" (41). In addition, Walsh argues that Lewis stumbles as a poet when he "tries to say weighty things," becomes "preachy or editorializes," and "fails to convert his ideas into effective symbols" (42). Other problems are his heavy reliance on formal meters and effusive use of mythological and literary allusions. Still, Walsh commends the volume as illustrating a young poet "willing to learn the craft" and well equipped by wide reading. In Lewis's determination to wrestle with the eternal questions of "life, death, meaning, emptiness, God, Satan, love," Walsh finds much to admire, since these are the ideas "toward which great poetry gravitates" (43).

In chronological order, the other critical essays are: Rodger Lancelyn Green and Walter Hooper, "C. S. Lewis and Andrew Lang," *Notes and Queries* 22 (May 1975): 208–9; George Musacchio, "War Poet," *The Lamp-Post of the Southern California C. S. Lewis Society* 2, no. 4 (Oct. 1978): 7 (revised and reprinted in George Musacchio, *C. S. Lewis: Man and Writer* [Belton, Tex.: U of Mary Hardin-Baylor P, 1994]); John Kirkpatrick, "Fresh Views of Humankind in Lewis's Poems," *Bulletin of the New York C. S. Lewis Society* 10 (Sept. 1979): 1–7; Stephen Thorson, "Thematic Implications of C. S. Lewis's *Spirits in Bondage*," *Mythlore* 8 (Summer 1981): 26–30; Joe R. Christopher, "C. S. Lewis Dances among the Elves: A Dull and Scholarly Survey of *Spirits in Bondage* and 'The Queen of Drum,'" *Mythlore* 9 (Spring 1982): 11–17, 47; Walter Hooper, preface to *SB;* Roland Kawano, "C. S. Lewis's Early Poems," *The Living Church* 186 (Feb. 13, 1983): 9–10; Peter Schakel, *Reason and Imagination in C. S. Lewis: A Study of* Till We Have Faces (Grand Rapids, Mich.: Eerdmans, 1984); George Sayer, *Jack:*

C. S. Lewis and His Times (San Francisco: Harper and Row, 1988); Joe R. Christopher, "Is 'D' for Despoina?" *The Canadian C. S. Lewis Journal: The Inklings, Their Friends, and Their Predecessors* 85 (Spring 1994): 48–59; John Bremer, "From Despoina to Diotima: The Mistress of C. S. Lewis," *The Lewis Legacy* 61 (Summer 1994): 6–18; and Don King, "C. S. Lewis's *Spirits in Bondage:* World I Poet as Frustrated Dualist," *The Christian Scholar's Review* 27 (Summer 1998): 454–74.

2. Walter Hooper's preface to the 1984 reprint of *Spirits in Bondage* offers a helpful overview of the volume. Hooper's great contribution is less literary analysis than literary history; his preface is long on how the volume came to be and short on literary analysis. For example, he reveals that many of the poems later published in *Spirits in Bondage* were originally included in a hand-copied notebook entitled "The Metrical Meditations of a Cod." Furthermore, he argues convincingly that certain poems were probably written while Lewis lived and studied with Kirkpatrick. We learn from Hooper that while Lewis's father was privy to the typescript of the poems, "it seems doubtful if Mr. Lewis understood the 'general idea' behind the cycle" (xiii–xiv). Hooper goes on to provide an account of the important factors influencing Lewis while he was composing *Spirits in Bondage,* including his search for joy, his experiences at public school, his thrill at discovering "pure Northernness," his friendship with Arthur Greeves, his studies under Kirkpatrick, his acceptance at Oxford, his military service, his reading of philosophy, and his aspiration to achieve acclaim as a poet.

Also of value is Hooper's tracing of the publication history of the book from its initial rejection by Macmillan to its eventual publication by Heinemann under the pseudonym Clive Hamilton. We learn as well of its generally favorable evaluation by reviewers except for Lewis's father and brother, Warren. At the end of his preface Hooper challenges critical readers: "As tempting as it may be to think how much better everything [in *Spirits in Bondage*] could be said in prose, I urge that one at least consider the poems as *poems* [emphasis Hooper's]" (xxxix–xl). Hooper's challenge in the tradition of New Criticism is a worthy one, and one this book hopefully addresses.

3. Peter Schakel in his *Reason and Imagination in C. S. Lewis: A Study of* Till We Have Faces devotes a thoughtful chapter to Lewis's poetry in *Spirits in Bondage* and *Dymer.* Arguing that the poetry demonstrates "a bifurcation and tension between the rationalism and the romantic" (93) aspects of Lewis's personality, Schakel says "in [*Spirits in Bondage*] its 'enlightened' rationalism on the one hand and deep sense of longing for a world of the spirit on the other, the collection provides an early and immature version of themes which would be treated much more satisfactorily in *Till We Have Faces*" (94). He then offers cogent though brief comments upon "De Profundis" (where he says these opposing themes are united), "The Philosopher," "The Escape," "Dungeon Grates," and "How He Saw Angus the God." Schakel says the volume as a whole "is uneven as a collection of poetry: there are a few gems, usually brief passages rather than entire poems. Its strength is expression of youthful emotions rather than handling of poetic skills. Its best quality as poetry is its visual imagery" (98).

4. Moreover, we see this frustrated dualism in earlier poems such as "The Hills of Down," "Couplets," and *Loki Bound.*

5. Why he did this for his war experience and not for his time in public school may be explained by the difference in kind between the alienation he felt as a young boy out of place

in Malvern with the stark terror of a young adult thrown into the hellish nightmare of no-man's-land on the WWI battlefields. Actually, we should also challenge the statements he made about some of his public school experiences, since Warren went to many of the same places and never shared his brother's gloomy assessment. Indeed, many portions of *Surprised by Joy* should be considered carefully, since the story being related is by an older person exercising selective filtering.

6. In another place Lewis admits to other kinds of masking in *Surprised by Joy:* "But before I say anything of my life there [Oxford *after* the war] I must warn the reader that one huge and complex episode will be omitted" (*SJ*, 198). The "complex episode" being omitted is the nature of his relationship with Mrs. Janie Moore.

7. Siegfried Sassoon describes such suppression in his *Memoirs of an Infantry Officer* (1930; reprint, London: Faber and Faber, 1965): "Someone . . . had sent me some details of the show they'd been in on April 23ʳᵈ [1917]. The attack had been at the place where I'd left them. A little ground had been gained and lost, and then the Germans had retreated a few hundred yards. Four officers had been killed and nine wounded. About forty other ranks killed, including several of the best N.C.O.s. It had been an episode typical of uncountable others, some of which now fill their few pages in Regimental Histories. Such stories look straightforward enough in print, twelve years later; but their reality remains hidden; even in the minds of old soldiers the harsh horror mellows and recedes" (170).

8. Warren Lewis writes in the Lewis Papers, 4:306:

It would be during this visit [From Albert's (Lewis) pocket diary:—"Thursday, April 1ˢᵗ., 1915. Jacks arrived for Easter"] to Little Lea that Clive wrote the first poetry which he himself considered worthy of preservation so late as 1917. In the two years intervening between Easter 1915 and Easter 1917, he wrote fifty two poems which he copied carefully into an old Malvern Upper Fifth Divinity note book, prefixing them with a chronological list of titles. The whole is entitled "The metrical meditations of a Cod." It is perhaps not irrelevant to explain here the Ulster word "cod", from which Clive formed for himself the diminutive "Kodotta" which appears so frequently in his letters. Patterson in his Glossary defines cod as, (1) "a silly, troublesome fellow", and (2) v. "to humbug or quiz a person; to hoax; to idle about. 'Quit your coddin'". It has however a third meaning, namely an expression of humourous and insincere self depreciation; an Ulsterman will say of himself, "Am'nt I the quare oul' cod to be doin' so and so", and it is in this latter sense that it is to be understood in this context. Of the poems included in the "Metrical meditations", three are marked as having been written in Easter 1915. Of the three, one was subsequently published, and does not therefore concern us at the moment; of the remaining two we select the following specimen" [what follows is "The Hills of Down"].

Warren's careful assessment of the development of "Meditations" is fascinating reading and can be found in the Lewis papers, vols. 4 and 5. Furthermore, the notebook "Early Poems" in the Wade Center may be a later version of the "Meditations." See appendix 6.

9. Lewis's experience in the trenches at this point suggests his battalion may have inherited German positions, since he describes his as being so comfortable, an uncommon circumstance for most in the British trenches. Lewis writes: "They are very deep, you go down to them by a shaft of about twenty steps: they have wire bunks where a man can sleep

quite snugly, and brasiers for warmth and cooking. Indeed, the chief discomfort is that they tend to get TOO hot, while of course the bad air makes one get headachy. I had a quiet pleasant time, and was only once in a situation of unusual danger, owing to a shell falling near the latrines while I was using them" (Jan. 4, 1918, *LL*, 71). However, according to Paul Fussell in *The Great War and Modern Memory* (London: Oxford UP, 1975), "The British trenches were wet, cold, smelly, and thoroughly squalid. Compared with the precise and thorough German works, they were decidedly amateur, reflecting a complacency about the British genius for improvisation" (43).

10. According to Everard Wyrall in his *The History of the Somerset Light Infantry (Prince Albert's): 1914–1919* (London: Methuen, 1927), the regimental history of Lewis's unit, vigorous fighting occurred during this battle. He reports: "The casualties of the 1st Battalion between 14th and 16th April were: 2/Lieut. L. B. Johnson died of wounds (15/4/18) and 2/Lieuts. C. S. Lewis, A. G. Rawlence, J. R. Hill and C. S. Dowding wounded: in other ranks the estimated losses were 210 killed, wounded or missing" (295).

11. *TST*, 212 (see his footnote).

12. Lewis, of course, is not the first person to turn to belief in transcendence because of service on a battlefield.

13. The self-doubt he expressed is something most writers experience, as is the constant tendency to revise.

14. The full text of Heinemann's letter to Lewis is given under note 45, chapter 2.

15. Fussell, *Great War*, 7.

16. John Johnston, *English Poetry of the First World War: A Study in the Evolution of Lyric and Narrative Form* (Princeton, N.J.: Princeton UP, 1964), 78, 155.

17. *The Collected Poems of Rupert Brooke* (New York: Dodd, Mead, 1961), 105. "1914" first appeared in the fourth and final issue of *New Numbers* (Dec. 1914).

18. Robert Nichols, ed., *Anthology of War Poetry, 1914–1918* (London: Nicholson and Watson, 1943), 35.

19. *The Letters of Charles Sorley* (Cambridge: Cambridge UP, 1919), 263.

20. Cited in Fussell, *Great War*, 176. The irony of the phrase, "French attack on our immediate right proceeds equally satisfactorily" is bitter.

21. In *Siegfried's Journey* (London: Faber and Faber, 1946) he writes, "In spite of my hatred of war and 'Empery's insatiate lust of power,' there was an awful attraction in its hold over my mind, which since childhood had shown a tendency towards tragic emotions about human existence. While at Lancaster Gate [where he was recovering from wounds] I was disquieted by a craving to be back on the Western Front as an independent contemplator. No longer feeling any impulse to write bitterly, I imagined myself describing it in a comprehensive way, seeing it like a painter and imbuing my poetry with Whitmanesque humanity and amplitude" (104–5).

22. *The War Poems of Siegfried Sassoon*, ed. Rupert Hart-Davis (London: Faber and Faber, 1983), 89 (originally published in the *Cambridge Magazine*, Sept. 22, 1917).

23. Originally published in the *Cambridge Magazine*, June 9, 1917.

24. See in *War Poems*: "The Prince of Wounds," "Golgotha," "Stand-to: Good Friday Morning," "At Carnoy," "To His Dead Body," "A Mystic as Soldier," "In the Church of St. Ouen," "Attack," "Reconciliation," "Vicarious Christ," and especially "Christ and the Soldier."

25. C. Day Lewis from his introduction to *The Collected Poems of Wilfred Owen* (Norfolk, Conn.: New Directions, 1963), 11.

26. Other poems with a similar sharpness include "Disabled," "The Last Laugh," "The Letter," "The Chances," "S[elf]. I[nflicted]. W[ound].," "Smile, Smile, Smile," and "Inspection."

27. Several years later after recounting a story from a friend who met Sassoon and said he "agonized in silence," Lewis adds, "Are all our modern poets like this? Were the old ones so? It is almost enough to prove R.[obert] Graves' contention that an artist is like a medium: a neurotic with an inferiority complex who gets his own back by attributing to himself abnormal powers. And indeed I have noticed in myself a ridiculous tendency to indulge in poetical complacency as a consolation when I am ill at ease thro' managing ordinary life worse than usual" (May 20, 1926, *DCSL*, 399).

Still later in an essay, "Talking about Bicycles" (in *Resistance*, Oct. 1946; reprinted in *Present Concerns*, 67–72), Lewis mentions Sassoon again. The focus of the essay is upon the four stages or "ages" a man goes through. The Unenchanted Age is when he is oblivious of the meaning of something, such as a toddler's lack of understanding of a bicycle. The Enchanted Age is when he discovers the wonders of the thing, such as a schoolboy's delight in riding all over the countryside on a bicycle. The Disenchanted Age is when he discovers the thing is actually just a tool or means to an end, such as when he has to ride through rain and wind to reach an appointment. The Re-enchanted Age is when he recaptures the joy of the Enchanted Age, enjoying the bicycle both for the happy memories of riding the countryside and for the sheer pleasure he now experiences. Lewis then moves to discuss this phenomenon in the context of war:

> Most of our juniors were brought up Unenchanted about war. The Unenchanted man sees (quite correctly) the waste and cruelty and sees nothing else. The Enchanted man is in the Rupert Brooke or Philip Sidney state of mind—he's thinking of glory and battle-poetry and forlorn hopes and last stands and chivalry. Then comes the Disenchanted Age—say Siegfried Sassoon. But there is also a fourth stage, though very few people in modern England dare to talk about it. You know quite well what I mean. One is not in least deceived: we remember the trenches too well. We know how much of the reality the romantic view left out. But we also know that heroism is a real thing, that all the plumes and flags and trumpets of the tradition were not there for nothing. They were an attempt to honour what is truly honourable: what was first perceived to be honourable precisely because everyone knew how horrible war is. (69–70)

Lewis goes on to say the war poetry of Homer or *The Battle of Maldon* is Re-enchantment, while that of the *Lays of Ancient Rome* or *Lepanto* is Enchantment, since "the poets obviously have no idea what a battle is like" (70). Similarly, he continues, with Unenchantment and Disenchantment, and he implicitly refers to Sassoon: "[Suppose] you read an author in whom love is treated as lust and all war as murder—and so forth. But are you reading a Disenchanted man or only an Unenchanted man? Has the writer been through the Enchantment and come out on to the bleak highlands, or is he simply a subman who is . . . free from the heroic mirage as a coward is free? If Disenchanted, he may have something worth hearing to say, though less than a Re-enchanted man. If Unenchanted, into the fire with his book. He is talking of what he doesn't understand. But the great danger we have to guard against in this age is the Unenchanted man, mistaking himself for, and mistaken by others for, the Disenchanted man" (70–71). In addition to what Lewis implies here about Sassoon—his Unenchantment being mistaken for Disenchantment—he also offers insight into his own suppressed view of war. That is, the question becomes whether his own "enchanted" view of the war is "no more than an illusion of memory . . . [since one remembers] a good many more exciting experiences than one really had" (71). Lewis answers this by noting "memory is the supreme example of the four ages. . . . But what then? Isn't the warehousing [of memories] just as much a fact as anything else? Is the vision any less important because a particular kind of polarized light between past and present happens to be the mechanism that brings it into focus?" (71).

28. Thorson, "Thematic Implications of C. S. Lewis's *Spirits in Bondage*."

29. Thorson himself labors admirably to force a cyclical reading and offers some thoughtful evidence at times; in the end, however, his effort to give *Spirits in Bondage* a unified reading as a cycle of lyrics does not work.

30. When possible, I give the earliest known date of composition; unfortunately, this will only be possible for a limited number of poems, since the earliest versions have not survived.

31. Furthermore, the prologue returns us to Lewis's penchant toward heavy allusion noted in his early poetry. Actually, *Spirits in Bondage* includes allusions to Greek, Latin, Celtic, Norse, Irish, English, and biblical sources. There are also numerous references to singing and music.

32. Walter Hooper, in the preface to *Spirits in Bondage*, suggests this poem dates somewhere around December 1917, within a month of Lewis reaching the trenches; see xxx.

33. In *Surprised by Joy* Lewis also notes that, even before he went to the trenches, "I attended almost entirely to what I thought awe-inspiring, or wild, or eerie, and above all to distance. Hence mountains and clouds were my especial delight; the sky was, and still is, to me one of the principal elements in any landscape" (152).

34. Lewis has in mind Shakespeare's "Sonnet 55" that begins: "Not marble, nor the gilded monuments / Of princes, shall outlive this powerful rhyme." Hooper speculates that Lewis's poem dates from Christmas 1916. See his preface to *Spirits in Bondage*, xxv–xxvi.

35. In the legends associated with Cuchulain, when he becomes enraged he is transformed into a hideous monster akin to a Scandinavian berserker.

36. In the preface to *Spirits in Bondage*, Hooper says this was one of the poems Lewis sent Heinemann as replacements for the five he rejected. I have been unable to verify Hooper's assertion, but if it is accurate this means the poem dates some time during or after October 1918, since Heinemann's letter to Lewis is dated October 8, 1918.

37. Two essays addressing the identity of Despoina are worth noting here. Joe R. Christopher's "Is 'D' for Despoina?" is fascinating speculation about whether Mrs. Moore is the inspiration for Despoina in both "Apology" and "Ode for New Year's Day." By referring to Lewis's diaries and letters (especially to Arthur Greeves) where Lewis often referred to Mrs. Moore as "D," Christopher patches together a convincing though not verifiable conjecture in support of this idea. He does not analyze the poems as such but uses them in terms of the dating he tries to establish, so that he concludes with "the mysterious 'D' and the literary use of *Despoina*, coming in the same general time period, are probably related; the discussion of the two poems does not invalidate this conjecture and, in a general way, tends to identify Janie Moore with Despoina; since she is already identified with 'D', the

triple identification of 'D', Despoina, and Moore seems likely (at least, to [Christopher])" (58–59).

John Bremer's discussion of this same topic in his "From Despoina to Diotima: The Mistress of C. S. Lewis" is more thorough and perceptive, and in the end Bremer disagrees with Christopher's identification of Janie Moore with Despoina. He begins by providing a detailed chronology of Lewis's life from his first connection to Oxford (Dec. 1916) through the publication of *Spirits in Bondage* (Mar. 1919), with special attention to any mention of Mrs. Moore in Lewis's letters, diaries, and other communications. He follows this with a carefully argued case for the development and nature of Lewis's relationship with Mrs. Moore, the dates and occasions for writing the poems in the volume, and the relationship, if any, between the two. With regard to the first, Bremer, following in the line of biographers such as Wilson, Green, and Hooper, and, more recently, Sayer, assumes that a sexual relationship between Lewis and Moore was a certainty, though admittedly not verifiable, and that it probably began as early as September 1917.

With regard to the second, Bremer follows with a helpful summary of the details we know about the writing, composition, and publication of the poems that finally make up *Spirits in Bondage.* He concludes the first part of his essay by arguing that it "is absolutely clear . . . that Janie Moore and Jack's feelings for her and his sexual relationship with her do not play any significant part in the composition, the literal putting together, of these poems into a lyric cycle. . . . Nor does she seem to have affected any individual poems" (11). Later, Bremer discusses "Apology," "Ode for New Year's Day," and "World's Desire" (poems where Despoina or a woman seems to be addressed) and claims that Mrs. Moore, in the sense that she inspired Lewis or was the object of admiration or veneration, "never touched his writings" (16). This fine essay ends with an intelligent discussion that posits possible references to "D" in the letters and diaries as Despoina (symbolically linked to the idea of "mistress" but not connected with the figure who is mentioned in *Spirits in Bondage*), Demeter (the Earth-mother), and Diotima (the introducer to love in Greek literature).

38. Again Lewis shows his indebtedness to Milton as the last line here recalls Satan in *Paradise Lost* (hereafter cited as *PL*) who claims, "The mind is its own place, and in itself / Can make a Heaven of Hell, a Hell of Heaven" (I, 254–55).

39. Lewis's allusion to the *Inferno* in these lines strengthens the argument that Despoina is being directed to speak to the dead.

40. *PL,* II, 269–70, 273.

41. The Tennysonian allusion to lyrics 55–57 of *In Memoriam* suggests "this creature" is man.

42. The implications of Lewis's theological dualism is beyond the scope of this study. While a poem like this clearly suggests that Lewis may have embraced such dualism for a brief time, it is not a position he holds very long. Much later in *Mere Christianity* he writes convincingly against holding this position, since logically it assumes even if there are two gods, a "good" one and a "bad" one, there must be another god behind these two that created them.

43. Hooper in the preface to *Spirits in Bondage* suggests this poem dates from around January 1918.

44. Interestingly, Lewis splits his Darwinian view of Nature from his malicious God here though both are equally deaf to man's pleas.

45. The title of Lewis's poem literally means "from the abyss," and is both an ironic allusion to Psalm 130:1–2 ("Out of the depths I cry to you, O Lord; O Lord, hear my voice. Let your ears be attentive to my cry for mercy") and a gloss to Oscar Wilde's *De Profundis* (1905). About the latter Lewis writes Greeves on September 18, 1919: "'De Profundis' is hardly more than a memory to me. I seem to remember that it had considerable beauties, but of course in his serious work one always wonders how much is real and how much is artistic convention. He must have suffered terribly in prison, more perhaps than many a better man. I believe 'The Ballad of Reading Gaol' [1898] was written just after he came out, and before he had had time to smelt down his experiences into artificiality, and that *it* [Lewis's emphasis] rather than 'De Profundis' represents the real effect on his mind. In other words the grim bitterness is true: the resignation not quite so true. Of course one gets very real bitterness in D. P. too" (*TST,* 260). Wilde, a fellow Irishman, rebel, and poet, clearly interested Lewis at this time in his life.

46. Lewis's view of God in *Spirits in Bondage* is similar to that of George Meredith, A. E. Housman, and Thomas Hardy, late-nineteenth-century British poets. In particular, this recalls Housman's lines from "The Chestnut Casts His Flambeaux": "We for certainty are not the first / Have sat in taverns while the tempest hurled / Their hopeful plans to emptiness, and cursed / Whatever brute and blackguard made the world."

47. In the preface to *Spirits in Bondage,* Hooper says this was one of the poems Lewis sent Heinemann as replacements for the five he rejected. I have been unable to verify Hooper's assertion, but if it is accurate this means the poem dates some time before or after October 1918, since Heinemann's letter to Lewis is dated October 8, 1918.

48. For another interesting comparison to *In Memoriam,* see "Lyric 22."

49. This dating would place the poem before the Easter 1916 Irish uprising and Yeats's subsequent poem with the same title.

50. Interestingly, poppies came to be the flower of WWI.

51. A nereid is a sea nymph.

52. An early version of this poem dates from Christmas 1915. See *LP,* 5:46.

53. Though it is impossible to date this poem precisely, it certainly was written while Lewis studied with Kirkpatrick.

54. This poem is first mentioned in a letter to Greeves on June 3, 1918, after Lewis returns from France to recover from his wounds. See *TST,* 220. Since Lewis refers in the poem to Oxford, it is possible he wrote the earliest version of the poem after he matriculated at University College, April 1917.

55. The three maidens may also be linked to the Norns of Norse mythology.

56. In the preface to *Spirits in Bondage,* Hooper says this was one of the poems Lewis sent Heinemann as replacements for the five he rejected. I have been unable to verify Hooper's assertion, but if it is accurate this means the poem dates some time during or after October 1918 since Heinemann's letter to Lewis is dated October 8, 1918.

57. In one of the many Celtic stories about Angus, Son of the Young, he gives his father, Dagda, good advice regarding the use of a heifer to gain advantage over a rival. In his poem, Lewis has Angus become a bull.

58. Lewis writes Greeves on August 4, 1917, saying he is happy to hear Greeves has enjoyed reading *Comus* and says his favorite song from that poem has allusions to "Hesperus and his daughters three / That sing about the golden tree" (198).

59. Lewis returns to this myth in *Perelandra* when Ransom discovers a similar garden and dragon living among the bubble trees that give him delightfully pleasant nourishment.

60. The earliest version of this poem dates from Summer 1916. See *LP*, 5:122. The context of this poem as a memory connects it with the Wordsworthian overtones of "Our Daily Bread."

61. See Hooper's preface to *Spirits in Bondage*, xxxiii, for additional information. In the preface to *Spirits in Bondage*, Hooper says this was one of the poems Lewis sent Heinemann as replacements for the five he rejected. I have been unable to verify Hooper's assertion, but if it is accurate this means the poem dates some time during or after October 1918, since Heinemann's letter to Lewis is dated October 8, 1918.

62. Joe R. Christopher's "C. S. Lewis Dances among the Elves: A Dull and Scholarly Survey of *Spirits in Bondage* and 'The Queen of Drum'" quickly surveys eleven poems in the volume with "poetic references to fairies and elves" (11). In most of these poems ("*Tu Ne Quaesieris*," "The Autumn Morning," "Victory," "Our Daily Bread," "In Praise of Solid People," "Ballade Mystique," "Night," "Song of the Pilgrims," "World's Desire," "Song," "Hymn (for Boys' Voices)," and "The Satyr") Christopher focuses upon how Lewis uses supernatural creatures "as a symbol of the mysterious, the Romantic, the dream of escape. In short, they are psychological symbols" (12). He concludes his comments on these poems by noting Lewis has established "the land of faerie as an ideal of Romantic escape and the faeries, with one or two clear exceptions, as the attractive inhabitants of this golden realm" (14).

63. This poem may later influence Lewis's portrayal of Mr. Tumnus in *The Lion, the Witch and the Wardrobe*. Christopher, in the essay mentioned above, also sees "The Satyr" as a depiction of the Victorian man—half human and half bestial.

64. Medea uses her powers as an enchantress to assist Jason to steal the golden fleece from her father King Aeetes of Colchis. Jason deserts her, after they marry, for the daughter of King Creon of Corinth; in revenge she kills Creon, his daughter, and her own two sons by Jason, taking refuge later in Athens.

65. In the preface to *Spirits in Bondage*, Hooper says this was one of the poems Lewis sent Heinemann as replacements for the five he rejected. I have been unable to verify Hooper's assertion, but if it is accurate this means the poem dates some time before or during September 1918, since Heinemann's letter to Lewis is dated October 8, 1918.

66. For more on this, see Schakel's *Reason and Imagination in C. S. Lewis*.

67. The hesitation of the dreamer may parallel the structure of *Spirits in Bondage*, since this poem appears as the first poem in the section "Hesitation."

68. Many readers will catch Lewis's possible allusion here to George Macdonald's *At the Back of the North Wind*.

69. Alternatively, the attraction to the commonplace may be a matter of hesitation before he leaps toward Romantic escape.

70. Lewis sends an early version of the poem to Greeves in a letter dated May 23, 1918, *TST*, 215–16.

71. The earliest version of this poem dates from Easter 1917. See *LP*, 11:255–56.

72. The earliest version of this poem dates from Easter 1916. See *LP*, 5:72.

73. "Death in Battle," *Reveille* 3 (Feb. 1919): 508 (under pseudonym Clive Hamilton).

4. EARLY OXFORD POEMS AND *DYMER*, 1920–26:
SIEGFRIED UNBOUND

1. Proving these dates is problematic and open to challenge. However, given my reading of Lewis's poetry corpus, I believe these autobiographical poem fragments may be reasonably dated within this time frame.

2. The common use of alexandrines for all three fragments is an argument in favor of the source autobiographical poem.

3. King, "Glints of Light," 79–80, and reprinted in appendix 2. Warren Lewis completes the story of Capron:

> We will here anticipate the end of the story of Robert Capron and Wynyard School. In 1907 (?) the list of scholastic successes comes to an end, and from that time onwards the school sank rapidly and uninteruptedly [*sic*], until in 1909 "Oldy" forestalled the inevitable by what he described as "giving up his school," though in point of fact his school had given him up, the number of boarders being then reduced to five. He retired from Watford, and was in 1910 presented to the tiny living of Radstock in the north of Hertfordshire. There, old, poor, stripped of his Lilliputian autocracy, deserted by the last of his slaves, his daughters, he shivered for a little in the cold wind of reality that had blustered harmlessly around Wynyard, and then did the only thing that was left him to do—he died. His tombstone in Watford cemetary [*sic*] records his death to have taken place on the 18ᵗʰ of November 1911 at the age of sixty. His epitaph is in two words— "JESU, MERCY." (*LP*, 3:41–42)

4. One conclusion we might draw from this and the other autobiographical fragments is that they served as source drafts for the later prose versions appearing in *Surprised by Joy*.

5. Lewis writes about Sennacherib in "Sonnet":

> The Bible says Sennacherib's campaign was spoiled
> By angels: in Herodotus it says, by mice—
> Innumerably nibbling all one night they toiled
> To eat his bowstrings piecemeal as warm wind eats ice.
> But muscular archangels, I suggest, employed
> Seven little jaws at labour on each slender string
> And by their aid, weak masters though they be, destroyed
> The smiling-lipped Assyrian, cruel-bearded king.
> (1–8; *The Oxford Magazine*, May 14, 1936, 575)

6. King, "Glints of Light," 80, and reprinted in appendix 2. These lines are perhaps an echo to Dante's *Inferno*, Canto I, lines 8–9: "Yet there I gained such good, that, to convey / The tale, I'll write what else I found therewith."

7. In *Surprised by Joy* Lewis comments on this phrase: "'Never let us live with *amousia*,' was one of [Smewgy's] favorite maxims: *amousia*, the absence of the Muses" (112).

8. King, "Glints of Light," 81, and reprinted in appendix 2.

9. Warren Lewis adds the following: "Mr. Smith died at his little house in the school grounds, South Lodge, where he lived alone, on the 13ᵗʰ November 1918, a victim of the epidemic of influenza which swept Europe and Africa in that year" (*LP*, 3:263).

10. King, "Glints of Light," 82, and reprinted in appendix 2. A. N. Wilson publishes a short excerpt from this fragment in *C. S. Lewis: A Biography* (San Francisco: HarperCollins, 1990), 251. The excerpt covers the twelve lines running from "Across my landscape" through "From Kirk's strong hand."

11. King, "Glints of Light," 82–83.

12. Ibid., 83.

13. Ibid.

14. Letter to the author, May 7, 1997.

15. Warren Lewis writes: "This fragment has been dated in Clive's handwriting 'probably 1922–23.' The 'room' in line 5 is 'the little end room,' the upstairs sitting room generally used by Warren and Clive when their father was out of the house, and the 'fretting' of the 'lost' wind was a familiar sound in the attic which in earlier days was their play room" (*LP*, 11:251). Given the tone of "The Carpet Rises in the Draught," I believe this is the poem Lewis is working on when he writes Greeves on January 3, 1923: "[I am working on] a new poem on my old theme of 'Alone in the House.' I soon found that I was creating rather too well in myself the creepy atmosphere wh. I was trying to create in the poem, and gave up" (*TST*, 169).

16. In King, "Glints of Light," 85, and reprinted in appendix 2.

17. Here we find no breath of life, no warm breeze of love, no spirit of joy, the very thing he also laments in "Song of the Pilgrims" in *Spirits in Bondage:*

> Dwellers at the back of the North Wind,
> What have we done to you? How have we sinned
> Wandering the Earth from Orkney unto Ind?
> . . .—The red-rose and the white-rose gardens blow
> In the green Northern land to which we go,
> Surely the ways are long and the years are slow.
> We have forsaken all things sweet and fair,
> We have found nothing worth a moment's care
> Because the real flowers are blowing there. (*SB*, 47)

18. Letter to the author, May 7, 1997.

19. In both the preface to *Narrative Poems* (xi) and a footnote in *The Diary of C. S. Lewis* to the September 9, 1923, entry (266), Hooper says there are seventy-eight lines. I explain our different count by assuming he counts two half-lines as if they are separate lines. I do not believe any of these lines have ever before been published. The complete text is published in appendix 1.

20. Lewis provides us with another version of the last six lines immediately following this ending:

> But when I rest my eyes
> Upon that house, I see far otherwise.
> First it is weeping shapes: then these begin
> To come apart. And here is Psyche's twin,
> A brother, not a sister, fair as she
> And prettier than a boy would choose to be,

Reading his book, self pleased in hazy thought.
Now, on my life, I'll guess it's he that taught
The story, as we have it, to the world. (*LP,* 8:164)

21. In a September 18, 1919, letter to Greeves, Lewis writes: "I sent 'Hippolytus' to the Odds & Ends Magazine, but I haven't seen it yet" (*TST,* 261–62). Lewis offers additional insights in *The Diary of C. S. Lewis:* "I sat in and worked on the first chunk of the 'King of Drum', wh. is to consist, I hope, of three chunks—about 130 lines each. This chunk is a new version of a piece I began writing about two years ago, wh. itself was a re-writing of the 'Wild Hunt' (about 1920), which in its turn was based on something I started at Bristol in 1918" (Jan. 16, 1927, 430). Unfortunately, no copies of the *Odds & Ends Magazine* have survived. The relationship between these pieces which have not survived and "The Queen of Drum" has been discussed by Hooper in his preface to *Narrative Poems* (1969), xii–xiv.

22. The complete text is published in appendix 1. Furthermore, Lewis's use of Hippolytus may suggest he was reading Euripides' *The Bacchae* around the time these lines were composed.

23. H. A. Guerber, *Myths of the Norsemen* (London: Harrap & Co., 1908), 23.

24. We know Lewis is working on this poem before April 18, 1922: "In the evening I copied out 'Joy' and worked a new ending: it is now ready to be typed" (*DCSL,* 22). Interestingly, the editor who accepted it for publication in *The Beacon* was Owen Barfield: "A letter from Barfield accepting 'Joy' for the *Beacon* and saying nice things" (May 2, 1922, *DCSL,* 28). However, it was two years before the poem was published in *The Beacon* 3, no. 31 (May 1924): 444–45 (under pseudonym Clive Hamilton); reprinted in *CP,* 243–44.

25. *Surprised by Joy* has numerous passages in which Lewis discusses joy; see in particular 16–18 and 165–70. In addition, see Lewis's preface to *The Pilgrim's Regress* (London: Geoffrey Bles, 1933) (hereafter *PR*) where he offers an extended definition of what he means by joy.

26. It is interesting to note Lewis and Yeats use Leda in a poem at about the same time; see Yeats's "Leda and the Swan" (1923).

27. I list all the critical articles on *Dymer* in the bibliography.

28. She compared her first reading to "watching a ballet," and though her essay is brief, she argues convincingly that *Dymer* is a poem infused and empowered by its mythic elements ("conflict-leading-to-death-and-rebirth," "Paradise-Hades: Heaven and Hell," and "the poet's relation to his Muse"). She concludes her panegyric with this unintended hyperbole: "Those . . . who are not unwilling to read a 'classic' because it appears ahead of its time may, I fancy, read and re-read *Dymer* and enjoying Mr. Lewis once again as myth-maker may discover him as poet" (173).

29. "C. S. Lewis," an address given at Wheaton College, Oct. 16, 1964.

30. Most impressive is his linking of several of the poems from *Spirits in Bondage* to his discussion of *Dymer,* including "Death in Battle," "Victory," "De Profundis," "Despoina," "Satan Speaks," and "*Tu Ne Quaesieris.*"

31. Sayer, "C. S. Lewis's *Dymer,*" 97.

32. He supports this thesis by referring to illustrative passages in Lewis's diary. Lewis's intent in the poem is to show how destructive the Christina Dream can be. Citing from a letter to Green, Sayer notes that, for Lewis at the time of the writing of *Dymer,* romanticism

was full of dangers, "'a sickness of the soul' and one that could prove fatal. In his case the Christina Dream was undoubtedly accompanied by a strong sense of guilt, especially sexual guilt" (97–98).

33. In addition, Sayer notes the functions of Nature and joy in the poem, and he articulates the role of other characters effectively. Regarding the master-magician, Sayer reminds us Lewis says "'the physical appearance of the Magician owes something to Yeats as I saw him'" (107), and he cites passages from the poem illustrating this point. Furthermore, he shows how the magician "sets out to tempt Dymer to dream again and more deeply. He must close his eyes to the real world, to his own mistakes and failures, and live as far as possible in the world of fantasy" (108). Sayer correctly points out how crucial it is to distinguish between Dymer's early experience with the mysterious bride and the old hag: "The union with the mysterious bride is one unblessed and unsanctified by the moral laws. . . . So he suffers from a guilt, personified in the ancient matriarch. But the brief meeting supplies him with an ideal to pursue. His experience in the Master's house is merely one of sexual fantasy" (110).

In Sayer's conclusion he offers additional insights. He notes that Lewis privately "thought the best passages [in *Dymer*] were among the pieces of writing by which he would most like to be remembered" (113). About the psychological nature of the poem, Sayer admits Lewis's approach is outdated but adds, "There is no verse treatment of the subject comparable to *Dymer* in depth and complexity" (113). He also reinforces other critics who admire Lewis's technical achievements in the poem while noting its unfashionable form: "At a time when free verse was coming into fashion, it is written in complex stanzas that rhyme and scan perfectly. Again it is quite free from the fashionable sort of obscurity—all its lines make sense" (113).

34. See the "Preface by the Author to the 1950 Edition," reprinted in *Narrative Poems.* Lewis writes:

> My hero was to be a man escaping from illusion. He begins by egregiously supposing the universe to be his friend and seems for a time to find confirmation of his belief. Then he tries, as we all try, to repeat his moment of youthful rapture. It cannot be done; the old Matriarch sees to that. On top of his rebuff comes the discovery of the consequences which his rebellion against the City has produced. He sinks into despair and gives utterance to the pessimism which had, on the whole, been my own view about six years earlier [note this would mean anytime between 1917–19, corresponding with Lewis's battlefield experiences]. Hunger and a shock of real danger bring him to his senses and he at last accepts reality. But just as he is setting out on the new and soberer life, the shabbiest of all bribes is offered him; the false promise that by magic or invited illusion there may be a short cut back to the one happiness he remembers. He relapses and swallows the bait, but he has grown too mature to be really deceived. He finds that the wish-fulfillment dream leads to the fear-fulfillment dream, recovers himself, defies the Magician who tempted him, and faces his destiny. (*NP,* 5–6)

35. The complete reference is:

> I ween that I hung on the windy tree
>   Hung there for nights full nine:

> With the spear I was wounded, and offered I was
>> To Othin, myself to myself,
> On the tree that none may ever know
>> What root beneath it runs.

From *The Poetic Edda*, trans. Henry Adams Bellows (New York: The American-Scandinavian Foundation, 1923), 60. The windy tree refers to the "ash Yggdrasil (literally 'the Horse of Othin,' so called because of this story), on which Othin, in order to win the magic runes, hanged himself as an offering to himself, and wounded himself with his own spear."

36. Sayer makes a similar observation but does not detail the parallels.

37. All references to *Dymer* are to the version printed in *Narrative Poems.*

38. Similarly Sigurd murders Regin in William Morris's *The Story of Sigurd the Volsung and the Fall of the Nibelung* (London: Ellis & White, 1877).

39. Wagner, *The Ring of the Nibelung*, 229.

40. This is similar to the persona in Francis Thompson's "The Hound of Heaven," when, early in the poem, he proposes to run from God by losing himself in nature.

41. For more on this see Joe R. Christopher's "Comments on *Dymer*" *The Lamp-Post of the Southern California C. S. Lewis Society* 20 (Autumn 1996): 17–22.

42. The connection here between Dymer's state and that of King Lear as he wanders on the heath is clear.

43. Fussell notes that both the Allies and the Germans accused the other of such atrocities throughout the war.

44. Though distasteful to many who only know the post-Christian Lewis, it must be admitted Lewis struggled with sexual temptation, including masturbation, throughout his early life. His letters to Greeves include veiled and not-so-veiled references to such temptations. For instance, in a letter of June 1, 1930, Lewis confides in Greeves:

> Just to give you the other side of the picture (I shall not often tell you these things)— I have "fallen" twice since you left after a long period of quite untroubled peace in that respect. Serves me right, for I was beginning to pat myself on the back and even (idiotically) beginning to fancy I had really escaped, if not for good, at any rate for an indefinite time. The interesting thing was that on both occasions the temptation arose when I was almost asleep, quite suddenly, and carried me by storm before I really had my waking mind fully about me. I don't mean to disclaim responsibility on this account, but I feel grateful that the enemy has been driven to resort to *strategems* (not by me, but by God) whereas he used to walk boldly up to me for a frontal attack in the face of all my guns. I hope I don't delude myself in thinking that this is an improvement. (*TST*, 354–55)

Elsewhere he warns against self-sexual gratification for the "imaginary harems of the mind" it encourages. Lewis's struggles are very human, and rather than clouding our view of him, remind us he was no plaster saint unacquainted with the human condition. Indeed, it is his rather perceptive insights into human nature that help him write so effectively.

45. Lewis says in his introduction to the 1950 edition of the poem that the physical description of the magician is based on his memories of having twice met W. B. Yeats as an undergraduate in Oxford.

46. Isaiah 1:18: "'Come now, let us reason together,' says the Lord. 'Though your sins be as scarlet, they shall be as white as snow; though they are red as crimson, they shall be like wool.'"

47. Almost certainly Lewis bases this descent into madness upon Mrs. Moore's brother, Dr. John Askins ("the Doc"). In *The Diary of C. S. Lewis,* Lewis records the following on February 23, 1923: "[I was told] the Doc was very bad and must stay here. After lunch he began raving. Quieted later and explained that he was haunted by horrible blasphemous and obscene thoughts. . . . Had two more bad attacks before tea—very violent. The third was the worse. Thinks (while in the fit) that he is going to Hell" (202). He also comments upon this in *Surprised by Joy:* "It had been my chance to spend fourteen days, and most of the fourteen nights as well, in close contact with a man who was going mad. He was a man whom I had dearly loved, and well he deserved love. And now I helped to hold him while he kicked and wallowed on the floor, screaming out that devils were tearing him and he was that moment falling down into Hell. And this man, as I well knew, had not kept the beaten track. He had flirted with Theosophy, Yoga, Spiritualism, Psychoanalysis, what not" (202–3).

48. Here is another echo to *Paradise Lost,* specifically to Sin's description of the birth of her son, Death: "Pensive here I sat / Alone, but long I sat not, till my womb / Pregnant by thee [Satan], and now excessive grown, / Prodigious motion felt and rueful throes" (II, 777–80).

49. These lines recall stanzas 10–15 of Browning's "Childe Roland to the Dark Tower Came."

50. Richard Hodgens, "Notes on *Narrative Poems,*" *Bull. of the New York C. S. Lewis Society* 7 (April 1976): 3.

51. Walsh, *Literary Legacy,* 46.

52. Other important essays on *Dymer* include the following. Walter Hooper's preface to *Narrative Poems* is primarily concerned with historical background on *Dymer;* he reveals the titles of other poems Lewis was working on at the time, including (besides those later published in *Spirits in Bondage*), *Loki Bound,* "The Quest of Bleheris" [a prose romance], and "Medea's Childhood." According to a manuscript version of *Dymer,* Lewis toyed with the idea of making it a dream version, since "Lewis added one further stanza after Canto IX, 35, in which he, the dreamer, awakes" (x).

Joe R. Christopher's first study of *Dymer,* "A Study of C. S. Lewis's *Dymer*" (*Orcrist* 6 [Winter 1971–72]: 17–19), is really more a note; this is not surprising since it is a short chapter from his dissertation. In it he links the poem to Northrop Frye's taxonomy of romance; according to Frye, the romance "often radiates a glow of subjective intensity." Christopher sees the "upwelling from the unconscious," "the feast prepared in the empty palace," "Dymer as the Wanderer," and "the failure to ask the proper questions" as romance motifs in the poem (17). Further, he argues that *Dymer* is more in the tradition of *The Faerie Queene* than *King Horn* or *Havelock the Dane.* In very brief fashion, he touches on elements in several cantos to support his contention. Unfortunately, Christopher struggles in his reading of the poem as a whole. At first he posits a possible Freudian reading: "[The poem] is so obviously a Oedipal complexioned story, that the temptation is to read it in terms of Lewis's life—the death of his mother when he was ten (hence the vanishing goddess), the difficulties with his father. Perhaps the fairest interpretation is to put the story in Freudian terms" (18). But then he argues against this, since readers identify with Dymer (why this should negate the Freudian reading he never says). His concluding lines are most disappointing: "All I can do is testify that to me the shift [of point of view at the end of the poem] is too sudden to be successful: I am left feeling not 'what a glorious rebirth!' but 'How odd!'" (18). Christopher's second piece, "Comments on *Dymer*," is essentially a plot summary, although he is helpful in suggesting links from episodes in the poem to later Lewis works including *The Pilgrim's Regress, Surprised by Joy,* and *The Great Divorce* (London: Geoffrey Bles, 1946).

Richard Hodgens's essay on Lewis's *Narrative Poems* ("Notes on *Narrative Poems*," *Bulletin of the New York C. S. Lewis Society* 7 [Apr. 1976]: 1–14) discusses more than *Dymer*, but he is the first critic to dignify the poem with an extended and thoughtful discussion. In his introduction, he notes the important role narrative poetry played in Lewis's literary development, pointing out how aggressively the young Lewis defended such poetry from the prevailing English verse of the 1920s. After this he makes a series of helpful points. First, he argues that, though Lewis's intention in narrative poetry is to tell a story first and execute the mechanics of poetry second, in *Dymer* he reverses this: "I think it is only fair to grant that *Dymer* is not altogether lacking in understanding, or beauty, or vitality or solidity. Certainly no one could object to the execution of the verse itself. But the poem fails, as it approaches its conclusion, to tell its story clearly, and the conclusion itself is obscure" (4). Second, after a short summary of the poem, Hodgens investigates the literary history of *Dymer* and tries to reconcile how elements of both an earlier prose version and an earlier verse version may have contributed to the flawed character of the final verse version. Third, he suggests possible literary influences, including *Paradise Lost,* Arnold's "Sohrab and Rustum," and a series of other poems Lewis was writing while working on his versions of *Dymer.* Fourth, Hodgens posits "the conflict of generations," particularly the murder of a parent by a child, as uppermost in Lewis's mind during this time. Fifth, he commends Lewis for several technical achievements, including the regularity of the poem's meter, the effectiveness of the dialogue, and vividness of the visual images. Hodgens's thoughtful comments on *Dymer* advance our understanding of this difficult poem.

Michael Slack gives an interesting reading of *Dymer;* he argues the poem's *Sehnsucht* "is essentially similar to the Platonic Eros." ("Sehnsucht and the Platonic Eros in *Dymer,*" *Bulletin of the New York C. S. Lewis Society* 11 [Aug. 1980]: 3–7). To this he adds: "Both are similarly self-corrective, are unsatisfiable in this world, and have as their goals union with 'ultimate reality'" (4). While this is a valuable critical perspective, the essay is flawed on several accounts. Some are minor, as when Slack claims *Dymer* was published three years prior to Lewis's conversion in 1929; actually, in *Surprised by Joy,* Lewis dates his conversion to Christ as occurring in 1931. Others are more serious. For instance, after citing that "Plato defines the soul's natures as the appetitive, the passionate, and the rational, each characterized by a form of desire with its peculiar object" (4), Slack argues, "It is appropriate that Dymer learns of sexual passion as his last sampling of Eros as physical desire because the intensity of sexual desire and, more subtly, the fact that procreation is one way of achieving immortality make it the most deceptive appetitive form of Eros" (5). Awkward syntax aside, what does this mean? Unfortunately, there are many similar passages. Still, this essay deserves critical attention for its fresh approach to our understanding of *Dymer.*

Peter Schakel's comments about *Dymer* are filtered by his argument that, as with *Spirits in Bondage* noted above, the tension is between rationalism and Romanticism. Consequently, he believes "*Dymer* is a review and modification of Lewis's earlier romanticism, both the romantic protest and idealism and the romantic longing and emotional indulgence" (*Reason and Imagination,* 99). He gives an accurate summary of the poem read in this way and notes significant differences in handling this tension from *Spirits in Bondage:* "*Dymer,* more than *Spirits in Bondage,* develops the Platonic theme, or Lewis's adaptation of a Platonic theme, implicit in the earlier title and the ideas about nature expressed there. Dymer, like all humanity, is imprisoned within his mortal body; he must seek to become free of it, to keep his attention on higher things. But that effort is hindered by the world, especially by nature, which is 'diabolical' in that its attractions and beauties create longings and satisfactions which invite one to be content with the world and this life. . . It is a neat, abstractly satisfying means of dealing with the problems of suffering and evil in the world, and a good deal more sophisticated than the simple materialism of *Spirits in Bondage*" (101). Like Sayer, Schakel rightly connects *Spirits in Bondage* and *Dymer;* however, as his larger purpose is a discussion of *Till We Have Faces,* he focuses upon showing the affinities between *Dymer* and *Till We Have Faces.* Still, Schakel's criticism of both these volumes of poetry broadens our understanding of Lewis as poet.

Almost as effective is Patrick Murphy's essay in which he argues for our reading *Dymer* as "a long, continuous narrative poem that begins as a hesitation fantasy but is resolved as supernatural (marvelous) fantasy" ("C. S. Lewis's *Dymer:* Once More with Hesitation," *Bull. of the New York C. S. Lewis Society* 17 [June 1986]: 2). That is, readers following the narrative hesitate "over the more fantastic elements of the story, wondering whether they are products of the fictional world or products of Dymer's fantasizing mind" (3); the dissonance this creates draws readers deeper into the narrative and "induces reader hesitation and intensifies the experiencing of Dymer's journey of self-discovery and enlightenment" (5). As Dymer comes to a series of realizations about himself, readers remain uncertain, "impaired by hesitation over the nature of the events that led to Dymer's enlightenment" (6); another way to put this is that, while readers follow Dymer through his adventures, they wonder whether what he describes is dream or reality. For Murphy, this tension is resolved in Canto VIII when Dymer learns his mysterious lover is a spirit: "At that point, but not before it, Dymer's and the reader's hesitation ends and the hesitation fantasy becomes clearly a supernatural fantasy, a marvelous story, moving inexorably toward Dymer's destruction" (6).

5. Narrative Poems: The Grand Tradition

1. Hugh L'Anson Fausett reviewed *Dymer* ("Review of *Dymer*") for *The Times Literary Supplement* (July 13, 1927, 27). In a letter to Lewis before the review appeared, Fausett wrote, "I wish to send you a line to say what a remarkable achievement I consider your poem to be. I have not read any poem recently which has impressed me by its inevitability of expression and by the profundity of its metaphysic . . . which is wholly and quite incalculably translated into terms of image and symbolism, and this seems to me the final test of greatness in poetry" (*LP,* 9:130–31).

2. Sayer, "C. S. Lewis's *Dymer*," 94.

3. Shaw, "Looking Back to Eden . . . ," *Radix* 21, no. 3 (1993), 14.

4. Lewis received a letter from Barfield informing him of a friend's judgment of *Dymer*: "The metrical level is good, the vocabulary is large: but Poetry—not a line" (Jan. 26, 1927, *DCSL*, 438).

5. About these lines, Green and Hooper write: "In the spring of 1932 he [Lewis] had another go at writing the story of Joy leading on to conversion. This, like the first attempt, was to be in the form of a long narrative poem. Only 34 lines of it [in their book they only quote the first twelve] have survived in a letter written to Owen Barfield on 6 May 1932 in which he says: 'I am not satisfied with any part I have yet written and the design is ludicrously ambitious. But I feel it will be several years anyway before I give it up'" (*C. S. Lewis: A Biography*, 127). Later they refer to this as "a new verse autobiography" beginning with "an idea of [Lewis's] Chestertonian 'voyage'" (127). Still later, they add: "Lewis added another 100 lines of this new autobiography before he went on his annual spring walking tour with Barfield and Dom Bede Griffiths shortly after Easter of 1932" (128). As of this writing I have not discovered where the "100 lines" to which Green and Hooper refer are located.

Kathryn Lindskoog's *Finding the Landlord: A Guidebook to C. S. Lewis's Pilgrim's Regress* (Chicago, Ill.: Cornerstone Press, 1995) adds the following about the thirty-four-line fragment:

> Written in hexameter like Homer's *Odyssey* . . . [after Lewis's poem begins] with the lines "I will write down the portion that I understand / Of twenty years wherein I went from land to land," Lewis went on to claim that he went halfway round the world searching for a home. . . . The unpublished second stanza is a prayer to God for nurture and guidance to enable Lewis to complete this book well for the sake of readers who might be helped by it. In this stanza he likens God to a self-kindled flame and likens himself to a fading candle; he describes God as an unquivering light and the warmth of the world. He feels too reverent to use the word God. In the third stanza, Lewis recalls that in his childhood he heard the Christian story, but it didn't interest him. He was much more interested in the joys of being alive in the world than in any news about his soul. (xxv)

Lindskoog believes this poem is the source for Lewis's allegorical *The Pilgrim's Regress*.

6. Lindskoog correctly points out this word is "whose"; see "'Odyssey' Poem Left Out; Glaring Error Left In," *The Lewis Legacy*, 65 (Summer 1995): 3. In the Green and Hooper biography, they print this word as "whole."

7. King, "Glints of Light," 86–87, and reprinted in appendix 2. Original found in a letter to Owen Barfield, May 6, 1932, *OB*, vol. 2 (1932–1940), cat. no. 26–50, index no. 0065, Wade Center.

8. Again we see the subtle influence of Wordsworth, who finds both memory (see "Tintern Abbey") and experience ("Let Nature be your teacher" from "The Tables Turned") important for cognitive development.

9. See Hooper's preface to *Narrative Poems*, xii.

10. Almost no critical work has been done on this poem. Caroline Geer's thesis on Lewis's narrative poems excluding *Dymer* begins with an obligatory brief biography in which she assumes but never proves Lewis "was at best a minor poet" ("The Posthumous Narrative Poems of C. S. Lewis," M.A. thesis, North Texas State University, 1976, 6). She

concentrates upon the "posthumous narrative poems" and so, conveniently, does not have to consider *Dymer,* although she does briefly nod her head in its direction, noting "the tone of the poem is anti-totalitarian, vindictive, and romantic" (10). Her intent throughout is to "explore common motifs found in the stories of the three poems ["Launcelot," "The Nameless Isle," and "The Queen of Drum"]" (11). In addition to Arthurian myth (especially the grail legend), Greek mythology, and Romanticism, she investigates the theme of the quest. Suggesting both Charles Williams and Tennyson as influences, Geer summarizes the basic content of "Launcelot," offers a review of the grail legend, and notes that the theme ("The Sangrail has betrayed us all") is so powerful it dominates Lewis's characterizations of Guinevere, Arthur, Gawain, and Launcelot; she claims theme, not character, drives the poem.

Walter Hooper offers little criticism, though he does indulge in several literary judgments. He says, "There is little I can say of *Launcelot* except that it reflects [Lewis's] deep love for the 'matter of Britain' (especially Malory)" (preface to *NP,* xii).

11. Malory, *Le Morte D'Arthur,* 284.

12. Although Caroline Geer finds the poem "an effective dramatic narrative, . . . [and] the story is a dramatization of the quest as the real struggle in men's lives as they search for truth and strive to consecrate themselves to the holy journey" (30), her evaluation is not supported by a close reading.

13. Lewis may owe some of his imagery here to Tennyson's description of Launcelot and his horse in "The Lady of Shalott": "His broad clear brow in the sunlight glowed; / On burnished hooves his war horse trode; / From underneath his helmet flowed / His coal-black curls as on he rode, / As he rode down to Camelot."

14. This poem may be the result in part of Lewis's essay "A Metrical Suggestion," *Lysistrata* 2 (May 1935): 13–24. Later published as "The Alliterative Metre" in *Selected Literary Essays,* 15–26.

15. Like "Launcelot," this poem has received little critical commentary. Noting the poem's alliterative style, Geer speculates that Lewis writes it in conjunction with his teaching of *Beowulf* and other Anglo-Saxon poetry, perhaps as an experiment. Then she summarizes the poem, comments briefly on Anglo-Saxon metrics, and says the poem draws upon Greek and English mythological and biblical motifs. Noticeable in this poem is the flatness of characterization; characters are significant only as they contribute "to the unfolding of the story" (39). She argues for a reading that sees the shipwrecked master mariner as an Odysseus figure, though not as heroic; other elements she finds compelling are the love quest and the magic flute.

Hooper attributes "The Nameless Isle" to Lewis's love of the Old English alliterative line as well as his desire to write a long story in verse (preface to *NP,* xii). Roland Kawano studies "The Nameless Isle" and suggests that, because it was written during the years of Lewis's move to Christian faith, it "reflects Lewis's own preoccupation with the pilgrimage which eventually brought him into orthodoxy" ("C. S. Lewis and 'The Nameless Isle': A Metaphor of Major Change," *Bull. of the New York C. S. Lewis Society* 15 [Mar. 1984], 2). After a summary, Kawano says the poem reflects for the first time in Lewis's writing the image of the great dance; further, he says the theme of the poem "is that of edenic reversal" (3), linking it therefore to *Perelandra.* He also identifies other spiritually infused motifs including genuflection, reference to All Saints' Eve, and the Exodus simile; about the latter, Kawano speculates: "Is it also possible that through the Exodus simile Lewis is speaking of a change in himself, or a personal exodus?" (3–4). Though Kawano acknowledges such an argument opens him to the charge of practicing the "personal heresy," he maintains this reading of the poem.

16. Lewis was profoundly influenced by Mozart's *The Magic Flute,* a work he wrote about to Greeves as early as July 11, 1916 (*TST,* 121). In *The Diary of C. S. Lewis* there are two passages that underscore this influence. On October 2, 1922, Lewis writes: "I . . . looked into a book on Mozart and read the story of the *Magic Flute* which I found very suggestive. The opposition of Sarastro and the Queen and the meeting ground in the girl makes a good myth. . . . I thought curiously of how this might be used for a big poem some day" (112). A week later he adds: "I also looked into the book on Mozart where I read that Goethe had written a continuation to the story of the *Magic Flute*. It is really extraordinary how much this subject has been on my mind lately" (115). Although Lewis may have waited more than ten years to write a "big poem" on a theme suggested by Mozart's *The Magic Flute,* "The Nameless Isle" is certainly this attempt. For instance, the conflict between the King and the Queen in "The Nameless Isle" is akin to that of Sarastro and the Queen of Night in *The Magic Flute;* similarly, the conflict in both stories turns upon who will have control of the daughter.

17. Lewis may have been influenced here by Dante's ship of saved souls in Canto II of *Purgatorio,* in *Paradise Lost.*

18. Cited in *NP,* 179.

19. A long narrative poem in varied stanzas is certainly legitimate; Tennyson's *Maud* is only one of many examples Lewis would have known well.

20. More critical work has been done on this poem than either "Launcelot" or "The Nameless Isle." Walter Hooper admits "The Queen of Drum" is his favorite of Lewis's narrative poems: "Besides the poem's poetical merits, I would say that *The Queen of Drum* is a Christian work, though not written from Lewis's usual objective basis: the Christianity emerges, and even the theme of Drumland (Romanticism) is developed on its own merits, and not as Christian byway" (xiv). William Linden's piece on "The Queen of Drum" argues that the geographical references to Drum in the poem suggest it is located "in the region of Narnia-Archenland." He also believes there was a Drummian Revolution akin to the French Revolution, though "one may conjecture that the Revolution was suppressed by the neighboring states" ("New Light on Narnia; or, Who Beat the Drum?" *Bull. of the New York C. S. Lewis Society* 2 [Apr. 1971], 9). Such conjectures define this brief analysis. James Purcell adds little to our understanding of it in his review essay; his impatience with reading the poem as a poem is clear in the following statement: "Unfortunately, Lewis worked in his [narrative] poetry within the critical limits of British Victorian taste" ("*Narrative Poems,*" *Bull. of the New York C. S. Lewis Society* 2 [Nov. 1972], 2). Richard Hodgens's essay mentioned above in reference to *Dymer* also discusses "The Queen of Drum." After reviewing the plot and relating how Lewis's *The Discarded Image* provides helpful information on his view of the *longaevi,* the long-lived ones, Hodgens turns his attention to criticizing several sudden and ineffective plot turns as well as Lewis's use of a mixed meter rather than a consistent one. His argument about meter is informed, literate, and interesting. Carol Ann Brown's short note on "The Queen of Drum" reflects on the three roads available to the characters in the poem: Heaven, Hell, or Elfland. She moralizes in her conclusion: "The three ways are a reality in our lives. It is futile to comment on Heaven or Hell. Our conscience will take care

of that, but Elfland is a present danger" ("Three Roads: A Comment on 'The Queen of Drum,'" *Bull. of the New York C. S. Lewis Society* 7 [Apr. 1976], 14).

After giving a careful review of its literary development and following her summary of "The Queen of Drum," Caroline Geer offers helpful insight and analysis. She reads the poem as contrasting "the philosophy which acknowledges a physical, closed universe [represented by the General and the Council of Drum] opposed to one which recognizes a spiritual, open universe" [represented by the Queen and the Archbishop] (58). Helpful, too, is her suggestion that since *drum* has Celtic connections to the idea of faery, readers are prepared for the Queen's eventual movement into Elfland, even at the risk of damnation. When she links the General with fascism and nazism because the poem uses the words "duce" and "fuhrer," she is on target; she claims "He is the epitome of the philosophy of modern Materialism—vulgar, efficient, insensitive" (62). In its contrast between dreams and materialism, Geer posits that the poem restates "man's deep, and often unfulfilled, need to long for something Other—either the pure emotional pleasure of Faerie or deep spiritual fulfillment in a personal relationship with God—which may be approached through, though never realized in, dreams" (65). Her thesis concludes by noting Lewis's use of the third-person narrator in each poem (giving them, she claims, "a measure of authenticity") as well as the ubiquitous quest theme; this is a piece of criticism worth reading if only for its earnest look at these three poems.

Finally, Roland Kawano maintains that the poem is concerned with the tension for the Queen between the Kingdom of Light and the Land of Faerie. He cannot resist wondering "how far-fetched it would be to recognize in the alternatives given the Queen, the kind of alternatives that Lewis recognized he was wrestling with prior to becoming a Christian" (12). He adds later: "Perhaps the poet was telling us of a choice that he had made in his priate [*sic*] life, a choice that could not help but have consequences in his poetry." ("C. S. Lewis' *The Queen of Drum*," *The Lamp-Post of the Southern California C. S. Lewis Society* 11 [Nov. 1987], 10–14.)

21. An alternative reading would see these parenthetical lines as the dreams of the people of Drumland; they go to the mountains in their dreams, while the Queen goes there physically.

22. Moreover, while Hooper dates the poem as 1933–34, it is possible it was written before Lewis's conversion to Christ in 1931. If so, it reveals his very thoughtful exploration of this tension, suggesting he feared how Christianity might impact his own love of faery, and, by extension, his imaginative world.

6. Comic and Satiric Verse

1. *Poems* lacks a unified structure such as we see in *Spirits in Bondage* and *Dymer;* however, some of Lewis's best poetry is found in this volume. Hooper gives the book a four-part structure: Part I: The Hidden Country; Part II: The Backward Glance; Part III: A Larger World; and Part IV: Further Up & Further In.

2. In Hooper's appendix to *Poems,* he cites the sources of 75 of these 77; the two he omits are "Angel's Song" from *The Pilgrim's Regress,* 198–99, and "Re-Adjustment" from *Fifty-Two: A Journal of Books and Authors* 14 (Autumn 1964): 4.

3. The three poems are revisions of ones appearing in *Fear No More: A Book of Poems for the Present Time by Living English Poets* (Cambridge: Cambridge UP, 1940). "A Pageant Played in Vain" from *Poems* (96) is a revision of "Break, Sun, My Crusted Earth" from *Fear No More* (72); "Poem from Psychoanalysts and/or Theologians" from *Poems* (113) is a revision of "The World is Round" from *Fear No More* (85); and "After Prayers, Lie Cold" from *Poems* (130) is a revision of "Arise My Body" from *Fear No More* (89).

4. *Letters to Malcolm: Chiefly on Prayer* (London: Geoffrey Bles, 1964), 67.

5. Happily, in the fall of 1997 Hooper deposited in the Bodleian Library both the typescript manuscript of *Young King Cole and Other Pieces* as well as holographs of many poems published in *Poems*. Those interested in these concerns should examine the holographs in the Bodleian Library. Appendix 4 contains a complete list of the contents of this deposit as well the publication history of each poem. Other topical poems include those appearing in the "Miscellany" of *Collected Poems* and a handful of miscellaneous poems.

6. "Abecedarium Philosophicum" (coauthored by Owen Barfield), *The Oxford Magazine* 52 (Nov. 30, 1933): 298; "After Kirby's *Kalevala*," *The Oxford Magazine* 56 (May 13, 1937): 505; "Awake, My Lute!" *The Atlantic Monthly* 172 (Nov. 1943): 113, 115; "From the Latin of Milton's *De Idea Platonica Quemadmodum Aristoteles Intellexit*" (a translation), *English* 5, no. 30 (1945): 195; "To Mr. Kingsley Amis on His Late Verses," *Essays in Criticism* 4 (Apr. 1954): 190; "Epitaph for Helen Joy Davidman," in *C. S. Lewis: Images of His World*, ed. Douglas Gilbert and Clyde S. Kilby (Grand Rapids, Mich.: Eerdmans, 1973), 65; "Re-Adjustment," *Fifty-Two: A Journal of Books and Authors* 14 (Autumn 1964): 4.

7. Walter Hooper's preface to *Poems* is notable, primarily because of his explanations about how and why the volume came to be published. He reveals that Lewis had been collecting a number of his poems, many previously published, with an eye toward publishing the compilation as *Young King Cole and Other Pieces*. Unfortunately, Lewis died and left unfinished this effort. Accordingly, Hooper felt "justified in collecting everything I could find among his literary remains and in following my judgements as to what should be printed" (vii). Furthermore, Hooper says it was not always easy to determine the final version of some poems because, even among those previously printed, there were multiple versions; in addition, he says Lewis used to dictate poems to him and "even after he [Lewis] thought one was completed he might suggest a change here. Then a change there" (vii–viii). All this is problematic for scholars since unless all variants are available for scrutiny, the question of which version of each poem Lewis intended as "final" is unknown. Compounding this problem is *Collected Poems*. Prompted at least in part by the publication of *Collected Poems*, a series of articles over several issues in *The Lewis Legacy* questions the validity of the introductory letter purported to be by Lewis in the latter volume, the incompleteness of *Collected Poems*, and revisions to poems Lewis published during his lifetime; see *The Lewis Legacy* 64 (Spring 1995). Also targeted are specific poems and their variants, especially "Finchley Avenue," first published in *Occasional Poets: An Anthology* (1986) and subsequently published in *Collected Poems*; see *The Lewis Legacy* 65 (Summer 1995). Finally, whole-text variants of "March for Drum, Trumpet, and Twenty-One Giants," "The Day with a White Mark," and "Under Sentence" (published as "The Condemned" in *Poems*) with notes and commentary are published in *Collected Poems*; see *The Lewis Legacy* 66 (Autumn 1995).

8. In order to see the growth of Lewis as a poet, ideally these poems should be discussed in the chronological order in which they were first published. However, a thematic

approach along the lines I suggest provides an effective way to access the important ideas in his poetry.

9. Of these forty-two, I have reviewed holographs of all but a few poems and epigrams and epitaphs. In my judgment, Walter Hooper's editorial decisions regarding these holographs—many often existing in several versions—have been judicious. The versions he eventually publishes in *Poems* reflect what he believes are Lewis's *intended* versions. While I do not share in Hooper's view that the *intended* version is the one that should be published (how can we really know which version is the intended one?), I accept his explanation.

10. Lewis often linked comic and satiric poems. For example, in his *English Literature in the Sixteenth Century* (Oxford: Oxford UP, 1944) he writes that "a third group of [William Dunbar's] poems is comic; if you will, satiric, though 'abusive' would be a better word" (93).

11. *The Oxford Magazine* 52 (Nov. 30, 1933): 298 (with Owen Barfield). An earlier version of this poem appears in the Lewis Papers, 9:164–65.

12. *The Atlantic Monthly* 172 (Nov. 1943): 113, 115. Reprinted in *CP*.

13. Lewis may be imitating songs of W. S. Gilbert in his poem. For instance, his use of internal rhyme and meter is (loosely) akin to Little Buttercup's opening aria in *H. M. S. Pinafore or The Lass that Loved a Sailor*: "I've snuff and tobaccy and excellent jacky, / I've scissors, and watches, and knives; / I've ribbons and laces to set off the faces / Of pretty young sweethearts and wives." Compare to the opening of "Awake, My Lute": "I stood in the gloom of a spacious room / Where I listened for hours (on and off) / To a terrible bore with a beard like a snore / And a heavy rectangular cough." Even more influential may be the Lord Chancellor's song in *Iolanthe*: "When you're lying awake with a dismal headache, and repose is taboo'd by anxiety, / I conceive you may use any language you choose to indulge in, without impropriety; / For your brain is on fire—the bedclothes conspire of usual slumbers to plunder you: / First your counterpane goes, and uncovers your toes, and your sheet slips demurely from under you . . . ."

14. See *The Complete Works of Lewis Carroll* (New York: The Modern Library, n.d.), 920–21.

15. Ibid., 901.

16. *Punch* 225 (Nov. 4, 1953): 553 (N.W.). Revised and reprinted in *P* and *CP* as part 2 of "Narnian Suite." No less than four different versions of this poem exist in holograph, indicating either Lewis's enjoyment of the sounds he fashions for the poem or his frustrations in trying to get the right combination of sounds.

17. In the satiric poems, the percussive tone is brittle, pedantic, querulous, combative, or acidic. I am indebted to James Prothero for the term "percussive."

18. *P*, 31; reprinted in *CP*. A holograph of this poem is available in the Bodleian Library. Interestingly, another holograph, "A Wedding has been Arranged," is a slightly different version of "The Small Man Orders His Wedding." Still another version is in the Bodleian, MS. Eng. c. 2724, fol. 55; it has the title, "An Epithalamium for John Wain feigned to be spoken in his person giving orders for his wedding," signed C.S.L., June 1947. There also appear to be fragments of early drafts of this version of the poem.

19. *LL*, 293.

20. Warren Lewis, *Brothers and Friends: The Diaries of Major Warren Hamilton Lewis*, ed. Clyde S. Kilby and Marjorie Lamp Mead (San Francisco, Calif.: Harper and Row, 1982), 99.

21. Ibid., 192.

22. Sayer, *Jack: C. S. Lewis and His Times*, 150.

23. In King, "Glints of Light," 89, and reprinted in appendix 2. The holograph is available from MS. Eng. lett. c. 220/7, fols. 1–3, Bodleian Library.

24. Joe R. Christopher says: "In the poem to Mrs. Dyson, note that one of her names is Margaret. This means *pearl*, so the reference in the poem to Pearl is explained. (I know it because 'Pearl' by the Pearl Poet is sometimes guessed to be about a dead child named Margaret)" (e-mail to the author, Apr. 7, 1997).

25. Published poems reflecting a similar jocularity include the previously discussed "Abecedarium Philosophicum" and "Awake, My Lute."

26. *The Oxford Magazine* 55 (May 6, 1937): 565 (N.W.). Reprinted in *P* and *CP*.

27. *Punch* 225 (July 15, 1953): 91 (N.W.). Reprinted in *P* and *CP*. He uses the Sapphic stanza here.

28. Lewis takes up the same issue in his essay "On Three Ways of Writing for Children" where he defends his love of fairy tale: "Now the modern critical world uses 'adult' as a term of approval. It is hostile to what it calls 'nostalgia' and contemptuous of what it calls 'Peter Pantheism.' Hence a man who admits that dwarfs and giants and talking beasts and witches are still dear to him in his fifty-third year is now less likely to be praised for his perennial youth than scorned and pitied for arrested development. If I spend some little time defending myself against these charges, this is not so much because it matters greatly whether I am scorned and pitied as because the defence is germane to my whole view of the fairy tale and even of literature in general" (in *Of Other Worlds: Essays and Stories*, ed. Walter Hooper [New York: Harcourt Brace Jovanovich, 1966], 25).

29. *The Times Literary Supplement* (June 11, 1954): 375. Revised and retitled "Science-Fiction Cradlesong" in *P* and *CP*.

30. *The Magazine of Fantasy and Science Fiction* 16, no. 6 (June 1959): 47. Reprinted in *P* and *CP*.

31. *Of Other Worlds*, 61–62. For more on this, see in the same volume "On Stories" as well as the complete text of "On Science Fiction."

32. *The Cambridge Review* 79 (Nov. 30, 1957): 227 (N.W.). Reprinted in *P* and *CP*. Some have suggested Joy Davidman assisted Lewis in composing this poem and that they sang it as a parody of *Joyful, Joyful We Adore Thee* or *Lead Us, Heavenly Father, Lead Us*.

33. *Punch* 215 (Dec. 1, 1948): 510 (N.W.). Revised and reprinted in *P* and *CP*.

34. David Landrum's essay "Pindar, Prodigality, and Paganism: Natural Law Ethics in the Poetry of C. S. Lewis" (*The Lamp-Post of the Southern California C. S. Lewis Society* 19 [Summer 1995], 4–13) is very good and should be mentioned here. He considers the poems on these subjects in light of what were "Lewis's ideas on what is proper, desirable, and captivating in art as well as in life" (4). Of special interest, Landrum points out that Lewis uses "unbelievers, classical pagans and worshippers of the Olympian gods, and followers of Islam" as models of such principles rather than Christian ones. Accordingly, "these unbelievers are presented as the moral and artistic antithesis of a post-Christian world where true sentiments have been lost and, as a result, art has become distorted and cut off from what Lewis believed to be its humane intellectual moorings." When Landrum turns to analyze the poems, he notes Lewis's "disquieting range of rhetorical excess" (5) and links this to Lewis's same tactic in his apologetics. A good deal more needs to be done in

examining Lewis's poetic rhetoric, and Landrum does much to advance such study in this interesting essay.

35. *Essays in Criticism* 4 (Apr. 1954): 190; cf. Kingsley Amis, "Beowulf," ibid. (Jan. 1954): 85.

36. *The Cherwell* 56 (May 6, 1939): 35 (N.W.). Revised and retitled "The Author of *Flowering Rifle*" in *P* and *CP*.

37. British slang for a fool or a white man.

38. "To Mr. Roy Campbell," in *Poems*, 66–67; reprinted in *CP*. A holograph of this poem is available in the Bodleian Library.

39. Interestingly, on November 28, 1946, Warren Lewis writes in *Brothers and Friends*: "A pretty full meeting of the Inklings to meet Roy Campbell . . . whom I was very glad to see again; he is fatter and tamer than he used to be I think" (197). Apparently, Lewis and Campbell eventually found common ground. For more on Lewis and Campbell, see Joe R. Christopher's "Roy Campbell and the Inklings," *Mythlore* 22 (Autumn 1997): 33–34, 36–46.

40. In King "Glints of Light," 90–91, and reprinted in appendix 2. The holograph is available in MS. Eng. lett. c. 861, fol. 69, Bodleian Library. Beneath the poem is the following, apparently in Lewis's handwriting: "C. S. Lewis, Magdalen College, Oxford." Further down are the words "Femine, livy, fright (?)," still in Lewis's hand; I suppose Lewis was using these as he struggled for rhymes. Finally, in a different hand, is the following: "Fell out of Jack's Latin Dictionary. ACH(arwood)." I believe this is Hooper's handwriting as he notes where this poem was discovered.

41. According to Marjorie Mead, Lewis takes issue publicly on this point in his letter to the Editor, "Poetic Licence," *The Sunday Times* (Aug. 11, 1946): 6. Mead says Lewis discusses the "poetic licence" granted writers when working on a rhyme scheme using foreign names, adding it is not necessary for an English poet to retain ancient pronunciations in English. Such assimilation into English vernacular indicates the health of the language. In his letter, Lewis is responding to several others which criticize the freedom of rhyme in "Thoughts of England" by John Gwynne-Hughes, *The Sunday Times* (June 23, 1946): 4. A letter by H. Lang Jones (July 7, 1946) complains of other poets who rhyme Aphrodite with white, thus the occasion for Lewis's letter. These letters may help date the poem on Mackenzie to this general time. See Jeffrey D. Schultz and John G. West, eds., *The C. S. Lewis Readers' Encyclopedia* (Grand Rapids, Mich.: Zondervan, 1998), 327.

42. Although the precise occasion that moved Lewis to write this poem is not clear, since the poem contains references to the mythological Romulus, Lewis may be reacting to his reading Mackenzie's *Marathon and Salamis* (1934) or to any of his numerous histories of military activity in Greece and Rome written during World War I.

43. *Nine: A Magazine of Poetry and Criticism* 2 (May 1950): 114. Revised (a second stanza is added) and reprinted in *P* and *CP*.

44. *The Month* 11 (May 1954): 272. Revised and reprinted in *P* and *CP*.

45. Lewis himself fell under the gaze of such tabloids when a woman claimed Lewis was going to marry her. See Walter Hooper's *C. S. Lewis: A Companion and Guide* (London: HarperCollins, 1996), 55–65.

46. *Poems*, 56–57; reprinted in *CP*. A holograph of this poem is available in the Bodleian Library.

47. In "Religion and Rocketry" Lewis puts it this way: "We know what our race does to strangers. Man destroys or enslaves every species he can. Civilized man murders, enslaves, cheats, and corrupts savage man. Even inanimate nature he turns into dust bowls and slag-heaps. There are individuals who don't. But they are not the sort who are likely to be our pioneers in space. Our ambassador to new worlds will be the needy and greedy adventurer or the ruthless technical expert. They will do as their kind has always done. What that will be if they meet things weaker than themselves, the black man and the red man can tell" (*The World's Last Night and Other Essays* [New York: Harcourt Brace Jovanovich, 1952], 89).

48. *Poems*, 60; reprinted in *CP*. A holograph of this poem is available in the Bodleian Library.

49. *Punch* 227 (Dec. 1, 1954): 685 (N.W.). The title means "Spartan having obtained." Revised and retitled "A Confession" in *P* and *CP*.

50. *Poems*, 62; reprinted in *CP*. Two holograph versions of this poem are available in the Bodleian Library; one is titled "Government" and is signed by Lewis as having been written at Magdalen College, Oxford. Unfortunately, neither version is dated. This poem has connections to "The Future of Forestry," "Under Sentence," "Prelude to Space," and "On a Vulgar Error."

51. *Poems*, 63–64; reprinted in *CP*.

52. *The Spectator* 181 (July 30, 1948): 142. Revised and retitled "Epigrams and Epitaphs, No. 14" in *P* and *CP*.

53. Of course, a literal reading gives it that democracy is the tyranny of majority rule that will not permit the radio to be turned off.

54. *CP*, 249. A holograph of this poem is available in the Bodleian Library.

55. Vortigern, also spelled Wyrtgeorn (fl. 425–450), was king of the Britons at the time of the arrival of the Saxons. He accepted the assistance of the Saxons in order to protect his kingdom against the Picts and Scots, granting them land as compensation. Later the Britons made war on the Saxons in their Kentish strongholds. After the death in battle of Vortemir, Vortigern's son, against the Saxons, the *Historia Brittonum* records the massacre of the British nobles and Vortigern's subsequent grant of Essex and Sussex to the invaders. Except for this poem, Lewis does not write much poetry about World War II. In part, this is because he was not in active service or on the battlefield; in part, because he is older, more mature, and no longer angry with God; and, in part, because he uses prose primarily to deal with the war, especially *The Screwtape Letters* and his essay "Learning In War-time."

7. Contemplative Verse

1. *CP*, 250–52. A holograph of this poem exists and may be viewed in the Bodleian Library. London has a Finchley Lane, Finchley Court, Finchley Park, Finchley Place, Finchley Road, and a Finchley Way, but it does not have a Finchley Avenue. Kathryn Lindskoog has questioned the legitimacy of "Finchley Avenue," first published in *Occasional Poets: An Anthology* (1986) and subsequently published in *Collected Poems*.

2. This recalls a passage from *Surprised by Joy*: "The New House [Little Lea] is almost a major character in my story. I am a product of long corridors, empty sunlit rooms, upstairs

indoor silences, attics explored in solitude, distant noises of gurgling cisterns and pipes, and the noise of wind under the tiles" (10).

3. In *Surprised by Joy* Lewis writes: "One dominant factor in our [Lewis and Warren's] life at home was the daily absence of our father from about nine in the morning till six at night. . . . From the very first we built up for ourselves a life that excluded him" (40, 119).

4. *The Oxford Magazine* 56 (Feb. 10, 1938): 383 (N.W.). Reprinted in *P* and *CP*.

5. Besides the inverted biblical allusion seen in "trees as men walking," this phrase may anticipate Tolkien's Ents.

6. *The Spectator* 175 (Sept. 7, 1945): 219. Revised and retitled "The Condemned" in *P* and *CP*.

7. See Johnson's *London*, Cobbett's *Rural Rides*, Landor's *Imaginary Conversations*, and Blake's *Songs of Innocence and Experience*.

8. The poem also has affinities with Lewis's warnings about "conditioners" like Gaius and Titius in his *The Abolition of Man*.

9. *Punch* 212 (Jan. 15, 1947): 71 (N.W.). Reprinted in *P* and *CP*.

10. *Punch* 221 (Sept. 12, 1951): 303 (N.W.). Reprinted in *P* and *CP*. He uses the Asclepiadean stanza here.

11. In this regard, the poem links to *The Abolition of Man* (New York: Macmillan, 1947) since it is not just the loss of the meaning of language that concerns Lewis; he is as concerned with the loss of objective truth that follows the destruction of language: "You can hardly open a periodical without coming across the statement that what our civilization needs is more 'drive,' or dynamism, or self-sacrifice, or 'creativity.' In a sort of ghastly simplicity we remove the organ and demand the function. We make men without chests and expect of them virtue and enterprise. We laugh at honour and are shocked to find traitors in our midst. We castrate and bid the geldings to be fruitful" (35).

12. *Fifty-Two: A Journal of Books and Authors* 14 (Autumn 1964): 4. Reprinted in *P* and *CP*.

13. "*De Descriptione Temporum*" is reprinted in *Selected Literary Essays*.

14. Lewis's "timeless rays" may be thought of as objective truths reflected in the "dew drop" of the present moment.

15. *P*, 114–15; reprinted in *CP*.

16. The poem recalls passages from *Spirits in Bondage*.

17. The language in the poem anticipates the more belligerent attitude of the dwarfs in *The Last Battle* who refuse to believe they are enjoying a feast in the stable in celebration of Aslan's return. Refusing to "be taken in," they taste hay, turnips, old cabbage leaves, and trough water instead of pies, pigeons, ices, and rich wine. They insist at the end: "We haven't let anyone take us in. The Dwarfs are for the Dwarfs." Aslan notes, "They have chosen cunning instead of belief. Their prison is only in their own minds, yet they are in that prison; and so afraid of being taken in that they can not be taken out" (148). At least initially, the persona in the poem has the same reluctance to enter into joy; he does not want to be "taken in" yet again.

18. Also helpful regarding the theme and language of this poem is Stephen Metcalf, "Language and Self-Consciousness: The Making and Breaking of C. S. Lewis's Personae," in

Word and Story in C. S. Lewis, ed. Peter Schakel and Charles Huttar (Columbia, Mo.: U of Missouri P, 1991), 109–44.

19. *Punch* 215 (Sept. 15, 1948): 237 (N.W.). Revised and reprinted in *P* and *CP*.

20. An ironic reading of the poem would have it that the search will go on and on, one false hope after another since "the Hesperides' Country . . . is not men's." However, the renewed vision of the men ("Hope died . . . rose again . . . flickered and increased in us: / Strenuous our longing; we re-embarked") mitigates against this ironic reading.

21. *Punch* 217 (Aug. 17, 1949): 170 (N.W.). Revised and reprinted in *P* and *CP*.

22. The sentiment expressed here links the poem to Lewis's earlier "Joy." See chapter 4.

23. *Punch* 218 (Mar. 15, 1950): 294–95 (N.W.). Revised and reprinted in *P* and *CP*. He uses the Alcaic stanza here.

24. All the poems in this volume are published anonymously; however, six copies contain an additional leaf giving the names of the authors of the poems; one of these is in the Bodleian Library, Oxford.

25. *Fear No More: A Book of Poems for the Present Time by Living English Poets,* 4. Reprinted in *CP*.

26. Ibid., 72. This is an alternative version of "A Pageant Played in Vain," found in *P* and *CP*.

27. Matthew Arnold's "The Buried Life" is an interesting poem to compare with Lewis's. Lewis comments on other attributes of the sun in *The Discarded Image,* 106. Another interesting gloss is the invocation in book 3 of *Paradise Lost* that begins: "Hail holy Light, offspring of Heav'n first-born, / Or of th' Eternal Coeternal beam / May I express thee unblam'd? since God is Light, / And never but in unapproachable Light / Dwelt from Eternity, dwelt then in thee, / Bright effluence of bright essence increate" (1–6).

28. *Fear No More,* 85. Revised and retitled "Poem for Psychoanalysts and/or Theologians" in *P* and *CP*. The poem is also lyrical in the tradition of Wordsworth's "Tintern Abbey."

29. Some readers may find a connection here to the opening lines of "The Queen of Drum."

30. *The Month* 7 (May 1952): 275. Reprinted in *P* and *CP*.

31. What does the map represent? His settled way of seeing the world, one characterized by "stock responses" and tradition? His spiritual convictions? Biblical texts? While we cannot be certain what the map represents, the significant point is that he momentarily questioned its validity. Such contemplation may be seen by some as disturbing; nonetheless, the poem reveals one who was always thinking, reflecting, and musing.

32. This poem appears in the Lewis Papers, 2:79–80. Hooper publishes it in *Collected Poems,* 245.

33. *The Spectator* 174 (June 8, 1945): 521. See erratum: "Poet and Printer," ibid. (June 15, 1945): 550. Reprinted in *P* and *CP*.

34. Of course the salamander could be the butt of Lewis's satire if Lewis is subtly glossing the poem to Plato's myth of the cave from book 7 of *The Republic*.

35. His genetic propensity toward pessimism and the general gloom and darkness of the world because of the competing philosophies of World War II—nazism, communism, socialism, totalitarianism, capitalism, and so on—may have gripped Lewis at this time.

36. *P,* 73–76; reprinted in *CP.* In *DCSL* Walter Hooper says: "The first version of this sonnet sequence survives in the same notebook as the last portion of the Diary. A revised version of it, entitled 'Infatuation,' is found in Lewis's *Poems*" (403). If accurate, this means Lewis first worked on the poem in 1926.

37. See Shakespeare's sonnets "129," "138," and "147."

38. Lewis also uses the idea of Venus's infernal in Letter XX of *The Screwtape Letters.*

39. *P,* 81; reprinted in *CP.*

40. Kathryn Lindskoog's fascination with this poem turns on her seeing in Lewis's use of reason and imagination in the poem a confirmation of the right brain/left brain polarity. She brings in references to *Till We Have Faces* and *The Pilgrim's Regress,* as well as allusions to right brain/left brain authorities to bolster her contention. See her "Getting It Together: Lewis and the Two Hemispheres of Knowing," *Journal of Psychology and Theology* 3 (Fall 1975): 290–93. Also, a very fine discussion of the poem may be found in Schakel's *Reason and Imagination in C. S. Lewis: A Study of* Till We Have Faces, ix, 179–88.

41. *P,* 125–27; reprinted in *CP.* Holographs of these poems are available in the Bodleian Library.

42. Lionel Adey offers a cursory analysis of this sequence and links the sonnets to *A Grief Observed* in his *C. S. Lewis: Writer, Dreamer & Mentor* (Grand Rapids, Mich.: Eerdmans, 1998), 219.

43. Consider, for instance, James 1:2–4: "Consider it pure joy, my brothers, whenever you face trials of many kinds, because you know that the testing of your faith develops perseverance. Perseverance must finish its work so that you may be mature and complete, not lacking anything."

44. *The Spectator* 169 (Oct. 9, 1942): 335. Revised and retitled "To a Friend" in *P* and *CP.* Hooper says this poem was originally entitled "To C. W." (preface to *Poems,* viii).

45. *Britain Today* 112 (Aug. 1945): 14. Revised and retitled "To Charles Williams" in *P* and *CP.* Williams died May 15, 1945.

46. *P,* 83; reprinted in *CP.*

47. Joe Christopher offers criticism of these poems assuming Lewis was writing about Joy Davidman. See his "C. S. Lewis, Love Poet" (*Studies in the Literary Imagination* 22 [Fall 1989]: 161–73) and "C. S. Lewis's Poems to Joy Davidman" (*The Canadian C. S. Lewis Journal* 94 [Autumn 1998]: 20–37).

48. *P,* 108; reprinted in *CP.* A holograph of this poem is available in the Bodleian Library.

49. I am indebted to Dabney Hart for her helpful insight on this point.

50. *P,* 109; reprinted in *CP.* A holograph of this poem is available in the Bodleian Library.

51. Ibid., 109–10; reprinted in *CP.* See the earlier discussion of this poem in chapter 1.

52. Joe Christopher argues similarly in his essay "C. S. Lewis, Love Poet." He says that "Joys That Sting," "Old Poets Remembered," and "As the Ruin Falls" are sonnets probably written to Joy Davidman: "In all of them the woman addressed is dying: they could have been written during Davidman's first bout with cancer, but—since Lewis only began to know he loved her during that time—the probability is stronger for the second and final bout with cancer" (167–68). His analyses of these poems are more prosaic than enlightening, though he is right when he says these are among "Lewis's best verse, clever, polished, and . . . highly successful" (173).

8. Religious Verse

1. "C. S. Lewis," Barfield address given at Wheaton College, Oct. 16, 1964.

2. Given the popularity of *The Problem of Pain, Miracles,* and *Mere Christianity,* attention should be given to his religious verse, since many of these poems offer commentary on his prose apologetics as well as powerful insights into his maturation in Christ.

3. *SJ,* 228–29.

4. In the introduction to *Collected Poems,* Hooper notes that a number of these poems may have existed in early variants: "Fourteen of [his] religious lyrics were sent to Owen Barfield during the summer of 1930 under the general title 'Half Hours with Hamilton,' and they are some of the most beautiful poems Lewis wrote. Most of these same poems were to appear a couple of years later in his semi-autobiographical *The Pilgrim's Regress* (1933). They were always Lewis's favourites of his own poems" (xv). "Half Hours with Hamilton" in holograph is available at the Wade Center. Appendix 5 contains a complete listing of the poems in "Half Hours with Hamilton" and their publication history.

5. In *Poems,* Hooper titles this "Footnote to All Prayers" (129).

6. Must reading in connection with *The Pilgrim's Regress* is Kathryn Lindskoog's *Finding the Landlord: A Guidebook to C. S. Lewis's Pilgrim's Regress.* Because my focus is upon the poetry of *The Pilgrim's Regress,* I will discuss the poems in isolation from the prose text of *The Pilgrim's Regress.* However, I will offer commentary about the context of the poem's placement in *The Pilgrim's Regress* in the accompanying notes.

7. In *Poems,* this is "Caught" (115–16). The poem is found in *PR,* bk. 8, chap. 6, entitled "Caught." John, having thought he had escaped from the Landlord, suddenly awakened to the fact that there was nowhere to escape from him: "In one night the Landlord—call him by what name you would—had come back to the world, and filled the world, quite full without a cranny. His eyes stared and His hand pointed and His voice commanded in everything that could be heard or seen. . . . All things said one word: CAUGHT—caught into slavery again, to walk warily and on sufferance all his days, never to be alone; never the master of his own soul, to have no privacy, no corner whereof you could say to the whole universe: This is my own, here I can do as I please" (147).

8. In *Poems,* this is "The Naked Seed" (117). The poem is found in *PR,* bk. 8, chap. 10, entitled "Archetype and Ectype." John and the hermit (History) discuss John's fear that "the things the Landlord really intends for me may be utterly unlike the things he has taught me to desire." The hermit assures him that the Landlord is the author of desire and that only He can fulfill John's desire. Furthermore, the hermit affirms that John's loss of his initial desire is normal: "First comes delight: then pain: then fruit. And then there is joy of the fruit, but that is different again from the first delight. And mortal lovers must not try to remain at the first step: for lasting passion is the dream of a harlot and from it we wake in despair. You must not try to keep the raptures: they have done their work. Manna kept, is worms" (162). The hermit sings the poem and is overheard by John.

9. From *The English Poems of George Herbert,* ed. C. A. Patrides (London: Dent, 1974), 127.

10. In *Poems,* this is "Wormwood" (87). The poem is found in *PR,* bk. 10, chap. 1, entitled "The Same yet Different." John and Vertue are off on their regress, for John the start

of his life in Christ. John complains that "Mother Kirk [the church] treats us very ill. Since we have followed her and eaten her food the way seems twice as narrow and twice as dangerous as it did before" (*PR*, 177). Virtue sings the poem as John and he start their journey.

11. In *Poems*, this is "Divine Justice" (98). The poem is found in *PR*, bk. 10, chap. 3, entitled "Limbo." John learns from his Guide (Slikisteinsauga) that human wisdom is not adequate to know the Landlord. Sadly, those who rely upon wisdom cut themselves off from hope and God's mercy: "The Landlord does not condemn them to lack of hope: they have done that themselves. The Landlord's interference is all on the other side. Left to itself, the desire without the hope would soon fall back to spurious satisfactions, and these souls would follow it of their own free will into far darker regions at the very bottom of the black hole [hell]. What the Landlord has done is to fix it forever: and by his art, though unfulfilled, it is uncorrupted" (*PR*, 179–80). The Guide then sings the poem to John. For more on the triolet, see Joe R. Christopher, "A Theological Triolet," *Bull. of the New York C. S. Lewis Society* 2 (Sept. 1971): 4–5.

12. In *The Great Divorce*, George Macdonald puts it differently: "There are only two kinds of people in the end: those who say to God, 'Thy will be done,' and those to whom God says, in the end, '*Thy* will be done. All that are in Hell, choose it.' Without that self-choice there could be no Hell" (72).

13. In *Poems*, this is "Nearly They Stood" (102–3). The poem is found in *PR*, bk. 10, chap. 4, entitled "The Black Hole." John questions the goodness of the Landlord for having created the black hole. The Guide counters with the argument that the Landlord created humans with a free will able to make free choices. If they end up in the black hole, it is because that is where they want to be. Returning to his argument of the previous chapter, the Guide underscores that the black hole is actually merciful since it limits the sufferings of those who choose to be there: "A black hole is blackness enclosed, limited. . . . But evil of itself would never reach a worst: for evil is fissiparous and could never in a thousand eternities find any way to arrest its own reproduction. . . . The walls of the black hole are the tourniquet on the wound through which the lost soul else would bleed to a death she never reached. It is the Landlord's last service to those who will let him do nothing better for them" (181). The Guide then sings the poem to John. Lewis's three eight-line stanzas follow a set pattern of six lines of trimeter, one line of pentameter, and one line of dimeter with a rhyme scheme of *ababcdcd*.

14. *PL*, 4:58–67.

15. Spiritual pride is also a central theme in his fiction.

16. In *Poems*, this is "Virtue's Independence" (88). The poem is found in *PR*, bk. 10, chap. 5, entitled "Superbia." As John and Virtue continue their regress, they come upon a gaunt woman who was "scrabbling and puddering to and fro on what appeared to be a mirror; but it was only the rock itself scraped clean of every speck of dust and fibre of lichen and polished by the continued activity of this famished creature" (182). The Guide tells them she is one of the Enemy's [Satan's] daughters. As they pass she "croaks out" the poem.

17. In *Poems*, this is "Posturing" (89). It is also in "Superbia" when Virtue sings this song after the Guide warns him and John about the dangers of self-sufficiency. Lewis's *ababcc* rhyme scheme (the last stanza adds *cc*) recalls the rhyme scheme of Wordsworth's "I Wandered Lonely as a Cloud."

18. This recalls an incident Lewis recounts in a letter to Greeves: "What worreys [*sic*] me much more is *Pride* [Lewis's emphasis]—my besetting sin. . . . During my afternoon 'meditations' . . . I have found out ludicrous and terrible things about my own character. Sitting by, watching the rising thoughts to break their necks as they pop up, one learns to know the sort of thoughts that do come. And, will you believe it, one out of every three is a thought of self-admiration: when everything else fails, having had its neck broken, up comes the thought 'What an admirable fellow I am to have broken their necks!' I catch myself posturing before the mirror, so to speak, all day long" (*TST*, Jan. 30, 1930, 339).

19. *The English Poems of George Herbert,* 140.

20. In *Poems,* this is "Deception" (90). The poem is found in *PR,* bk. 10, chap. 6, entitled "Ignorantia." The Guide tells John and Vertue that the shift to a machine age is cutting people off from a knowledge of the truth: "Their labour-saving devices multiply drudgery; their aphrodisiacs make them impotent: their amusements bore them: their rapid production of food leaves half of them starving, and their devices for saving time have banished leisure from their country" (187). He then sings this poem. Lewis experiments with the unusual rhyme scheme of *abbbbbcd* in the three stanzas.

21. One wonders what Lewis would have said about the popular TV "talk-shows" of today. Also see his "*Odora Canum Vis:* A Defence of Certain Modern Biographers and Critics" discussed in chapter 6.

22. Appropriately, both poems appear in the chapter entitled "Luxuria."

23. In *Poems,* this is "Forbidden Pleasure" (116). The poem is found in *PR,* bk. 10, chap. 7, entitled "Luxuria." John notices on the side of the road men who "seemed to be suffering from some disease of a crumbling and disintegrating kind" (188). As he looks closer, he sees tumors detach themselves from the bodies and turn into writhing reptiles. In a passage that merges elements of Cantos XXV and XXIX of Dante's *Inferno,* Lewis takes John through Luxuria, "a very dangerous place." He sees a witch (sexual indulgence) holding out a cup to the sufferers. In particular he sees a young man, who, though like the others is diseased, "was still a well-looking person. And as the witch came to him the hands shot out to the cup, and the man drew them back again: and the hands went crawling out for the cup a second time, and again the man wrenched them back, and turned his face away" (189). The young man then cries out the poem.

24. The request here that God break in to override human will is similar to that of "He Whom I Bow To" and "Legion."

25. *The Complete Poetry of John Donne,* ed. John T. Shawcross (Garden City, New York: Anchor, 1967), 344.

26. In *Poems,* this is "Lilith" (95). An earlier version of this poem appears in *They Stand Together,* 353–54 (letter of Apr. 29, [1930]). This poem is also in "Luxuria." After John sees the young man sink into a horrible swamp, the witch approaches him with this temptation: "I will not deceive you. . . . You see there is no pretence. I am not trying to make you believe that this cup will take you to your Island [the good that John has always desired—heaven]. I am not saying it will quench your thirst for long. But taste it, none the less, for you are very thirsty" (189–90). John continues his walk without acknowledging her. She tries two more times to tempt him, appealing primarily to the immediate satisfaction he will receive by succumbing to her offer, but he continues on, never even speaking to her. The temptation she offers him is very real, but he uses the poem he speaks to help put her temptation out of

his mind. Lewis uses a variation on rhyme royal; instead of the traditional *ababbcc,* he uses *ababccb.*

27. In *Poems,* this is "The Dragon Speaks" (92–93). The poem is found in *PR,* bk. 10, chap. 8, entitled "The Northern Dragon." John journeys to face the northern dragon (avarice, hardness, and coldness), but before he confronts it, John hears the dragon sing this poem. After hearing the poem, John almost feels pity for the dragon, but he recovers his senses and manages to slay the dragon after he is attacked.

28. Lewis explores this again in *The Voyage of the Dawn Treader* in the person of Eustace Clarence Scrubb, a boy, who because he harbored "dragonish thoughts in his heart," is transformed into one in order to learn the extent of his selfishness and need for Aslan.

29. The dragon (a symbol of evil here) is overcome by the warrior (the faithful believer) who exercises his prowess (God's blessing).

30. In *Poems,* this is "Dragon-Slayer" (94). The poem is found in *PR,* bk. 10, chap. 9, entitled "The Southern Dragon." Vertue returns from his victory with the southern dragon (unrestrained emotion) and appears dazzling: "At first they thought that it was the sun upon his arms that made Vertue flash like flame as he came leaping, running, and dancing towards them. But as he drew nearer they saw that he was veritably on fire. Smoke came from him, and where his feet slipped into the bog holes there were little puffs of steam. Hurtless flames ran up and down his sword and licked over his hand. His breast heaved and he reeled like a drunk man" (195). Delighting in his newfound passion, Vertue shouts out this poem as John and the Guide draw near.

31. Leviathan and Behemoth allude to legendary creatures of enormous size as found in Job 3:8 and 40:15.

32. RESVRGAM is "I shall rise again," and IO PAEAN is the cry of praise a Greek warrior would have made celebrating his victory over a foe.

33. Although there is always the temptation to reserve for self some of the glory that should rightly go to God, this poem intimates that the warrior here manages to delight in a job well done without giving in to the pull of vainglory.

34. In *Poems,* this is "When the Curtain's Down" (97). The poem is found in *PR,* bk. 10, chap. 10, entitled "The Brook." John and Vertue are now back in Puritania approaching the final stream (death). Vertue speaks this poem as evidence of his newly acquired passion, and he reflects that death is no longer a thing to fear.

35. Consider: "Where can I go from your Spirit? Where can I flee from your presence? If I go up to the heavens, you are there; if I make my bed in the depths, you are there. If I rise on the wings of the dawn, if I settle on the far side of the sea, even there your hand will guide me, your right hand will hold me fast. If I say, 'Surely the darkness will hide me and the light become night around me,' even the darkness will not be dark to you; the night will shine like the day, for darkness is as light to you" (Ps. 139:7–12).

36. In *Poems,* this is "Scazons" (118). Also in *PR,* bk. 10, chap. 10, "The Brook." The melancholic theme of this poem links it to both "Angel's Song" and "Lines Written in a Copy of Milton's Works." John reflects briefly on the Landlord's wisdom in creating humans with the capacities to love people and places before speaking this poem.

37. In *Poems,* this is "Angel's Song" (107). The poem is also in "The Brook" and ends *The Pilgrim's Regress.* John and Vertue pass over the brook, and the voice of the Guide is heard singing this poem.

38. Lewis's debt to Milton is evident in this poem, as it recalls Adam's speech to Raphael in book 8 of *Paradise Lost* where he thanks the angel for counseling him to be "lowly wise" regarding the ways of God:

> How fully hast thou satisfi'd me, pure
> Intelligence of Heav'n, Angel serene,
> And freed from intricacies, taught to live
> The easiest way, nor with perplexing thoughts
> To interrupt the sweet of Life, from which
> God hath bid dwell far off all anxious cares,
> And not molest us, unless we ourselves
> Seek them with wand'ring thoughts, and notions vain. (8:180–87)

39. The independent "life" of the poems is clearly established by many having originally been a part of Lewis's "Half Hours with Hamilton" written in 1930, three years before the publication of *The Pilgrim's Regress*. See appendix 5.

40. For more on the relationship between the poems and the text of *The Pilgrim's Regress*, see Kathryn Lindskoog's *Finding the Landlord*.

41. See *Atlantic Monthly* 203 (Jan. 1959): 59–61. Reprinted in Lewis's *The World's Last Night* and *Fern-Seed and Elephants and Other Essays on Christianity* (Glasgow: Fontana, 1975).

42. *The Oxford Magazine* 54 (May 14, 1936): 575 (N.W.). Reprinted in *Poems*.

43. *The Month* 13 (Apr. 1955): 210. Revised and reprinted in *Poems*.

44. First published in *Letters to Malcolm*, 67–68. Revised and retitled "Prayer" in *Poems*.

45. In *Letters to Malcolm*, Lewis offers the following: "*Dream* makes it too like Pantheism and was perhaps dragged in for the rhyme. But is he not right in thinking that prayer in its most perfect state is a soliloquy? If the Holy Spirit speaks in the man, then in prayer God speaks to God" (68).

46. For this reason it is an interesting gloss on *Surprised by Joy*. It is in *Poems*, 124–25. A holograph of this poem is available in the Bodleian Library.

47. *Fear No More*, 89. Revised and retitled "After Prayers, Lie Cold" in *P* and *CP*. The poem works at two levels. On the one hand, it is a preparation for sleep with an awakening the next morning; on the other hand, it is a preparation for death with an eventual resurrection. Thematically it has connections with "Hermione in the House of Paulina."

48. *The Month* 2 (July 1949): 8. Retitled "Epigrams and Epitaphs, No. 17" in *P* and *CP*. Lewis later reworked this poem at Joy's request and used the revision as the epitaph marking her memorial at the Oxford Crematorium, "Epitaph for Helen Joy Davidman." Hooper publishes this in *Collected Poems*, 252. In the introduction to *Collected Poems* Hooper explains how these variations came about: "Sometimes [*sic*] before his marriage Lewis wrote two versions of an 'Epitaph.' The one he planned to use in *Young King Cole* appears as Epitaph 17. . . . When Joy read this poem she knew she was dying and she asked that it be used as her epitaph. In July 1963 Lewis revised the epitaph with her in mind and arranged for it to be cut into marble and placed in the Oxford Crematorium" (xviii).

49. This opening may owe something to the microcosm/macrocosm we find in Donne's "A Valediction: Of Weeping": "Let me pour forth / My tears before thy face whilst I stay

here, / For thy face coins them, and thy stamp they bear, / And by this mintage they are something worth, / For thus they be / Pregnant of thee."

50. For more on this, see Joe R. Christopher's "C. S. Lewis, Love Poet."

51. *Poems*, 128; reprinted in *CP*. A holograph of this poem is available in the Bodleian Library.

52. *P*, 129. A holograph of this poem is available in the Bodleian Library. Joe R. Christopher in "An Analysis of 'The Apologist's Evening Prayer'" (*Bull. of the New York C. S. Lewis Society* 5 [Oct. 1974]: 2–4) looks at how the tone of this poem "is much like Donne" (2). He notes similarities in the use of pronouns (for example, "Thou"), the parallelism of the "from all" phrase, and the balanced, antithetical phrasing. Christopher sidesteps the question of whose poetry is best and ends with "we are left with a simpler-than-Donne poem in Donne's tradition" (4).

53. Although Hooper refers to this poem in his 1992 bibliography of Lewis's poems, the poem first appears in the Green and Hooper biography, 183.

54. The biblical narrative is found in Genesis 6–9.

55. *Punch* 215 (Aug. 11, 1948): 124 (N.W.). Revised and retitled "The Late Passenger" in *P* and *CP*.

56. Lewis's portrayal of Ham supports the biblical narrative. For instance, in Genesis 9:20–27, Ham brings shame upon his father by viewing the nakedness of his drunken father and then telling his brothers about it. After Shem and Japheth take discreet measures to cover their father's nakedness and Noah awakens to discover what has happened, he blesses the older two but curses Ham: "Cursed be Canaan [Ham]; / A servant of servants / He shall be to his brothers."

57. *P*, 125; reprinted in *CP*. A holograph of this poem is available in the Bodleian Library. For an account of Stephen's martyrdom, see Acts 6:8–8:1. Lewis treats the same subject in *A Grief Observed* (London: Faber and Faber, 1961) (N. W. Clerk, pseudonym), 34.

58. *Punch* 210 (May 8, 1946): 402 (N.W.). Revised and reprinted in *P* and *CP*. This poem has obvious affinities with "I Know Not, I" from *The Pilgrim's Regress*.

59. Lewis writes Ruth Pitter about this humor: "The bathos about angels having no nose etc. was intended: I wanted a serio-comic effect" (*RP*, Aug. 10, 1946, 009).

60. *Perelandra* (New York: Macmillan, 1944; paperback edition, 1965), 17, 18 (pb. edition).

61. *Punch* (Almanac) 215 (Nov. 1, 1948): n.p. (N.W.). Revised and reprinted in *P* and *CP*.

62. Among the many similarities the two poems share include beginning with a frozen landscape, use of pagan and Christian imagery, the reviving power of music, the symbolic rebirth of the world at Christ's birth, similar lines (Milton's "The Oracles are dumb" becomes Lewis's "That oracle was dumb"), and an ending focusing upon the poignancy of Christ in the manger.

63. This is akin to Father Christmas's influence on the winter of Narnia in *The Lion, the Witch and the Wardrobe*.

64. *P*, 122; reprinted in *CP*. A holograph of this poem is available in the Bodleian Library.

65. *P*, 114; reprinted in *CP*.

66. The passage continues: "'And I will be gracious to whom I will be gracious, and will show compassion on whom I will show compassion.' But He said, 'You cannot see My face, for no man can see Me and live!' Then the Lord said, 'Behold, there is a place by Me, and you shall stand there on the rock; and it will come about, while My glory is passing by, that I

will put you in the cleft of the rock and cover you with My hand until I have passed by. Then I will take My hand away and you shall see My back, but My face shall not be seen'" (Ex. 33:19b–23).

67. *That Hideous Strength* (New York: Macmillan, 1946; paperback edition, 1965), 323 (paperback edition).

68. *P*, 121; reprinted in *CP*. A holograph of this poem is available in the Bodleian Library. Joe R. Christopher's essay "No Fish for the Phoenix" (*Bull. of the New York C. S. Lewis Society* 23 [July 1992]: 1–7) is frustrating; that is, he follows a lengthy, involved, technical discussion of the poem's metrics (for which he apologizes) with an analysis that raises more questions than it answers. After taking us through Lewis's use of the poulter's measure (the alternation of iambic heptameter and iambic hexameter), Christopher tries to explain what the poem means. He considers the images of the phoenix and the fish, but he has trouble deciding how they work in the poem. When he does attempt interpretation, he is tentative and halting. For example, about the line, "I had dreamed that I had caught / . . . a silver, shining fish," he says, "It is difficult to know what his metaphor means" (4). Though he argues the persona speaking in the poem is a man, he is uncertain even of this: "I say the speaker is a man for what is implied in the poem is that the woman is attracted to the man" (5), yet the poem could sustain a reading with a female persona. More unsatisfying is his conclusion: "Is this an autobiographical poem on Lewis's part ? . . . The male spiritual leader attracts women followers, who may even think they are being pious while they daydream of being closer to the leader, rather than to God" (6).

69. "On Another Theme from Nicolas of Cusa," *The Times Literary Supplement* (Jan. 21, 1955): 43. Revised and retitled "On a Theme from Nicolas of Cusa" in *P* and *CP*.

70. *P*, 91–92; reprinted in *CP*.

71. The best study of the seven deadly sins is found in Morton W. Bloomfield's *The Seven Deadly Sins: An Introduction to the History of a Religious Concept, with Special Reference to Medieval English Literature,* (East Lansing: Michigan State College P, 1952; reprint, 1967).

72. *The Allegory of Love: A Study in Medieval Tradition* (Oxford: Oxford UP, 1936), 159–60.

73. There has also been work on the possible relationship between Lewis's seven Narnia tales and the seven deadly sins. See my "Narnia and the Seven Deadly Sins," *Mythlore* 10 (Spring 1984): 14–19.

74. William Langland, *Piers Plowman: A New Translation of the B-Text*, trans. A. V. C. Schmidt (Oxford: Oxford UP, 1992).

75. *Poems*, 122–23. A holograph of this poem is available in the Bodleian Library.

76. In A. M. Hardie and K. C. Douglas, *Augury: An Oxford Miscellany of Verse and Poetry* (Oxford: Blackwell, 1940), 28. Revised and reprinted in *P* and *CP*. Lewis uses cross rhyme, and each of the three stanzas has four alexandrines, one tetrameter, and three pentameters.

77. For a more extensive treatment of this poem, see Joe R. Christopher's "C. S. Lewis's Shakespearean Poem, Part One" and "Part Two" (*The Lamp-Post of the Southern California C. S. Lewis Society* 22 [Summer 1998]: 7–17 and 22 [Fall 1998]: 8–15).

78. Lewis apparently invested more time in refining his religious poems than others. In a letter to Greeves dated August 28, 1930, less than a year before his conversion to

Christianity, he writes: "It is a very remarkable thing that in the few religious lyrics which I have written during the last year, in which I had no idea of publication & at first very little idea even of showing them to friends, I have found myself impelled to take infinitely more pains, less ready to be contented with the fairly good and more determined to reach the best attainable, than ever I was in the days when I never wrote without the ardent hope of successful publication" (*TST,* 385). In the introduction to *Collected Poems,* Hooper adds that Lewis did not revise his prose very much, but his poems "went through endless revisions, the best examples of which are the religious lyrics of 1930 which he was still revising up to the time he died" (xvi).

9. Poetic Prose: Lewis's Poetic Legacy

1. Daniel, "The Taste of the Pineapple: A Basis for Literary Criticism," 9, 11.

2. Consider the following critical evaluations. In the preface to Pitter's *First and Second Poems* (London: Sheed & Ward, 1927), Hilaire Belloc praises her poetry as "an exceptional reappearance of the classical spirit amongst us" (7). He likens her verse to a strong stone building and argues that really good verse "contrasted with the general run of that in the midst of which it appears, seems to me to have a certain quality of *hardness* [Belloc's emphasis]; so that, in the long run, it will be discovered, as a gem is discovered in mud" (9). In her poetry he finds "beauty and right order" (10). Belloc also writes in the preface to her *A Mad Lady's Garland* (London: Cresset Press, 1934) that Pitter has two peculiar poetic gifts: "A perfect ear and exact epithet. How those two ever get combined is incomprehensible— one would think it was never possible—but when the combination does appear then you have verse of that classic sort which is founded and secure of its own future" (vii). In his *Four Living Poets* (Santa Barbara, Calif.: Unicorn, 1944) Rudolph Gilbert calls Pitter "the poet of purity" and notes "what the poetry reader values most in Pitter's poems is her eloquence . . . In Pitter one almost looks through the language, as through air, discerning the exact form of the objects which stand there, and every part and shade of meaning is brought out by the sunny light resting upon them" (48–49). Later he adds: "She has a first-rate intuitive gift of observation, a control of poetic language and magical perception that is always to found in great poetry" (52). In addition, in the *festschrift, Ruth Pitter: Homage to a Poet* (London: Rapp and Whiting, 1969), David Cecil says "she is the most moving of living English poets, and one of the most original" (13). John Arlott refers to her as "a poet's poet" (43), while Thom Gunn notes she "is the most modest of poets, slipping us her riches as if they were everyday currency" (64). Kathleen Raine is more lavish in her praise: "I now see her as one of the poets whose best work will survive as long as the English language, with whose expressiveness in image and idea she has kept faith, remains" (106). In the introduction to Pitter's *Collected Poems* (London: Enitharmon, 1996), Elizabeth Jennings appreciates her "acute sensibility and deep integrity"; Jennings continues to say her poems "are informed with a sweetness which is also bracing, and a generosity which is blind to nothing, neither the sufferings in this world nor the quirky behavior of human beings" (15).

3. Her volumes of poetry are listed in the bibliography.

4. In her "There is a Spirit," the preface to *Collected Poems* (1968), she writes, "My purpose [as a poet] has never varied. . . . It has been simply to capture and express some of the secret meanings which haunt life and language: the silent music, the dance in stillness, the

hints and echoes and messages of which everything is full; the smile on the face of the tiger, or of the Bernini seraph. The silent music is within oneself too, or it would not be detected elsewhere. In the face of mundane joy it says '. . . but all the same'! and in the face of horror '. . . but all the same'! As though the normal targets of consciousness were somehow unreal; life, bursting with its secret, sits hugging itself until we have read the riddle" (xi–xii).

5. This poem has striking affinities with Lewis's "The Day with a White Mark," *Punch* 217 (Aug. 17, 1949): 170. That poem begins with the speaker realizing a surprising turn of events: "All ahead is dark or splashed with hideous light. / My garden's spoiled; my holidays are cancelled; the omens harden; / The plann'd and the unplann'd miseries deepen; the knots draw tight. / Yet I—I could have kissed the very scullery taps. The colour of / My day was like a peacock's chest." Finding unexpected delight in the midst of an otherwise drab day is the thematic focus of the poem. In its conclusion, we see Lewis using a phrase that appears as Pitter's title: "Who knows if ever it [unexpected delight] will come again, now the day closes? / No one can give me—or take away—the key. All depends / on the elf, the bird, the angel. I question if the angel himself / Has power to choose when *sudden heaven* for me begins or ends" (emphasis added).

6. She noted, "I had to be intellectually satisfied as well as emotionally, because at that time of one's life one doesn't just fall into religion with adolescent emotion. But at last I was satisfied at every point that it was the one way for me. It wasn't the easy road but it was the only possible one" (Cecil, *Homage*, 28).

7. July 13, 1946; MS. Eng. lett. c. 220/3, fol. 18, Bodleian Library. Because Lewis apparently did not save many of Pitter's letters, she compiled a journal that reconstructed and summarized the correspondence she had sent to Lewis.

8. "Pitter to C. S. Lewis," CSL /L-Pitter/ 1a, Wade Center. This is the only letter Pitter sent to Lewis known to survive. During a research trip to the Wade Center, I discovered it inside the copy of *A Mad Lady's Garland* Pitter had sent Lewis.

9. On July 23, 1985, Lyle Dorsett and his wife, Mary, did an oral interview with Ruth Pitter in her home in Long Crendon, Buckinghamshire, England. In the interview, Pitter's recollection of this first meeting is quite different:

D: How did you come to meet C. S. Lewis? . . .

P: . . . I forced myself on him. I wrote to him and said how his work had delighted, and indeed, more than delighted me. And, would he see me. And he seemed rather grumpy when I got there and said, "I can spare half an hour." Has a deep voice. That was all—

D: Did you go to his—

P: I went to his rooms in—

D: In Magdalen College.

P: In, the college, what was the name of it now?

D: Magdalen.

P: Magdalen, that's right. Yes.

D: About what year was this, Miss Pitter?

P: Oh dear.

D: Was this after the war?

P: No, no it would be while the war was still on. . . . And, well—I think, now I left my book and I don't know whether he wrote to me. But he did say to me at some point,

"Why did nobody ever tell me of this?" He was very much struck. He thought the quality of the work was very high.

D: So you went to see him that day and he was a bit grumpy. He said he'd give you about a half an hour.

P: Yes.

D: And while you were there you showed him some of your poetry or you left it with him, did you?

P: Yes, I think it must have been—

D: Did you stay just about a half an hour?

P: Yes. I don't—well, after what he said it was up to me to rise when the end of the of the half hour. I didn't want to—

D: Did he get any friendlier?

P: What?

D: Did he get any friendlier after you'd been there?

P: Yes, a bit. Not very. I fancy he was always a good deal on the defensive with all sorts of tiresome people.

D: So you left this volume of your verse there. Then did he write to your after that?

P: I think he must have . . .

D: Did you—well, you obviously became a good friend.

P: Yes.

D: The two of you became friends.

P: Oh, I may say that, yes, I think so, yes. Yes, we were.

D: What did he think of your poetry?

P: Thought it was very good . . .

This interview is available in the Wade Center; the transcription covers pp. 9–11.

10. MS. Eng. lett. c. 220/3, fols. 63–64, Bodleian Library.

11. The question of whether the focus here is prose poetry or poetic prose should be addressed here. According to *The New Princeton Encyclopedia of Poetry and Poetics*, prose poetry is characterized by "unity even in brevity and poetic quality even without the line breaks of free verse: high patterning, rhythmic and figural repetition, sustained intensity, and compactness" (Alex Preminger and T. V. F. Brogan, eds. [Princeton, N.J.: Princeton UP, 1993], 977). *A Handbook to Literature* defines prose poetry as "a form of prose with marked (although preferably not too regular) cadence and frequently with extensive use of figurative language and imagery" (William Thrall and Addison Hibbard, eds., revised and enlarged by C. Hugh Holman [New York: The Odyssey Press, 1960], 383). On the other hand, poetic prose has been defined as "ordinary spoken and written language (prose) that makes use of cadence, rhythm, figurative language, or other devices ordinarily associated with poetry" (Harry Shaw, *Concise Dictionary of Literary Terms* [New York: McGraw-Hill, 1972], 213). Accordingly, the focus of this essay is upon Lewis's poetic prose.

12. Lewis himself thought the novel was one of his two best, the other being *Till We Have Faces:* "Which do I like best? Now, the answer wd. be *Till We Have Faces* and *Perelandra*" (*Letters to Children* [New York: Macmillan, 1985], 95).

13. In brief, the chapters may be summarized as follows. Chapters 1–2 are primarily exposition providing us the background on how Ransom is assisted by Lewis both upon his

going to Perelandra and returning to Earth. Chapters 3–4 are heavily poetic, filled with numerous lyrical passages describing Ransom's richly sensuous experiences in the Perelandrian ocean. Chapters 5–6 deal with Ransom's encounter with the Green Lady and provide additional historical details about her and Maleldil. Chapters 7–11 are primarily rhetorical, as the Green Lady, Weston, and Ransom discuss many matters and play out a second temptation in this paradisal world. Chapter 11 is Ransom's internal debate wherein he realizes finally why he has been sent to Perelandra and what is required of him. Chapters 12–14 cover Ransom's brutal fight with Weston. Chapter 15 chronicles Ransom's journey out of the cave into the Perelandrian sun once again; it is heavily poetic. Chapter 16 concerns Ransom's conversation with Malacandra (Mars) and Perelandra (Venus); it is heavily poetic. Chapter 17 is Ransom's conversation with the King, Tor, and the Queen/Green Lady, Tinidril; it is heavily poetic, culminating in the Great Dance.

14. Thomas Peters, "The War of the Worldviews: H. G. Wells and Scientism and C. S. Lewis and Christianity," *Mission and Ministry* 11, no. 4 and 12, no. 1 (1998): 47, and Kath Filmer, "The Polemic Image: The Role of Metaphor and Symbol in the Fiction of C. S. Lewis," *SEVEN: An Anglo-American Literary Review* 7 (1986): 74.

15. See "Unreal Estates" in *Of Other Worlds*, 87. The passage continues: "And then of course the whole story about an averted fall developed. This is because . . . having got your people to this exciting country, something must happen" (87).

16. Cited in Hooper, *C. S. Lewis: A Companion and Guide*, 220. This fragment first appears in a footnote to Green and Hooper's *C. S. Lewis: A Biography*, 171.

17. *Perelandra*, 33.

18. For more on this see Filmer, "The Polemic Image," 61–76.

19. MS. Eng. lett. c. 220/3, fol. 52, Bodleian Library.

20. The complete transcription is published in appendix 1.

21. Many of the passages relating to the Great Dance have echoes to the book of Revelation. Here, for instance, there is a hint of Rev. 2:7: "'He who has an ear, let him hear what the Spirit says to the Churches. To him who overcomes, I will grant to eat of the tree of life, which is in the Paradise of God'" (New American Standard version).

22. Indeed, of Lewis's twenty-three paragraphs concerning the Great Dance, twelve make similar reference (1, 7–10, 12–16, 18, and 22). In Pitter's transcription, however, only eight of her twenty-three stanzas make similar reference (I, X, XII, XIV–XVI, XVIII, and XXII). The lack of interconnection by reference to "centre of the worlds" in Pitter's stanzas as compared to Lewis's paragraphs is especially noteworthy in its appearance in his 7–10 while only appearing in Pitter's X.

23. A similar identification of the Creator overmuch with the creation occurs in her interpolation of "His by right" in line seven, leaving "Himself" in line eight as an appositive.

24. The entire passage reads: "For by him all things were created: things in heaven and on earth, visible and invisible, whether thrones or powers of rulers or authorities; all things were created by him and for him. He is before all things, and in him all things hold together. And he is the head of the body, the church; he is the beginning and the firstborn from among the dead, so that in everything he might have the supremacy. For God was pleased to have all his fullness dwell in him, and through him to reconcile to himself all things, whether things on earth or things in heaven, by making peace through his blood, shed on the cross" (Col. 1:16–20).

25. Kate O'Brien, "Review of *Perelandra*," *The Spectator* 170 (May 14, 1943): 458.

26. Before leaving this discussion, it is worth noting the significant role language plays throughout the Ransom trilogy. In addition to the poetry of *Perelandra*, the poetry of the *hrossa*, the acquisition of language by Ransom upon his arrival upon Malacandra, and the advantage this subsequently gives him over Weston and Divine are central foci of *Out of the Silent Planet*. In contrast, poetry is relatively absent in *That Hideous Strength*, in part because a key strategy of N.I.C.E. is to manipulate language and meaning, stripping words of both truth and beauty.

27. *Still by Choice* (London: Cresset Press, 1966), 24.

28. In his 1985 interview, Dorsett asked Pitter several questions about the nature of her personal relationship with Lewis; we may take Pitter's own statement as the last word on this subject:

> D: Someone said that if C. S. Lewis was ever going to marry [attributed to Hugo Dyson], that he would marry Miss Ruth Pitter.
>
> P: Oh. Think of that! Did he say that?
>
> D: That is what I've read somewhere that he said to one of his friends.
>
> P: You can't be—
>
> D: No, no, I take that back. I want to correct that. That one of his friends surmised that was what was said, that if he were to marry, he would marry Miss Ruth Pitter.
>
> P: Well, it's slender, isn't it? All the same it's very gratifying to the feelings. I'm glad to have heard it.
>
> D: Yes, yes, it's a nice thing to have said, isn't it? . . . Well, do you think it would be fair to say that if Miss Ruth Pitter had ever married, maybe she would have married C. S. Lewis?
>
> P: Don't put it to me like that, because honestly I don't know. I think on the whole, I've never been the marrying sort. I think it may be the case, it was just as well I were not called upon to make that decision. Well, I—I'm left with the hope that we shall meet again in heaven (p. 11 of the transcription of the interview).

29. In the end, a shared love of poetry and faith in Christ connect the two writers, yet these links transcend both time and death. A fitting irony occurs in *The Oxford Book of 20th Century English Verse* (Oxford: Oxford UP, 1973) when Philip Larkin, who chose the entries, lists Pitter and Lewis back-to-back; Pitter's "The Eternal Image," "Time's Fool," "But for Lust," and "Hen Under Bay-Tree" immediately precede Lewis's "On a Vulgar Error."

30. That Lewis knew this would be the case explains why it was published under the pseudonym N. W. Clerk, the N.W. a return to the way he signed many of his topical poems. In fact, the book was never published under Lewis's name while he lived.

31. "*A Grief Observed*: Fact or Fiction?" *Mythlore* 16 (Summer 1990): 4–9, 26. This quote is from p. 9. See also George Musacchio, "C. S. Lewis' *A Grief Observed* as Fiction," *Mythlore* 12 (Spring 1986): 25ff.

32. John Beversluis, *C. S. Lewis and the Search for Rational Religion* (Grand Rapids, Mich.: Eerdmans, 1985), 141, 161. See also his "Beyond the Double Bolted Door," *Christian History* 4, no. 3 (1985): 28–31.

33. Lewis also manages a deft rhyme here in *believe:conceive*.

34. For a thoughtful comparison of *A Grief Observed* and Tennyson's *In Memoriam*, see Joe R. Christopher's *C. S. Lewis* (Boston: Twayne, 1987).

35. Early in life he writes Greeves: "When you are fed up with life start writing: ink is the great cure for all human ill, as I have found out long ago" (May 30, 1916, *TST*, 104).

36. Lewis only slightly veils Joy here, using the initial of her first name, Helen.

37. Sometimes the tone is not far from that of some of the Psalms. For instance: "I say to God my Rock, 'Why have you forgotten me? Why must I go about mourning, oppressed by the enemy?' My bones suffer mortal agony as my foes taunt me, saying to me all day long, 'Where is your God?' Why are you so downcast, O my soul? Why so disturbed within me? Put your hope in God, for I will yet praise him, my Savior and my God" (Psalm 42:9–11; NIV).

Appendix One

1. The transcription covers pages 214–19 of *Perelandra*.

2. There is an alternative word written above "makes"; it is "making."

3. The line "All the magnificence that He has planned" was inadvertently dropped by Pitter when she copied her transcriptions in the notebook dated 1970. However, earlier drafts of the poem include this line. See "A Passage from 'Perelandra,' by C. S. Lewis Transcribed into Irregular Spenserian Stanzas," Pitter "Poems-Unpublished & TSS," (uncatalogued) box 19, Bodleian Library. In another draft, Pitter toyed with arranging the stanzas into a spoken chorus for a duet. In still another manifestation, she included stanzas I, VIII, IX, XI, XII, and XX in the choral verse-speaking of the Oxford Worship and the Arts Conference of 1950 (see Pitter Worship & Arts Conference, 1950–59 [uncatalogued] box 25, Bodleian Library).

Bibliography

CHRONOLOGICAL LISTING OF LEWIS'S POEMS

Whenever possible, I have indicated where holograph versions of the poems are available, as well as publication information.

DATED POEMS:

"The Old Grey Mare" (1908?) in *LP*, 3:166–67. Published in R. L. Green's "C. S. Lewis," *Puffin Post* 4, no. 1 (1970): 14–15.

"Descend to Earth, Descend, Celestial Nine" (1912–13?). In *LP*, 3:321–36. Published in appendix 1.

"*Quam Bene Saturno*," *Cherbourg School Magazine* (July 1913). Also in *LP*, 4:51–52; there it is dated July 29, 1913. A holograph version appears in Douglas Gilbert and Clyde S. Kilby's *C. S. Lewis: Images of His World*. Grand Rapids, Mich.: Eerdmans, 1973, 113.

"'Carpe Diem' after Horace" (Oct. 1913). In *LP*, 4:88. Published in King, "Glints of Light." Reprinted in appendix 2.

"In Winter When the Frosty Nights Are Long" (late 1913–early 1914). In *LP*, 4:121. Published in King, "Glints of Light." Reprinted in appendix 2.

"Ovid's '*Pars Estis Pauci*'" (June 1914). In *LP*, 4:191–92. Published in King, "Glints of Light." Reprinted in appendix 2.

Loki Bound (1914). In *LP*, 4:217–20. Published in appendix 1.

"Hills of Down" (Easter 1915). In *LP*, 4:306. Revised and reprinted in *CP*.

"Against Potpourri" (Aug. 1915). In *LP*, 5:14. Revised and reprinted in *CP*.

"A Prelude" (Aug. 1915). In *LP*, 5:14. Revised and reprinted in *CP*.

"Ballade of a Winter's Morning" (Christmas 1915). In *LP*, 5:46. Revised and reprinted in *CP*.

"*Laus Mortis*" (Easter 1916). In *LP*, 5:72. Revised and reprinted in *CP*.

"Sonnet—To Sir Philip Sydney" (Autumn 1916). In *LP*, 5:122. Revised and reprinted in *CP*.

"Of Ships" (Christmas 1916). In *LP*, 5:170. Revised and reprinted in *CP*.

"Couplets" (Christmas 1916). In *LP*, 5:170. Revised and reprinted in *CP*.

"Circe—A Fragment" (Apr. 1917). In *LP*, 5:197. Revised and reprinted in *CP*.

"Exercise" (Apr. 1917). In *LP*, 5:197. Revised and reprinted in *CP*.

"Death in Battle," *Reveille* 3 (Feb. 1919): 508 (under pseudonym Clive Hamilton). Reprinted in *SB* and *CP*.

"Nimue" (Sept. 1919). In *They Stand Together,* 261.
Spirits in Bondage: A Cycle of Lyrics (1919). Containing:
    "Prologue"
    "Satan Speaks" (I)
    "French Nocturne"
    "The Satyr"
    "Victory"
    "Irish Nocturne"
    "Spooks"
    "Apology"
    "Ode for New Year's Day"
    "Night" (IX)
    "To Sleep"
    "In Prison"
    "De Profundis"
    "Satan Speaks" (XIII)
    "The Witch"
    "Dungeon Grates"
    "The Philosopher"
    "The Ocean Strand"
    "Noon"
    "Milton Read Again"
    "Sonnet"
    "The Autumn Morning"
    "L'Apprenti Sorcier"
    "Alexandrines"
    "In Praise of Solid People"
    "Song of the Pilgrims"
    "Song"
    "The Ass"
    "Ballade Mystique"
    "Night" (XXIX)
    "Oxford"
    "Hymn (for Boys' Voices)"
    "Our Daily Bread"
    "How He Saw Angus the God"
    "The Roads"
    "Hesperus"
    "The Star Bath"
    "Tu Ne Quaesieris"
    "Lullaby"
    "World's Desire"
    "Death In Battle"
    (These are reprinted in *CP.*)

"On Robert Capron" (1920–23). In *LP*, 3:41–42. Published in King, "Glints of Light." Reprinted in appendix 2.

"On Henry Wakelyn Smith" (1920–23). In *LP*, 3:262–63. Published in King, "Glints of Light." Reprinted in appendix 2.

"On W. T. Kirkpatrick" (1920–23). In *LP*, 4:64–65. Published in King, "Glints of Light." Reprinted in appendix 2.

"The Carpet Rises in the Draught" (1922–23). In *LP*, 9:251. Published in King, "Glints of Light." Reprinted in appendix 2.

"On Cupid and Psyche" (1923). In *LP*, 8:163–64. Published in appendix.

"The Silence of the Night" (1923). In *LP*, 8:164–67. Published in appendix.

"Joy," *The Beacon* 3, no. 31 (May 1924): 444–45 (under pseudonym Clive Hamilton). Reprinted in *CP*.

Dymer. London: J. M. Dent, 1926 (under pseudonym Clive Hamilton). Reprinted by Dutton in 1950 with a preface by C. S. Lewis. Also reprinted in *NP*.

"Leaving For Ever the Home of One's Youth" (1930). In *LP*, 2:79–80. Published in *Occasional Poets: An Anthology*. Ed. Richard Adams. Harmondsworth, Middlesex: Penguin Books, 1986. Reprinted in *CP*. Holograph version available in the Hooper deposit in the Bodleian Library, Oxford.

"The Nameless Isle" (Hooper dates as Aug. 1930). In *NP*.

"I Will Write Down the Portion that I Understand" (May 1932). Holograph version available in a letter to Owen Barfield, May 6, 1932, in *OB*, vol. 2 (1932–40), cat. no. 26–50, index no. 0065, Marion E. Wade Center, Wheaton College, Wheaton, Ill. Published in King, "Glints of Light." Reprinted in appendix 2.

"Launcelot" (Hooper dates as 1930–33?). Holograph version available in Dep. d. 809, fols. 2–8, Bodleian Library. In *NP*.

"The Queen of Drum" (Hooper dates as 1933–34). In *NP*.

The Pilgrim's Regress (1933). Containing:

"He Whom I Bow To." Revised and retitled "Footnote to All Prayers" in *P* and *CP*. Holograph versions available in the Hooper deposit in the Bodleian, in a notebook Hooper holds, and in "Half Hours with Hamilton."

"You Rest Upon Me All My Days." Revised and retitled "Caught" in *P* and *CP*. Holograph versions available in a notebook Hooper holds and in "Half Hours with Hamilton."

"My Heart Is Empty." Revised and retitled "The Naked Seed" in *P* and *CP*. Holograph version available in a notebook Hooper holds.

"Thou Only Art Alternative to God." Revised and retitled "Wormwood" in *P* and *CP*. Holograph version available in a notebook Hooper holds.

"God in His Mercy." Revised and retitled "Divine Justice" in *P* and *CP*.

"Nearly They Stood Who Fall." Revised and retitled "Nearly They Stood" in *P* and *CP*. Holograph versions available in the Hooper deposit in the Bodleian, in a notebook Hooper holds, and in "Half Hours with Hamilton."

"I Have Scraped Clean the Plateau." Revised and retitled "Virtue's Independence" in *P* and *CP*. Holograph versions available in the Hooper deposit in the Bodleian and in a notebook Hooper holds.

"Because of Endless Pride." Revised and retitled "Posturing" in *P* and *CP*. Holograph versions available in a notebook Hooper holds and in "Half Hours with Hamilton."

"Iron Will Eat the World's Old Beauty Up." Revised and retitled "Deception" in *P* and *CP*.

"Quick!" Revised and retitled "Forbidden Pleasure" in *P* and *CP*. Holograph versions available in a notebook Hooper holds and in "Half Hours with Hamilton."

"When Lilith Means to Draw Me." Revised and retitled "Lilith" in *P* and *CP*. Holograph versions available in a notebook Hooper holds and in "Half Hours with Hamilton."

"Once the Worm-laid Egg Broke in the Wood." Revised and retitled "The Dragon Speaks" in *P* and *CP*. Holograph versions available in a notebook Hooper holds and in "Half Hours with Hamilton."

"I Have Come Back with Victory Got." Revised and retitled "Dragon-Slayer" in *P* and *CP*. Holograph versions available in a notebook Hooper holds and in "Half Hours with Hamilton."

"I Am not One that Easily Flits Past in Thought." Revised and retitled "When the Curtain's Down" in *P* and *CP*. Holograph versions available in a notebook Hooper holds and in "Half Hours with Hamilton."

"Passing To-day by a Cottage, I Shed Tears." Revised and retitled "Scazons" in *P* and *CP*. Holograph versions of this poem available in the Hooper deposit in the Bodleian, in a notebook Hooper holds, and in "Half Hours with Hamilton."

"I Know Not, I." Revised and retitled "Angel's Song" in *P* and *CP*. Holograph version available in the Hooper deposit in the Bodleian.

"Abecedarium Philosophicum," *The Oxford Magazine* 52 (Nov. 30, 1933): 298 (with Owen Barfield). An earlier version of this poem appears in *LP*, 9:164–65.

"The Shortest Way Home," *The Oxford Magazine* 52 (May 10, 1934): 665 (under the pseudonym Nat Whilk, hereafter N.W.). Revised and retitled "Man is a Lumpe Where All Beasts Kneaded Be" in *P* and *CP*. Holograph versions of this poem are available in the Hooper deposit in the Bodleian, in a notebook Hooper holds, and in "Half Hours with Hamilton."

"Scholar's Melancholy," *The Oxford Magazine* 52 (May 24, 1934): 734 (N.W.). Reprinted in *P* and *CP*. Holograph version available in a notebook Hooper holds.

"The Planets," *Lysistrata* 2 (May 1935): 21–24 (a portion of this poem is quoted in Lewis's essay "A Metrical Suggestion"). Reprinted in *P* and *CP*. Holograph version available in a notebook Hooper holds.

"Sonnet," *The Oxford Magazine* 54 (May 14, 1936): 575 (N.W.). Reprinted in *P* and *CP*. Holograph version available in a notebook Hooper holds.

"Coronation March," *Oxford Magazine* 55 (May 6, 1937): 565 (N.W.). Reprinted in *P* and *CP*.

"After Kirby's *Kalevala*" (a translation), *Oxford Magazine* 55 (May 13, 1937): 595 (N.W.).

"The Future of Forestry," *The Oxford Magazine* 56 (Feb. 10, 1938): 383 (N.W.). Reprinted in *P* and *CP*.

"*Chanson D'Aventure*," *The Oxford Magazine* 56 (May 19, 1938): 638 (N.W.). Revised and retitled as "What the Bird Said Early in the Year" in *P* and *CP*. Holograph versions available in the Hooper deposit in the Bodleian and in a notebook Hooper holds.

"Experiment," *The Spectator* 161 (Dec. 9, 1938): 998. The poem is also found in *Augury: An Oxford Miscellany of Verse and Prose*. Ed. A. M. Hardie and K. C. Douglas. Oxford: Blackwell, 1940, 28. There it is a slightly different version called "Metrical Experiment." Still another version appears as "Pattern" in *P* and *CP*. Holograph versions available in the Hooper deposit in the Bodleian and in a notebook Hooper holds.

"To Mr. Roy Campbell," *The Cherwell* 56 (May 6, 1939): 35 (N.W.). Revised and retitled "The Author of *Flowering Rifle*" in *P* and *CP*. Holograph version available in the Hooper deposit in the Bodleian.

"Hermione in the House of Paulina," *Augury: An Oxford Miscellany of Verse and Poetry.* Ed. A. M. Hardie and K. C. Douglas. Oxford: Blackwell, 1940, 28. Revised and reprinted in *P* and *CP*. Holograph versions available both in the Hooper deposit in the Bodleian and in a notebook Hooper holds.

"Essence," *Fear No More: A Book of Poems for the Present Time by Living English Poets.* Cambridge: Cambridge UP, 1940, 4. Reprinted in *CP*. All the poems in this volume are published anonymously; however, six copies contain an additional leaf giving the names of the authors of the poems; one of these is in the Bodleian Library. Holograph versions of this poem are available both in a notebook Hooper holds and in "Half Hours with Hamilton."

"Break, Sun, my Crusted Earth," *Fear No More,* 72. This is an alternative version of "A Pageant Played in Vain," in *P* and *CP*. Holograph version available in a notebook Hooper holds.

"The World is Round," *Fear No More,* 85. Revised and retitled "Poem for Psychoanalysts and/or Theologians" in *P* and *CP*. Holograph version available in a notebook Hooper holds.

"Arise my Body," *Fear No More,* 89. Revised and retitled "After Prayers, Lie Cold" in *P* and *CP*. Holograph version available in a notebook Hooper holds.

"Epitaph," *Time and Tide* 23 (June 6, 1942): 460. Retitled "Epigrams and Epitaphs, No. 11" in *P* and *CP*. Holograph versions available in the Hooper deposit in the Bodleian.

"To G. M.," *The Spectator* 169 (Oct. 9, 1942): 335. Revised and retitled "To a Friend" in *P* and *CP*. Holograph version available in the Hooper deposit in the Bodleian.

"Awake, My Lute!" *The Atlantic Monthly* 172 (Nov. 1943): 113, 115. Reprinted in *CP*.

"The Salamander," *The Spectator* 174 (June 8, 1945): 521. See erratum: "Poet and Printer," ibid. (June 15, 1945): 550. Reprinted in *P* and *CP*.

"From the Latin of Milton's *De Idea Platonica Quemadmodum Aristoteles Intellexit,*" (a translation), *English* 5, no. 30 (1945): 195.

"On the Death of Charles Williams," *Britain Today* 112 (Aug. 1945): 14. Revised and retitled "To Charles Williams" in *P* and *CP*. Holograph version available in the Hooper deposit in the Bodleian.

"Under Sentence," *The Spectator* 175 (Sept. 7, 1945): 219. Revised and retitled "The Condemned" in *P* and *CP*. Holograph version available in the Hooper deposit in the Bodleian.

"On the Atomic Bomb (Metrical Experiment)," *The Spectator* 175 (Dec. 28, 1945): 619. Reprinted in *P* and *CP*.

"On Receiving Bad News," *Time and Tide* 26 (Dec. 29, 1945): 1093. Retitled "Epigrams and Epitaphs, No. 12" in *P* and *CP*. Holograph version available in the Hooper deposit in the Bodleian.

"The Birth of Language," *Punch* 210 (Jan. 9, 1946): 32 (N.W.). Revised and reprinted in *P* and *CP*. Holograph version available in the Hooper deposit in the Bodleian.

"On Being Human," *Punch* 210 (May 8, 1946): 402 (N.W.). Revised and reprinted in *P* and *CP*. Holograph version available in the Hooper deposit in the Bodleian.

"Solomon," *Punch* 211 (Aug. 14, 1946): 136 (N.W.). Revised and reprinted in *P* and *CP*. Holograph version available in the Hooper deposit in the Bodleian.

"The True Nature of Gnomes," *Punch* 211 (Oct. 16, 1946): 310 (N.W.). Reprinted in *P* and *CP*.

"The Meteorite," *Time and Tide* 27 (Dec. 7, 1946): 1183. Reprinted in *P* and *CP*. Holograph version available in the Hooper deposit in the Bodleian.

"Pan's Purge," *Punch* 212 (Jan. 15, 1947): 71 (N.W.). Reprinted in *P* and *CP*. Holograph version available in the Hooper deposit in the Bodleian.

"The Romantics," *The New English Weekly* 30 (Jan. 16, 1947): 130. Revised and retitled "The Prudent Jailer" in *P* and *CP*. Holograph version available in the Hooper deposit in the Bodleian.

"Dangerous Oversight," *Punch* 212 (May 21, 1947): 434 (N.W.). Revised and retitled "Young King Cole" in *P* and *CP*. Holograph version available in the Hooper deposit in the Bodleian.

"Two Kinds of Memory," *Time and Tide* 28 (Aug. 7, 1947): 859. Revised and reprinted in *P* and *CP*. Holograph version available in the Hooper deposit in the Bodleian.

"*Le Roi S'Amuse*," *Punch* 213 (Oct. 1, 1947): 324 (N.W.). Revised and reprinted in *P* and *CP*. Holograph version available in the Hooper deposit in the Bodleian.

"Donkey's Delight," *Punch* 213 (Nov. 5, 1947): 442 (N.W.). Revised and reprinted in *P* and *CP*. Holograph version available in the Hooper deposit in the Bodleian.

"The End of the Wine," *Punch* 213 (Dec. 3, 1947): 538 (N.W.). Revised and retitled "The Last of the Wine" in *P* and *CP*. Holograph version available in the Hooper deposit in the Bodleian.

"*Vitrea Circe*," *Punch* 214 (June 23, 1948): 543 (N.W.). Revised and reprinted in *P* and *CP*. Holograph version available in the Hooper deposit in the Bodleian.

"Epitaph," *The Spectator* 181 (July 30, 1948): 142. Revised and retitled "Epigrams and Epitaphs, No. 14" in *P* and *CP*. Holograph version available in the Hooper deposit in the Bodleian.

"The Sailing of the Ark," *Punch* 215 (Aug. 11, 1948): 124 (N.W.). Revised and retitled "The Late Passenger" in *P* and *CP*. Holograph version available in the Hooper deposit in the Bodleian.

"The Landing," *Punch* 215 (Sept. 15, 1948): 237 (N.W.). Revised and reprinted in *P* and *CP*. Holograph version available in the Hooper deposit in the Bodleian.

"The Turn of the Tide," *Punch: Almanac* 215 (Nov. 1, 1948): n.p. (N.W.). Revised in *P* and *CP*. Holograph version available in the Hooper deposit in the Bodleian.

"The Prodigality of Firdausi," *Punch* 215 (Dec. 1, 1948): 510 (N.W.). Revised and reprinted in *P* and *CP*.

"Epitaph in a Village Churchyard," *Time and Tide* 30 (Mar. 19, 1949): 272. Retitled "Epigrams and Epitaphs, No. 16" in *P* and *CP*. Holograph versions available in the Hooper deposit in the Bodleian.

"On a Picture by Chirico," *The Spectator* 182 (May 6, 1949): 607. Revised and reprinted in *P* and *CP*. Holograph version available in the Hooper deposit in the Bodleian.

"Adam at Night," *Punch* 216 (May 11, 1949): 510 (N.W.). Revised and retitled "The Adam at Night" in *P* and *CP*. Holograph version available in the Hooper deposit in the Bodleian.

"Arrangement of Pindar," *Mandrake* 1, no. 6 (1949): 43–45. Revised and retitled "Pindar Sang" in *P* and *CP.* Holograph version available in the Hooper deposit in the Bodleian.

"Epitaph," *The Month* 2 (July 1949): 8. Retitled "Epigrams and Epitaphs, No. 17" in *P* and *CP.* Holograph version available in the Hooper deposit in the Bodleian.

"Conversation Piece: The Magician and the Dryad," *Punch* 217 (July 20, 1949): 71 (N.W.). Revised and retitled "The Magician and the Dryad" in *P* and *CP.* Holograph version available in the Hooper deposit in the Bodleian.

"The Day with a White Mark," *Punch* 217 (Aug. 17, 1949): 170 (N.W.). Revised and reprinted in *P* and *CP.* Holograph version available in the Hooper deposit in the Bodleian.

"A Footnote to Pre-History," *Punch* 217 (Sept. 14, 1949): 304 (N.W.). Revised and retitled "The Adam Unparadised" in *P* and *CP.* Holograph version available in the Hooper deposit in the Bodleian.

"As One Oldester to Another," *Punch* 218 (Mar. 15, 1950): 294–95 (N.W.). Revised and reprinted in *P* and *CP.* Holograph version available in the Hooper deposit in the Bodleian.

"A Cliché Came Out of its Cage," *Nine: A Magazine of Poetry and Criticism* 2 (May 1950): 114. Revised (a second stanza is added) and reprinted in *P* and *CP.* Holograph version available in the Hooper deposit in the Bodleian.

"Ballade of Dead Gentlemen," *Punch* 220 (Mar. 28, 1951): 386 (N.W.). Reprinted in *P* and *CP.*

"The Country of the Blind," *Punch* 221 (Sept. 12, 1951): 303 (N.W.). Reprinted in *P* and *CP.*

"Pilgrim's Problem," *The Month* 7 (May 1952): 275. Reprinted in *P* and *CP.*

"Vowels and Sirens," *The Times Literary Supplement,* Special Autumn Issue (Aug. 29, 1952): xiv. Revised and reprinted in *P* and *CP.* Holograph version available in the Hooper deposit in the Bodleian.

"Impenitence," *Punch* 225 (July 15, 1953): 91 (N.W.). Reprinted in *P* and *CP.*

"March for Drum, Trumpet, and Twenty-one Giants," *Punch* 225 (Nov. 4, 1953): 553. Revised and reprinted in *P* and *CP.* Holograph version available in the Hooper deposit in the Bodleian.

"To Mr. Kingsley Amis on His Late Verses," *Essays in Criticism* 4 (Apr. 1954): 190; cf. Kingsley Amis, "Beowulf," ibid. (Jan. 1954): 85.

"*Odora Canum Vis* (A defence of certain modern biographers and critics)," *The Month* 11 (May 1954): 272. Revised and reprinted in *P* and *CP.*

"Cradle-Song Based on a Theme from Nicolas of Cusa," *The Times Literary Supplement* (June 11, 1954): 375. Revised and reprinted in *P* and *CP.* Holograph version available in the Hooper deposit in the Bodleian.

"*Spartan Nactus,*" *Punch* 227 (Dec. 1, 1954): 685 (N.W.). Revised and retitled "A Confession" in *P* and *CP.* Holograph version available in the Hooper deposit in the Bodleian.

"On Another Theme from Nicolas of Cusa," *The Times Literary Supplement* (Jan. 21, 1955): 43. Revised and retitled "On a Theme from Nicolas of Cusa" in *P* and *CP.* Holograph version available in the Hooper deposit in the Bodleian.

"Legion," *The Month* 13 (Apr. 1955): 210. Revised and reprinted in *P* and *CP.* Holograph version available in the Hooper deposit in the Bodleian.

"After Aristotle," *The Oxford Magazine* 74 (Feb. 23, 1956): 296 (N.W.). Reprinted in *P* and *CP.*

"Epanorthosis (for the end of Goethe's *Faust*)," *The Cambridge Review* 77 (May 26, 1956): 610 (N.W.). Revised and retitled "Epigrams and Epitaphs, No. 15" in *P* and *CP*. Holograph version available in the Hooper deposit in the Bodleian.

"Evolutionary Hymn," *The Cambridge Review* 79 (Nov. 30, 1957): 227 (N.W.). Reprinted in *P* and *CP*.

"An Expostulation (against too many writers of science fiction)," *The Magazine of Fantasy and Science Fiction* 16, no. 6 (June 1959): 47. Reprinted in *P* and *CP*.

"Epitaph for Helen Joy Davidman" (a photograph; summer 1963) in Douglas Gilbert and Clyde S. Kilby, *C. S. Lewis: Images of His World*. Grand Rapids, Mich.: Eerdmans, 1973, 65. This is a revision of the "Epitaph" above and marks her memorial at the Oxford Crematorium. Reprinted in *CP*. Holograph versions available in the Hooper deposit in the Bodleian.

"They tell me, Lord" in *Letters to Malcolm: Chiefly on Prayer*. London: Geoffrey Bles, 1964. Revised and retitled "Prayer" in *P* and *CP*. Holograph versions in a notebook Hooper holds and in "Half Hours with Hamilton."

"Re-Adjustment," *Fifty-Two: A Journal of Books and Authors* [from Geoffrey Bles] no. 14 (Autumn 1964): 4. Reprinted in *P* and *CP*. Holograph version available in the Hooper deposit in the Bodleian.

UNDATED POEMS:

Poems contains the following:

"The Small Man Orders His Wedding." *P*, 31; reprinted in *CP*. Holograph version available in the Hooper deposit in the Bodleian. Interestingly, another holograph in the Bodleian, "A Wedding has been Arranged," is a slightly different version of "The Small Man Orders His Wedding." Still another version is in the Bodleian, MS. Eng. c. 2724, fol. 55; it has the title "An Epithalamium for John Wain feigned to be spoken in his person giving orders for his wedding" signed C.S.L., June 1947. There also appear to be fragments of early drafts of this version of the poem.

"The Ecstasy." *P*, 36–37; reprinted in *CP*. Holograph version available in the Hooper deposit in the Bodleian.

"The *Saboteuse*." *P*, 38–40; reprinted in *CP*. Holograph version available in the Hooper deposit in the Bodleian.

"Prelude to Space: An Epithalamium." *P*, 56–57; reprinted in *CP*. Holograph version available in the Hooper deposit in the Bodleian.

"On a Vulgar Error." *P*, 60; reprinted in *CP*. Holograph version available in the Hooper deposit in the Bodleian.

"Lines During a General Election." *P*, 62; reprinted in *CP*. Holograph versions available both in the Hooper deposit in the Bodleian and in a notebook Hooper holds.

"The Genuine Article." *P*, 63–64; reprinted in *CP*. Holograph version available in a notebook Hooper holds.

"To Roy Campbell." *P*, 66–67; reprinted in *CP*. Holograph version available in the Hooper deposit in the Bodleian.

"Infatuation." *P*, 73–76; reprinted in *CP*.

"*Aubade* [Eight Strokes Sound from Within]." *P*, 78; reprinted in *CP*. Holograph version available in the Hooper deposit in the Bodleian.

"Reason." *P,* 81; reprinted in *CP.* Holograph version available in a notebook Hooper holds.

"To Andrew Marvell." *P,* 82; reprinted in *CP.*

"Lines Written in a Copy of Milton's Work." *P,* 83; reprinted in *CP.*

"Deadly Sins." *P,* 91–92; reprinted in *CP.* Holograph version available in a notebook Hooper holds.

"Eden's Courtesy." *P,* 98; reprinted in *CP.* Holograph version available in a notebook Hooper holds.

"Relapse." *P,* 103–4; reprinted in *CP.* Holograph version available in a notebook Hooper holds.

"Late Summer." *P,* 104; reprinted in *CP.* Holograph versions available in the Hooper deposit in the Bodleian and in a notebook Hooper holds.

"After Vain Pretence." *P,* 106; reprinted in *CP.* Holograph version available in a notebook Hooper holds.

"Joys That Sting." *P,* 108; reprinted in *CP.* Holograph versions available in the Hooper deposit in the Bodleian.

"Old Poets Remembered." *P,* 109; reprinted in *CP.* Holograph version available in the Hooper deposit in the Bodleian.

"As the Ruin Falls." *P,* 109–10; reprinted in *CP.* Holograph versions available in the Hooper deposit in the Bodleian.

"Noon's Intensity." *P,* 114; reprinted in *CP.* Holograph version available in a notebook Hooper holds.

"Sweet Desire." *P,* 114–15; reprinted in *CP.* Holograph version available in a notebook Hooper holds.

"The Phoenix." *P,* 121; reprinted in *CP.* Holograph version available in the Hooper deposit in the Bodleian.

"The Nativity." *P,* 122; reprinted in *CP.* Holograph version available in the Hooper deposit in the Bodleian.

"Love's As Warm As Tears." *P,* 122–23; reprinted in *CP.* Holograph version available in the Hooper deposit in the Bodleian.

"No Beauty We Could Desire." *P,* 124–25; reprinted in *CP.* Holograph version available in the Hooper deposit in the Bodleian.

"Stephen to Lazarus." *P,* 125; reprinted in *CP.* Holograph version available in the Hooper deposit in the Bodleian.

"Five Sonnets." *P,* 125–27; reprinted in *CP.* Holograph versions available in the Hooper deposit in the Bodleian.

"Evensong." *P,* 128; reprinted in *CP.* Holograph version available in the Hooper deposit in the Bodleian.

"The Apologist's Evening Prayer." *P,* 129; reprinted in *CP.* Holograph version available in the Hooper deposit in the Bodleian.

"Epitaphs and Epigrams 1." *P,* 133; reprinted in *CP.* Holograph version available in the Hooper deposit in the Bodleian.

"Epitaphs and Epigrams 2." *P,* 133; reprinted in *CP.* Holograph version available in the Hooper deposit in the Bodleian.

"Epitaphs and Epigrams 3." *P,* 133; reprinted in *CP.* Holograph versions available both in a notebook Hooper holds and in the "Half Hours with Hamilton" manuscript.

"Epitaphs and Epigrams 4." *P,* 133; reprinted in *CP.* Holograph version available in a notebook Hooper holds.

"Epitaphs and Epigrams 5." *P,* 133; reprinted in *CP.* Holograph version available in the Hooper deposit in the Bodleian.

"Epitaphs and Epigrams 6." *P,* 134; reprinted in *CP.* Holograph version available both in the Hooper deposit in the Bodleian and in the "Half Hours with Hamilton" manuscript.

"Epitaphs and Epigrams 7." *P,* 134; reprinted in *CP.* Holograph version available in a notebook Hooper holds.

"Epitaphs and Epigrams 8." *P,* 134; reprinted in *CP.* Holograph version available in the Hooper deposit in the Bodleian.

"Epitaphs and Epigrams 9." *P,* 134; reprinted in *CP.* Holograph version available in the Hooper deposit in the Bodleian.

"Epitaphs and Epigrams 10." *P,* 134; reprinted in *CP.* Holograph version available in the Hooper deposit in the Bodleian.

"Epitaphs and Epigrams 13." *P,* 135; reprinted in *CP.* Holograph version available in the Hooper deposit in the Bodleian.

Collected Poems contains the following:

"Consolation." In *CP.* Holograph version available in the Hooper deposit in the Bodleian.

"Finchley Avenue," *Occasional Poets,* 102–4. Reprinted in *CP.* Holograph version available in the Hooper deposit in the Bodleian.

OTHER POEMS

"West Germanic to Primitive Old English" (fifteen lines of a mnemonic poem) quoted in Walter Hooper's "Preface" to Lewis's *Selected Literary Essays.* Ed. Walter Hooper. Cambridge: Cambridge UP, 1969, xv.

"Prayer for My Brother." In the Hooper and Green biography, 183.

"To Mrs. Dyson, Angrie." From MS. Eng. lett. c. 220/7, fols. 1–3; Bodleian Library. Published in King, "Glints of Light."

"Lines to Mr. Compton Mackenzie." From MS. Eng. lett. c. 861, fol. 69; Bodleian Library. Published in King, "Glints of Light."

OTHER WORKS BY LEWIS

Lewis, C. S. *The Abolition of Man.* London: Oxford UP, 1943.

———. *All My Road before Me: The Diary of C. S. Lewis, 1922–1927.* Ed. Walter Hooper. New York: Harcourt Brace Jovanovich, 1991.

———. *The Allegory of Love: A Study in Medieval Tradition.* Oxford: Oxford UP, 1936.

———. *The Collected Poems of C. S. Lewis.* Ed. Walter Hooper. London: Fount, 1994.

———. *The Discarded Image: An Introduction to Medieval and Renaissance Literature.* Cambridge: Cambridge UP, 1964.

———. *English Literature in the Sixteenth Century.* Oxford: Oxford UP, 1944.

———. *An Experiment in Criticism.* Cambridge: Cambridge UP, 1961.

———. *Fern-seed and Elephants and Other Essays on Christianity.* Glasgow: Fontana, 1975.

————. *The Four Loves.* New York: Harcourt Brace Jovanovich, 1960.

————. *The Great Divorce.* London: Geoffrey Bles, 1946.

————. *A Grief Observed* (N. W. Clerk, pseudonym). London: Faber and Faber, 1961.

————. *The Last Battle.* New York: Macmillan, 1956.

————. *Letters of C. S. Lewis.* Memoir and ed. Warren Lewis. Revised edition, ed. Walter Hooper. 1966. Reprint, London: Fount, 1988.

————. *Letters to Children.* Ed. Lyle W. Dorsett and Marjorie Lamp Mead. New York: Macmillan, 1985.

————. *Letters to Malcolm: Chiefly on Prayer.* London: Geoffrey Bles, 1964.

————. Lewis to Dom Bede Griffiths. Letters of CSL to Dom Bede Griffiths, Vol. 1, Apr. 22, 1954, 0070, Wade Center.

————. Lewis to Leo Kingsley Baker. Miscellaneous Letters, Easter Vacation, Apr. 1920 (?), 0087, and Sept. 1920, 0092–0093, Wade Center.

————. Lewis to Martyn Skinner. Miscellaneous Letters, Oct. 11, 1950, 942, Wade Center.

————. Lewis to Owen Barfield. Mar. 16, 1932, 0054; May 6, 1932, 0063; Feb. 8, 1939, 0088, Wade Center.

————. Lewis to Rhona Bodle. Miscellaneous Letters, June 24, 1949, 0192–0193, Wade Center.

————. Lewis to Albert Lewis. Unpublished letter in Warren Lewis's unpublished "C. S. Lewis: A Biography," Wade Center.

————. Lewis to Ruth Pitter. July 13, 1946, 001; July 19, 1946, 002–003; July 24, 1946, 005; Aug. 10, 1946, 0008; Jan. 4, 1947, 016; Feb. 2, 1947, 017 and 019; July 6, 1947, 028; July 21, 1947, 030; Aug. 31, 1948, 032; Sept. 29, 1948, 034; Aug. 24, 1949, 041; Nov. 17, 1949, 043; May 12, 1953, 060–061; May 15, 1953, 062–063; Mar. 19, 1955, 0073, Wade Center.

————. *The Lion, the Witch, and the Wardrobe.* London: Geoffrey Bles, 1950.

————. *Narrative Poems.* Ed. Walter Hooper. New York: Harcourt Brace Jovanovich, 1969.

————. *Of Other Worlds: Essays and Stories.* Ed. Walter Hooper. New York: Harcourt Brace Jovanovich, 1966.

————. *Out of the Silent Planet.* London: Bodley Head, 1938; paperback edition New York: Macmillan, 1965.

————. *Perelandra.* New York: Macmillan, 1944; paperback edition 1965.

————. *The Pilgrim's Regress.* London: Geoffrey Bles, 1933.

————. *Poems.* Ed. Walter Hooper. New York: Harcourt Brace Jovanovich, 1964.

————. *A Preface to Paradise Lost.* London: Oxford UP, 1942.

————. *Present Concerns.* London: Fount, 1986.

————. *Reflections on the Psalms.* New York: Harcourt Brace Jovanovich, 1958.

————. "The Quest of Bleheris." MS. Eng. lett. c. 220/5. fols. 5–43. Dated 1916. The Bodleian Library.

————. *Selected Literary Essays.* Cambridge: Cambridge UP, 1969.

————. *Spirits in Bondage: A Cycle of Lyrics.* London: Heinemann, 1919. Reprint, with an introduction by Walter Hooper, New York: Harcourt Brace Jovanovich, 1984.

————. *Surprised by Joy: The Shape of My Early Life.* New York: Harcourt, Brace and World, 1955.

————. *That Hideous Strength.* New York: Macmillan, 1946; paperback edition, 1965.

————. *They Stand Together: The Letters of C. S. Lewis to Arthur Greeves (1914–1963).* Ed. Walter Hooper. New York: Macmillan, 1979.

————. *The World's Last Night and Other Essays.* New York: Harcourt Brace Jovanovich, 1952.

Lewis, C. S., and E. M. W. Tillyard. *The Personal Heresy.* London: Oxford UP, 1939.

RELATED WORKS AND CRITICISM OF LEWIS'S POETRY

Adams, Richard, ed. *Occasional Poets: An Anthology.* New York: Viking, 1986.

Adey, Lionel. "Failed Poet?" In his *C. S. Lewis: Writer, Dreamer, and Mentor.* Grand Rapids, Mich.: Eerdmans, 1998, 194–220.

Alden, Raymond MacDonald, ed. *English Verse: Specimens Illustrating Its Principles and History.* 1929. Reprint, New York: AMS, 1970.

Anderson, Margaret. "'Fresh Robed/In Flesh': The Incarnation Theme in the Poetry of C. S. Lewis." M.A. thesis, Old Dominion University, 1975.

Arlott, John, ed. "The Cool, Clear Voice." *Ruth Pitter: Homage to a Poet.* London: Rapp and Whiting, 1969, 41–44.

Barfield, Owen. "C. S. Lewis." An address given at Wheaton College, Wheaton, Ill., Oct. 16, 1964. Marion E. Wade Center, Wheaton College.

————. *Owen Barfield on C. S. Lewis.* Ed. G. B. Tennyson. Middletown, Conn.: Wesleyan UP, 1989.

Beversluis, John. "Beyond the Double Bolted Door." *Christian History* 4, no. 3 (1985): 28–31.

————. *C. S. Lewis and the Search for Rational Religion.* Grand Rapids, Mich.: Eerdmans, 1985.

Bloomfield, Morton W. *The Seven Deadly Sins: An Introduction to the History of a Religious Concept, with Special Reference to Medieval English Literature.* East Lansing: Michigan State College P, 1952; reprint 1967.

Borhek, Mary. "A Grief Observed: Fact or Fiction?" *Mythlore* 16 (Summer 1990): 4–9, 26.

Bremer, John. "From Despoina to Diotima: The Mistress of C. S. Lewis." *The Lewis Legacy* 61 (Summer 1994): 6–18.

Brooke, Rupert. *The Collected Poems of Rupert Brooke.* New York: Dodd, Mead, 1961.

Brown, Carol Ann. "Three Roads: A Comment on 'The Queen of Drum.'" *Bulletin of the New York C. S. Lewis Society* 7 (Apr. 1976): 14.

Carroll, Lewis. *The Complete Works of Lewis Carroll.* New York: Modern Library, n. d.

Carter, Margaret. "Joy and Memory: Wordsworth as Illuminated by C. S. Lewis." *Mythlore* 17 (Autumn 1990): 9–13.

Cecil, David, ed. *Ruth Pitter: Homage to a Poet.* London: Rapp and Whiting, 1969.

Christopher, Joe R. "An Analysis of 'Old Poets Remembered.'" *The Lamp-Post of the Southern California C. S. Lewis Society* 19 (Fall 1995): 16–18.

————. "An Analysis of 'The Apologist's Evening Prayer.'" *Bulletin of the New York C. S. Lewis Society* 5 (Oct. 1974): 2–4.

————. "Comments on *Dymer.*" *The Lamp-Post of the Southern California C. S. Lewis Society* 20 (Autumn 1996): 17–22.

————. *C. S. Lewis.* Boston: Twayne, 1987.

———. "C. S. Lewis Dances among the Elves: A Dull and Scholarly Survey of *Spirits in Bondage* and 'The Queen of Drum.'" *Mythlore* 9 (Spring 1982): 11–17, 47.

———. "C. S. Lewis' Lingusitic [*sic*] Myth." *Mythlore* 21 (Summer 1995): 41–50.

———. "C. S. Lewis, Love Poet." *Studies in the Literary Imagination* 22 (Fall 1989): 161–73.

———. "C. S. Lewis's Poems to Joy Davidman." *The Canadian C. S. Lewis Journal* 94 (Autumn 1998): 20–37.

———. "C. S. Lewis's Shakespearean Poem ["Hermoine in the House of Paulina"], Part One." *The Lamp-Post of the Southern California C. S. Lewis Society* 22 (Summer 1998): 7–17; "Part Two." *The Lamp-Post of the Southern California C. S. Lewis Society* 22 (Fall 1998): 8–15.

———. "'From the Master's Lips': W. B. Yeats as C. S. Lewis Saw Him." *Bulletin of the New York C. S. Lewis Society* 6 (Nov. 1974): 14–19.

———. "Is 'D' for Despoina?" *The Canadian C. S. Lewis Journal* 85 (Spring 1994): 48–59.

———. "No Fish for the Phoenix." *Bulletin of the New York C. S. Lewis Society* 23 (July 1992): 1–7.

———. "Roy Campbell and the Inklings." *Mythlore* 22 (Autumn 1997): 33–34, 36–46.

———. "A Serious Limerick." *The Chronicle of the Portland C. S. Lewis Society* 1, no. 8 (Sept. 8, 1972): 4–5.

———. "A Study of C. S. Lewis's *Dymer*." *Orcrist* 6 (Winter 1971–72): 17–19. This is a revision of chapter 2: *Dymer* (17–25) from his Ph.D. dissertation, "The Romances of Clive Staples Lewis," University of Oklahoma, 1969.

———. "A Theological Triolet." *Bulletin of the New York C. S. Lewis Society* 2 (Sept. 1971): 4–5.

———. "Transformed Nature: 'Where Is It Now, the Glory and the Dream?'" *Bulletin of the New York C. S. Lewis Society* 7 (Sept. 1976): 1–7.

Coghill, Nevill. "The Approach to English." In *Light on C. S. Lewis*. Ed. Jocelyn Gibb. New York: Harcourt Brace Jovanovich, 1965, 51–66.

Daniel, Jerry. "The Taste of the Pineapple: A Basis for Literary Criticism." In *The Taste of the Pineapple: Essays on C. S. Lewis as Reader, Critic, and Imaginative Writer*. Ed. Bruce L. Edward. Bowling Green, Ohio: Bowling Green State U Popular P, 1988, 9–27.

Dante. *The Divine Comedy*. Translated by Dorothy L. Sayers. London: Penguin, 1949.

Donne, John. *The Complete Poetry of John Donne*. Ed. John T. Shawcross. Garden City, New York: Anchor, 1967.

Fausett, Hugh L'Anson. "Review of *Dymer*." *The Times Literary Supplement*. July 13, 1927, 27.

Fear No More: A Book of Poems for the Present Time by Living English Poets. Cambridge: Cambridge UP, 1940.

Filmer, Kath. "The Polemic Image: The Role of Metaphor and Symbol in the Fiction of C. S. Lewis." *SEVEN: An Anglo-American Literary Review* 7 (1986): 61–76.

Fussell, Paul. *The Great War and Modern Memory*. London: Oxford UP, 1975.

Geer, Caroline. "The Posthumous Narrative Poems of C. S. Lewis." M.A. thesis, North Texas State University, 1976.

Gilbert, Douglas, and Clyde S. Kilby. *C. S. Lewis: Images of His World*. Grand Rapids, Mich.: Eerdmans, 1973.

Gilbert, Rudolph. *Four Living Poets.* Santa Barbara, Calif.: Unicorn P, 1944.

Green, Roger Lancelyn. "C. S. Lewis." *Puffin Post* 4, no. 1 (1970): 14–15.

Green, Roger Lancelyn, and Walter Hooper. *C. S. Lewis: A Biography.* New York: Harcourt Brace Jovanovich, 1974.

———. "C. S. Lewis and Andrew Lang." *Notes and Queries* 22 (May 1975): 208–9.

Guerber, H. A. *Myths of the Norsemen.* London: Harrap and Co., 1908.

Gunn, Thom. "Urania as Poet." In *Ruth Pitter: Homage to a Poet.* Ed. David Cecil. London: Rapp and Whiting, 1969, 63–65.

Hamer, Enid. *The Metres of English Poetry.* London: Methuen and Co., 1930.

Hardie, A. M., and K. C. Douglas. *Augury: An Oxford Miscellany of Verse and Poetry.* Oxford: Blackwell, 1940.

Hart, Dabney. "Editor's Comment." *Studies in the Literary Imagination* 22 (Fall 1989): 125–28.

Herbert, George. *The English Poems of George Herbert.* Ed. C. A. Patrides. London: Dent, 1974.

Hodgens, Richard. "Notes on *Narrative Poems.*" *Bulletin of the New York C. S. Lewis Society* 7 (Apr. 1976): 1–14.

Hooper, Walter. *C. S. Lewis: A Companion and Guide.* London: HarperCollins, 1996.

———. Preface to *Poems* by C. S. Lewis. New York: Harcourt Brace Jovanovich, 1964, v–ix.

———. Preface to *Narrative Poems* by C. S. Lewis. New York: Harcourt Brace Jovanovich, 1969, vii–xiv.

———. Preface to *Spirits in Bondage: A Cycle of Lyrics* by C. S. Lewis. New York: Harcourt Brace Jovanovich, 1984, xi–xl.

———. Introduction and Introductory Letter to *The Collected Poems of C. S. Lewis* by C. S. Lewis. London: Fount, 1994, ix–xxi.

Horace. *The Complete Works of Horace.* Ed. Caspar Kraemer, Jr. Trans. J. H. Deazeley. New York: Modern Library, 1936.

———. *Horace: The Odes and Epodes.* Ed. C. E. Bennett. Cambridge: U of Massachusetts P, 1914.

Housman, A. E. *Housman: Collected Poems.* Ed. John Sparrow. New York: Penguin, 1995.

Howard, Thomas. "*Poems*: A Review." *Christianity Today* 9 (June 18, 1965): 30.

Huttar, Charles. "A Lifelong Love Affair with Language: C. S. Lewis's Poetry." In *Word and Story in C. S. Lewis.* Ed. Peter Schakel and Charles Huttar. Columbia, Missouri: U of Missouri P, 1991, 86–108.

Johnston, John. *English Poetry of the First World War: A Study in the Evolution of Lyric and Narrative Form.* Princeton, N.J.: Princeton UP, 1964.

Kawano, Roland. "C. S. Lewis and 'The Nameless Isle': A Metaphor of Major Change." *Bulletin of the New York C. S. Lewis Society* 15 (Mar. 1984): 1–4.

———. "C. S. Lewis's Early Poems." *The Living Church* 186 (Feb. 13, 1983): 9–10.

———. "C. S. Lewis: Public Poet." *Mythlore* 9 (Autumn 1982): 20–21.

———. "C. S. Lewis' *The Queen of Drum.*" *The Lamp-Post of the Southern California C. S. Lewis Society* 11 (Nov. 1987): 10–14.

King, Don W. "A Bibliographic Review of C. S. Lewis as Poet: 1952–1995, Part One." *The Canadian C. S. Lewis Journal* 91 (Spring 1997): 9–23.

———. "A Bibliographic Review of C. S. Lewis as Poet: 1952–1995, Part Two." *The Canadian C. S. Lewis Journal* 91 (Autumn 1997): 34–56.

———. "*The Collected Poems of C. S. Lewis*" (124–26); "*Dymer*" (144–46); "*Narrative Poems*" (289–90); "*Poems*" (325–27); "*Spirits in Bondage*" (385–87); and eighty other short entries in *The C. S. Lewis Readers' Encyclopedia.* Ed. Jeffrey D. Schultz and John G. West. Grand Rapids, Mich.: Zondervan, 1998.

———. "C. S. Lewis's *Spirits in Bondage:* World War I Poet as Frustrated Dualist." *The Christian Scholar's Review* 27 (Summer 1998): 454–74.

———. "C. S. Lewis' 'The Quest of Bleheris' as Prose Poetry." *The Lamp-Post of the Southern California C. S. Lewis Society* 23, no. 1 (Spring 1999): 3–15.

———. "Glints of Light: The Unpublished Short Poetry of C. S. Lewis." SEVEN: *An Anglo-American Literary Review* 15 (1998): 73–96.

———. "Making the Poor Best of Dull Things: C. S. Lewis as Poet." SEVEN: *An Anglo-American Literary Review* 12 (1995): 79–92.

———. "Narnia and the Seven Deadly Sins." *Mythlore* 10 (Spring 1984): 14–19.

———. "The Distant Voice in C. S. Lewis's *Poems.*" *Studies in the Literary Imagination* 22 (Fall 1989): 175–84.

———. "The Poetry of Prose: C. S. Lewis, Ruth Pitter, and *Perelandra.*" *Christianity and Literature* 49 (Spring 2000): 331–56.

———. "The Religious Verse of C. S. Lewis: Part One." *The Canadian C. S. Lewis Journal* 97 (Spring 2000): 12–27.

Kirkpatrick, Hope. "An Approach to *The Personal Heresy.*" *Bulletin of the New York C. S. Lewis Society* 7 (June 1976): 1–8.

———. "The Final Essay in *The Personal Heresy.*" *Bulletin of the New York C. S. Lewis Society* 9 (May 1978): 1–8.

Kirkpatrick, John. "Fresh Views of Humankind in Lewis's Poems." *Bulletin of the New York C. S. Lewis Society* 10 (Sept. 1979): 1–7.

Landrum, David. "Pindar, Prodigality, and Paganism: Natural Law Ethics in the Poetry of C. S. Lewis." *The Lamp-Post of the Southern California C. S. Lewis Society* 19 (Summer 1995): 4–13.

Langland, William. *Piers Plowman: A New Translation of the B-Text.* Translated by A. V. C. Schmidt. Oxford: Oxford UP, 1992.

Larkin, Philip, ed. *The Oxford Book of Twentieth Century English Verse.* Oxford: Oxford UP, 1973.

Lewis, Warren. *Brothers and Friends: The Diaries of Major Warren Hamilton Lewis.* Ed. Clyde S. Kilby and Marjorie Lamp Mead. San Francisco, Calif.: Harper and Row, 1982.

———. "C. S. Lewis: A Biography." Unpublished manuscript. Marion E. Wade Center, Wheaton College, Wheaton, Ill.

———. "The Lewis Papers: Memoirs of the Lewis Family, 1850–1930." 11 volumes. Wade Center, Wheaton College, Wheaton, Ill.

Linden, William. "New Light on Narnia; or, Who Beat the Drum?" *Bulletin of the New York C. S. Lewis Society* 2 (Apr. 1971): 9–10.

Lindskoog, Kathryn. "C. S. Lewis on Christmas." *Christianity Today* 27 (Dec. 16, 1983): 24–26.

———. "Fear No More: C. S. Lewis and Laureate Masefield." *The Lewis Legacy* 65 (Summer 1995): 8.

———. *Finding the Landlord: A Guidebook to C. S. Lewis's Pilgrim's Regress.* Chicago, Ill.: Cornerstone P, 1995.

———. "Fit for Psychoanalysts and/or Theologians Needed." *The Lewis Legacy* 65 (Summer 1995): 3.

———. "Getting It Together: Lewis and the Two Hemispheres of Knowing." *Journal of Psychology and Theology* 3 (Fall 1975): 290–93. Reprinted in *Mythlore* 6 (Winter 1979): 43–45. Also revised and published as "Appendix Two" in *Finding the Landlord.*

———. "G. F. Ellwood: 'Finchley Ave. Wastes a lot of Space." *The Lewis Legacy* 65 (Summer 1995): 5.

———. "Here We Go Again: Two New Lewis Forgeries." *The Lewis Legacy* no. 64 (Spring 1995): 1.

———. "'How Can I Ask?' Poem Presents Ongoing Puzzle." *The Lewis Legacy* 65 (Summer 1995): 3.

———. "Laureate Richard Wilbur Critiques 'Finchley Ave.'" *The Lewis Legacy* 65 (Summer 1995): 1.

———. "Lindskoog: Detour Ahead, Analyzing Finchley Ave." *The Lewis Legacy* 65 (Summer 1995): 7.

———. "No Rhyme or Reason in the Handling of Lewis's Poetry." *The Lewis Legacy* 65 (Summer 1995): 1.

———. "'Odyssey' Poem Left Out; Glaring Error Left In." *The Lewis Legacy* 65 (Summer 1995): 3.

———. "Opinions of Robert Evans: It Seems Ridiculous to Me." *The Lewis Legacy* 65 (Summer 1995): 7.

———. "'A Paeant Played in Vain,' A Prank that Causes Pain?" *The Lewis Legacy* 65 (Summer 1995): 1.

———. "Poet Laureate Richard Wilbur on 'Finchley Avenue.'" *The Lewis Legacy* 65 (Summer 1995): 12.

———. "Vanauken: 'Finchley Ave. . . Peculiar in Some Ways." *The Lewis Legacy* 65 (Summer 1995): 5.

———. "Walter Hearn: A Diamond in the Dust of Finchley Ave." *The Lewis Legacy* 65 (Summer 1995): 7.

———. "Walter Hearn: 'An Editor Ambles Down Finchley Ave." *The Lewis Legacy* 65 (Summer 1995): 5.

———. "Why Aren't These in Lewis's Collected Poems?" *The Lewis Legacy* 65 (Summer 1995): 8.

Malory, Thomas. *Le Morte D'Arthur.* 2 volumes. London: The Medici Society, 1920.

McLaughlin, Sara Park, and Mark O. Webb. *A Word Index to the Poetry of C. S. Lewis.* West Cornwall, Conn: Locust Hill P, 1988.

Metcalf, Stephen. "Language and Consciousness: The Making and Breaking of C. S. Lewis's Personae." *Word and Story in C. S. Lewis.* Ed. Peter Schakel and Charles Huttar. Columbia, Missouri: U of Missouri P, 1991, 109–44.

Milne, Marjorie. "*Dymer:* Myth or Poem?" *The Month* 194 (Sept. 1952): 170–73.

Morris, William. *The Story of Sigurd the Volsung and the Fall of the Nibelung.* London: Ellis and White, 1877.

Murphy, Patrick. "C. S. Lewis's *Dymer:* Once More with Hesitation." *Bulletin of the New York C. S. Lewis Society* 17 (June 1986): 1–8. Reprinted in *The Poetic Fantastic: Studies in an Evolving Genre.* Ed. Patrick Murphy and Vernon Hyles. Westport, Conn.: Greenwood, 1989, 63–78.

Musacchio, George. "C. S. Lewis' *A Grief Observed* as Fiction." *Mythlore* 12 (Spring 1986): 25ff.

———. "War Poet." *The Lamp-Post of the Southern California C. S. Lewis Society* 2, no. 4 (Oct. 1978): 7. Revised and reprinted in George Musacchio. *C. S. Lewis: Man and Writer.* Belton, Tex.: U of Mary Hardin-Baylor P, 1994.

Nichols, Robert, ed. *Anthology of War Poetry, 1914–1918.* London: Nicholson and Watson, 1943.

O'Brien, Kate. "Review of *Perelandra*." *The Spectator* 170 (May 14, 1943): 458.

Owen, Wilfred. *The Collected Poems of Wilfred Owen.* Ed. C. Day Lewis. Norfolk, Conn.: New Directions, 1963.

Peters, Thomas. "The War of the Worldviews: H. G. Wells and Scientism and C. S. Lewis and Christianity." *Mission and Ministry* 11, no. 4, 12, no. 1 (1998): 44–49.

Pitter, Ruth. *The Bridge: Poems 1939–1944.* London: Cresset, 1945.

———. *Collected Poems.* London: Enitharmon, 1996.

———. *Collected Poems: 1990.* Petersfield: Enitharmon, 1990.

———. *End of the Drought.* London: Barrie and Jenkins, 1975.

———. *The Ermine: Poems 1942–1952.* London: Cresset, 1953.

———. *First and Second Poems.* London: Sheed and Ward, 1927.

———. *First Poems.* London: Cecil Palmer, 1920.

———. *A Heaven to Find.* London: Enitharmon, 1987.

———. "Interview with Lyle Dorsett." July 23, 1985, Wade Center.

———. Letters from Lewis to Ruth Pitter, Wade Center.

———. *A Mad Lady's Garland.* London: Cresset, 1934.

———. "Passages from *Perelandra*." MS Pitter Verse (uncataloged), Box 28. The Bodleian Library.

———. *Persephone in Hades.* Privately printed, 1931.

———. "Pitter Journal Recollections of Correspondence with C. S. Lewis." Ms. Eng. lett. c. 220/3. Bodeleian Library, Oxford.

———. *Pitter on Cats.* London: Cresset, 1946.

———. "Pitter to C. S. Lewis." July 17, 1946; CSL /L-Pitter/ 1a; Wade Center.

———. *Poem.* Southampton: Shirley P, 1943.

———. *Poems 1926–1966.* London: Barrie and Rockcliff/Cresset, 1968.

———. *The Rude Potato.* London: Cresset, 1941.

———. *The Spirit Watches.* London: Cresset, 1939.

———. *Still by Choice.* London: Cresset, 1966.

———. *A Trophy of Arms: Poems 1926–1935.* London: Cresset, 1936.

———. *Urania* (selections from *A Trophy of Arms, The Spirit Watches,* and *The Bridge*). London: Cresset, 1950.

The Poetic Edda. Translated by Henry Adams Bellows. New York: The American-Scandinavian Foundation, 1923.

Preminger, Alex, and T. V. F. Brogan, eds. *The New Princeton Encyclopedia of Poetry and Poetics.* Princeton, NJ: Princeton UP, 1993.

Prothero, James. "Lewis's Poetry: A Preliminary Exploration." *Bulletin of the New York C. S. Lewis Society* 25 (Mar.–Apr. 1994): 1–6.

Purcell, James. "*Narrative Poems.*" *Bulletin of the New York C. S. Lewis Society* 2 (Nov. 1972): 2–3.

Raine, Kathleen. "A Homecoming." In *Ruth Pitter: Homage to a Poet*. Ed. David Cecil. London: Rapp and Whiting, 1969, 103–6.

Robson, W. W. "The Poetry of C. S. Lewis." *The Chesterton Review* 17, nos. 3–4 (Aug.–Nov. 1991): 437–43.

———. "The Romanticism of C. S. Lewis." *Cambridge Quarterly* 1 (Summer 1966): 252–72. Reprinted in W. W. Robson. *Critical Essays*. London: Routledge and Kegan Paul, 1966.

Russell, Arthur, ed. *Ruth Pitter: Homage to a Poet*. London: Rapp and Whiting, 1969.

Saintsbury, George. *A History of English Prosody from the Twelfth Century to the Present Day*. 3 volumes. London, 1908. Reprint, New York: Russell and Russell, 1961.

Sassoon, Siegfried. *Memoirs of an Infantry Officer*. London, 1930. Reprinted, London: Faber and Faber, 1965.

———. *Siegfried's Journey*. London: Faber and Faber, 1946.

———. *The War Poems of Siegfried Sassoon*. Ed. Rupert Hart-Davis. London: Faber and Faber, 1983.

Sayer, George. "C. S. Lewis's *Dymer*." SEVEN: *An Anglo-American Literary Review* 1 (1980): 94–116.

———. *Jack: C. S. Lewis and His Times*. San Francisco, Calif.: Harper and Row, 1988.

Sayers, Dorothy L. *Further Papers on Dante*. New York: Harper and Brothers, 1957.

Schakel, Peter. *Reason and Imagination in C. S. Lewis: A Study of* Till We Have Faces. Grand Rapids, Mich.: Eerdmans, 1984.

Schakel, Peter, and Charles Huttar, eds. *Word and Story in C. S. Lewis*. Columbia, Missouri: U of Missouri P, 1991.

Schultz, Jeffrey D., and John G. West, eds. *The C. S. Lewis Readers' Encyclopedia*. Grand Rapids, Mich.: Zondervan, 1998.

Shaw, Harry. *Concise Dictionary of Literary Terms*. New York: McGraw-Hill, 1972.

Shaw, Luci. "Looking Back to Eden: The Poetry of C. S. Lewis." *Bulletin of the New York C. S. Lewis Society* 23 (Feb. 1992): 1–7. Reprinted in *Radix* 21, no. 3 (1993): 12–15, 30.

Shelley, Percy Bysshe. *Shelley: Poetical Works*. Ed. Thomas Hutchinson. London: Oxford UP, 1970.

Slack, Michael. "Sehnsucht and the Platonic Eros in *Dymer*." *Bulletin of the New York C. S. Lewis Society* 11 (Aug. 1980): 3–7.

Sorley, Charles. *The Letters of Charles Sorley*. Cambridge: Cambridge UP, 1919.

Tennyson, Alfred. *Poems of Tennyson*. Ed. Jerome H. Buckley. Cambridge, Mass.: Riverside, 1958.

Tetreault, James. "C. S. Lewis and T. S. Eliot." *Bulletin of the New York C. S. Lewis Society* 8 (Dec. 1976): 1–5. Revised and expanded as "Parallel Lines: C. S. Lewis and T. S. Eliot." *Renascence: Essays on Value in Literature* 38, no. 4 (Summer 1986): 256–69.

Thorson, Stephen. "Thematic Implications of C. S. Lewis's *Spirits in Bondage*." *Mythlore* 8 (Summer 1981): 26–30.

Thrall, William, and Addison Hibbard, eds. *A Handbook to Literature*. Revised and enlarged by C. Hugh Holman. New York: Odyssey, 1960.

Wagner, Richard. *The Ring of the Nibelung*. Vol. 2, *Siegfried and the Twilight of the Gods*. Translated by Margaret Armour. Illustrations by Arthur Rackham. London: Heinemann, 1911.

Walsh, Chad. *The Literary Legacy of C. S. Lewis.* New York: Harcourt Brace Jovanovich, 1979.

Wilson, A. N. *C. S. Lewis: A Biography.* San Francisco: HarperCollins, 1990.

Wordsworth, William. *William Wordsworth.* Ed. Stephen Gill. Oxford: Oxford UP, 1984.

Wyrall, Everard. *The History of the Somerset Light Infantry (Prince Albert's): 1914–1919.* London: Methuen, 1927.

Index

C. S. Lewis, Poet
was designed by Christine Brooks;
composed in 10/13.5 Minion in Quark XPress
by The Bookpage, Inc.;
printed on 50# Supple Opaque stock
and notch bound in signatures
by Thomson-Shore, Inc.;
and published by
The Kent State University Press
KENT, OHIO 44242